CONTENTS

INTRODUCTION

Culture is an influential force in an individual's life. In the United States, the population is becoming more culturally diverse. This poses new challenges, opportunities, as well as responsibilities for not only classroom teachers but educators in general. *Cultural diversity* refers to an individual's ethnicity, race, religion, language, sexual orientation, values, gender, social class, age, and many other factors. The goal of this book is to explain how culture plays a significant role in the learning process of individuals. Since it is common that people continually change their beliefs and points of view about existence and cultural diversity, it is critical as educators to have extensive knowledge of culture and diversity among students. This text is designed for multicultural education courses as well as to help educators understand diversity and equality in early childhood studies. An additional goal of this book is to assist professionals who wish to expand their knowledge about multiculturalism and diversity in the educational field. *Diversity and Child Development* offers an essential perspective on theories, definitions, and implementing different techniques in culturally relevant settings. Moreover, this textbook provides numerous studies that help students appreciate and understand the diversity in different social categories in terms of race, ethnic background, class, sexual orientation, language, religions, exceptions, and disabilities.

Section one of this book explains the importance of recognizing, respecting, and helping individuals build positive and healthy internal identities in terms of their race and ethnicity in an early childhood classroom. In the process of identity development from an early stage of life, many individuals may encounter discrimination, sexism, racism, teasing, and rejection. As a result, multiple articles in this chapter discuss how an educator or adult can help children develop understanding and learn about many elements of diversity, such as race, language, culture, ability, and gender, as well as rising tolerance and awareness about sensitive and controversial issues regarding individual similarities and differences.

Section two provides comprehensive information for educators, childcare personnel, and students in the early childhood field concerning individuals with disabilities. The goal is to raise awareness about exclusion and discrimination that individuals with physical, intellectual, or developmental disabilities may face in the education system. This chapter discusses how recognition and acceptance of the children's disabilities and specific needs are essential for successful teaching, the learning process, and the overall performance outcome. Educators need to acknowledge that active learning for special needs children takes place in the context of a supportive and inclusive environment. This section of the book review articles that focus on inclusive settings and how effective teachers should respond to children with disabilities and provide support for students, particularly those with special needs.

Section three focuses on cultural sustainability, tolerance, and respecting diversity among immigrant children and their families. The United States is experiencing an immigration wave of historic proportions, which is profoundly affecting large and small population centers across social, cultural, economic, and political dimensions of society. In this section of the book, we will review pieces of literature that relate to migrant and refugee children and their families in the early childhood education field. An educator needs to know that culture plays an essential role in how children perceive the worlds around them and how understanding cultural variations in early childhood education can affect the development of this perception.

Mainstream culture in the United States tends to associate more with the values and beliefs of White middle-class people living in the country. As a result, individuals who identify with subcultures can sometimes experience relegation, discrimination, and institutional racism.

Nowadays, the primary challenge facing many early childhood educators is the effect of children's culture on their development and learning process. Therefore, one of the main emphases of this section is to clarify how an individual's family cultural traditions shape a child's development cognitively, physically, of language, and of expression of emotions. Multiple articles in this chapter describe and support the concept that children's development and learning depends on the adoption of the appropriate cultural tools such as language, expression of emotion, beliefs, and perception.

In general, this book intends to gather pieces of literature concerning diversity and equality in the field of child development together in a single volume based on their importance and effects on children's lives. The content in each section helps readers understand that culturally relevant education acknowledges the importance of encouraging equity and equality in the education system. This book has clear and direct relevance to diversity and child development, and each of the chapters in *Diversity and Child Development* clarifies particular areas of diversity through the review of theories and research.

UNIT I

CULTURE AND HUMAN DEVELOPMENT

Human Development

Culture and Biology

Krum Krumov and Knud S. Larsen

A central concern in cross-cultural and cultural psychology is how people acquire behaviors that we identify as *culturally unique*. While we are interested in what is different between cultures of the world, there is also the potentially larger area of research into what we have in common. Although recent thinking point to universal psychic unity as rooted in biology supporting what is commonly called human universals, that universalism has been challenged by recent cultural and cross-cultural work. For example, cultural psychology has demonstrated that higher mental functioning is created by cultural activity and communication. Further, results from cultural neuroscience show that long term interaction with cultural settings may actually modify brain pathways and the very architecture of the brain (Kolstad, 2012). In particular acquiring culture is partly the outcome of parenting styles employed in the process of socialization. However, broader social institutions including the educational system and dominant religious or political organizations are considered important factors in producing cultural ideologies. Children also grow up with siblings and peers that have an influence on socialization. Since culture emerged out of the struggle to survive, the particular environmental contexts have produced some of the cultural variability we can observe in the world today. Survival requires competencies that in turn vary with the ecological context (Kagitcibasi, 1996). To a large extent cultural learning is implicit perhaps governed by social learning and imitation, but by the time we are adults most of us have learned the cultural rules and customs and they are so integrated in our lives that few people even notice or pass judgment on habitual rituals or behaviors. Other forms of learning have also played a role in the acquisition of cultural values through reinforcement in the educational system based on operant conditioning or by the association of cultural and unconditioned stimuli that occurs in classical conditioning.

[...] Socialization or Enculturation?

Psychologists investigating comparative cultures make a distinction between socialization and enculturation in how cultures are transmitted from one generation to the next. Socialization as a concept has a long history in both social psychology and sociology. In particular *socialization* refers to the process of individual development that is shaped by cultural values through the deliberate teaching by culture bearers and enforcers especially the child's parents. Cultural values are learned when someone deliberately shapes the behavior of children in society. On the other hand, Herskovits (1948) used the concept of *enculturation* to define the end product of socialization. Enculturation refers to the assimilation of the components of culture considered essential in order to function adequately in a society. Enculturation describes the influence of the cultural context and the possibilities offered by that environment. In other words, enculturation describes the subjective end products manifested in behavior and represent the psychological internalization of cultural values throughout the process of development. Socialization refers more to the actual means of how children learn the rules of their societies, whereas enculturation is the end product manifested in subjective psychology. We can think of culture as the subjective psychological experience resulting from socialization, and enculturation as the resulting society that surrounds members of the culture with an inescapable context.

The processes of socialization and enculturation are not the only determinants of individual behavior. Members of a culture must also respond to the ecological environment and develop behaviors that support survival and successful adaptation. The transmission of culture is aimed at creating skills in children that support successful living. Still culture must also adapt to changing circumstances. The transmission of culture is not fixed, but is a more fluid process that prevents chaos and promotes social stability (Boyd & Richerson, 1995).

The study of child rearing practices in various cultures has a long history. For example, Whiting and Child (1953) examined child training study archives and concluded that in some ways child training is identical all over the world since parents everywhere confront similar problems. However, there are also some salient cultural differences in how child training differs between cultures. These observations are consistent with a biological perspective of all that we have in common as a species, but also a cultural comparative view based on enculturation and socialization. According to Barry, Bacon and Child (1957), and Barry, Child and Bacon (1959) six dimensions of child rearing were similar in all societies studied. These included training for obedience, responsibility, nurturance, achievement, self-reliance, and independence. Gender differences were also universally similar across cultures with girls being socialized to take on more responsibility and nurturance, and boys being encouraged to be assertive through achievement and self-reliance. However, later investigators found comparative cultural variations in socialization described as either narrow or broad (Arnett, 1995). Obedience was emphasized in the narrow transmission of a culture that required conformity as a cultural product, whereas broad transmission emphasized personal independence.

[...] Enculturation and Choice

The growing child develops within a niche from which he/she learns cultural values. The major components that form the context of development are the ecological environment, the socio-political context, customs of child rearing, and the psychology that motivates parents and child care givers (Super & Harkness, 1994, 2002). These niche components interact with the child's unique genetically based temperamental traits. However, it is well to keep in mind that children are not just acted upon by the cultural environment, but are *behavioral actors* in their own right and through their choices influence family life and the broader cultural context. As Bronfenbrenner (1979) noted children are not passive recipients of cultural knowledge, but dynamically interact with the choices provided by culture. The micro-systems with the most immediate influence on development are the interaction of the child with the family, educational system, and peers. The exo-system influences development indirectly, for example, by the opportunities provided by the social standing of parents. The macro-system refers to the major normative influences that require conformity to cultural values, religion, and ideology. Nevertheless, according to Bronfenbrenner it is important to remember that members of a culture are not passive observers, but children contribute to self-development by the choices they make and through the willingness to conform or risk alternatives.

The effect of quality of life variables can be observed in studies on child development. Technological development has been practically ubiquitous in the world the last decades and has affected family life in significant ways (Berry, 1997). Differences in outcomes for family life have been found between wealthy individualistic countries compared to collectivistic countries (Georgas, Christakopoulou, Poortinga, Angleitner, Goodwin, & Charalambous, 1997). Although the search for material wealth is ubiquitous it is also associated with a decreasing frequency of helping behavior among second or third generation Mexican-American children. A salient outcome with psychological consequences is the less important role of family solidarity in the survival of children from more affluent families (Knight & Kagan, 1977).

Parents and other child caregivers generally share culturally appropriate ideas about child rearing. In a given culture parents have assimilated beliefs about the correct ways to help a child achieve developmental goals and the role of parents in creating the best learning climate. Cultural values frame the way that child caregivers express affection and love for the child and determine when the child should be fed and the appropriate time for weaning. Cultural values also create expectations about the right time to master the beginnings of speech, when the child should walk, and other developmental goals (Harkness & Super, 1995).

Differences in *child rearing ideology* were found in a study comparing Japanese with U.S. teachers (Tobin, Wu, & Davidson, 1989). For example, Japanese teachers preferred larger class rooms believing the greater number of students to constitute a more appropriate forum to teach children to get along with others. The beliefs about children's misbehavior also varied between the samples with Japanese teachers believing that misbehavior occurred when something went wrong in the relationship between child and mother, whereas U.S. teachers were more likely to attribute the cause to some inherent deficit in the child. The attribution of either individual or relationship causes is also consistent with generally recognized differences between collectivistic and individualistic cultures represented by Japan and the U.S.

LeVine (1977) suggested that early childrearing practices were created and motivated by parental goals. Initially the survival of the infant is paramount and therefore parents focus on infant health. However, at some point children in all cultures must develop self-sufficiency. Childrearing inculcates the cultural values of the broader society as mediated by parents. However, children raised in affluent cultures do not face the same struggles for survival as those raised in poverty with subsequent long-term psychological consequences. When parents have to struggle daily to put food on the table there is not much time to develop the assets and abilities of the child, and family bonding becomes a primary goal in order to create survival security. The harshness of the environment may be so extreme that mothering is directly influenced.

Frequency and length of breastfeeding also depend on the socio-economic status of society. The more advanced societies encourage the use of formula to create earlier independence between mother and child. In turn that may affect attachment and later development. Infant weakness in extremely impoverished communities is conceptualized by mothers as representing a low likelihood for survival. Hence mothers in these cultures are in some cases tentative in committing total affection for the child as the baby may be only a short-term visitor in the home. In other words, bonding is promoted when there is a chance that it will have utility in the survival of the child (Scheper-Hughes, 1992).

Parental ideology referred to as parental *ethno-theories* describes integrated beliefs about parenting (Edwards, Knoche, Aukrust, Kimru, & Kim, 2006; Harkness & Super, 2006). *The belief system about parenting determines the methods which direct the child in learning important elements of the cultural context.* Parental beliefs serve as an organizing tool in governing the daily activities of the child.

[...] Authoritative Versus Authoritarian Childrearing Approaches and Cultural Differences

Research on child rearing in the United States identified three styles of parenting (Baumrind, 1971). *Authoritative* parents provide the child with care that is firm, but also reasonable and fair. Control in authoritative child rearing is dependent on the child's maturity, and parents typically display warm and open affection for their children. Guidelines are provided by authoritative parents, but not rigidly enforced as children are given freedom to choose dependent on their level of development and responsibility. In the second style of parenting *authoritarian* parents demand obedience first and foremost and provide strict control over the child. Authoritarianism may have grown out of harsh environments where parents see their role as keeping their children out of harm's way. Baumrind's research also identified *permissiveness* as a parental style. Permissive parents allow their children to live their own lives without much interference or discipline. This style of parenting seems close to that of the uninvolved parents identified by Maccoby and Martin (1983). However, permissive parents are involved with their children and exhibit warmth in their relationships, whereas uninvolved parents are just indifferent.

The initial results from American studies supported the superiority of the authoritative style in many studies. Children who grow up with parents that use the authoritative childrearing style develop more useful traits including more positive emotions, more self-confidence and self-reliance (Karavasilis, Doyle, & Markiewicz, 2003). The authoritative parenting style prepares the child well for life resulting in children that are psychologically healthy and competent, and who live with fewer anxieties compared to children brought up by other parenting styles. By contrast children of authoritarian parents displayed more anxiety and develop cognitive styles that lack spontaneity and curiosity. The benefits for children of authoritative parents are not just confined to childhood. Studies of adolescents produced similar positive results. Adolescents with authoritative parents are more socially adept, tend to have higher self-esteem and display more creativity (Collins & Laursen, 2004; Spera, 2005). The authoritative style of parenting seems to have a positive effect on the child's sense of optimism and helps create the belief that the child lives in a well-ordered world with developmental goals that are attainable. These effects are carried over into university life where students from authoritative homes displayed less depression and greater social adaptability (Jackson, Pratt, Hunsberger, & Pancer, 2005).

For comparative psychology an important question is whether these styles are manifested in other cultures than the United States, or to what degree are they culturally specific? Are the positive outcomes of authoritative parents limited to children living in the United States? Chao (2001) argued that it is important to understand the dominant cultural values before investigating parental styles. The efficacy of parental styles may well depend on underlying values to which the child must conform. Chao argued that the role of training in Chinese culture is unique and not covered by the Baumrind's parental styles. However, in another study in China authoritarian parenting was related negatively to school adjustment, whereas children from authoritative homes fared better in overall social adjustment (Chen, Dong, & Zhou, 1997). In a multi-cultural society like the U.S. perhaps the efficacy of authoritative approaches to childrearing depends on the child's ethnic or cultural group? However, a review of more recent studies confirms the continuous advantage of authoritative approaches to childrearing that are independent of the larger cultural values associated with collectivistic or individualistic cultures (Sorkhabi, 2005). Parental warmth and acceptance of the child are important factors in positive outcomes every-where, and authoritative parenting takes on universal value as the advantages are not limited by culture. Comparative studies have largely confirmed the advantages of authoritative versus authoritarian parenting as it produces more solidarity in families and better mental functioning (Dwairy, Achoui, Abouserie, & Farah, 2006).

[...] Creating the Climate of Home: Cultural and Cross-Cultural Studies

Parents are the principal conduits of cultural learning. Differences in social attitudes, however, reflect the broader cultural values. For example, Asian parents think effort is more important in education than ability, whereas American parents believe innate ability is responsible for success (Stevenson & Zusho, 2002). These cultural attributions for success are consistent with the cultural underpinnings of collectivistic and individualistic societies.

Differences in parental values are reflected in the parent's involvement with the school system. American parents of European background are more likely to pay attention to in-school activities and the children's teachers, whereas Asian parents are more concerned with outside events like museum and library visits as contributors to the child's education (Sy & Schulenberg, 2005). Asian parents also emphasize high expectations and explicit rules about activities that interfere with learning. Since American parents believe limits are set by ability they are less likely to emphasize high expectations and are more concerned with shoring up their child's self-esteem.

[...] The Sleeping Arrangements of Childhood

The home climate is the earliest cultural influence on members of a society and the *sleeping arrangements* are thought to be very significant to the security of the child. Cultural studies demonstrate varying patterns in sleeping arrangements as parents in societies like the United States seek to create child independence from the very beginning. Mothers in the U.S. strive to have their babies sleep through the night and in a location separate from parents. The American culture is characterized by values of individualism and early independence, and separate sleeping arrangements support these values. In place of the security and warmth of parental bodies the child is often offered a soft toy or security blanket that the child carries around for several years.

Cultural studies of other societies show that independent sleeping arrangements are not ubiquitous. For example, in Sweden children often sleep with their parents through early childhood (Welles-Nystrom, 2005). This is believed by parents to provide the security essential to normal development. Likewise in Mayan cultures children often sleep with their mothers through early childhood creating bonds important to the survival of families. It is probably true that bonding through early childhood is emphasized more in societies where strong bonds are essential for survival, and sleeping arrangements have supported such collectivistic values. Socio-economic factors may also play a role as separate sleeping facilities may not be affordable in poor families (Morelli, Rogoff, Oppenheim, & Goldsmith, 1992). In some collectivistic societies parents would be amazed at the early separation of the infant from the mother's presence during the night.

The establishment of sleeping patterns is an early concern by young parents. Super, Harkness, Van Tijen, Van der Vlugt, Fintelman, and Dijkstra (1996) found differences in regulating sleeping patterns between Dutch and American parents. Dutch parents established early regularity in sleeping patterns believing that otherwise children with inadequate sleep would be more difficult to handle. The parents in the U.S. were more likely to adopt a non-directive attitude believing that as they age children will eventually sleep properly. The child's relative alertness also varied as measured by diaries of parents. Dutch children displayed quieter arousal, whereas U.S. children were more active. Contributing to the difference was the finding that U.S. mothers spent more time talking to and touching their children. Dutch parents found it more important to organize family time for their children, whereas U.S. mothers emphasized the importance of finding special time with just the child.

Ethnic groups within a society may also practice different sleeping arrangements. The United States is a multi-cultural society, and it is not surprising that subgroups have different child-rearing practices. One study demonstrated that parents sleeping with their children in early childhood are expected in the struggling communities of Appalachia (Small, 1998). Likewise in a study comparing a matched sample of white children with a sample of Latinos living in Harlem, a larger proportion of the Harlem children slept with their parents. Perhaps these studies are pointing to socio-economic differences in communities that are struggling with poverty and the acceptance of longer periods of sleeping with parents as essential for stronger bonding for survival. Sleeping arrangements reflect subliminal cultural values not articulated explicitly that still may reach into the earliest phases of life and children.

[...] Attachment in Childhood

Temperament is thought to be a genetically based trait present in infancy and related to attachment (Buss & Plomin, 1984). Many mothers observe differences in child reaction to stimuli with some children temperamentally difficult and others easy. These differences may later have personality consequences as parents respond differentially dependent on the child's temperament. Cross-cultural studies suggest some important comparative attachment differences. A study of middle-class mothers in the United States were compared to a sample of mothers from Kenya. Important similarities were found in the desire of mothers to touch and hold the child. However, American mothers talked more to their infants whereas Kenyan mothers communicated more with physical touch (Berger, 1995). Perhaps differences in the mother's verbal communication have a broader effect on cognitive development required in an industrial society, and U.S. mothers reflect in their communication style a cultural evolution to provide this advantage in the U.S. sample.

An important developmental achievement in infancy is *the formation of attachment*, first to the mother and later to the broader extended family and community. The recognition of the face of the mother and members of the family are important precursors to attachment. Studies have shown that most infants form attachment to the immediate family at about age seven months, but react differentially to strangers. However, the manner that infants react in the presence of strangers appears to follow universal patterns (Gardiner, Mutter, & Kosmitzki, 1998). Some children are anxious and avoidant, others anxious and resistant, and yet others are secure and are not threatened by the presence of strangers. However, the prevalence of these types has been found to vary by cultures (Van Ijzendoorn & Kroonenberg, 1988). Secure attachment is the basis for other developmental tasks that follow.

[...] Relationships with Siblings

Our relationships with brothers and/or sisters play important roles in socialization. In large families older siblings may be delegated roles as caregivers (Weisner & Gallimore, 1977). When children are close in age siblings are present along with parents for the most important events of a child's life. *The significance of family and cultural life is filtered through the eyes of siblings who struggle with similar family and cultural values.* Cultural values including interdependence are taught via sibling relationships. Our social assessment of right and wrong develop in sibling relationships whether cultivating aggression or empathy (Parke, 2004). As time moves on appropriate sex role behavior and gender relationships are learned primarily from siblings. Of all the influences in life the role of siblings is likely to be the most enduring as parents typically pass from the scene, but relationships with brothers and sisters are sustained until the end. However, the main focus of research has been on the child-parent relationship and we have only modest information on what must be the very significant influence of siblings (McHale, Crouter, & Whiteman, 2003).

[...] The Influence of the Extended Family and Peers

Research on the self demonstrates the profound influence of the extended family and peers on the development of the self. Self-concept research draws on information from the fields of personality theory and social psychology (Yang & Bond, 1990). Triandis noted that aspects of the self are influenced by cultural values like individualism-collectivism. Childrearing and other interpersonal relationships are the means by which the self is formed consistent with cultural values. Kagitcibasi (1996) discussed the relational self based on a family model of material and emotional interdependence. *Societies fostering the relational self are often pre-industrial where families have to rely on one another for subsistence and survival. Individualistic Western societies are more likely to nurture a separated self where children in the extended family live lives separate and distinct from one another.* Although emotional relatedness exists in individualistic families this feeling is not extended to the rest of society or the world.

These considerations brought Markus and Kitayama (1991a) to make a distinction between the *independent and interdependent* self. They argued that the self is construed differentially in various cultures with consequences for interpersonal relationships. In the extended family and peer relationships the child first experiences the construal of the social self that becomes the model for behavior in the larger society. In collectivistic societies the self is not separate from others, but seen as interdependent and connected. On the other hand, the self is incomplete in collectivistic societies when independent from others since only in relationships is the self seen as fully functioning.

However, Matsumoto (1999) reviewed 18 studies that examined differences between Japan as a collectivistic society, and the individualistic United States on the individualism-collectivism construct. The results showed that only one study supported differences between the two countries in the direction predicted. Takano and Osaka (1999) in a review of 15 studies came to a similar conclusion calling into question the validity of the existence of individualistic and collectivistic societies. However, Kitayama, Markus, Matsumoto and Norasakkunit (1997) in other studies found evidence for the utility of the collectivistic-individualistic construct. Nevertheless, we must exercise caution in accepting results that might be more stereotypic impression management especially in a globalized world of cultural change.

Extended families are more involved in childrearing in non-European collectivistic cultures. In these societies extended families are the main source for cultural transmission. In a multi-cultural society like the United States, extended families continue to play a role transmitting expectations related to gender appropriate behavior, and emphasizing the importance of family loyalty, cooperation among family members, and duties related to childrearing (Nydell, 1998; Tolson & Wilson, 1990). Where extended families play a role children experience more frequent interaction with other family members and provide useful models for the growing child of expected duties and contributions. In polygamous extended families children are provided with mothering from several individuals, and as in other collectivistic societies the entire community takes an interest in the well-being of children and in the requirement of obedience to cultural values. In the U.S. poverty plays a role where parents utilize the extended family in support of childrearing. Since the nuclear family has lost ground in recent decades and many children are born out of wedlock grandparents and in many cases great-grandparents play a socializing role in the lives of the affected children. The grandmother is particularly important as she is often more responsive to the children of teen age mothers and is a role model for childrearing (Leadbeater & Way, 2001).

The peer group influences socialization in all societies, but probably plays distinct roles in individualistic versus collectivistic cultures. In the modern society parents are often so busy with career issues that they are unable to invest time in teaching their children cultural values. When the nuclear family cannot play that socializing role, children learn from peers the common stereotypes, norms and customs of a culture. In more industrialized societies parents have little time for family life, and children spend more time with their peers (Fugligni & Stevenson, 1995).

During the teenage years, the role of the mentor is also very important. The mentor could be a teacher, a coach, a relative, a family friend or an elder friend of the teenager. As for the teenager since this is a time for rebellion against their parents the influence of a mentor is invaluable (Dolto, 1988).

[...] Culture and the Educational System

Same aged peers make important contributions to socialization in societies with regular educational systems. While not all cultures have formal educational systems, there is little doubt that schools are major socializing agents in the vast majority of countries. The educational system in a given country inculcates children with the dominant cultural values and implicitly conveys stereotypes or attitudes, and more explicitly salient culture through music and rituals. *What is taught in the educational system is dependent on cultural values.* In the United States conservative forces prohibited for a long time the teaching of evolutionary principles, so that history shows that cultural values can determine the very educational curriculum. In individualistic societies success is seen as a consequence of achievement that is individual and relative. Hence the emphasis in the educational system on grading and ranking of students in Western societies as such presumably prepares the student for a competitive society. Although American schools have explored non-grading alternatives and cooperative learning these efforts represent decidedly minority perspectives in education.

When the child enrolls in the school system the influence of peers increases and the majority of waking hours are spent with school mates. Together the educational system and peers play dominant roles in enforcing cultural values through both positive learning events but also by sanctioning behavior that is divergent and non-conformist. The educational system reflects what society thinks is important in order to function optimally. In some societies education is not formal as elders or other experts may teach the next generation cultural competencies and social structures. As the child grows older, however, peer acceptance is very important and only few children can escape the pressures of norms and customs.

[...] Socio-Economic Climate

The home climate and broader socio-economic environment have primary effects on child development. Some cultural environments require the development of motor skills at an earlier age since such learning contributes to coping with harsher environments. For example, the motor skills of African infants develop several months earlier than in comparable groups of white children, and different techniques are used to encourage walking (Gardiner, Mutter, & Kosmitzki, 1998). We know that birth death rates vary by culture and country reflecting different socio-economic circumstances and different social values about medical treatment for the poor and disadvantaged. When many children die at birth or in infancy mothers and family will focus their attention on creating the optimal conditions for survival and there is little time for other developmental tasks beneficial to children. In many societies there is little possibility for parents to foster the cultural or spiritual development of children as the harshness of the socio-economic environment direct parental attention totally on day by day survival.

Although the U.S. is commonly defined as an affluent society there is relatively low social acceptance of medical treatment as a common human right, whereas the reverse is true in Cuba a relatively poor country with nevertheless equal access to quality medical science and treatment. Within the United States there are large differences in medical access by people driven by costs and socio-economic differences. These health-related differences in child care may well produce long-term consequences not only for well-being, but also for the child's sense of security and view of the world as dangerous or benign.

[...] Social Identity

The individual's social identity grows from the home climate, and interactions away from the home. Research shows that children very early begin to identify with ingroups and reference groups. School children show a clear preference for their nation's flag, and can easily identify themselves in terms of ethnic and national groups (Lawson, 1975). The cultural context is important as children from individualistic societies demonstrate more competiveness than children from other cultures (Madsen, 1971). Competitive orientations have utility where cultural values of individualism and achievement are dominant and the welfare of the group is secondary. The effect of cultural values has been confirmed in comparative studies. For example, Thailand is a country dominated by Buddhist values of non-violence and respect for others. Problems of over-control among children are more commonly reported in Thailand and are manifested by withdrawal from social interaction. On the other hand, for parents in North America disorderly behavior and violence among children are a more dominant concern (Weisz, Suwanlert, Chaiyasit, & Walter, 1987).

[...] Comparative Studies in Child Rearing Behaviors

Do attachment patterns vary by culture? Studies on collectivistic versus individualistic societies suggest that the attachment experiences of childhood vary with cultural values. For example, in Japan people are conceived as being interdependent defined by the idea of "amae." This concept refers to the tendency by the Japanese to construe the self as merging with others (Doi, 1989). Amae is encouraged by Japanese mothers and is thought to be different from the concept of dependency in Western societies which describes the child's need for attention and approval. However, the two concepts prove to be similar in the actual descriptions used (Vereijken, Riksen-Walraven, & Van Lieshout, 1997). Different labels in comparative psychology may in fact describe the same behaviors.

The impact of culture can be observed at even the neonate stage. For example Asian neonate tends to be calmer and less irritable when compared to white American neonates. After birth the response to crying varies by culture. In cultures where infants are carried around all day prolonged episodes of crying are rarely observed whereas American infants cry for much longer periods. For example Korean mothers respond much more quickly to infant crying compared to American mothers (Arnett, 2012).

Cross-cultural comparative observation studies have demonstrated further differences in the infant's home climate. A survey frequently used is the "Home Observation and Measurement of the Environment Measure" commonly called the Home Inventory. The researcher visits the home and observes the interaction between the child and parents and follows up with some questions (Bradley, Caldwell, & Corwyn, 2003; Bradley & Corwyn, 2005). In studies employing this inventory cultures vary along several dimensions. For example, while parental warmth and responsiveness is present in all the cultures studied they are not expressed the same way. In some cultures parents do not express affection physically, but rather use the voice to indicate warmth. In Western countries being responsive to a child is measured by the frequency of spontaneous and unplanned conversations with the child. In other cultures like India spontaneous conversations are less frequent since it is expected that children will respect their parents and wait for permission to speak. The comparative studies show that the home environment corresponds to the broader cultural values present in society. At the same time comparative research has also yielded significant similarities in child rearing between cultural groups as most parents' in all cultures desire their children to develop social and emotional skills, and display similar assertion in disciplining their children for infractions. *The comparative research supports the presence of differences and similarities in the home climate that implicitly teaches the child during childhood and beyond.*

The *parental ethno-theories* and goals are seen as affecting varying childrearing in Gusii mothers in Kenya compared to U.S. mothers. The cultural context of agriculture in the Kenyan sample led mothers to emphasize the protection of infants, and keeping the child physically close. In the U.S. sample mothers encouraged more social engagement and more social exchange. American mothers believe stimulation begins in the earliest moments of infancy and try to talk to their babies. By contrast Gusii mothers believe such child rearing will create a more self-centered child (LeVine, LeVine, Dixon, Richman, Leiderman, Keefer, & Brazelton, 1994). Japanese mothers are more directly responsive when babies play with them, whereas U.S. mothers reinforce babies' behavior when they play with physical objects. A significant difference between Japanese and U.S. parenting is the amount of time spent with their children. While U.S. mothers will occasionally depend on babysitters Japanese mothers will rarely leave their infants. Some believe this difference in childrearing explains the higher anxiety of Japanese children in the absence of their parents (Bornstein & Tamis-LeMonda, 1989). Consistent with the broader cultural values Japanese mothers in one study were more concerned about lack of cooperativeness and social insensitivity in their children, compared to U.S. mothers who expressed greater worry about disruptive or aggressive behavior (Olson, Kashiwagi, & Crystal, 2001).

Working class parents in the U.S. and parents in pre-industrial communities believe that children can grow up by themselves, and do not need special tutoring. Obviously children raised with differences in parental ideology will develop characteristics unique to the child rearing strategy. What is required for the child to transit to successful adulthood may also play a role in the ethnotheories of parents and in child rearing practices. In the U.S. parents believe they are required to play a very active role in directing the development of their children (e.g. Goodnow, 1988). However, in other societies the focus is more on enjoying the parent-child relationship and allowing the child to grow up without excessive direction (Kagitcibasi, 1996).

Research on collectivism and individualism demonstrates the effect of these cultural values on parental childrearing. Collectivistic societies emphasize behavioral controls of children often making strict demands and providing sanctions for behavior that do not meet expectations (Rudy & Grusec, 2001). Parental authoritarianism is often associated with other authoritarian cultural practices derived from social instability, lower levels of education, and socio-political authoritarianism. For example, Russian adolescents see similar efforts to control behavior by both parents and teachers, and perceive that they are under more control when compared to U.S. students (Chirkov & Ryan, 2001). Comparative differences have also been found between white and Mexican-American parents, although no differences in authoritarianism were found between white and Mexican parental childrearing styles (Varela, Vernberg, Sanchez-Sosa, Riveros, Mitchell, & Mashunkashey, 2004). Obedience has great utility in societies that are struggling with survival. Children that face difficult or harsh ecological environments are likely to be raised with strict controls (Schonpflug, Silbereisen, & Schulz, 1990).

The age of mastery of various childhood skills varies by culture. Western cultures place competitive demands on the child from the very beginning reflected in expectations for early mastery. In a study of Dutch, Turkish immigrants, and Zambian mothers six types of skills were investigated. The childhood skills included physical, perceptual, cognitive, intra-individual, inter-individual, and social competencies. The expected developmental differences between cultures for physical skills across developmental stages were insignificant supporting the common biological basis of these competencies for all humans. However, for other domains like social skills the expectations by Zambian mothers were for later development compared to the other samples. Parents and other participants in a culture transmit the rules and customs of their society when rearing their children. Their specific socialization practices reflect these cultural beliefs (Segall, Dasen, Berry, & Poortinga, 1999). Once childrearing norms are established they are passed on from one generation to the next.

Childhood represents a period of continuous growth and development. Cognitive skills gradually develop to help the child cope with the complexities of the environment and social skills are developed appropriate to cultural values. Concern with the child's health causes mothers to encourage their children to eat properly and nutritiously. Although eating habits can be a way for the child to control powerful parents, it drives many mothers and fathers to distraction with worries. Worries over children's nutritional health seem, however, restricted to cultures where food is plentiful. In impoverished cultures children are just happy to fill their stomachs and are unlikely to put up a fuss over taste or texture. Eating preferences are laid down in early childhood and affect eating habits later in life.

Cultural history may also encourage competitive modes at an early age. For example, Israeli mothers from European background expected earlier development of cognitive skills compared to Israeli mothers from non-European families (Ninio, 1979). Compared to U.S. mothers Japanese mothers expected earlier development of emotional control, whereas U.S. mothers by comparison expected earlier development of assertive behavior (Hess et al, 1980).

[...] Human Development is Incorporation of Culture

Studies like the *"Wild boy of Averyon"* (Itard, 1962) call into question whether human nature exists in isolation from culture. In this early historical study Itard investigated the lack of development in a boy found in the forest of the district of Averyon in France, a boy thought to have survived in the wild without human contact. The boy was devoid of human qualities including the use of speech or recognizable emotional responses. *These and similar studies of children brought up in the wild suggest that there are no discernible human qualities developed apart from the interaction of the child with others.* Vygotsky had that right when he argued that the origin of human cognition is social interaction (Vygotsky, 1978; see also discussion by another Soviet psychologist Luria, 1976). All cultural development occurs as a result of interaction at the social level, and later represented intra-psychologically. Biological foundations are important as we shall see, however culture is what gives us human features and variations in behavior.

Human development is a function of many influences. Culture mediates between the child and the biological and environmental imperatives. Cole (1996), for example, maintained that biology does not interact directly with the ecological context but via the social environment. There is a basic distinction between the ecological context and the environment. More precisely, it is the complex interactions of biology, phylogenetic contributions, and cultural-historical factors that determine individual development. Biological influences are not directly responsible for behavior, as the impact on the child occurs through the filter of cultural values. Culture frames the social interactions that are eventually responsible for the internalization of cultural values.

Cultural values also play important roles in lifespan development (Baltes, 1997). Here biology and culture also interact dynamically. Evolutionary selection benefits derived from biology decrease in effectiveness with increasing age as the genome of older people produces more dysfunctional genes. The benefits of biological selection for fitness really have no role to play in later life, since evolutionary pressures for selection have passed with the end of the child-bearing age at around 30 years. Biological decline is associated with greater demand on culture for a variety of support resources that provide culturally based functioning in the later stage of the lifespan. Lifespan development through all the stages of life is dependent on the continual interaction of genetic heritage with what culture can offer in support. Culture can help offset the lower functioning produced by aging through, for example, improving skills in reading or writing that allows the individual to continue to participate and live actively at a time in life not possible in the dawn of humankind.

[...] Stage Theories of Human Development: Culturally Unique or Universal

Several prominent theorists in developmental psychology have proposed stages of development thought universal for all humans. There is evidence to support this assertion as we now have theories describing stages of cognitive, moral and psychosocial development. Nevertheless the universality is far from established as cultural ideology and the ecological context may prove more influential.

[...] The Evolution of Cognition

Developmental theory has been enriched by several stage theories of human cognitive development. If these theories are validated in all societies investigated it would lend support to the presence of universal cognitive structures, and by inference point to the biological basis for development. Piaget (1963) was the most influential researcher in the field of *cognitive development*. In-depth studies of children, some his own grandchildren, led him to formulate a theory of cognitive development in four stages. Stage one is called sensorimotor where the infant learns from direct sensory engagement with the environment. This stage last from infancy to about two years. The child understands his world through sensory perceptions and motor behaviors that occur in the process of interacting with the demands of the environment. Other cognitive achievements include learning to imitate others and learning by observation. Also the child begins language acquisition at this stage an achievement significant for later communication.

Stage two from about 2 to 7 years of age is called the preoperational stage where egocentrism is supreme as children do not understand the perspectives of others. However, this stage is also fundamental to language acquisition as the child expands vocabulary and understanding. Children's thinking is dominated by conservation defined as the ability to understand that changes in appearance do not change objects volume or weight. Centration is another characteristic of cognition in stage 2 that allows the child to focus on solitary objects or problems. The child also masters irreversibility which is the ability to reverse the process of problem solving. Egocentrism that is manifested at this stage shows that children cannot yet see problems from the perspectives of others. Finally, animism is the child's fantasy that all objects have life. A doll is living and may take on aspects of personality as children at this stage do not operate by logic.

Stage three is the concrete operations stage and lasts from about 7 to 11 years of age. At this stage cognition actually increases in complexity as children are able to view problems from a variety of perspectives. Taking the perspectives of others is considered a significant cognitive achievement. Children at this stage begin the development of more abstract thinking since they can assess more than one aspect of a problem or issue.

Finally, children learn to think abstractly in the fourth stage called formal operations. That stage lasts from about 11 years of age until the end of life. The individual operating at this stage can think logically about abstractions like notions of democracy and justice. As life progresses thinking becomes more systematic in problem solution. Formal operations is a cognitive process that allows for stage movement called assimilation where the individual fits new concepts into what is already understood, and accommodation where the individual changes his understanding by integrating concepts that do not fit the preexisting conceptual structure.

Piaget in fact believed that these stages of cognitive development were universal and each followed the preceding sequentially. Dasen (1984, 1994) found evidence for the universality of the stage sequence across cultures. However, methodological problems make valid comparisons difficult (Gardiner, Mutter, & Kosmitzki, 1998). Although Piaget valued the final stage of formal operations there is little evidence that it is a form of universal cognition as people can indeed have reproductive success in Western cultures and other societies without abstract thinking.

However, some support is present in the literature. The invariance of the stages was found in a study on school age children in several countries that showed that these children learned problem solving in the order predicted by Piaget (Shayer, Demetriou, & Perez, 1988). However, the ages that children achieved these stages varied by culture (Dasen, 1984). Some research indicated that Piaget's cognitive stages are not invariant as the children do not achieve the skills in the same order (Dasen, 1975). Finally, abstract thinking found in formal operations may be a cognitive development especially favored in societies that have benefitted from scientific development. Islamic cultures focus more on the rigid cultural transmission of faith that is less adaptable to abstract thinking required in a world of transition. Cole argued that formal operations required a Western education demonstrating the dependence of the Piagetian model of cognition on cultural values (Cole, 2006).

[...] The Evolution of Moral Development

As the child develops cognitively, he/she is able to bring these skills to bear in moral judgment. Cultural values are at least partially based on how people solved problems of morality. To a large extent these values serve as a guide for behavior in social interaction. Consequently, it is not possible to understand culture without an appreciation of the underlying morality and value system.

Kohlberg (1981) proposed 6 stages of *moral development* thought invariable for all people. The preconventional stage 1 evolves out of fear of punishment framing the child's perception of what is moral. In stage 2 the child recognizes that immoral conduct has negative consequences and moral conduct positive outcomes and the child has developed the ability to make choices. In the third stage the child enters the conventional level where what is good is defined by approval from significant others, in particular the child's parents and other important persons. In stage four, obedience to law becomes dominant determining what is considered good or bad. At stage five the child enters the postconventional level where morality is determined by the protection of individual rights and by the flexibility required by varying social requirements and circumstances. Finally, at stage six the individual becomes independent of institutions and social pressure, and moral conduct is determined by universal ethical principles. Kohlberg's theory moves in stages from initial concern with punishment when the child is very young, to stages where social institutions and conformity define moral conducts, to finally individually defined moral principles. In support of Kohlberg's theory are the studies that confirm that moral development progresses with age as predicted by his stage theory (Arnett, 2012).

In a review of 45 studies conducted in 27 countries Kohlberg's theory was evaluated (Snarey, 1985). The research literature provided evidence for the universality of the first two stages, but not the following. Others have found similar results (Ma & Cheung, 1996). These research reviews call into question whether the higher stages of moral development proposed by Kohlberg are in fact universal. However, we must keep in mind that it is also at the higher stages where culture produces the greater variability. Further, we must note that Kohlberg, like other stage theorists, developed his morality concepts from studies of Western samples. It is in fact a major complaint that Kohlberg's stages seem encapsulated in Western thought, and at least the last two have primarily emerged from Western liberal societies. Postconventional thinking would not get people much traction in Saudi Arabia or other totalitarian societies, where people who display this level of morality would spend their lives contemplating their noble thoughts from prison cells or worse.

Others have found evidence for the powerful influence of *cultural axioms* that can cancel moral development (Matsumoto, 1994). Chinese culture, for example, emphasizes collectivistic moral choices as influenced by working toward consensus, obeying law, and striving for harmony. These powerful cultural values would in most cases trump any moral stage development. Nevertheless there are probably dissidents in any culture with the moral courage to operate by universal principles of ethics developed individually. Further, Kohlberg's theory has also been attacked for gender bias based since males and females view relationships in different ways affecting moral choices (Gilligan, 1982). Consequently the higher stages of moral development are not invariant, but heavily influenced by culture as one would expect when the child moves from family circles to social conformity required by prevailing cultural values. Edwards (1986) believed that comparative differences in moral stages pointed directly to differences in social organization and underlying cultural values. In particular to understand morality it is essential to examine the culture's social structure and the broader environment.

Kohlberg largely agreed with these criticisms (Kohlberg, Levine, & Hewer, 1983). However, the theory is subject to many additional criticisms. Shweder, Mahapatra and Miller (1990) argued that Kohlberg's constructs were based on individualistic cultures and offered alternative moral views rooted in natural law using the family as a model. From this collectivistic perspective morality is based on duty to others rather than on rights of individuals (Shweder, Minow, & Markus, 2002). Ma (1988) offered an alternative based on Chinese morality that requires a person to behave consistently with the morality of the majority of society.

The review by Eckensberger and Zimba (1997) addressed the criteria that must be met in order to accept Kohlberg's moral stages as universal. The first criterion is whether the moral stages are found in all cultures investigated. The answer is mainly in the affirmative as long as invariance in stage sequence is not expected. However, stage invariance is supported by the .85 correlation between age and stage suggesting the sequence of moral behavior is the same for most respondents. Do the stages appear in all the cultures examined? Here the authors found support for some of the early moral stages, but not the latter. Although research supports universal development of moral reasoning in the early stages, the differences in the later moral stages may be what really counts in intercultural relations. For example, differences in moral development and the meaning of morality are real sources of conflict today between the Islamic world and the West. Acts considered blasphemy in Pakistan and other Islamic countries are behaviors governed by free speech in the West. These same acts of "free speech" produce the death penalty or vigilante action for the "offender" in Islamic countries.

[...] Evolution of Psychosocial Development

The relationship between the individual and his social environment was examined by Erickson (1950) in his theory on *psychosocial development*. Erickson believed that all human beings went through 8 developmental stages starting at birth and ending with death. At each stage the individual is faced with a developmental crisis which can have either a positive or negative resolution. A positive outcome in Erickson's stage theory results in a stronger ego as the individual is better able to adapt and consequently develop a healthy personality. The positive outcome produces individuals who have hope, will, purpose, competence, fidelity, love, care and wisdom, each the outcome of facing separate developmental crises as a person moves through life. If a person has not successfully mastered a stage it was in Erickson's theory possible to reverse the outcome through psychotherapy (Erickson, 1968).

Although some evidence has been found for the presence of these stages in other cultures (Gardiner, Mutter, & Kosmitzki, 1998) the theory is vulnerable to criticism. The main criticism is that Erickson is merely reflecting the normative culture of the West. Within Christian ethics the positive outcomes in Erickson's theory can be seen as lofty goals that permit the individual to live a complete and fearless life. This ideal is not likely replicated where people are struggling for survival. When it comes to the cross-cultural validity of the theory it should be noted that many people in both the West and in other cultures have no hope for developing "competency" or even "intimacy," goals that are valued outcomes in Erickson's theory, since survival is the daily theme of life. A Western college professor or other professional may struggle with issues of "stagnation" toward the end of professional careers, but for others less fortunate the dominant motivator is finding bread for the table. What Erickson calls "generativity" (finding new ways to make contributions in latter stages of life) never becomes a developmental issue for billions of people. People living from paycheck to paycheck who have mounting immediate problems do not have the luxury to contemplate the meaning of life in maturity or achieve wisdom and will despair from just the sheer inability to find economic security. Also despite Erickson theory there is really no struggle over "identity" in many societies since these are established at birth in cultures that define identity through obedience to ideology and social institutions. The theory has applications in societies called individualistic where individuals have some freedom to choose, but as noted even in these situations choices are limited by socio-economic circumstances.

Nevertheless that human development takes place in stages is widely accepted. That there are biological influences is very likely. However, how these stages of developmental achievement take place and when they occur is dependent on unique cultural factors. Therefore there is evidence for both universal and culturally specific behavior in these stage theories.

[...] Human Development is the Expression of Biology: The Presence of Universal Values

Only half of the story of cultural transmission is told in cross-cultural psychology. *The emphasis in the discipline of cross-cultural psychology is on the transfer of culture within the socio-cultural context. This bias ignores a growing body of research that points to the essential biological basis for cultural and social behavior.* The selective adaptation that has occurred over time as a result of evolution is transmitted via the genes and passed from one generation to the next (Mange & Mange, 1999). In evolution and the adaptation of humans to their environment we can understand the important story of cultural survival and the improved chances of reproductive success brought about by gene modification. Biology forms the basis of cultural transmission over the course of our evolutionary history. The key to understanding evolution is the idea that genetic material changes over time by means of natural selection.

When a heritable trait contributes to survival and therefore to successful reproduction the frequency of that trait will increase over time. If the trait contributes to greater fitness and therefore survival members of a species that do not carry the trait disappear from the evolutionary record. Natural selection is the process where the inclusion of a trait that improves fitness leads to systematic and significant changes affecting reproductive success over many generations. In modern times these changes have been associated with modification of the gene and the essential DNA sequences. Changes in genetic material called mutations are often adverse to the organism, but given sufficient time occasionally mutations may confer benefits to those that carry the modification. Other factors that affects the presence of heritable traits include selection caused by migration and isolation from the original mating population, and social rules for mating that favor or disfavor certain biological characteristics. Specified mating rules in some cases lead to inbreeding that affect the frequency of genetic components.

In some societies cousins are expected to marry, whereas in other cultures such a union is viewed as incest. Although genetic contributions to behavior is thought independent of environmental factors there is increasing evidence that environmental events can at least influence the regulatory processes of these heritable factors (Gottlieb, 1998).

Natural selection will favor those individuals who possess traits that result in improved adaptation. From the perspective of evolutionary science adaptation occur through interaction with the environment. In social science adaptation refer more specifically to changes occurring within individuals as they cope with the environment. However, in some cases the environmental pressure is so significant that the impact causes changes in the surface of genes carried from one generation to the next. For example, during the war on Vietnam the U.S. military sprayed enormous amounts of Agent Orange on Vietnam. The principal component dioxin is the strongest poison known to man (Bouny, 2007), and the spraying produced 4,800,000 victims that now span three generations (Stellman, Stellman, Christian, Weber, & Tomasallo, 2003). The new field of epigenetics shows that the environment can in fact affect cellular modifications that are transmitted intergenerationally and which produces outcomes that are lasting. Although the common scientific belief in the past was that the environment could only affect the current generation, results reported by Cloud (2010) show that powerful environmental events can leave an imprint on the genetic material in both eggs and sperm and thereby short circuit evolution and pass the trait to the next generation. The change does not occur in the genetic material, but rather on the cellular material placed on top of the gene that tells the gene to switch on or off. These epigenetic changes represent the biological reactions to extreme environmental events like the poisoning by Agent Orange in Vietnam. The young discipline of epigenetics does not provide a definitive answer as to whether the genetic changes will eventually fade away in the absence of stressor, but regardless there is a cautionary tale in that our extreme disruption of the environment may produce immediate genetic consequences that formerly took many generations (Larsen & Van Le, 2010).

Human beings are not passive in the face of their environmental challenges, but are active participants in shaping the conditions that create selective success. The environment places limits on what solutions are possible, but within these parameters human beings create a variety of cultural responses. Cultural responses to environmental challenges include in the most abstract sense also religion and cultural values. Biology has long recognized the existence of behavior traits that are relatively invariable for species other than humans and coded in the genes of the organism. As science is opening the possibilities of genetic modifications including artificial mutations we are learning more about gene based behavior. Can this science also be applied to human culture?

[...] The Evolutionary Basis for Human Behavior: Maximizing Inclusive Fitness

According *to sociobiological explanations all human behavior is aimed at maximizing inclusive fitness that motivates people to promote the interests of genetically related people.* The concept of inclusive fitness for the human species is not limited to offspring, but includes also maximizing the interest of other kin including nephews and nieces (Wilson, 1975). The promotion of the interest of kin is central to evolutionary reproductive success for social species like humans. Sociobiology extends the argument of genetic determinants of human behavior on a very broad scale. Wilson suggests that most of the branches of human knowledge in social sciences or humanities are reducible to the biology or sociobiology of a species.

[...] Perspective in the Transmission of Culture

It is the obligation of researchers to examine both cultural as well as genetic bases in cultural transmission. The genetic underpinnings of culture are essential components in the development of cultural solutions to environmental problems. However, cultural information is transmitted by social interaction from one generation to the next. The capacity for learning is limited by our genetic inheritance, but the cultural information channels offer the possibility to pass on cultural knowledge to our offspring. Life teaches us what is useful to survival or social success, and that information is conveyed by parents and other cultural guardians. Social learning theory explains many of the differences found in comparative studies as people learn by observation and imitation. It is important to remember that members of society are not passive spectators in cultural transmission. People interact with their cultures for evolutionary benefit and create niches that serve the purpose of reproductive success (Laland, Odling-Smee, & Feldman, 2000). Members of cultural groups participate in creating niches, for example, some population groups have dominated certain professions like medicine or the sale of jewelry as these were found over time to be successful niches ensuring survival through several generations.

Summary

The central concern of cross-cultural psychology is how people acquire culturally unique traits as well as communalities in behaviors across cultures. All theories of learning apply to the transmission of culture in interactions with parents, siblings, the educational system, and the ecological context. Socialization is the deliberate teaching of cultural values by parents and others whereas enculturation refers to the internalized psychological end product. In other words, socialization is the means to the encultural ends. Through the transmission of culture society passes on the skills and values thought important to survival and successful living.

There are both important similarities between cultures, but also distinct differences in chil-drearing as some cultures emphasize conformity and obedience and other societies promote personal independence. The ecological context, socio-political environment, customs, and psychology of caregivers provide the important niche components defining child development. However, the child is not a passive observer but actively interacts with these developmental forces and in the process affects the construal of the self. Childrearing ideology describes the dominant parental beliefs in society about the best way to raise children, and how to nurture and express warmth and affection. These and other values are inculcated in all members of a culture in the process of development. Affluent societies have more resources and time to develop unique assets of the child, whereas parents in poor societies are just struggling to stay afloat and survive.

Childrearing styles identified as authoritative and authoritarian have been found to have significant outcomes. Authoritative parents provide child care that is firm, but also reasonable and fair. The context of authoritative child rearing includes the consistent expression of warmth and affection. Authoritarian parents, on the other hand, demand obedience and practice strict control. Research has demonstrated the superiority of the authoritative style producing more positive emotions in the child more self-confidence, with long-lasting consequences.

The climate of home life is the major context in the transmission of cultural values. Differences have been observed between collectivistic and individualistic societies in the interaction of parents with the educational system. Sleeping with the mother is the earliest form of security in the home and also varies by culture. In the U.S. parents generally try to create early independence in all aspects of childrearing, and as a substitute for sleeping with the mother the child is provided with security blankets and sleep in separate quarters at the earliest moment possible. However, parents in other societies believe that keeping the child physically close provides essential security for later development. Socio-economic factors may also play a role in sleeping arrangements. Bonding has more utility in societies struggling to survive and that context may favor intimate sleeping patterns. Further, poverty may prevent the creation of additional space for separate sleeping arrangements.

The means of creating attachment in childhood varies by culture. The use of physical touch and verbal stimulation are dependent on cultural values and beliefs. Attachment is considered an important psychological achievement essential for later cultural learning. Relationships to siblings represent an early cultural influence. In fact the significant events of family and cultural life are sifted through the eyes of siblings, and cultural interdependence is taught by these relationships. How to act properly in social interaction and in gender relationships is primarily mediated by sibling relationships.

The extended family is also a source of cultural knowledge. Peers and the extended family reinforce the important cultural values in society. Material and emotional interdependence is particularly important in pre-industrial societies and in those cultures where people struggle to survive. By contrast interdependence is limited to the immediate family in Western countries and Western societies foster the separated and independent self. Although the research results are ambiguous it is thought that the self is construed differentially in collectivistic and individualistic cultures. Extended families are more involved in child rearing in collectivistic cultures. Ethnic groups in multi-cultural societies may continue to transmit the cultural expectation on gender related behavior and loyalty unique to their own group.

Culture is mediated by the country's educational system. Schools are major socializing agents in most societies in the world and serve to inculcate cultural values. In individualistic societies the educational system serves to prepare the student for a competitive future through the emphasis on grading, ranking, and competitive sports. The influence of peers on cultural learning increases in the school years. The socio-economic climate also affects development. In societies struggling for survival children learn motor skills at an earlier age compared to children from affluent communities. These motor skills are more salient to aid survival in harsh environments. Birth death rates vary by culture. Where the rates are high mothers must concentrate all their efforts on the survival of their infants and few parental resources are available to promote other assets of the child or provide enriching learning experiences. Eventually social identity grows out of the home climate and children learn early to identify with ingroups and reference groups. Children from individualistic societies also learn early the utility of competiveness for success and achievement.

Comparative studies in child rearing show that attachment experiences vary by culture as parental warmth and affection are not expressed in the same way in all cultures. In some cultures parents use physical touch to express loving feelings whereas in other cultures parents utilize their voices and intonation to express warmth. However, in all cultures parents have a desire for their children to learn emotional and social skills. Parents everywhere also use assertive behavior when disciplining their children for infractions. Parental ideology or ethnotheories play important but varying roles in different societies. These theories define play time interactions and the actual time spent with their children. Adherence to cultural values is a parental concern in all societies; however, mothers in collectivistic cultures are more concerned when the child displays a lack of cooperation, whereas American mothers are more worried about their children's disruptive behavior.

In some cultural or social groups parents have no childrearing ideology believing that their children can manage development without interference. However, in most cultures parents believe they must play an active role in raising their children. In collectivistic societies parents demand strict obedience and provide sanctions for behavior that does not meet expectations. Parental authoritarianism is related to a lack of cultural and socio-economic stability. The emphasis on competition leads Western parents to have expectations for the early development of skills.

The origin of human cognition is human interaction. In fact human "nature" does not exist in isolation from culture. Culture is the mediating variable between biological and environmental factors. Individual development is determined by the interaction of biology, phylogenetic development, and cultural variables. Culture provides the framework for the social interactions and mediates the internalization of cultural values. Culture also plays a role in lifespan development since it provides support services needed in the later stages of aging without which a person would not survive.

Stage theories in cognition, moral development and psychosocial development describe individual change in processes thought universal. Piaget's theory examines the evolution of cognition in four stages. Evidence from the comparative literature supports the universality of the early cognitive stage sequences. However, there is little evidence for the universality of "formal operations" as this type of abstract thinking probably requires a Western education. The ages at which children master the early stages also appear to vary by culture. Moral development is evaluated in Kohlberg's theory in 6 stages. Some evidence for the universality of the first two stages is supported by comparative research. However, the higher stages appear to reflect

Western moral traditions. The stability of moral stages is questioned since circumstances and powerful situations may cancel any stage of moral development. Kohlberg has also been criticized for gender bias since males and females view relationships differentially. Other criticisms focus on the influence of individualistic cultures on the higher stages of moral development. Erickson believed that all human beings pass through 8 psychosocial stages starting at birth and ending with death. At each stage a crisis occurs that if solved in a positive way leads to stronger egos and better adaptability. The main criticism of psychosocial development theory is that it reflects the normative culture of the West. Psychosocial development takes a different road in societies struggling for survival, and social identity is prescribed in some societies and not the outcome of crisis. The aforementioned discussion has emphasized cultural transmission from the perspective of the socio-cultural context. The chapter concludes with a discussion of the biological underpinnings of cultural behavior. The important study of survival and cultural adaptation is based on evolutionary principles.

References

Arnett, J. J. (1995). Broad and narrow socialization: The family in the context of a cultural theory. *Journal of Marriage and the Family, 57*, 617–628.

Arnett, J. J. (2012). *Human development : a cultural approach,* (1st ed.). Pearson Education, Inc.

Baltes, P. (1997). On the incomplete architecture of human ontogeny: Selection, optimization, and compensation as foundation of developmental theory. *American Psychologist, 52*, 366–380.

Barry, H., Bacon, M., & Child, I. (1957). A cross-cultural survey of some sex differences in socialization. *Journal of Abnormal and Social Psychology, 55*, 327–332.

Barry, H., Child, I., & Bacon, M. (1959). Relation of child training to subsistence economy. *American Anthropologist, 61*, 51–63.

Baumrind, D. (1971). Current patterns of parental authority. *Developmental Psychology monographs, Part 2, 4*(1), 1–103.

Berger, K. S. (1995). *The developing person through the lifespan*. New York: Worth Publishers.

Berry, J. W. (1997). Immigration, acculturation, and adaptation. *Applied Psychology: An International Review, 46*(1), 5–68.

Bornstein, M. H., & Tamis-LeMonda, C. (1989). Maternal responsiveness and cognitive development in children. In M. H. Bornstein (Ed.), *Maternal responsiveness: Characteristics and consequences*. San Francisco: Jossey-Bass.

Bouny, A. (2007). The effects of Agent Orange and its consequences. *Global Research*. January 4th. Retrieved from: http://www.globalresearch.ca/index. php?context=va&aid=4490, Last access April 9, 2012.

Boyd, R., & Richerson, P. J. (1995). Why does culture increase human adaptability? *Ethnology and Sociobiology, 16*, 125–143.

Bradley, R. H., & Corwyn, R.F. (2005). Caring for children around the world: a view from HOME. *International Journal of Behavioral Development, 29*(6), 468–478.

Bradley, R. H., Caldwell, B. M., & Corwyn, R. F. (2003). The child care HOME inventories: Assessing the quality of family child care homes. *Early Childhood Research Quarterly, 18*(3), 294–309.

Bronfenbrenner, U. (1979). *The ecology of human development: Experiments by nature and design.* Cambridge, MA: Harvard University Press.

Buss, A. H., & Plomin, R. (1984). *Temperament: Early developing personality traits.* Hillsdale, NJ: Erlbaum.

Chao, R. (2001). Extending research on the consequences of parenting style for Chinese Americans and European Americans. *Child Development, 72*(6), 1832– 1843.

Chen, X., Dong, Q., & Zhou, H. (1997). Authoritative and authoritarian parenting practices and social and school performance in Chinese children. *International Journal of Behavioral Development, 21*(4), 855–873.

Chirkov, V., & Ryan, R. (2001). Parent and teacher autonomy-support in Russian and U.S. adolescents: Common effects on well-being and academic motivation. *Journal of Cross-Cultural Psychology, 32*(5), 618–635.

Cloud, J. (2010, January 18). Why genes aren't destiny. *Time*, 49–53.

Cole, M. (1996). *Cultural psychology: A once and future discipline.* Cambridge, MA: Belknap/Harvard.

Cole, M. (2006). Culture and cognitive development in phylogenetic, historical, and ontogenetic perspective. In W. Damon & R. M. Lerner (Gen. Eds.), *Handbook of child psychology* (6th ed.), D. Kuhn & R.S. Siegler (Vol. Eds.), *Cognition, perception, and language*, (Vol. 2, pp. 636–683). New York: Wiley.

Collins, W., & Laursen, B. (2004). Changing relationships, changing youth: Interpersonal contexts of adolescent development. *Journal of Early Adolescence, Special Issue: Memorial Issue: Adolescence: The Legacy of Hershel & Ellen Thornberg. 24*(1), 55–62. doi 10.1177/0272431603260882

Dasen, P. (1975). Concrete operational development in three cultures. *Journal of Cross-Cultural Psychology, 6*, 156–172.

Dasen, P. R. (1984). The cross-cultural study of intelligence: Piaget and the Baoule. *International Journal of Psychology, 19*, 407–434.

Dasen, P. R. (1994). Culture and cognitive development from a Piagetian perspective. In. W. J. Lonner & R. Malpass (Eds.), *Psychology and culture* (pp. 141–150). Boston: Allyn and Bacon.

Doi, T. (1989). The concept of Amae and its psychoanalytic applications. *International Review of Psychoanalysis, 16*, 349–354.

Dolto, F. (1988). *La cause des adolescents*, Robert Laffont (Ed), Paris.

Dwairy, M., Achoui, M., Abouserie, R., & Farah, A. (2006). Parenting styles, individuation, and mental health of Arab adolescents: A third cross-regional research study. *Journal of Cross-Cultural Psychology, 37*(3), 262–272.

Eckensberger, L. H., & Zimba, R. F. (1997). The development of moral judgment. In J. W. Berry, P. R. Dasen, & T. S. Saraswathi (Eds.), *Handbook of cross-cultural psychology: Basic processes and human development* (Vol. 2., pp. 299–338). Boston, MA: Allyn and Bacon.

Edwards, C. P. (1986). Cross-cultural research on Kohlberg's stages: The basis for consensus. In S. Modgil & C. Modgil (Eds.), *Lawrence Kohlberg: Consensus and controversy* (pp. 419–430). London: The Falmer Press.

Edwards, C. P., Knoche, L., Aukrust, V., Kimru, A., & Kim, M. (2006). Parental ethnotheories of child development: Looking beyond independence and individualism in American belief systems. In U. Kim, K. S., Yang, & K. K. Hwang, (Eds.), *Indigenous and cultural psychology: Understanding people in the context* (pp. 141–162). New York: Springer Science and Media.

Erickson, E. H. (1950). *Childhood and society.* New York: Norton.

Erickson, E. H. (1968). *Identity: Youth and crisis.* New York: Norton.

Fugligni, A., & Stevenson, H. (1995). Time-use and mathematics achievement among American, Chinese, and Japanese high school students. *Child Development, 66,* 830–842.

Gardiner, H. W., Mutter, J. D., & Kosmitzki, C. (1998). *Lives across cultures: Cross-cultural human development.* Boston, MA: Allyn & Bacon.

Georgas, J., Christakopoulou, S., Poortinga, Y., Angleitner, A., Goodwin, R., & Charalambous, N. (1997). The relationship of family bonds to family structure and function across cultures. *Journal of Cross-Cultural Psychology, 28*(3), 303–320.

Gilligan, C. (1982). *In a different voice: Psychological theory and women's development.* Cambridge, MA: Harvard University Press.

Goodnow, J. J. (1988). Parents' ideas, actions and feelings: Models and methods from developmental and social psychology. *Child Development, 59,* 286–320.

Gottlieb, G. (1998). Normally occurring environmental and behavioral influences on gene activity: from central dogma to probabilistic epigenesist. *Psychological Review, 105,* 792–802.

Harkness, S., & Super, C. H. (1995). *Parent's cultural belief system: their origins, expressions, and consequences.* New York: Guildford Press.

Harkness, S., & Super, C. M. (2006). Themes and variations: Parental ethnotheories in Western cultures. In K. Rubin & O. Chung (Eds.), *Parenting beliefs, behaviors, and parent-child relations: A Cross-Cultural Perspective* (pp. 61–79). New York: Psychology Press.

Herskovits, M. J. (1948). *Man and his works: The science of cultural anthropology.* New York: Knopf.

Hess, R. D., Kashiwagi, K., Azuma, H., Price, G. G., & Dickinson, W. P. (1980). Maternal expectation for mastery of developmental tasks in Japan and the United States. *International Journal of Psychology, 15,* 259–271.

Itard, J. M. G. (1962). *The wild boy of Aveyron.* New York: Appleton-Century-Crofts.

Jackson, L. M., Pratt, M., W. Hunsberger, B., & Pancer, S. (2005). Optimism as a mediator of the relation between perceived parental authoritativeness and adjustment among adolescents: Finding the sunny side of the street. *Social Development, 14*(2), 273–304.

Kagitcibasi, C. (1996).*Family and human development across cultures: A view from the other side.* Hillsdale, NJ: Erlbaum.

Karavasilis, L., Doyle, A., & Markiewicz, D. (2003). Associations between parenting style and attachment to mother in middle childhood and adolescence. *International Journal of Behavioral Development, 27*(2), 153–164.

Kitayama, S., Markus, H. R., Matsumoto, H., & Norasakkunit, V. (1997). Individual and collective processes in the construction of the self: Self-enhancement in the United States and self-criticism in Japan. *Journal of Personality and Social Psychology, 72*, 1245–1267.

Knight, G., & Kagan, S. (1977). Acculturation of prosocial and competitive behaviors among second- and third-generation Mexican-American children. *Journal of Cross-Cultural Psychology, 8*(3), 273–285.

Kohlberg, L. (1981). *The philosophy of moral development: Moral stages and the idea of justice.* San Francisco: Harper & Row.

Kohlberg, L., Levine, C., & Hewer, A. (1983). Moral stages: a current formulation, and a response to critics. In J. A. Meacham (Ed.), *Contributions to human development* (Vol. 10), New York: Kargen.

Kolstad, A. (2012) . Inter-functionality between mind, biology and culture: Some epistemological issues concerning human psychological development. In Seidl-de-Moura, M. L. (Ed.). *Human development–Different perspectives.* Published by InTech, ISBN 978-953-51-0610-4.

Laland, K. N., Odling-Smee, J., & Feldman, M. W. (2000). Niche construction, biological evolution, and cultural change. *Behavioral and Brain Sciences, 23*, 131–175.

Larsen, K. S., & Van Le, H. (2010). Agent Orange and war related stress: Physical and psychological disorders. *Journal of Social Management, 8*(2), 73–88.

Lawson, E. (1975). Flag preference as an indicator of patriotism in Israeli children. *Journal of Cross-Cultural Psychology, 6*(4), 490–497.

Leadbeater, B. J., & Way, N. (2001). *Growing up fast: Transitions to early adulthood of inner-city adolescent mothers.* Mahwah, NJ: Erlbaum.

LeVine, R. A. (1977). Child rearing as cultural adaptation. In P. H. Leiderman, S. R. Tulkin, & A. Rosenfeld (Eds.), *Culture and infancy: Variations in the human experience* (pp. 15–27). New York: Academic Press.

LeVine, R. A., LeVine, S. E., Dixon, S., Richman, A., Leiderman, P. H., Keefer, C. & Brazelton, T. B. (1994). *Child care and culture: Lessons from Africa.* Cambridge, UK: Cambridge University Press.

Luria, A. R. (1976). *Cognitive development: Its cultural and social foundations.* Cambridge, MA: Harvard University Press.

Ma, H. K. (1988). The Chinese perspective on moral judgment development. *International Journal of Psychology, 23*, 201–227.

Ma, H. K., & Cheung, C. K. (1996). A cross-cultural study of moral stage structure in Hong Kong Chinese, English, and Americans. *Journal of Cross-Cultural Psychology, 27*(6), 700–713.

Maccoby, E. E., & Martin, J. A. (1983). Socialization in the context of the family: Parent-child interaction. In P. H. Müssen (Series Ed.) & E. M. Hetherington (Vol. Ed.), *Handbook of child psychology: Socialization, personality, and social development* (Vol. 4, pp. 1–101). New York: Wiley.

Madsen, M. C. (1971). Developmental and cross-cultural differences in the cooperative and competitive behavior of young children. *Journal of Cross-Cultural Psychology, 2*, 365–371.

Mange, E. J., & Mange, A. (1999). *Basic human genetics* (2nd ed.). Sunderland, MA: Sinauer.

Markus, H. R., & Kitayama, S. (1991a). Culture and the self: Implications for cognition, emotion, and motivation. *Psychological Review, 98*(2), 224–253.

Matsumoto, D. (1994). *People: Psychology from a cultural perspective*. Pacific Grove, CA: Brooks/ Cole.

Matsumoto, D. (1999). Culture and the self: An empirical assessment of Markus and Kitayama's theory of independent and interdependent self-construals. *Asian Journal of Social Psychology, 2*, 289–310.

McHale, S. M., Crouter, A. C., & Whiteman, S. D. (2003). The family contexts of gender development in childhood and adolescence. *Social Development, 12*(1), 125–148.

Morelli, G. A., Rogoff, B., Oppenheim, D., & Goldsmith, D. (1992). Cultural variations in infants' sleeping arrangements: Questions of independence. *Developmental Psychology, 28*(4), 604–613.

Ninio, A. (1979). The naive theory of the infant and other maternal attitudes in two subgroups in Israel. *Child Development, 50*, 076–980.

Nydell, M. K. (1998). *Understanding Arabs: A guide for Westerners*. Yarmouth, ME: Intercultural Press.

Olson, S., Kashiwagi, K., & Crystal, D. (2001). Concepts of adaptive and maladaptive child behavior: A comparison of U.S. and Japanese mothers of Preschool-Age Children. *Journal of Cross-Cultural Psychology, 32*(1), 43–57. doi:10.1177/0022022101032001007 SAGE Publications.

Parke, R. (2004). Developments in the family. *Annual Review of Psychology, 55*, 365–399.

Piaget, J. (1963). *The child's conception of the world*. Paterson, NJ: Littlefield, Adams.

Rudy, D., & Grusec, J. (2001). Correlates of authoritarian parenting in individualist and collectivist cultures and implications for understanding the transmission of values. *Journal of Cross-Cultural Psychology, 32*(2), 202–212.

Scheper-Hughes, N. (1992). *Death without weeping: The violence of everyday life in Brazil*. Berkeley: University of California Press.

Schonpflug, U., Silbereisen, R.K., and Schulz, J. (1990). Perceived decision-making influence in Turkish migrant workers' and German workers' families: the impact of social support. *Journal of Cross-Cultural Psychology, 21*(3), 261–282.

Segall, M. H., Dasen, P. R., Berry, J. W., & Poortinga, Y. H. (1999). *Human behavior in global perspective: An introduction to cross-cultural psychology* (2nd ed.). Boston: Allyn & Bacon.

Shayer, M., Demetriou. A., & Pervez, M. (1988). The structure and scaling of concrete operational thought: three studies in four countries. *Genetic, Social and General Psychology Monographs, 114*(3), 307–376.

Shweder, R. A., Mahapatra, M, & Miller, J. G. (1990). Culture a moral development. In J. W. Stigler, R. A. Shweder, & G. Herdt (Eds.), *Cultural psychology: Essays on comparative human development* (pp. 130–204). Cambridge, UK: Cambridge University Press.

Shweder, R. A., Minow, M., & Markus, H. R. (Eds.). (2002). *Engaging cultural differences: The multicultural challenge in liberal democracies*. New York: Russell Sage Foundation.

Small, M. F. (1998). *Our babies, ourselves: How biology and culture shape the way we parent*. New York: Anchor.

Snarey, J. (1985). Cross-cultural universality of social-moral development: A critical review of Kohlbergian research. *Psychological Bulletin, 97*(2), 202–232.

Sorkhabi, N. (2005). Applicability of Baumrind's parent typology to collective cultures: Analysis of cultural explanations of parent socialization effects. *International Journal of Behavioral Development, 29*(6), 552–563.

Spera, C. (2005). A review of the relationship among parenting practices, parenting styles, and adolescent school achievement. *Educational Psychology Review, 17*(2), 125–146.

Stellman, J. M., Stellman, S. D., Christian, R., Weber, T., & Tomasallo, C. (2003). The extent and patterns of usage of agent orange and other herbicides in Vietnam. *Nature, 422*, 681–687.

Stevenson, H., & Zusho, A. (2002). Adolescence in China and Japan: Adapting to a changing environment. In B. Brown, R. Larson, & T. Saraswathi (Eds.), *The world's youth: Adolescence in eight regions of the globe* (pp. 141–170). New York: Cambridge University Press.

Super, C. M., & Harkness, S. (1994). The developmental niche. In W. Lonner & R. Malpass (Eds.), *Psychology and culture* (pp. 95–99). Boston: Allyn and Bacon.

Super, C. M., & Harkness, S. (2002). Culture structures the environment for development. *Human Development, 45*(4), 270–274.

Super, C. M., Harkness, S., Van Tijen, N., Van der Vlugt, E., Fintelman, M., & Dijkstra, J. (1996). The three Rs of Dutch childrearing and the socialization of infant arousal. In Harkness & C. M. Super (Eds.), *Parent's cultural belief system: Their origins, expressions, and consequences* (pp. 447–465). New York: Guildford Press.

Sy, S., & Schulenberg, J. (2005). Parent beliefs and children's achievement trajectories during the transition to school in Asian American and European American families. *International Journal of Behavioral Development, 29*(6), 505–515.

Takano, Y., & Osaka, E. (1999). An unsupported common view: Comparing Japan and the U.S. on individualism/collectivism. *Asian Journal of Social Psychology, 2*, 311–341.

Tobin, J. J., Wu, D. Y. H., & Davidson, D. H. (1989). *Preschool in three cultures: Japan, China, and the United States*. New Haven, CT: Yale University Press.

Tolson, T. F., & Wilson, M. N. (1990). The impact of two- and three-generational Black family structure on perceived family climate. *Child Development, 61*, 416–428.

Van Ijzendoorn, M. H., & Kroonenberg, P. M. (1988). Cross-cultural patterns of attachment: A meta-analysis of the strange situation. *Child Development, 59*, 147–156.

Varela, R. E., Vernberg, E., Sanchez-Sosa, J., Riveros, A., Mitchell, M., & Mashunkashey, J. (2004). Parenting style of Mexican, Mexican American, and Caucasian-Non-Hispanic families: Social context and cultural influences. *Journal of Family Psychology, 18*(4), 651–657.

Vereijken, C., Riksen-Walraven, J. M., & Van Lieshout, C. (1997). Mother-infant relationships in Japan: Attachment, dependency, and amae. *Journal of Cross-Cultural Psychology, 28*(4), 442–462.

Vygotsky, L. S. (1978). *Mind in Society*. Cambridge MA: Harvard University Press.

Weisner, T. S., & Gallimore, R. (1977). My brother's keeper: Child and sibling care-taking. *Current Anthropology 18*, 169–190.

Weisz, J., Suwanlert, S., Chaiyasit, W., Walter, B. (1987). Over- and undercontrolled referral problems among children and adolescents from Thailand and the United States. *Journal of Counsulting and Clinical Psychology, 55*, 719–726.

Welles-Nystrom, B. *(2005)*. Co-sleeping as a window into Swedish culture: Considerations of gender and health care. *Scandinavian Journal of caring Sciences, 19*(4), 354–360.

Whiting, J. W. M., & Child, I. (1953). *Child training and personality.* New Haven. CT: Yale University Press.

Wilson, E. O. (1975). *Sociobiology: The new synthesis.* Cambridge, MA: Belknap Press of Harvard University Press.

Yang, K. S., & Bond, M. H. (1990). Exploring implicit personality theories with indigenous or imported constructs: The Chinese case. *Journal of Personality and Social Psychology, 58*, 1087–1095.

Diversity in Early Childhood Education

Olivia Saracho

A critical issue in the United States is the everlasting challenge to education that develops from the Americans' belief that all are created equal and that all children deserve an equal chance to learn, to work, to contribute, and to prosper (Raudenbush, 2009, p. 169).

Early childhood teachers have assumed responsibility for the education of an increasingly diverse group of children (children of diverse cultures and children with diverse abilities) in their classes. Therefore, the early childhood education teachers need to become more sensitive to individual differences among these children and become more competent in providing an appropriate education for children who have been retained from school before or who were segregated in regular classes. Children who were kept out of school or who received their education in segregated classrooms have been integrated in the regular classes among children who have a wide range of abilities. Integration is perceived to be a way to provide some educational equity that has not been available to these children. Also educating children from diverse cultures and children with a range of abilities in an integrated classroom is considered to be more effective for all children in the classroom (Zimiles, 1991).

Children with Disabilities

Children with disabilities have attended segregated education programs. For example, children who were unable to move in the school's stairways and halls due to an orthopedic problem received their education in a separate school or at home and had no contact with any children without disabilities. There were limited resources in the public schools to help children who had any disability such as vision, hearing, or behavior problems.

Laws and Regulations

New laws and regulations have affected a variety of changes in the schools. Public schools are required to educate children with disabilities, provide them with resources such as wheelchair access and accessible bathrooms at all levels in the school buildings. Courts ruled that the law protects these children in order that they have equal access to a high quality education. Consequently, public schools offer educational opportunities to a range of diverse children (Spodek & Saracho, 1994) including those children who are at risk of failure or children with disabilities.

Changes for children with disabilities are the result of Public Law 94-142 (1975), which is the Education for All Handicapped Children Act. President Gerald Ford signed Public Law 94-142[1] into law on November 29, 1975. Such legislation acknowledges the "Bill of Rights" for children with disabilities and their families. In addition, the legislation integrates the following six essential constituents, which are reiterated by the Project on Informing and Designing Education For All Learners (Project Informing and Designing Education For All Learners, 2008):

- *A free appropriate public education.* All children, regardless of the severity of the disability, must be provided an education appropriate to their unique needs at no cost to the parent(s)/guardian(s). Included in this principle is the concept of related services, which requires that children receive, for example, occupational therapy, physical therapy, orientation and mobility, as well as other services as necessary in order to benefit from special education.
- *The least restrictive environment.* Children with disabilities are to be educated, to the maximum extent appropriate, with students without disabilities. Placements must be consistent with the pupil's education needs. Each state is required to provide a full continuum of alternate placements.
- *An individualized education program (IEP).* This document, developed with the parent(s)/guardian(s), is an individually tailored statement describing an educational plan for each learner with exceptionalities. The IEP is required to address (1) the present level of academic functioning; (2) annual goals and accompanying instructional objectives; (3) educational services to be provided; (4) the degree to which the pupil will be able to participate in general education programs; (5) plans for initiating services and length of service delivery; and (6) annual evaluation procedures specifying objective criteria to determine if instructional objectives are being met.
- *Procedural due process.* The Act affords parent(s)/guardian(s) several safeguards as it pertains to their child's education. Briefly, parent(s)/guardian(s) have the right to confidentiality of records; to examine all records; to obtain an independent evaluation; to receive written notification (in the parents' native language) of proposed changes to their child's educational classification or placement; and the right to an impartial hearing whenever

disagreements arise regarding educational plans for their child. Furthermore, the student's parent(s)/guardian(s) have the right to representation by legal counsel.

- *Nondiscriminatory assessment.* Prior to placement, a child must be evaluated by a multidisciplinary team in all areas of suspected disability by tests that are neither racially, culturally, nor linguistically biased. Students are to receive several types of assessments, administered by trained personnel; a single evaluation procedure is not permitted for either planning or placement purposes.
- *Parental participation.* Public Law 94-142 mandates meaningful parent involvement. This legislation requires that parents participate fully in the decision-making process that affects their child's education.

The legal decisions of Public Law 94-142 support the integration of children with disabilities and grants them the rights (1) to a free public education, (2) to be educated in the least restrictive educational environment, and (3) to have parents evaluate and agree to any educational decisions related to their children with disabilities (Spodek & Saracho, 1994). Bud (Spodek, 1982) believed that this law had an impact on regular early childhood education teachers, but it also affected special education teachers who were used to their segregated classrooms. Therefore, he wrote several articles on the responsibilities of both regular and special education teachers in early childhood education programs.

Teachers Responsibilities

In "What Special Educators Need to Know About Regular Early Childhood Classes," Bud (Spodek, 1982) is concerned about the overwhelming consequences that Public Law 94-142 had on how the schools would function. Regular classroom teachers had to plan, work, and interact with children with disabilities, their parents, and a host of professionals (e.g., special educators, school psychologists, social workers, physicians). Such changes can leak and affect relationships between educational personnel and others who are involved in all of the children's education. Bud puts forward several issues and provides several recommendations. For example,

- Special education teachers rather than the regular classroom teachers prescribe instruction for the children with disabilities who are in the regular classroom. Special educators have specialized knowledge; but their practice differs from the regular classroom teachers' knowledge, experience, and values. Since special education teachers may not understand the classroom situation, Bud suggests that the special education teachers and regular classroom teachers become instructional partners and work together.
- Special educators affirm that their knowledge and practices are stronger for children with disabilities than those of the regular classroom teachers. This allegation becomes an imposition on the regular classroom teachers who have to accept the special education teachers' instructional methods and materials. Special education strategies may have been tested in segregated classes but may have different consequences in the regular classroom. Bud recommends that both regular and special education teachers negotiate meanings based on mutual respect and validity of their points of view.

- Some special educators work with children with disabilities outside of their regular class-room. The continued physical seclusion, as in pullout programs, or conceptual segregation lead to new ways of isolating both teachers and children. Bud believes that this segrega-tion is useless, because it does not improve the children's learning. He recommends that special educators become aware of the regular classroom teachers' validation of their classroom practices, dialogue, and work together.
- Sometimes special educators develop the IEP without the input of the regular classroom teachers. Bud points out that the regular classroom teachers, more than the special education teachers, work with the children with disabilities for a longer period of time and are able to provide them with information that can differ from that of the special education teachers. He suggests that the regular classroom teacher become part of the team in developing an IEP.

Bud (Spodek, 1982) contemplated on the following assumptions:

1. The classroom setting and the social environment within it are important elements of the learning process that can only be understood in terms of the interactions within it (p. 297).
2. The beliefs that teachers hold about schools, teachers, learning, children, individual differences, school content, and a host of other elements in the educative process rep-resent the parameters within which all resource personnel ought to operate (p. 300).
3. The techniques of classroom management used by regular educators are very effective means of working with a class of children from all sorts of backgrounds (p. 302).
4. The instructional strategies used by regular classroom teachers are powerful and effective means of aiding all children's learning (p. 304).

The requirement that children with disabilities be educated in the least restrictive environ-ment has increased the opportunities for regular and special educators to work together. Bud is concerned that improving the situations for the children with disabilities in regular classrooms may have been rushed and the strengths of the regular classroom environments may be ignored. He stated:

> regular classroom environments and regular classroom teachers might not be viewed as powerful educational forces. My fear is that teaching practices that have served children well and have valid theoretical and empirical justifications may be disregarded. I also fear that regular classroom teachers will feel imposed upon because of the way mainstreaming may be implemented. It is not that regular classroom teachers are unconcerned about the education of young children with disabilities, but they have, in some cases been alienated by the imposition of special educators lacking an understanding of what goes on in regular classes and what the regular teacher can and cannot do. There are potentials in the regular class as well as limitations. (Spodek, 1982, p. 305)

Bud recommends that regular classroom teachers and special educators need to engage in a deep dialogue at different educational levels. He concludes:

> As we move toward the greatest possible integration of children with disabilities in regular classroom facilities, there must be a similar move toward the integration of educational personnel. Only by working together, acting together, talking together, planning together, and thinking together (and even fighting together at times) will we be able to serve the best interests of all children, including children with disabilities. (Spodek, 1982, p. 306)

Children of Poverty

For several decades, equality of educational opportunity has been part of the discourse of American political life. Unfortunately, reality differs from this discourse. For example, poor children attend schools with scarce resources and are taught by unprepared teachers (Murnane, 2007). Children living in poverty are from families who have an income below the federal poverty level. For example, a family of four would have an income of $22,050 a year. Unfortunately, between 2000 and 2008 there was a 21% increase on the number of children living in poverty (Wight, Chau, & Aratani, 2010). In 2009, an income of $44,100 for a family of four characterized them as low income. Forty-one percent of the nation's children, which in 2008 was more than 29 million, are from low-income families (Wight & Chau, 2009). Presently, there has been an increase of 2.5 million more children living in poverty since the year 2000 (Wight, Chau, & Aratani, 2010). These statistics and the official poverty measure are disturbing. In addition, studies indicate that, on the average, families require an income of approximately twice the federal poverty level to make ends meet (Forry, 2008, Martínez-Beck & George, 2009). Regardless of the families' economic situation, it is essential that all children have equal access to a high quality education.

Poverty and Education

In "Poverty, Education, and the Young Child," Bud (Spodek, 1965) advocates the importance of helping children as students. He views the decennium of the sixties as the era of the "disadvantaged" just like society was concern for all children, especially poor children who were entering public education at that time. Although at that time, the word "disadvantaged" was a proper term. In my discussions with Bud, he said he disagreed with the label; because each child has some strengths that are considered advantages. Thus, there are no "disadvantaged" children. He explained that in the sixties, the term "disadvantaged" referred to those children who were living in poverty and were deprived of resources, experiences, and learning opportunities that kept them from succeeding in school. Children who did not have access to these learning opportunities became at risk of failing at school. The poor had a recurring nature where the poor from one generation launched conditions where poverty continued to the following generation.

Education assumed the responsibility of breaking this cycle. Educators soon realized that the educational problems of the poor became more complex, because their poor conditions had existed for a long time, which made important changes difficult.

Intervention Programs

Effective preschool interventions may assist in ending the disparity between prosperous children and poor children (Frede, 1995). Preprimary programs that were developed for children of poverty were considered to be a "new" approach, although this was actually an old approach. Historically, an effort to meet these children's needs has been attempted. At the turn of the 20th century, kindergarten associations throughout the United States and England offered free kindergarten programs in slum areas to children from families who were unable to afford to pay for private kindergartens. The first nursery school was initially established in the middle of London for young children who were growing up in an urban slum community. Unfortunately, the lack of financial support in the United States has caused the nursery schools to exclude the poor children. Child care centers became the poor children's nursery school (Spodek, 1965).

Historical concerns validated the importance of programs for poor children. In addition, several theoretical scholars (e.g., Piaget, Hunt, Bloom) supported that preprimary education would nurture the poor children's intellectual performance and academic achievement. Numerous preschool programs emerged for children of poverty. Federal funding became available through grants from the United States Children's Bureau and the Office of Economic Opportunity. Bud proposed the following recommendations.

> It will be exceedingly important that the developers of these programs base new curricula on knowledge of the effects of long established traditional approaches to early childhood education as well as on newer practices that are shown to be effective by contemporary research. Presently, developing research could be more valuable to the field if there were a concerted effort to factor out the effects of traditional nursery school practices from those of the more innovative practices. (Spodek, 1965, p. 601)

Bud (Spodek, 1965) predicted that preschool programs for children of poverty would continue to increase in future years. The children of poverty have been euphemistically identified as "culturally deprived," "disadvantaged," "disaffected," "alienated," and "socially unready." Sadly, these children are enrolled in the public schools of America, the American "common" schools that were established to prepare individuals "to live adequately in a republican society and to exercise effectively the prerogatives of citizenship" (Cremin, 1951, pp. 213-214). Several problems have surfaced in these schools. A foremost problem has been their approach to children who are culturally and linguistically different. The Americans' cultural, ethnic, religious, and linguistic discrepancies affect their social status and too often have been coerced to drastic socioeconomic deprivation. The concern for inequality is a persisting affliction, even though a number of modifications have taken place to diminish this inequality.

Children Who are Culturally and Linguistically Different

Throughout the 1990s, early childhood researchers recognized the need to provide programs and services for young children from diverse cultural and linguistic families. Their studies indicate that each cultural group benefits from their own unique teaching approach, which suggests that early childhood teachers need to use a range of strategies in working with young children from diverse cultural and linguistic backgrounds. Researchers show that early childhood teachers usually belong to a different cultural group from the one they are teaching (Saluja, Early, & Clifford, 2002), lack successful experiences with linguistically and culturally diverse children (Hollins & Guzman, 2005), and have trouble discussing race (Gay & Howard, 2000).

The education system in an open-ended American society offers opportunities for social mobility. The schools in the United States convey society's values to children of various cultures and languages, which are the leading essentials in the children's lives. Culture identifies their unique experiences whereas language helps them to reveal their culture in society (Saracho, & Spodek, 1995).

Culture and the School Curriculum

Culture and the school curriculum have a complex relationship, particularly at the "preschool" level, before the young children's entry to the first grade in the elementary or primary school. The degree of this relationship depends on educational goals, which could provide support to the children's development. One's definition of culture determines this relationship (Spodek & Saracho, 1996).

Culture can be understood through a society's values, beliefs, behaviors, language, customs, traditions (Saracho & Martínez-Hancock, 2005), assumptions, customs, physical objects, clothing, houses, food, tools, and art that a group of people have approved to give structure to their daily lives (Stassen-Berger & Thompson, 2000). In addition, culture is characterized through geography, history, architecture, religion, folk medicine, music, dance, and socialization practices. A society's culture is the knowledge that groups of people need to recognize or believe to effectively function and perform in an acceptable way in their society. Culture defines how individuals think, perceive, associate, and interpret (Goodenough, 1957) their world. It is an "information pool" (Goodenough, 2001) that people should know concerning their heritage to behave appropriately within their society. Stassen-Berger and Thompson (2000) believe that culture and ethnicity are analogous with a linkage to each other. An ethnic group is made of a cluster of individuals with the same antecedent attributes (e.g., national origin, religion, upbringing, language), beliefs, values, and cultural experiences. The children's cultural differences need to be recognized, understood, respected, and accepted to nourish their development (Saracho & Martínez-Hancock, 2005).

In his article, "Culture and the Early Childhood Curriculum" Bud (Spodek & Saracho, 1996) states that culture and child development have been considered to be two mutually exclusive sources of the early childhood education curriculum. Since culture has a profound influence on the children's development, both are actually directly related. The effect of culture on the children's development becomes evident in early childhood education programs from different countries. It is obvious the way each country's culture influences the content of the country's early childhood education curriculum.

Early childhood education is definitely a worldwide field. Each country's early childhood education program has affected programs from other countries. American early childhood education has widely influenced programs throughout the world, although American early childhood education was also influenced by programs from abroad. Most of the publications in early childhood education had their origins in America. There were no boundaries on the availability of early childhood education books and other printed materials. Abroad publications consistently cited American publications. Email messages and the Internet facilitated the transmission of ideas including information about the other countries' programs, such as those early childhood programs of Reggio Amelia in Italy, in Scandinavian countries, in France, and Japanese kindergartens. The exchange of ideas and practices with countries from abroad demonstrate "the one universality of early childhood education: A search for improved programs serving all children" (Spodek & Saracho, 1996, p. 12).

Cultural Traditions in Chinese Kindergartens

In "Chinese Kindergarten Education and its Reform," Bud (Spodek, (1989) analyzes the Chinese kindergartens in relation to (a) the provision of kindergarten education, (b) the only child, (c) teacher training, (d) the knowledge base of kindergarten education, and (e) reform of the kindergarten curriculum. His results reveal that the Chinese kindergarten reform focuses on creativity and individuality. Kindergarten educators use Western educational theories to transform their content, methods, and materials. Chinese kindergarten educators adapt the curriculum to respond to the children's needs and their evolving culture. However, Bud is concerned when one culture assumed the educational practices of another. He recommends that Chinese educators preserve those components that are rooted in their cultural traditions and are important to the children. In addition, Bud suggests that they use the early childhood education knowledge from abroad only as a source to modify their programs.

Cultural Traditions in the Preparation of Teachers

In the Chinese kindergarten reform, the administration of kindergarten education was transformed while the qualifications for kindergarten teachers were improved. Improvement through reform required supplementary resources for new kindergarten classes. An improvement became evident in the qualifications, preparation, and increase of incoming teachers. For example, in Taiwan the preparation of early childhood teachers initially took place in preservice training programs. When in-service programs became available, the teachers' preparation was altered. Presently, preservice training programs have been reestablished. Initially, preservice teacher preparation programs were 3 years in normal schools. Afterward 2-year preparation programs for kindergarten teachers were in normal junior colleges and teachers' colleges. At present time, teacher preparation programs are 4 years.

In "Early Childhood Teacher Preparation in Taiwan" Bud (Lin & Spodek, 1992) provides the historical and current perspectives on the preparation of early childhood education teachers in

Taiwan. He also offers recommendations to improve the preparation of early childhood teachers in that country.

Bud briefly reviews the history of early childhood education in China and a more exiguous one for Taiwan. The kindergarten development has remarkably influenced early childhood teacher preparation programs. In 1949, the Republic of China was transferred to Taiwan, which initiated a 40-year developmental era. For example, Taiwan was transformed from a rural province to an urbanized, industrialized country. Since Taiwan progressed from an underdeveloped domain to a developed one, educational institutions (like kindergartens) were modernized and transformed.

Taiwan's early childhood education teacher preparation and its problems can easily be recognized through an international development context in the field. Bud believes that reforms are necessary to improve the quality of Taiwan's early childhood teacher preparation such as the following.

- establishing a suitable and flexible certification system;
- extending the student teaching period;
- improving the salaries and benefits of kindergarten teachers; and
- improving the supervision system.

In summary, Taiwan's early childhood education teacher preparation had a brief history and was somewhat a novel discipline. Although in this modernization several problems have surfaced, Bud believes that these problems have solutions but will need an expansion of economic resources. As Taiwan continues to gain uniformity with western developed countries, Bud anticipates that its education will reinforce its children's educational development, which will generate the indispensable improvements.

Concluding Remarks

Although many modifications have occurred in Taiwan, other countries, and the United States, a major issue that persists is inequality, Bud (Saracho & Spodek, 2010) perceives that society

- feels threatened with how the various ethnic groups of immigrants and native populations are formed;
- views immigrants and ethnic minorities as realistic and symbolic threats; and
- believes that there is a conflicting logic for the national and the multicultural groups.

Public disputes on immigrants and ethnic minorities focus on the suspected threat to national identity and culture. Those who oppose such groups believe that national interests, beliefs, and values are threatened by newcomers and minorities; therefore, they are in opposition of multiculturalism and minority rights. Bud (Saracho & Spodek, 2010) promotes the multicultural recognition and equal rights for all society members (including immigrants, ethnic minorities, children with disabilities). He believes that in this democratic society, all children have the right to succeed in school. Verkuyten (2009) and Raudenbush (2009) support Bud's point of view.

They believe that it is important that everybody has the right to live in a multicultural and minority society (Verkuyten, 2009). They also have the right to succeed in our society. Bud proposes that the enduring challenge founded on the Americans' statement that all are created equal and that all children deserve an equal chance to learn, to work, to contribute, and to prosper (Raudenbush, 2009, p. 169) continue to a be the most important responsibility in early childhood education and the United States.

Note

1   Public Law 94-142- Education of All Handicapped Children Act has been amended, which also includes an amendment in its title, Individuals with Disabilities Education Act (IDEA). The 2004 and last amendment requires schools to offer services to eligible infants, toddlers, children and youth with disabilities (H.R. 1350).

References

Cremin, L. A. (1951). *The American common school: An historic conception.* New York, NY: Bureau of Publications, Teachers College, Columbia University.

Frede, E. C. (1995). The role of program quality in producing early childhood program benefits. *The Future of Children, 5*(3), 115–132.

Forry, N. D. (2008). The impact of child care subsidies on low-income single parents: An examination of child care expenditures and family finances. *Journal of Family and Economic Issues, 30*(1), 43–54.

Gay, G., & Howard, T. C. (2000). Multicultural teacher education for the 21st century. *The Teacher Educator, 36,* 1–16.

Goodenough, W. (1957). *Cultural anthropology and linguistics.* Report of the 7th Annual Round Table Meeting on Linguistics and Language Study. Monograph Series on Languages and Linguistics, no. 9. Washington, DC: Georgetown University.

Goodenough, W. (2001). *Theory and methodology. Lecture 17: Cognitive anthropology.* Retrieved from http://www.neurognosis.com/54.310/Lecture%2017%20-%20Cognitive20Anthropology.rft

Hollins, E., & Guzman, M. T. (2005). Research on preparing teachers for diverse populations. In M. Cochran-Smith & K. M. Zeichner (Eds.), *Studying teacher education: The report of the AERA Panel on research and teacher education* (pp. 477–548). Mahwah, NJ: Erlbaum.

H.R. 1350—*Individuals with Disabilities Education Improvement Act of 2004.* 108th Congress. Retrieved from http://thomas.loc.gov/cgi-bin/query/z?c108:h.1350.enr

Lin, Y., & Spodek, B. (1992). Early childhood teacher preparation on Taiwan. *Early Child Development and Care, 78,* 95–110.

Martínez-Beck, I., & George, R. M. (2009). *Employment outcomes for low-income families receiving child care subsidies in Illinois, Maryland, and Texas.* Final Report to the United States Department of Health and Human Services Administration for Children and Families. Chicago, IL: Office of Planning, Research, and Evaluation. Chicago, Chapin Hall at the University of Chicago.

Murnane, R. J. (2007). Improving the education of children living in poverty. *The Future of Children*, *17*(2), 161–182.

Project Informing and Designing Education For All Learners (IDEAL). (2008). *Introduction to special education public policy.* Lubbock, TX: Texas Tech University, College of Education. Retrieved from http://www.projectidealonline.org/publicPolicy.php

Public Law 94-142, Education for All Handicapped Children Act of 1975, November 28, 1975, Section 612 (2(B)).

Raudenbush, S. W. (2009). The *Brown* legacy and the O'Connor challenge: Transforming schools in the images of children's potential. *Educational Researcher*, *38*(3), 169–180.

Saluja, G., Early, D. M., & Clifford, R. M. (2002). Demographic characteristics of early childhood teachers and structural elements of early care and education in the United States. *Early Childhood Research and Practice*, *4*(1), 1–19.

Saracho, O. N., & Spodek, B. (1995). The future challenge of linguistic and cultural diversity in the schools. In E. E. García, B. McLaughlin, B. Spodek, & O. N. Saracho (Eds.), *Meeting the challenge and cultural diversity in early childhood education* (pp. 170–173). New York, NY: Teachers College Press.

Saracho, O. N., & Spodek, B. (Eds.). (2010). Classroom diversification: A strategic future perspective for equal rights. *Contemporary perspectives in language and cultural diversity in early childhood education* (pp. 253–264). Charlotte, NC: Information Age.

Saracho, O. N., & Martínez-Hancock, F. (2005). Mexican American families: Cultural and linguistic influences. In O. N. Saracho & B. Spodek (Eds.), *Contemporary perspectives on families, communities and schools for young children* (pp. 203–224). Greenwich, CT: Information Age.

Spodek, B. (1965). Poverty, education, and the young child. *Educational Leadership, 22,* 593–603 (Reprinted in Young Children, 21, 2–8).

Spodek, B. (1982). What special educators need to know about regular early childhood classes. *Educational Forum, 46,* 295–307.

Spodek, B. (1989). Chinese kindergarten education and its reform. *Early Childhood Research Quarterly, 4,* 31–50.

Spodek, B., & Saracho, O. N. (1994). *Dealing with individual differences in the early childhood classroom.* New York, NY: Longman.

Spodek, B., & Saracho, O. N. (1996). Culture and the early childhood curriculum. *Early Child Development and Care, 123,* 1–13.

Stassen-Berger, K., & Thompson, R. A. (2000). *Developing person through the life span* (5th ed.). New York, NY: Worth.

Verkuyten M. (2009). Support for multiculturalism and minority rights: The role of national identification and out-group threat. *Social Justice Research, 22*(1), 31–52.

Wight, V. R., & Chau, M. (2009). *Basic facts about low-income children, children under age 18.* New York, NY: National Center for Children in Poverty, Columbia University, Mailman School of Public Health.

Wight, V. R., Chau, M., & Aratani, Y. (2010). *Who are America's poor children? The official story.* New York, NY: The National Center for Children in Poverty, Mailman School of Public Health at Columbia University.

Zimiles, H. (1991). Diversity and change in young children: Some educational implications. In B. Spodek & O. N. Saracho (Ed.), *Issues in early childhood curriculum: Yearbook in early childhood education* (Vol. 2, pp. 21–45). New York, NY: Teachers College Press.

Conflict and Diversity in Democratic Classrooms

Christina Parker

> "Washing one's hands" of the conflict between the powerful and the powerless means to side with the powerful, not to be neutral.
>
> —Paulo Freire, *The Politics of Education*

Why are Peacebuilding, Citizenship, and Identity Important in Education?

Conflict can provide opportunities to learn for everyone, even young students. Conflict dialogue processes have been described in various contexts; in elementary classrooms, teachers may use conflict dialogue processes to facilitate open and inclusive social and academic engagement and democratic opportunities to learn. For example, a cross-national study demonstrated how open, inclusive dialogue can support democratic learning outcomes when conflictual issues were being discussed in classrooms (Hahn, 1998).

Some citizenship education has been criticized for not attending sufficiently to issues of diversity or to critical reflection regarding social and cultural inequities (Joshee, 2004; Osborne, 1995; Sears & Hughes, 2006; Tupper, 2005; Westheimer & Kahne, 2004). Similarly, mainstream multicultural education theories and practices have paid insufficient attention to pedagogies of dialogue and deliberation, and to developing the critical inquiry skills necessary for citizenship in pluralist societies (Banks, 2006b; Dei, 2000; Dilworth, 2004; Ladson-Billings, 1995; Nieto, 2002).

However, scholars have examined where diversity and conflict issues intersect with goals of education for democracy, through many overlapping perspectives, including antiracism, critical multiculturalism, critical pedagogy, culturally relevant and responsive peda-gogy, and citizenship education. To conceptualize how critical reflection on conflict and difference may provide inclusive, democratic learning opportunities for diverse students, in this chapter I gather insights from these areas of work and place them in an overarching conceptual framework of *peacebuilding*. Acknowledging diverse viewpoints and critically reflecting on social power structures are key aspects of peacebuilding pedagogy and critical components of educating for democracy (Bickmore, 2006; Davies, 2004a).

Together, culturally relevant curricula and peacebuilding pedagogies can help diverse students recognize and respond to questions of power and justice in society.

Dialogue, Difference, and Conflict in Education for Democracy

A curriculum may normalize hegemonic assumptions about race, gender, sexuality, and power, thereby silencing or ignoring others (hooks, 1994; McCarthy, 1988). Moreover, when such curric-ulum adopts a so-called neutral stance, treating conflict as something to be avoided, it implicitly invites students to maintain White, male-centred, heterosexual, and middle-class/upper-class norms and values (Apple, 1979/2004; Kumashiro, 2000). Avoiding explicit critical attention on conflict limits opportunities for students to engage in discussion and to explore alternative per-spectives. In contrast, curriculum that airs conflicting perspectives invites and supports critical thinking, exposing the ideological underpinnings of the existing system.

Conflict dialogue processes prepare diverse students for democratic and inclusive learning. Inherently connected to questions of student diversity is the concept of the *hidden curriculum*, based on the work of Jackson (1968) and Apple (1979/2004). Freire's (1970/1994b) theory of *critical consciousness* and *dialogic pedagogy for liberation* and Lynn Davies' (2004a) *dialogue for democratic education* illustrate how critical dialogic education may help teachers and students engage in inclusive peacebuilding learning.

All curriculum includes "norms and values that are implicitly, but effectively, taught in schools and that are not usually talked about in teachers' statements of ends or goals" (Apple, 1979/2004, p. 84). Together, these norms and values are known as the *hidden curriculum* (Jackson, 1968). While the hidden curriculum in North American schooling typically avoids conflict, it is entirely possible for conflict, whether explicit or implicitly embedded in the curriculum, to cut against this grain. In fact, it can be used to encourage critical, inclusive engagement. Conflict dialogue can be purposefully generated to address issues of power and difference, creating spaces for inclusion of multiple histories, experiences, and perspectives (Bickmore, 2007).

The identities of people involved in any conflictual discussion can be expected to play a significant role in the ways they understand and approach social and political issues. In conflict dialogue processes in the classroom, students and teachers engage with their many identities, and draw on their diverse lived experiences and perspectives to interpret and respond to par-ticular issues. Diverse students can better navigate the multiple worlds of home, school, and

community when teachers' pedagogical strategies engage their personal experiences and identities (Phelan, Davidson, & Cao, 1991). To support diverse students' identities as they engage in
conflict dialogue, teachers need to be equipped with culturally appropriate pedagogies (Delpit,
2006; Ladson-Billings, 2004). By contrast, when power and difference are ignored, it is possible
for conflictual issues pedagogies to be detrimental, particularly for students who carry marginalized identities (Apple, 1970/2004; Hess & Avery, 2008).

In societies characterized by social inequality, the dominant group's ways of thinking are legit-
imated when unproblematized; that is, when dominant world views are embedded in curriculum
content, and delivered in a top-down manner (Anyon, 1981; Apple, 1979/2004). This inhibits
the possibility for authentic, critical dialogue, which Freire (1970/1994b) argued is crucial for
democracy and social development:

> True dialogue cannot exist unless the dialoguers engage in critical thinking—
> thinking which discerns an indivisible solidarity between the world and the people
> and admits of no dichotomy between them—thinking which perceives reality as
> process, as transformation, rather than as static entity-thinking which does not
> separate itself from action, but constantly immerses itself in temporality without
> fear of the risks involved. (p. 73)

Dialogue evolves through developing *critical consciousness*—understanding gained through a
combination of transformative dialogue and praxis, action and reflection: "Dialogue (the two
acts of speaking and listening) is actually about emergence: the bringing out of new and previously hidden meanings and understandings" (Davies, 2004b, p. 216). Dialogue and critical
and creative thinking are ways to engage and teach towards social transformation. However,
for such dialogue to be democratic and transformative, the hegemony of socially constructed
norms must be explicitly challenged (Davies, 2004b). Hegemony is the pervasive and uncritical
acceptance of particular ideologies and discourses that work to maintain the dominance of certain
groups (Giroux, 1981). Applying Gramsci's (1971) notion of hegemony to education, Giroux (1981)
explained that this domination is perpetuated by mutual (unconscious) consent, through the
"power of consciousness and ideology" (p. 16). Education typically assumes, repeats, and reinforces
hegemonic discourses (Apple, 1970/2004; Giroux, 1981); but, through naming and challenging
problems of inequity or domination, critical dialogue offers counterhegemonic possibilities.

Interruption, in which a challenging or alternative view is presented, invites students to
shift their initial tacit beliefs and to form new and potentially counterhegemonic questions or
perspectives (Haroutunian-Gordon, 2010). Conflict dialogue pedagogies that do not include
marginalized perspectives limit the potential for such interruptive discussion (Davies, 2004b;
Haroutunian-Gordon, 2010). On the other hand, conflict dialogue that includes marginalized
perspectives challenges and disrupts hegemonic ideologies, and presents a way to achieve
recognition of difference. Its very goal is to elicit diverse and critical perspectives that question
dominant assumptions.

In a healthy, inclusive classroom, diverse students can freely and confidently learn from and
with their peers and teachers, actively and respectfully exchanging multiple and divergent

perspectives (Fine, 1993; Hahn, 1998; Larson, 2003). A curriculum characterized by "interruptive democracy"—frequent generation of dialogue and deliberation—engages in praxis (Davies, 2004b). Teachers in such classrooms encourage students to challenge hegemonic assumptions, and create inclusive spaces for expressing and challenging multiple identities. Such a curriculum may include organized forms of conflict dialogue such as student councils, circle time, diverse student representation on governing bodies, and critical pedagogy to address inequalities such as class, ethnicity, gender, and global injustices (Davies, 2004b, p. 223). Overall, conflict dialogue that is inclusive of multiple and diverse perspectives may contribute to democratic learning experiences.

Conflictual Issues Across the Curriculum

Schools lie in the nexus of political manipulation, fear, and societal conflict but also can be a potent forum for change.

—Weinstein et al., "School Voices: Challenges Facing
Educational Systems after Identity-Based Conflicts"

Classroom discussions of social and political issues are an essential component of education for democratic citizenship because they encourage students to be active and critical participants, and because they denormalize the status quo (Bickmore, 1999; Hahn, 1998; Hess & Avery, 2008; Torney-Purta, 2001). However, many teachers do not feel confident in facilitating open dialogue about conflictual issues (Bickmore, 2005, 2008b; Goldston & Kyzer, 2009; Yamashita, 2006). Avoiding conflict and complexity is part of what McNeil (1986) called *defensive teaching*, which reinforces standardization of hegemonic school knowledge. But explicit conflict learning scenarios challenge such antidemocratic education, in several ways. Teachers can choose to position conflicting perspectives as teachable moments (Houser, 1996). In critical pedagogy, attention can be paid to conflicting perspectives, thus stimulating critical self-reflection and thoughtful, constructively critical discussion (Houser, 2008; Shor, 1992). Open, inclusive dialogue about diverse viewpoints on conflictual questions contributes to peacebuilding by creating space for critical democratic learning.

Topics that may spark conflict in the classroom are extremely diverse, ranging from concerns over human rights to alternative ways of interpreting science experiments (Claire & Holden, 2007). For instance, science teachers may present students with actual cases of conflicts among scientists in history (Barton & Yang, 2000; Settlage & Sabik, 1997). Lesson materials on questions of human rights, prejudices, stereotypes, gender biases, current events, Canadian immigration patterns, sex education, and social justice literature present opportunities for conflict learning.

As Freire (1970/1994b) and Apple (1979/2004) argued, there is no such thing as neutral curriculum: particular perspectives, acknowledged or not, underlie all curriculum content. Biases in curriculum emerge from teachers' own choices and beliefs, curriculum mandates, and students' own perspectives influenced by their cultural, ethnic, religious, and gender identities. Thus, conflictual issues and topics explicitly embedded in curriculum content provide opportunities for including divergent perspectives.

What are such conflictual issues? In one definition, they are "those on which society has not found consensus and which are considered so significant that each proposed way of dealing with them has ardent supporters and adamant opponents" (Johnson & Johnson, 2009, p. 39). Hess (2009) categorized two kinds of controversial political issues: *settled* issues (including prejudice, racism, and bullying), to which teachers believe there is one acceptable answer; and *unsettled* issues (including the death penalty, abortion, and same-sex marriage), where public opinion is still widely split and teachers accept the legitimacy of alternative viewpoints. Hess (2001, 2009) argued that unsettled issues are the best topics for issues discussions, because they provide the opportunity to take a legitimate stance on either side of a question. In issues discussions in classrooms, of course, "reflective dialogue [is promoted] among students, or between students and teachers, about an issue on which there is disagreement" (Harwood & Hahn, 1990, p. 1). Hess and Posselt (2002) studied how Grade 10 students in two social studies classrooms participated in discussions on such unsettled issues as gambling, physician-assisted suicide, and free speech. Through pre- and post-questionnaires, observations, and interviews, the authors found that students' engagement was affected by "knowing a lot about the topic, being interested in the topic, and recognition from classmates" (Hess & Posselt, 2002, p. 299). They argued that positioning curricular material as controversial can motivate students to work together to find evidence to support their opinions, thereby increasing their confidence and interest in the material, and their participation in dialogue processes. These authors did not examine the ways these issues and pedagogies might have differentially engaged diverse students. Clearly, any curriculum is culturally bound, and varies depending on the context in which the issue is being discussed.

Positioning curriculum material as conflictual clearly offers teachers and students opportunities to make diverse, plausible interpretations through examining and evaluating politically relevant academic content. However, students' diverse identities increase the complexity of addressing conflictual issues in the classroom (Kim & Markus, 2005; Peck, 2010). Thus, I challenge the notion that unsettled issues are necessarily the most fruitful topics for discussion (Hess, 2001; Hess & Avery, 2008; Hughes & Sears, 2007). Instead, in examining how diverse students engaged in reflective dialogue on a broad spectrum of conflictual issues, I discovered that they found meaning in relation to their diverse identities. For instance, historical oppression and marginalization of particular cultural groups, such as Japanese-Canadians during World War II, are represented in Canadian textbooks in ways that implicitly or explicitly reinforce or challenge the status and membership of diverse students' ethnocultural groups in society. As Apple (1979/2004) and Barton and Levstik (2003) argued, critically addressing such social conflicts creates opportunities for democratic citizenship learning that interrupts prevailing inequities (Davies, 2004a; see also Epstein, 2000; Seixas, Peck, & Poyntz, 2011).

Integrating into the curriculum opportunities for diverse students to examine, interpret, read, write, and speak about social conflicts encourages critical literacy. With critical literacy, diverse students can challenge social injustices, develop and take stands on social conflicts, and "analyze and understand the social realities of their own lives and of their communities" (Cummins, 2009, p. 6). Engaging students in higher-order thinking involves purposeful inclusion of diverse perspectives, which deepens discussion and engages critical reading and writing (Applebee, 2002). Applebee, Langer, Nystrand, and Gamoran (2003) studied 64 middle and high school English classrooms and found that discussion-based pedagogies and high academic standards positively influenced diverse students' literacy performance. Further, addressing conflictual issues that are clearly relevant to students' identities and life experiences can offer newcomer immigrant students and language learners greater opportunities to participate. For language learners, "opportunities to practice listening, speaking, reading, and writing" in the target language are vital for second-language acquisition (Norton & Toohey, 2011, p. 414). Such engagement encourages opportunities for literacy improvement as diverse students read and write about important social issues that are meaningful and engaging (Cummins, 2009, 2011).

Pace (2011) has reminded us that "teachers provide students access to particular educational experiences through the choices they make about content and methods" (p. 34). She studied how social studies content was taught in American schools that did not hold standardized achievement tests (Pace, 2008). She found variations between what was taught in more affluent schools with mostly White students, and in poorer schools with more visible minorities. Much of the literature points to social studies as the ideal curricula in which to raise conflictual social and political issues. However, accountability via standardized testing that may exclude social studies (especially beyond a narrow history and civics content) limits what content is taught and the extent to which it may be presented critically and inclusively.

Social studies and language arts classrooms offer many possibilities of engaging elementary students in dialogue about alternative perspectives. The majority of research on dialogue processes in schools has been done in these settings; considerable research has been done on the rationale, complexity, and consequences of teaching conflictual issues in social studies and history curricula (e.g., Barton & Levstik, 2003; Osborne, 1995). "Schools teach a version of history that reflects 'their' truth—a nationalist perspective using literature and historical sources as evidence for that perspective" (Weinstein, Freedman, & Hughson, 2007, p. 63), which may marginalize students who do not identify with that history. A case study of Palestinian and Israeli teachers who cowrote a dual-language narrative on their countries' conflict history showed how curriculum content might be constructed to teach students to make sense of contrasting interpretations of historical events, in order to facilitate de-escalation of violent conflict (Steinberg & Bar-On, 2009; see also Freedman, Weinstein, Murphy, & Longman, 2008). In contrast, curricula most often offer hegemonic narratives that ignore conflicting perspectives on history and social structures—such as those of immigrants or indigenous peoples—and the people who have been marginalized through that history (Bannerji, 2000; Nicholas, 1996). As discussed above, many social studies teachers avoid making choices to engage in such complex and conflictual pedagogies; instead, they encourage their students to memorize and reiterate stories and facts from the past (Hughes & Sears, 2007; McNeil, 1986; Tupper, 2005).

Conflict can indeed be used for learning opportunities in the classroom. Social studies and language arts curriculum content that presents diverse perspectives, in conjunction with inclusive, engaging pedagogical tools, supports conflict learning for diverse students. Critical study of dominant and alternative narratives helps teach students to understand how narratives work (Funk & Said, 2004). And the study of fictional characters or events represented in literature can address power relations among participants with different identities. Such engagement with difference can in turn support processes of empathizing with others (Zembylas, 2007).

Diversity, Identity, Power, Conflict, and Peacebuilding Education

Students' identity and social status influence the ways they may choose to participate in conflict dialogue: diverse students' multiple identities—including race, ethnicity, gender, and socioeconomic status—in particular. Studies have shown that students' personal identities, histories, experiences, and social class shape the ways in which they interpret curricular subject matter (Banks, 2006a, 2006b; Delpit, 2006; Ogbu, 1992). "Language learners' identities are always multiple and in process," depending on the context, according to Norton and Toohey (2011, p. 437). Cummins (2001) argued that when "students' developing sense of self is affirmed and extended through their interactions with teachers, they are more likely to apply themselves to academic effort and participate actively in instruction" (p. 2).

However, Dull and Murrow (2008) and Kahne and Sporte (2008) have found that students in lower-income schools with higher percentages of newcomer immigrant and minority students had fewer opportunities to participate in conflictual issues discussions in their social studies classes than students in affluent and homogenous classrooms. In one case, Subedi (2008) observed and interviewed two immigrant teachers who tried to engage students in conflict dialogue about cultural differences in their diverse social studies classes, and found that these teachers were met with significant resistance and challenges from mainstream and minoritized students alike.

Hahn's (1998) cross-national, mixed-methods study showed that students who participated in conflictual issues discussions developed skills and inclinations for greater democratic civic participation. However, in interviews Hahn also found that some students in the classrooms she observed feared they would be embarrassed if they voiced unpopular dissenting views in classroom discussions (see also Bekerman, 2009; King, 2009). She concluded that key elements of the instructional climate—content, pedagogy, and atmosphere—could "model democratic inquiry and discourse" (Hahn, 1998, p. 232).

Participating in classroom discussions is risky for anyone, and feared repercussions (such as peer or teacher reprisal) when participating in conflictual issues discussions are even greater for visible minority newcomer students in Canadian elementary schools. These students simply may not possess the social or cultural capital to present the nuanced, normative perspectives that dominate most classrooms. One approach to address this fear is to create opportunities for young people to connect their identities to the curriculum.

While such connections might contribute to promoting democracy and peacebuilding education, it is still a complex endeavour that involves negotiating identities amidst sometimes painful acculturations. In an attempt to fit in to their new society, many minority immigrant students sometimes attach negative connotations to their ethnicities. For example, in one American study, predominantly Mexican and Vietnamese minority high school students felt excluded because of how stereotypes and misperceptions concerning their ethnic identities and immigration histories were presented in the classroom (Urrieta & Quach, 2000). As some students strive to be fully accepted into mainstream society, they may try to dissociate themselves from their families by purposely not speaking their familial language or connecting with their cultural heritage (Cummins, 2001; C. A. Parker, 2010b).

A climate of social prejudice may also contribute to students' marginalization, silence, or exclusion during conflictual issues discussions that touch upon or imply linkages to their ethnic identities. In their study of Asian students in a predominantly White high school, Quach, Jo, and Urrieta (2009) found that in this majority White population, some visible minorities vigorously attempted to subscribe to this Whiteness, while others chose to emphasize their ethnocultural differences. There is minimal research on whether students in predominantly visible minority communities experienced similar processes. But, in a Canadian study, ethnic minority immigrant youth formed strong attachments to their ethnic cultures and identities—and, at the same time, also identified with the larger Canadian political community—when these were recognized positively at school (Lee & Hébert, 2006).

Acknowledging and relating diverse identities to issues being discussed contributes to peace-building education. Discussions that encourage such diverse, tolerant, and dissenting viewpoints carry democratic peacebuilding potential, but they also risk further marginalizing or silencing diverse students. However, when teachers connect students' identities to the curriculum content, this may motivate and empower students to participate safely in democratic dialogue in the classroom, lessening that risk (Hemmings, 2000).

Pedagogical Tools for Conflict Dialogue

Teachers often fear managing controversial and politically charged material in inclusive and constructive ways, especially in classrooms with diverse students (Bickmore, 2005, 2008b; Torney-Purta et al., 2001; Yamashita, 2006). Teachers' sense of their own expertise in curriculum content and pedagogy, as well as their positionality on ethnic and political conflicts, influences how they facilitate or avoid conflictual issues discussions (see above and also Bekerman et al., 2009; Oulton, Day, Dillon, & Grace, 2004). Studying diverse classrooms and students' experiences with conflictual issues discussions is an effective means of revealing ways in which teachers can better facilitate effective, inclusive conflict dialogue.

Many pedagogical tools are available to teachers for guiding and inviting students to participate in discussions of conflicting perspectives. Some pedagogies prescribe particular, "correct" ways of handling conflict, while others rely on broad principles for including the diverse experiences of the participants to guide the dialogue process. *Prescriptive* approaches to conflict education often reflect dominant norms and behaviours, by teaching an assumed-neutral package of "how tos" that emerge from dominant cultural contexts, leaving minimal space for diversity of experiences and perspectives of participants (Lederach, 1995, p. 5).

By contrast, *elicitive* pedagogies invite participants to make explicit cultural knowledges that were formerly implicit, through storytelling and critical analysis of language, proverbs, and cultural symbols (Lederach, 1995). Such approaches can uncover culturally rooted knowledge resources for critical, creative, and locally relevant conflict learning. In this way, conflict education is a type of cultural learning; participants identify the different understandings of conflict embedded in curriculum content, thereby co-creating a new body of knowledge. Explicitly inviting students to voice and examine their diverse experiences helps them question and resist prescriptive Western models for understanding conflict and their own so-called common-sense assumptions regarding prevailing social relations. The way can thereby be paved for democratization.

Other pedagogical tools for facilitating conflict dialogue include structured academic controversy (Johnson & Johnson, 2009), peacemaking circle processes, and controversial public issues discussions. In structured academic controversy, students are taught to take positions in small-group discussions, then later to reverse their perspectives, and finally to attempt to reach consensus. The purpose of these dialogues is not to solve any conflictual issue. In the final stage of the process, students analyze and integrate the best arguments and evidence presented. While there is some empirical research on structured academic controversy, there is little research on how such a small-group conflict dialogue process might differentially engage and support learning of diverse and/or marginalized students.

Another pedagogical tool for conflict dialogue is the circle process, types of which include talking circles and community circles. These may be used in classrooms to build community or resolve conflict (Bickmore & Scheepstra, 2011). Circles can also be used during class meetings, to offer all participating students the opportunity to speak in discussion and decision-making on issues they are concerned about. Some facilitators may circulate a "talking piece," to provide all students with the opportunity to participate—the person who holds the talking piece, which is passed sequentially around the circle, is the only one who is entitled to speak. In such a circle, everyone is given the opportunity to voice his or her perspective, and as the talking piece is passed around, everyone is encouraged to listen.

Circle processes invite those "who are quiet, shy, or struggling to find their voice in a group space … to share what's on their minds and hearts" (Pranis, Stuart, & Wedge, 2003, p. 93). Such pedagogies may contribute to creating inclusive spaces for students who may feel marginalized or less confident to voice their perspectives. Peacemaking circles are designed to facilitate discussion and resolution of particular problems or conflictual issues; they work towards transformation through open-ended dialogue. In general, my research investigated how various kinds of dialogue pedagogies reinforced marginalization and/or encouraged ethnic minority students to identify positively with their cultural and ancestral histories. The limited literature on circle processes in school settings (McCluskey et al., 2008; Morrison, 2007) did not show how or whether marginalized students might experience a reduction in their sense of inclusion through such processes.

In one Grade 9 world history class, Kohlmeier (2006) found that when historical events were presented to students as being debatable, the students became engaged and intellectually stimulated to gather evidence and take on various perspectives (see also Hahn, 1998; Hess & Avery, 2008; Johnson & Johnson, 2009). Kohlmeier used a discussion tool known as the Socratic seminar, in which students engage in critical dialogue about multiple perspectives on a question posed by the teacher. However, Kohlmeier's study did not address how diverse students in this classroom might have experienced this conflict dialogue process in different ways.

King (2009) used an ethnographic method to study a cross-cultural reconciliation program involving Catholic and Protestant Northern Irish high school students and their teachers. In addition to extensive classroom observations, he conducted semistructured interviews with teachers and students, to explore how multiple perspectives influenced students' experience and participation in conflictual issues discussions. He found that through the use of conflict dialogue processes (including structured academic controversy), these students were equipped to engage in critical self-reflection while also exploring multiple perspectives.

Overall, the above cases illustrate how dialogic practices are demonstrably possible in social studies classrooms. Children in highly conflictual and in relatively harmonious settings may develop different understandings and approaches to conflict (Kitson & McCully, 2005). Conflictual issues discussions are not inevitably constructive learning experiences (Bekerman et al., 2009). Students need to learn to address conflictual material in any setting, but they tend to build on different knowledge and skills learned informally in conflictual or peaceful contexts (Merelman, 1990). Educators in conflict zones initially need to set up their programs to address safer conflictual issues so that students can first learn basic skills and values and develop trust: "Attempting too early to debate group *political* aims would destroy trust, alienate students, and bring parental reprisals" (Merelman, 1990, p. 59; see also Hemmings, 2000; Hess & Avery, 2008; King, 2009; Schultz, Buck, & Niesz, 2000).

Discussing Conflicts with Young Students

A number of studies of conflictual issues discussions have investigated the experiences of high school students (Byford, Lennon, & Russell, 2009; Freedman et al., 2008; Hess, 2001; Hess & Posselt, 2002; Kohlmeier, 2006; A. Ross, 2007). A smaller body of theory and research challenges preconceived notions about the supposedly limited capabilities of elementary children to engage in such discussions (Angell, 2004; Beck, 2003; Kelly & Brooks, 2009).

It is vital to provide adequate support for teachers when they engage with sensitive material, especially with younger students. Fine (1993) described a vignette from her research in a Grade 7/8 classroom, in which two students voiced perspectives that differed from the teacher's views about the Holocaust and Israeli-Palestinian relations. In an effort to address one student's anti-Semitic bias regarding a so-called Jewish conspiracy, the teacher brought in a guest facilitator from Facing History and Ourselves[1] to facilitate a follow-up discussion. This organization's curriculum materials and teacher training helps students examine cases of genocide from various contexts, and guides them to explore their own identities and perspectives as citizens who can resist violence in their own societies.

Elementary students are capable of engaging in conflict dialogue, especially when they have the benefit of preparatory lessons and scaffolding content and process (Bickmore, 1999, 2014;

Bickmore & Parker, 2014; Parker, 2011, 2013). Beck (2003) studied a case in which a suburban American Grade 4 class engaged in a Civics Deliberation unit on rights and government. He reported that the teacher's preparatory lessons on how to engage in conflictual discussions had created a classroom climate where at least some students felt comfortable in expressing minority points of view. During classroom discussions, one student's point of view was that, if someone was accused of murder, he shouldn't get a lawyer: "He should just go to jail" (Beck, 2003, p. 326). Beck's study shed light on how young children could engage in conflict dialogue about issues that may be familiar to their lived experience.

In any context, children's experiences of conflict are closely connected to their social status, gender, and cultural identity, and form part of their citizenship learning. Children who grow up in diverse neighbourhoods tend to become aware of ethnic and racial differences at an earlier age than children who live in monoracial settings (Kendall, 1983; Parker, 2010a; Peck & Sears, 2005; Ramsey, 2004; Ramsey & Myers, 1990); some argue that such awareness develops by the age of four or five (e.g., Derman-Sparks, 2006; Hyun, 2007; Wolpert, 2006). It is therefore important to pay attention to the ways that these differences may influence the ways that diverse students in elementary schools experience conflictual issues associated with such diversities. Cultural sensitivity in discussions with young, diverse students can contribute to all students developing positive feelings about their racial and cultural identities (Biles, 1994; C. A. Parker, 2010b).

Literature circles that elicit conflict dialogue may encourage students to draw on and voice their lived experiences in response to conflictual issues. For instance, inviting students to express their viewpoint through a character in a story can provide safety for students to participate (Bickmore & Parker, 2014). In an urban American Grade 1/2 mixed classroom with predominantly Latina/Latino students, Fain (2008) studied how the teacher's use of literature circles facilitated the students' discussion about issues of oppression. The teacher purposely selected controversial literature; the narratives explicitly addressed issues of racism, discrimination, and social exclusion. Fain argued that the literature circle provided a "safe space" where the students "established their voices in democratic ways by taking multiple positions in the dialogue" (Fain, 2008, p. 207). DeNicolo and Franquiz (2006) described similar critical incidents during literature circles on cultural literacy in a diverse American Grade 4 classroom.

Stereotyped notions of "childhood innocence" may make educators reluctant to raise conflictual issues with young children (Bekerman et al., 2009; Davies, 2004a; Yamashita, 2006). Kelly and Brooks (2009) challenged these preconceptions in their study of how novice teachers in British Columbia approached social justice issues in their Grades 4, 5, and 6 classrooms. They found that the teachers' presumptions about students' innocence and indifference to political and social justice issues (such as death, drugs, or poverty) usually caused those teachers to report that they avoided discussing controversial issues in their classrooms.

However, conflict dialogue pedagogies can be infused into the curriculum safely enough to engage diverse students in inclusive, democratic learning opportunities. For example, one teacher in Kelly and Brooks's study facilitated a conflict dialogue with his Grade 2 class of primarily South Asian immigrant students. In a discussion of the conflict between India and Pakistan, a student raised the issue of atomic bombs. The teacher linked this issue of global conflict with a lesson the class had already done on interpersonal conflict, in order to reduce the "heaviness" of the topic (Kelly & Brooks, 2009, p. 208). Clearly, issues discussions with young children are not only possible—they are also necessary. Voicing divergent perspectives and stories in the curriculum may contribute to diverse students' understandings of how issues of power and inequity are associated with their and others' race, ethnicity, gender, and migration experiences.

Critical Multiculturalism and Culturally Relevant Pedagogy

As Delpit (2006) has argued, mainstream cultural codes for language and interaction are generally assumed in schools, rather than being taught explicitly: this inexplicitness tends to disadvantage culturally minoritized students, such as new immigrants, who do not have prior access to such cultural knowledge. Culturally relevant pedagogy aims to challenge mainstream hidden curricula that teach acceptance of the status quo, by making the dynamics of the dominant society explicit—accessible for learning and for critique (Howard, 2001; Ladson-Billings, 1995). It encourages a wider range of diverse students' voices through equity-oriented teaching methods (Gay, 2000; Ladson-Billings, 1995). A main tenet of culturally responsive pedagogy is cultural reflection; teachers facilitating dialogue about sensitive, identity-linked issues can encourage diverse students to reflect on how conflicts are connected to their identities through their race, ethnicity, or gender. Such pedagogies are often promoted for students of colour (Nieto, 1999).

Distinct approaches to diversity and multiculturalism influence how conflict is approached in schools and how possibilities for uncovering hidden curriculum are managed. Banks (2006a) identified four approaches to multicultural curriculum reform: the contributions approach; the ethnic additive approach; the transformation approach; and the decision-making and social action approach. The contributions approach is the typical default approach, in which mainstream ethnic heroes and holidays are added to the curriculum. In ethnic additive approaches, teachers include content from various ethnic groups without encouraging students to understand society from these diverse perpectives. The transformation approach is fundamentally different from the first two approaches, because it considers how dominant assumptions can be challenged by interrogating the multiple perspectives of several ethnic groups. The decision-making and social action approach includes all elements of the transformative approach, but also provides students with opportunities to critically reflect on social issues and make decisions about how to take action and solve these issues.

Kumashiro (2000) also identified four approaches to antioppressive education: education for the Other, education about the Other, education that is critical of privileging and Othering, and education that changes students and society. As in Banks's model, the first two approaches reflect liberal and additive approaches to address issues of diversity and oppression and the last two approaches promote critical transformative multiculturalism. The latter approach explicitly addresses conflicts and questions of power, to motivate and equip diverse students to engage in cultural critique and democratization.

Uncritical, liberal approaches to multiculturalism produce national histories that imagine Canada as a socially just and successful multicultural state; in this way, normative Canadian history produces Canada as a nation that is "tolerant" and "innocent" (St. Denis, 2011, p. 310). But these multicultural initiatives can work against Aboriginal sovereignty and anticolonialism, sometimes excluding them: "By inciting multiculturalism, public schools effectively limit meaningful incorporation of Aboriginal content and perspectives into public schools" (St. Denis, 2011, p. 307). Multiculturalism sometimes equates Aboriginals' history and that of immigrant groups, inaccurately assuming shared commonalities. By doing so, it erases the specific experiences of Aboriginal peoples, who are indigenous to the land—experiences that are very different for people who have newly arrived to the country.

In order to respond to the so-called problem of difference, multicultural education is often used to promote a discourse of hybridity, cosmopolitanism, and equality amongst all cultures (Gérin-Lajoie, 2008a, 2008b; May & Sleeter, 2010; Nieto, 1999). But practitioners and theorists understand, experience, and interpret *difference* differently (Gérin-Lajoie, 2008b; Nieto, 1999). In the dominant discourse of liberal multiculturalism, equity and diversity are promoted at a minimal, generic level and focus on "celebrating" differences (Gérin-Lajoie, 2008b; Harper, 1997; Nieto, 1999). Some teachers still believe that an adequate response to multiculturalism and diversity would be to hold a "holiday party" instead of a "Christmas party." While this is a step towards inclusiveness, such conventional views of liberal multiculturalism are presented as short-term "'feelgood' additives" to curriculum programs, meant to "boost self-esteem for 'minority' students" (Nieto, 1999, p. 27). But one of the core concepts of multicultural education has to do with facilitating inclusion of diverse students, through sustainable interventions. A critical approach to multiculturalism presents antiracist and social justice education as basic education that is pervasive and important for all students (Nieto, 2002). A critical multicultural praxis involves "moving beyond dysconsciousness and miseducation toward liberatory pedagogy" (King, 2004, p. 81). Mainstream views that perpetuate dysconsciousness are challenged by acknowledging that education is not neutral. Dysconsciousness means uncritically accepting social structures which maintain a limited awareness of inequity and diversity:

> Dysconscious racism is a form of racism that tacitly accepts dominant White norms and privileges. It is not the absence of consciousness (i.e., not unconsciousness) but an impaired consciousness or distorted way of thinking about race as compared to, for example, critical consciousness. (King, 2004, p. 73)

Critical multicultural education focuses on knowledge construction and praxis; it is an "anti-racist, egalitarian, inclusive process that is embedded in all aspects of school life: program, pedagogy, social interactions between school actors, and notions of learning and teaching" (Jacquet, 2008, p. 61). This kind of teaching is necessary in order to pay attention to race and racism, equality and equity, and inclusion and exclusion, in both the content and pedagogy that students are engaged in at school. When students are free to examine and present multiple perspectives in democratic classrooms, multicultural education becomes critical, transformative, and antioppressive (Banks, 1996; Nieto, 2002; Kumashiro, 2000).

Multicultural education is part of citizenship education; however, both have been taken up in various ways. Liberal, additive, and uncritical approaches focus on generic, top-down content that ignores conflict and uncertainty. For example, while there have been nation-wide shifts in educational policies that seek to promote greater understanding and respect for diversity, early assimilation-oriented educational policies "were meant to be a homogenizing force that would work with immigrant and native-born children and their families to create 'good Canadian citizens'" (Joshee, 2004, p. 135). Such assimilation policies promote liberal, additive approaches that educate for and about the Other but do not invite critical reflection about social issues. Canadian federal policies have since been repositioned to reflect a social cohesion approach, which recognizes diversity but still maintains an uncritical approach to multicultural and human rights education (Joshee, 2004).

When power and hegemony are ignored, liberal multicultural educational practices can easily be implemented in the curriculum. In contrast, critical, progressive, and transformative approaches embrace the inevitable (and potentially positive) consequences of conflict and explicitly surface the hidden curriculum. Such approaches encourage dialogue about diversity, conflictual issues, and the necessity of action for social change to produce justice.

Teaching marginalized students to be good citizens is a goal of both multicultural and citizenship education (Ladson-Billings, 2004; Osborne, 1995). Critical multicultural education allows students and teachers to draw on their diverse lived experiences and perspectives to interpret and respond to particular issues. A critical multicultural education program encourages diverse students to reflect on how their lived experiences are part of conflictual and social issues in the democratic society in which they live. When teachers explicitly acknowledge issues pertaining to ethnocultural difference, such as racism, they acknowledge social conflict, thus fulfilling the peacebuilding education mandate of including social conflict issues in the implemented curriculum (Bickmore, 2008a).

Through connecting curriculum content and students' experiences, teachers empower students to critically reflect on their social and cultural identities. Critical race theory scholars (e.g., Delgado, 1995; Lopez, 2003) argue that maintaining a false neutrality about race and racism ignores the impact and reality of racism in schools. By acknowledging counternarratives about racism and injustice, applied critical race theory provokes critical reflection and an open space to challenge the status quo (Delgado, 1995; Knaus, 2009). Knaus, a high school teacher, described his personal experience in applying critical race theory in his class of predominantly African American and Latino students in California; his students were able to share their personal experiences with racism and oppression. Bolgatz (2005) showed how the pedagogy of two teachers, one Black and one White, facilitated conversations about race and racism in a high school class. The two teachers team-taught lessons that asked students to discuss issues of race and racism. Key features of their practice included explicitly teaching students to listen, "back up their opinions with evidence, and make use of their own experiences in discussions," and engaging students in peer-to-peer discussion (Bolgatz, 2005, p. 30). Similarly, in a qualitative study of an American middle school history classroom, the teacher used counterstorytelling as a method of resistance to racism; including alternative narratives, students reflected on their social realities and engaged in dialogue about race (Howard, 2004). In these examples, culturally relevant pedagogies supported ethnocultural minority students to share personal experiences, thereby creating space for them to engage in critical dialogue about social issues.

In another study, two male teachers, one Black and one White, integrated multicultural content in their diverse middle school and high school social studies classrooms and found that the teachers' lived experiences influenced how they chose to present conflictual historical issues (Dilworth, 2004). In both classes, the teachers articulated their confidence about integrating multicultural content in their curriculum, but both still relied heavily on the classroom textbook that presented multicultural issues through limited additive approaches. They extended their implemented curriculum through the contributions approach, presenting multiple perspectives and encouraging students to critically reflect on the contributions of diverse groups of people to society. The study showed that while integrating multicultural content was a necessary component of citizenship education, teachers' personal choices strongly impacted the extent to which students were able to dialogue about conflictual issues and develop a deeper awareness of their sociopolitical communities.

Obviously, discussing sensitive issues can be detrimental to classroom social relations if adequate preparations have not been made. For instance, one Toronto teacher attempted to engage with his diverse Grade 3 students' cultural histories (Dudley-Marling, 1997). However, during a discussion about a folk tale, he mistakenly assumed one of his students, an Afghani, was from Pakistan. The student, who had spent a year at a Pakistani refugee camp, was hurt, and retorted, "I'm not from Pakistan." Like this student, others might be sensitive to discussions that highlight their perceived ethnicity and experiences based on stereotypes. While I advocate for dialogue about diversity, I also acknowledge that such practices are not a panacea; in fact they are risky pedagogy. Even though risky, however, such practices are necessary to disrupt the guise of neutrality and to address social injustices (Freire, 1985).

When teachers' pedagogical strategies engage diverse students' personal experiences, they affirm students' identities—encouraging their active engagement in the curriculum (Cummins, 2001; Nieto, 1992). To provide this support, teachers need to be equipped with culturally appropriate pedagogies (Delpit, 2006; Ladson-Billings, 2004). Particularly when teachers encourage diverse students to voice their perspectives, conflict dialogue processes can open space for discussion of alternative viewpoints across all subject areas. For example, in the language arts curriculum, studying conflictual issues in fiction and nonfiction plots and themes can help diverse students relate to conflicting perspectives of characters. In a previous research study (C. A. Parker, 2010b), I described a new immigrant student who initially showed reluctance to engage in a multicultural unit integrated to the Grade 4 English language arts curriculum. However, he spoke up during a class discussion following a read-aloud of the picture book *The Name Jar* by Yansook Choi. The book is about a girl named Unhei who is embarrassed by her Korean name when she first goes to school in America, because her classmates cannot pronounce it. After the class read the book the student chose to share cultural and language challenges he had experienced when he moved back to China for a few years after his family first came to Canada. Despite this student's limited English language skills, he became comfortable participating in a discussion about this story as he related it to his own troubling story of cultural transition. This study demonstrated that, when curriculum content and pedagogy supported diverse students' inclusion, students may indeed be encouraged to share sensitive or personal issues about cultural conflict.

In sum: cultural responsiveness and flexibility of power are key characteristics of peacebuilding education, because they address destructive social conflict and systemic violence (Bush & Saltarelli, 2000; Lederach, 1995). Critical multiculturalism and culturally relevant pedagogy are necessary components of this peacebuilding education. Transforming implemented curriculum by inviting dialogue about conflict and diversity increases the possibility of inclusion for all students, and contributes to building peace.

Conclusion: Conflict and Diversity In Democratic and Diverse Classrooms

When curriculum and pedagogy engage diverse students' identities, histories, and perspectives, the students increasingly become included in the class. Democratic peacebuilding education relies on dialogic pedagogies to offer opportunities for all students to participate and have their voices heard. In elementary classrooms there still remain shifting approaches to understanding how these processes are used and whom they include. Hidden curriculum embedded in classroom practices that teach acceptance of the status quo tend to exclude some diverse students. However, as many diverse immigrant students acculturate to classroom settings, they may also encounter cultural barriers in the explicit, planned classroom curriculum. Apple's (1979/2004), Freire's (1970/1994a, 1970/1994), and Davies' (2004a, 2004b) theories suggest that inviting students to explore conflicting perspectives on unresolved issues would facilitate education for democratization. Conflict dialogue pedagogies may or may not be sensitive to diverse students' identities. Equity issues embedded in curriculum (e.g., experiences of historically marginalized, oppressed groups) are often skimmed over or not mentioned at all. In contrast, the infusion of conflictual issues dialogue provides opportunities to voice multiple, contesting, perspectives—which may be relevant to diverse students' identities.

Note

1   Facing History and Ourselves is a North American organization that began as a way to support educators to teach about the Nazi Holocaust; it is an example of an organization that educators may consult for support in facilitating conflictual issues.

References

Angell, A. (2004). Making peace in elementary classrooms: A case for class meetings [Peacebuilding Citizenship Education theme issue]. *Theory and Research in Social Education, 32*(1), 98–104.

Anyon, J. (1981). Social class and school knowledge. *Curriculum Inquiry, 11*(1), 3–42.

Apple, M. (2004). *Ideology and curriculum* (3rd ed.). New York, NY: Routledge. (Original work published 1979)

Applebee, A. (2002). Engaging students in the discipline of English: What are effective schools doing? *English Journal, 91*(6), 30–36.

Applebee, A. N., Langer, J. A., Nystrand, M., & Gamoran, A. (2003). Discussion-based approaches to developing understanding: Classroom instruction and student performance in middle and high school English. *American Educational Research Journal, 40*(3), 685–730.

Banks, J. A. (1996). The canon debate, knowledge construction, and multicultural education. In J. A. Banks (Ed.), *Multicultural education, transformative knowledge, and action: Historical and contemporary perspectives* (pp. 3–29). New York, NY: Teachers College Press.

Banks, J. A. (2006a). Approaches to multicultural curriculum reform. In E. Lee, D. Menkart, & M. Okazawa-Rey (Eds.), *Beyond heroes and holidays* (pp. 193–197). Washington, DC: Teaching for Change.

Banks, J. A. (2006b). *Cultural diversity and education: Foundations, curriculum, and teaching* (5th ed.). Boston, MA: Pearson.

Bannerji, H. (2000). Geography lessons: On being an insider/outsider to the Canadian nation. In H. Bannerji (Ed.), *The dark side of the nation: Essay on multiculturalism, nationalism, and gender* (pp. 63–86). Toronto, ON: Canadian Scholars Press.

Barton, K. C., & Levstik, L. S. (2003). Why don't more history teachers engage students in interpretation? *Social Education, 67*(6), 358–361.

Beck, T. (2003). "If he murdered some, he shouldn't get a lawyer": Engaging young children in civics deliberation. *Theory and Research in Social Education, 31*(3), 326–346.

Bekerman, Z. (2009). Identity versus peace: Identity wins. *Harvard Educational Review, 79*(1), 74–83.

Bekerman, Z., Zembylas, M., & McGlynn, C. (2009). Working toward the de-essentialization of identity categories in conflict and postconflict societies: Israel, Cyprus, and Northern Ireland. *Comparative Education Review, 53*(2), 213–234.

Bickmore, K. (1999). Elementary curriculum about conflict resolution: Can children handle global politics? *Theory and Research in Social Education, 27*(1), 45–69.

Bickmore, K. (2005). Foundations for peacebuilding and discursive peacekeeping: Infusion and exclusion of conflict in Canadian public school curricula. *Journal of Peace Education, 2*(2), 161–181.

Bickmore, K. (2006). Democratic social cohesion (assimilation)? Representations of social conflict in Canadian public school curriculum. *Canadian Journal of Education, 29*(2), 259–386.

Bickmore, K. (2007). Taking risks, building peace: Teaching conflict strategies and skills to students aged 6 to 16+. In H. Claire & C. Holden (Eds.), *The challenge of teaching controversial issues* (pp. 131–145). Stoke-on-Trent, UK: Trentham Books.

Bickmore, K. (2008a). Peace and conflict education. In J. Arthur, I. Davies, & C. Hahn (Eds.), *The Sage handbook of education for citizenship and democracy* (pp. 438–454). Los Angeles, CA: Sage.

Bickmore, K. (2008b). Social justice and the social studies. In L. Levstik & C. Tyson (Eds.), *Handbook of research in social studies education* (pp. 155–171). New York, NY: Routledge.

Bickmore, K. (2014). Peacebuilding dialogue pedagogies in Canadian classrooms. *Curriculum Inquiry, 44*(4), 553–582.

Bickmore, K., & Parker, C. A. (2014). Constructive conflict talk in classrooms: Pedagogies for engaging hearts and minds in social justice and divergent perspectives. *Theory and Research in Social Education, 42*(3), 291-335.

Bickmore, K., & Scheepstra, T. (2011, May). *Circle processes for community building and problem solving in elementary classrooms.* Paper presented at the Canadian Society for Studies in Education (CSSE) annual conference, Fredericton, NB.

Biles, B. (1994). Activities that promote racial and cultural awareness. *Family Child-Care Connections, 4*(3), 1–9.

Bolgatz, J. (2005). Teachers initiating conversations about race and racism in a high school class. *Multicultural Perspectives, 7*(3), 28–35.

Bush, K., & Saltarelli, D. (2000). *The two faces of education in ethnic conflict: Towards a peacebuilding education for children.* Florence, Italy: UNICEF Innocenti Research Centre.

Byford, J., Lennon, S., & Russell, W. B., III. (2009). Teaching controversial issues in the social studies: A research study of high school teachers. *The Clearing House, 82*(4), 165–171.

Claire, H., & Holden, C. (2007). *The challenge of teaching controversial issues.* Stoke-on-Trent, UK: Trentham Books.

Cummins, J. (2001). *Negotiating identities: Education for empowerment in a diverse society* (2nd ed.). Los Angeles, CA: California Association for Bilingual Education.

Cummins, J. (2009). Transformative multiliteracies pedagogy: School-based strategies for closing the achievement gap. *Multiple Voices for Ethnically Diverse Exceptional Learners, 11*(2), 1–19.

Davies, L. (2004a). Education for positive conflict and interruptive democracy. In L. Davies (Ed.), *Education and conflict: Complexity and chaos* (pp. 203–224). London, UK: RoutledgeFalmer.

Davies, L. (2004b). Gender and violence. In L. Davies (Ed.), *Education and conflict: Complexity and chaos* (pp. 57–73). London, England: RoutledgeFalmer.

Dei, G. S. (2000). Towards an anti-racism discursive framework. In G. S. Dei & A. Calliste (Eds.), *Power, knowledge, and anti-racism education* (pp. 23–40). Halifax, NS: Fernwood.

Delgado, R. (1995). Legal storytelling: Storytelling for oppositionists and others: A plea for narrative. In R. Delgado (Ed.), *Critical race theory: The cutting edge* (pp. 64–74).

Delpit, L. (2006). *Other people's children: Cultural conflict in the classroom.* New York, NY: New Press. (Original work published 1995)

DeNicolo, C. P., & Franquiz, M. E. (2006). "Do I have to say it?": Critical encounters with multicultural children's literature. *Language Arts, 84*(2), 157–170.

Derman-Sparks, L. (2006). Activism and preschool children. In E. Lee, D. Menkart, & M. Okazawa-Rey (Eds.), *Beyond heroes and holidays* (pp. 193–197). Washington, DC: Teaching for Change.

Dilworth, P. P. (2004). Multicultural citizenship education: Case studies from social studies classrooms. *Theory and Research in Social Education, 32*(2), 153–186.

Dudley-Marling, C. (1997). "I'm not from Pakistan": Multicultural literature and the problem of representation. *The New Advocate, 10,* 123–134.

Dull, L., & Murrow, S. (2008). Is dialogic questioning possible in social studies classrooms? *Theory and Research in Social Education, 36*(4), 391–412.

Epstein, T. (2000). Adolescents' perspectives on racial diversity in U.S. history: Case studies from an urban classroom. *American Educational Research Association, 37*(1), 185–214.

Fain, J. G. (2008). Um, they weren't thinking about their thinking: Children's talk about issues of oppression. *Multicultural Perspectives, 10*(4), 201–208.

Fine, M. (1993). "You can't just say that the only ones who can speak are those who agree with your position": Political discourse in the classroom. *Harvard Educational Review, 63*(4), 412–433.

Freedman, S. W., Weinstein, H., Murphy, K., & Longman, T. (2008). Teaching history after identity-based conflicts: The Rwanda experience. *Comparative Education Review, 52*(4), 663–690.

Freire, P. (1985). *The politics of education: Culture, power and liberation.* South Hadley, MA: Bergin & Garvey.

Freire, P. (1994a). *Pedagogy of hope.* New York, NY: Continuum. (Original work published 1970)
Freire, P. (1994b). *Pedagogy of the oppressed.* New York, NY: Continuum. (Original work published 1970)

Funk, N., & Said, A. A. (2004). Islam and the West: Narratives of conflict and conflict transformation. *International Journal of Peace Studies, 9*(1), 1–28.

Gay, G. (2000). *Culturally responsive teaching: Theory, research, and practice.* New York, NY: Teachers College Press.

Gérin-Lajoie, D. (2008a). *Educators' discourses on student diversity in Canada: Context, policy, practice.* Toronto, ON: Canadian Scholars' Press.

Gérin-Lajoie, D. (2008b). The issues of diversity in the Canadian educational context. In D. Gérin-Lajoie (Ed.), *Educators' discourses on student diversity in Canada: Context, policy, practice* (pp. 9–28). Toronto, ON: Canadian Scholars' Press.

Giroux, H. A. (1981). Hegemony, resistance, and the paradox of educational reform. *Interchange, 12*(2–3), 3–26.

Goldston, M. J. D., & Kyzer, P. (2009). Teaching evolution: Narratives with a view from three southern biology teachers in the U.S.A. *Journal of Research in Science Teaching, 46*(7), 762–790.

Gramsci, A. (1971). *Selections from the prison notebooks.* London: Lawrence and Wishart.

Hahn, C. (1998). Democratic inquiry and discourse: Classroom climates in cross-national perspective. In C. Hahn & P. State University of New York (Eds.), *Becoming political: Comparative perspectives on citizenship education* (pp. 177–234).

Haroutunian-Gordon, S. (2010). Listening to a challenging perspective: The role of interruption. *Teachers College Record, 112*(11), 2893–2814.

Harper, H. (1997). Difference and diversity in Ontario schooling. *Canadian Journal of Education, 22*(2), 192–206.

Harwood, A. M., & Hahn, C. L. (1990). *Controversial issues in the classroom*. Retrieved from ERIC database. (EDO-SO-90-7)

Hemmings, A. (2000). High school democratic dialogues: Possibilities for praxis. *American Educational Research Journal, 37*(1), 67–91.

Hess, D. (2001). *Teaching students to discuss controversial public issues*. Retrieved from ERIC database. (EDO-SO-2001-7)

Hess, D. (2009). *Controversy in the classroom: The democratic power of discussion*. New York, NY: Routledge.

Hess, D., & Avery, P. (2008). Discussion of controversial issues as a form and goal of democratic education. In J. Arthur, I. Davies, & C. Hahn (Eds.), *Sage handbook of education for citizenship and democracy* (pp. 506–518). London, UK: Sage.

Hess, D., & Posselt, J. (2002). How high school students experience and learn from the discussion of controversial public issues. *Journal of Curriculum and Supervision, 17*(4), 283–314.

hooks, b. (1994). Theory as liberatory practice. In b. hooks (Ed.), *Teaching to transgress: Education as the practice of freedom* (pp. 59–75). New York, NY: Routledge.

Houser, N. O. (1996). Negotiating dissonance and safety for the common good: Social education in the elementary classroom. *Theory and Research in Social Education, 24*(3), 294–312.

Houser, N. O. (2008). Cultural plunge: A critical approach for multicultural development in teacher education. *Race, Ethnicity & Education, 11*(4), 465–482.

Howard, T. C. (2001). Telling their side of the story: African American students' perceptions of culturally relevant pedagogy. *Urban Review, 33*(2), 131–149.

Howard, T. C. (2004). "Does race really matter?" Secondary students' constructions of racial dialogue in the social studies. *Theory and Research in Social Education, 32*(4), 484–502.

Hughes, A., & Sears, A. (2007). Teaching the contested and controversial nature of democratic ideas: Taking the crisis out of controversy. In H. Claire & C. Holden (Eds.), *The challenge of teaching controversial issues* (pp. 83–93). Stoke-on-Trent, UK: Trentham Books.

Hyun, E. (2007). Cultural complexity in early childhood: Images of contemporary young children from a critical perspective. *Childhood Education, 83*(5), 261–266.

Jackson, P. (1968). *Life in classrooms*. New York, NY: Holt, Rinehart, and Winston.

Jacquet, M. (2008). The discourse on diversity in British Columbia public schools: From difference to in/difference. In D. Gérin-Lajoie (Ed.), *Educators' discourses on student diversity in Canada: Context, policy, practice* (pp. 51–80). Toronto, ON: Canadian Scholars' Press.

Johnson, D., & Johnson, R. (2009). Energizing learning: The instructional power of conflict. *Educational Researcher, 38*(1), 37–51.

Joshee, R. (2004). Citizenship and multicultural education in Canada: From assimilation to social cohesion. In J. A. Banks (Ed.), *Diversity and citizenship education: Global perspectives* (pp. 127–156). San Francisco, CA: Jossey-Bass.

Kahne, J., & Sporte, S. (2008). Developing citizens: The impact of civic learning opportunities on students' commitment to civic participation. *American Educational Research Journal, 45*(3), 738–766.

Kelly, D., & Brooks, M. (2009). How young is too young? Exploring beginning teachers' assumptions about young children and teaching for social justice. *Equity and Excellence in Education, 42*(2), 202–216.

Kendall, F. E. (1983). *Diversity in the classroom: A multicultural approach to the education of young children*. New York, NY: Teachers College Press.

Kim, H. S., & Markus, H. R. (2005). Speech and silence: An analysis of the cultural practice of talking. In L. Weis & M. Fine (Eds.), *Beyond silenced voices: Class, race, and gender in United States schools* (Rev. ed., pp. 147–161). New York, NY: State University of New York Press.

King, J. E. (2004). Dysconscious racism: Ideology, identity, and the miseducation of teachers. In G. Ladson-Billings & D. Gillborn (Eds.), *The RoutledgeFalmer reader in multicultural education: Critical perspectives on race, racism and education* (pp. 71–83). London, UK: RoutledgeFalmer.

King, J. T. (2009). Teaching and learning about controversial issues: Lessons from Northern Ireland. *Theory and Research in Social Education, 37*(2), 215–246.

Kitson, A., & McCully, A. (2005). "You hear about it for real in school": Avoiding, containing and risk-taking in the history classroom. *Teaching History, 120*, 32–37.

Knaus, C. B. (2009). "Shut up and listen": Applied critical race theory in the classroom. *Race Ethnicity and Education, 12*(2), 133–154.

Kohlmeier, J. (2006). "Couldn't she just leave?": The relationship between consistently using class discussions and the development of historical empathy in a 9th grade world history course. *Theory and Research in Social Education, 34*(1), 34–57.

Kumashiro, K. (2000). Toward a theory of anti-oppressive education. *Review of Educational Research, 70*(1), 25–53.

Ladson-Billings, G. (1995). Toward a theory of culturally relevant pedagogy. *American Educational Research Journal, 32*(3), 465–491.

Ladson-Billings, G. (2004). Culture versus citizenship: The challenge of racialized citizenship in the United States. In J. Banks (Ed.), *Diversity and citizenship education: Global perspectives* (pp. 99– 26). San Francisco, CA: Jossey-Bass/Wiley.

Larson, B. E. (2003). Comparing face-to-face discussion and electronic discussion: A case study from high school social studies. *Theory and Research in Social Education, 31*(3), 347–365.

Lederach, J. P. (1995). *Preparing for peace: Conflict transformation across cultures*. Syracuse, NY: Syracuse University Press.

Lee, J. W., & Hébert, Y. M. (2006). The meaning of being Canadian: A comparison between youth of immigrant and non-immigrant origins. *Canadian Journal of Education, 29*(2), 497–520.

Lopez, G. R. (2003). The (racially neutral) politics of education: A critical race theory perspective. *Educational Administration Quarterly, 39*(1), 68–94.

May, S., & Sleeter, C. E. (2010). *Critical multiculturalism: Theory and praxis*. New York, NY: Routledge.

McCarthy, C. (1988). Rethinking liberal and radical perspectives on racial inequality in schooling: Making the case of nonsynchrony. *Harvard Educational Review, 58*(3), 265–279.

McCluskey, G., Lloyd, G., Kane, J., Riddell, S., Stead, J., & Weedon, E. (2008). Can restorative practices in schools make a difference? *Educational Review, 60*(4), 405–417.

McNeil, L. (1986). Defensive teaching and classroom control. In L. McNeil (Ed.), *Contradictions of control* (pp. 157–190). New York, NY: Routledge.

Merelman, R. (1990). The role of conflict in children's political learning. In O. Ichilov (Ed.), *Political socialization, citizenship education, and democracy* (pp. 47–65). New York, NY: Teachers College Press.

Morrison, B. (2007). *Restoring safe school communities: A whole school response to bullying, violence alienation.* Leichhardt, Australia: Federation Press.

Nicholas, A. B. (1996). Citizenship education and aboriginal people: The humanitarian art of cultural genocide. *Canadian and International Education, 25*(2), 59–107.

Nieto, S. (1992). *Affirming diversity: The sociopolitical context of multicultural education.* White Plains, NY: Longman.

Nieto, S. (1999). Critical multicultural education and students' perspectives. In S. May (Ed.), *Critical multiculturalism* (pp. 191–215). London, UK: Falmer.

Nieto, S. (2002). *Language, culture, and teaching.* Mahwah, NJ: Lawrence Erlbaum Associates.

Norton, B., & Toohey, K. (2011). Identity, language learning, and social change. *Language Teaching, 44*(4), 412–446.

Ogbu, J. U. (1992). Understanding cultural diversity and learning. *Educational Researcher, 21*(8), 5–14, 24.

Osborne, K. (1995). "To the schools we must look for good Canadians": Developments in the teaching of history in Canadian schools since 1960. In K. Osborne (Ed.), *Defense of history: Teaching the past and the meaning of democratic citizenship* (pp. 49–82). Toronto, ON: Our Schools/Our Selves.

Oulton, C., Day, V., Dillon, J., & Grace, M. (2004). Controversial issues: Teachers' attitudes and practices in the context of citizenship education. *Oxford Review of Education, 30*(4), 489–507.

Pace, J. L. (2008). Inequalities in history-social science teaching under high stakes accountability: Interviews with fifth-grade teachers in California. *Social Studies Research and Practice, 3*(1), 24–40.

Pace, J. L. (2011). The complex and unequal impact of accountability on untested social studies across diverse school contexts. *Theory and Research in Social Education, 39*(1), 32–60.

Parker, C. A. (2010a). Finding our way home (at school): A study of students' experiences of bringing their home culture into the classroom. *Journal of Teaching and Learning, 7*(1), 17–29.

Parker, C. A. (2010b). A multicultural approach to teaching language arts within diverse elementary school settings. *English Quarterly, 41*(3/4), 67–78.

Parker, C. A. (2011). Conflictual dialogue pedagogies as learning opportunities for ethno-cultural minority immigrant students [Special issue]. *Citizenship Education Research Journal, 1*(1), 43–56.

Parker, C. A. (2013). Peacebuilding education: Pedagogical tools for democratic and inclusive learning opportunities for diverse students. *International Journal of Peace Studies, 18*(2), 1–24.

Peck, C. L. (2010). "It's not like [I'm] Chinese and Canadian. I am in between": Ethnicity and students' conceptions of historical significance. *Theory and Research in Social Education, 38*(4), 574–617.

Peck, C. L., & Sears, A. (2005). Uncharted territory: Mapping students' conceptions of ethnic diversity. *Canadian Ethnic Studies, 37*(1), 101–120.

Phelan, P., Davidson, A. L., & Cao, H. T. (1991). Students' multiple worlds: Negotiating the boundaries of family, peer, and school cultures. *Anthropology and Education Quarterly, 22*(3), 224–250.

Pranis, K., Stuart, B., & Wedge, M. (2003). *Peacemaking circles: From crime to community.* St. Paul, MN: Living Justice Press.

Quach, L., Jo, J. O., & Urrieta, L. (2009). Understanding the racialized identities of Asian students in predominantly White schools. In R. Kubota & A. Lin (Eds.), *Race, culture, and identities in second language education* (pp. 118–137). New York, NY: Routledge.

Ramsey, P. G. (2004). *Teaching and learning in a diverse world* (3rd ed.). New York, NY: Teachers College Press.

Ramsey, P. G., & Myers, L. C. (1990). Salience of race in young children's cognitive, affective, and behavioral responses to social environments. *Journal of Applied Developmental Psychology, 11*(1), 49–67.

Ross, A. (2007). Multiple identities and education for active citizenship. *British Journal of Educational Studies, 55*(6), 286–303.

Schultz, K., Buck, P., & Niesz, T. (2000). Democratizing conversations: Racialized talk in a post-desegregated middle school. *American Educational Research Journal, 37*(1), 33–65.

Sears, A., & Hughes, A. (2006). Citizenship: Education and indoctrination. *International Journal of Citizenship Teaching and Learning, 2*(1), 3–17.

Seixas, P., Peck, C. L., & Poyntz, S. (2011). "But we didn't live in those times": Canadian students negotiate past and present in a time of war. *Education as Change, 15*(1), 47–62.

Settlage, J., & Sabik, C. (1997). Harnessing the positive energy of conflict in science teaching. *Theory Into Practice, 36*(1), 39–45.

Shor, I. (1992). *Empowering education: Critical teaching for social change.* Portsmouth, NH: Heinemann.

St. Denis, V. (2011). Silencing the Aboriginal curricular content and perspectives through multiculturalism: "There are other children here." *Review of Education, Pedagogy, and Cultural Studies, 33*(4), 306–317.

Steinberg, S., & Bar-On, D. (2009). The other side of the story: Israeli and Palestinian teachers write a history textbook together. *Harvard Educational Review, 79*(1), 104–112.

Subedi, B. (2008). Fostering critical dialogue across cultural differences: A study of immigrant teachers' interventions in diverse schools. *Theory and Research in Social Education, 35*(4), 413–440.

Torney-Purta, J., Lehmann, R., Oswald, H., & Schultz, W. (2001). *Citizenship and education in 28 countries: Civic knowledge and engagement at age 14.* Amsterdam, the Netherlands: International Association for the Evaluation of Educational Achievement.

Tupper, J. A. (2005). *Searching citizenship: Social studies and the tensions of teaching.* Edmonton, AB: University of Alberta Press.

Urrieta, L., Jr., & Quach, L. H. (2000). My language speaks of me: Transmutational identities in L12 acquisition. *The High School Journal, 84*(1), 26–35.

Weinstein, H., Freedman, S., & Hughson, H. (2007). School voices: Challenges facing educational systems after identity-based conflicts. *Education, Citizenship and Social Justice, 2*(1), 41–71.

Westheimer, J., & Kahne, J. (2004). What kind of citizen? The politics of educating for democracy. *American Educational Research Journal, 41*(2), 237–269.

Wolpert, E. (2006). Redefining the norm: Early childhood. In E. Lee, D. Menkart, & M. Okazawa-Rey (Eds.), *Beyond heroes and holidays* (pp. 198–210). Washington, DC: Teaching for Change.

Yamashita, H. (2006). Global citizenship education and war: The needs of teachers and learners. *Educational Review, 58*(1), 27–39.

Zembylas, M. (2007). The politics of trauma: Empathy, reconciliation and peace education. *Journal of Peace Education, 4*(2), 207–224.

Discussion Questions

1. Explain whether or not the process of socialization and enculturation determines individual behavior. Use information from the text to support your answer.
2. Are the positive outcomes of authoritarian parents limited to children living in the United States? Explain.
3. In your opinion, why do many people continue to use race as a category for difference even though it has no biological basis?
4. What are some ways educators can explicitly teach students about complex social issues such as racism, culture, and race?

Activity

Think about when you felt you were mistreated because of your race, color, or background. Do you have any experience relating to racial discrimination and resistance?

UNIT II

DIVERSITY IN CHILDHOOD SETTINGS

Diversity in Early Childhood Settings

Suzanne L. Krogh and Kristine L. Slentz

When someone with the authority of a teacher, say, describes the world, and you're not in it, there is a moment of psychic disequilibrium, as if you looked into a mirror and saw nothing.

—Adrienne Rich

Chapter Objectives

After reading this chapter, you should be able to:

- Define diversity in broad terms and apply the concepts to early childhood education settings.
- Apply issues of diversity to previously read chapters.
- Identify characteristics of several U.S. cultures, particularly as they apply to interactions with families and young children.
- Begin establishing a classroom atmosphere that respects, values, nurtures, and provides equitable opportunities to all children.
- Begin establishing classroom practices that teach young children how to stand up for fairness and oppose bias, prejudice, and discrimination.

As you think about and apply the chapter content on your own, you should be able to:

- Recognize various characteristics of diversity among the children and families you encounter.
- Understand your own culture more fully.

- Embark on a lifelong process of learning about others.
- Collect a bank of ideas for handling diversity issues with skill.
- Incorporate issues of diversity into your developing philosophy of early education.
- Apply the four core goals of anti-bias education (ABE) to your own identity, life, and work in early childhood. Identify challenges, immediate goals, and long-term goals for development in each of the ABE goal areas.

One of the most intriguing aspects of early education is observing and supporting young children as they develop their individual identities. Discovering who they are can be a joyful journey of self-discovery as children learn about personal characteristics such as race, language, culture, ability, and gender. There can also be many bumps, potholes, and threats along the way as children encounter racism, sexism, discrimination, teasing, and exclusion. Helping young children build healthy and positive internal identities requires an understanding of the many facets of diversity, an awareness of opportunities to teach about similarities and differences, and a desire to expand your knowledge of self and others in collaboration with parents, other family members, and colleagues. And often it demands that early educators be courageous, stretch the boundaries of their comfort zones, and address issues that are sensitive and sometimes controversial.

It is critical that every child and every family feel recognized, valued, and included in early childhood programs. A child's identity is first awakened within the context of family, and early education is most effective when families are involved. One of your most important tasks as an early educator will be to establish and maintain positive relationships with all families, regardless

FIGURE 4.1 When Teachers Interact with Families of Cultures Other Than Their Own, They Will Generally Have More Ssuccess if They Take Time to Learn About the Families' Cultures and Communication Styles.

of their various backgrounds, family structures and membership, or *social economic status (SES)*. In this chapter we will provide an overview of the types of diversity you are likely to encounter in early childhood education settings, and suggest some useful strategies and resources to combat prejudice and inequity in your daily work with children.

Early childhood classrooms are becoming increasingly diverse. Preschool attendance has been increasing steadily for the last four decades, and a large majority of American children now spend time in classroom settings before they enter kindergarten. The increase in attendance in group settings prior to kindergarten reflects a greater need for out-of-home care among dual-career and single-parent families, as well as a rising demand for quality preschool education among the middle class (Barnett & Yarosz, 2007). Federal and state appropriations have increased over the same period for publicly funded preschool programs for children from families with low incomes, although children from affluent families are still more likely to attend preschool than their less advantaged peers. Along with the increase in preschool enrollment has come a marked increase in the diversity of children in early care and education programs.

Head Start, for example, has been a national leader in serving children from diverse cultures and language groups, and as early as 1993 served children from over 140 primary language groups. Estimates are that the number of cultures represented in Head Start programs is even larger. In 2008 almost 30% of enrolled children came from families who had home languages other than English, and nationwide just 16% of Head Start programs enrolled only *monolingual* English speaking children (U.S. Department of Health and Human Services, 2008). Head Start's mission is to serve children from families with low incomes, a population that often includes an unusually high number of families who have immigrated to this country and children who are not yet proficient in English. Nonetheless, Head Start programs also illustrate well the increasing diversity that early childhood educators will encounter in preschool programs.

Early childhood educators will also find increased emphasis on diversity in public schools during the primary years. There has been much national conversation and debate about the *achievement gap*, a term which describes unequal patterns of educational performance among groups of students in American schools. In specific, students of color (especially Hispanic, African-American, and American Indian) and those from lower income families tend to have poorer scores on measures of academic proficiency and higher drop-out rates than Caucasian peers from middle income and affluent families (U.S. Department of Education, 2003; Children's Defense Fund, 2008). Children from lower SES backgrounds start kindergarten with significantly lower achievement in the skills necessary for school success (Burkam & Lee, 2002), so early childhood educators have a very important role to play in closing the achievement gap during the primary years.

Cultural Influences

The term *diversity* as used in this chapter is defined in the broadest and most inclusive manner possible. We will discuss diversity among young children and their families that you are likely to encounter as an early educator, whether you work in home-based programs, center-based models, public schools, or private primary classrooms. Our discussion will address diversity among young children in areas of culture, race, language, social-economic status, family structure (including same-sex parents), ability, and gender identity. We will describe trends in demographics and education that have increased diversity in classrooms, introduce you to concepts related to gender and ability, and provide information to stimulate your thinking about the importance of your own heritage and the backgrounds of the children and families with whom you will soon be working.

Social scientists are forever creating new definitions for that elusive word *culture*, but the one that follows is sufficiently broad for use in this chapter's discussion of early education. *Culture: The knowledge, art, morals, laws, customs, values, attitudes, belief systems, behavioral expectations, and norms that give a society and the individuals in it their identity.* Another definition of culture is *life ways*, or the routines, activities, and roles of daily life for children and their families (Derman-Sparks & Olsen Edwards, 2010). For young children, important aspects of culture include daily routines and practices in their families: eating, sleeping, interacting, roles of children and adults, language, education, religion, and social activities. Although we have not yet addressed the issue of culture directly in this book's first chapters, it has been an important presence nonetheless.

For example, history and culture have a significant impact on our view of many of the central concepts of early learning: development, parenting, families, and the role of formal education in the lives of young children. An illustration of this impact is demonstrated by the variety of historical figures you met in Chapter One. All of these people observed children within approximately the same age range, witnessed approximately the same development and behaviors, yet emerged from their observations with very divergent ideas for education. In great part, these differences can be explained by variations in the cultures of the times, places, and people who have provided the foundation for our field.

In Chapter Two, a variety of career options were presented for your consideration, with the caveat that some of your choices would be of little financial benefit. In the culture of the United States, there has been a long history of strong reluctance to provide government support for the care and education of our youngest citizens. Without such support, living wages are out of reach for caregivers and teachers, and tuition rates are out of reach for many parents. Our cultural belief system includes both a desire for freedom from government intrusion, and the belief that young children are a valuable asset for the future. The inconsistency between two strong, opposing cultural values remains unresolved, and the result is a very tenuous foundation of early education in America, and young children and their teachers remain the unfortunate victims.

In Chapter Three, we visited several classrooms and centers, some of them influenced by the historic figures from Chapter One, all of them products, at least in part, of their own times and cultures. The project approach, for example, provides young children with the power to choose their own curricula, to decide their own methods of learning, and to make decisions as individuals and as groups both large and small. Giving such decision-making power might be dangerous in an autocratic culture; it is more appropriate, even expected, in a democratic society such as the United States.

These descriptions of cultural influences are but examples from each previous chapter. You are invited to discover other ways in which culture has shaped careers in early education, the views of educationists, and the various models of classrooms and centers.

The Role of Immigration

Complementary to influences of the immediate culture on early education are the diverse backgrounds of the children who attend the schools and centers. In the United States, such diversity has been growing in recent years as immigrants and refugees enter from an expanding number of countries and our own culture increasingly values and honors the backgrounds and variations in personal characteristics among all children. Arguing that we must look at the education of young children in new ways, one group of authors summarized the situation, particularly in relationship to immigration:

> The dramatic increase in immigration in the past 20 years, the young average age of immigrants, and the higher birth rate of several of these groups relative to that of white Americans is changing the face of America's people. This rapid demographic change has been called "the browning of America."

> (Swiniarski, Breitborde, & Murphy, 1999, p. 82)

In the decade between 1990 and 2000, the population of foreign-born people living in the United States increased by over half for naturalized citizens and non-citizens alike, from 19.8 million to 31.1 million. Over half of U.S. residents born elsewhere were from Latin America (Central America, South America, and the Caribbean), and 30% of the total immigrant population was from Mexico (U.S. Census Bureau, 2003). These statistics explain the fact that Spanish is the second most frequent home language in the United States. When countries were counted singly, Mexico was the greatest contributor of new arrivals, with China a distant second. Perhaps even more telling, the United Kingdom, the original source of American citizens and cultural heritage, was ranked 17th with just 1.5% of the new population. Germany, the leading contributor of new immigrants as recently as the 1950s, did not even make the top 30 countries listed by the U.S. Immigration and Naturalization Service.

From these statistics, it is possible to predict what school and child-care-center populations will look like in the near future. For example, it has been predicted that the 70% White population in 1990s American schools will be reversed by 2026 so that 70% will be non-White. Another prediction is that between 1990 and 2050, the percentage of Whites will fall from 74% to 52% (Swiniarski et al., 1999).

Many people believe it would be a good idea to close the door against the flood of outsiders who want to belong to the American family. The newspapers are full of stories that verify this opinion, and you may be or know someone who agrees that "America should remain American." This is not a new attitude, yet America has always been a nation of immigrants. After all, every group of citizens in the United States, with the exception of American Indians, comes from immigrant backgrounds. Despite the fact that most American families hailed originally from other countries, our country has a long history of anti-immigrant sentiment. Some members of immigrant groups and their heirs, ironically, have even become strong advocates for keeping out new immigrants.

Yet, immigrants continue to arrive, and their numbers steadily increase. Despite resentment and prejudice, the vilified groups of the last two centuries have managed to overcome most or all of the barriers erected against them, becoming full participants in the ever-changing U.S. culture. One of the most important tasks for early educators is to design environments and cultivate interactions with children that affirm and honor each and every family background, and to teach young children to follow that example.

The Demise of the Middle Class

> The United States has the unwanted distinction of being worst among industrialized nations in relative child poverty, in the gap between rich and poor, in teen birth rates, and in child gun violence, and first in the number of incarcerated persons.
>
> (Children's Defense Fund, 2008, p. 1)

Compared to other industrialized countries, the United States ranks first in the number of millionaires and billionaires, but close to last in the gap between rich and poor children.

We are first in health technology but 25th in infant mortality; our country's standing in infant mortality rates fell from 18th to 25th between 1998 and 2008, meaning that by 2008 more babies in America died before their first birthdays than in 24 other developed countries. The United States is ranked first in military technology but last in protecting children against gun violence. On the average, states spend almost three times as much for each person in prison as for each public school student (Children's Defense Fund, 2008). These statistics illustrate clearly that our society's collective desire for autonomy from government intervention is stronger than the combined will to protect and support the well-being of young children.

One in six children in the United States, a total of 13.3 million, lived in poverty in 2008, an increase of over 500,000 from 2006. Young children are more likely to live in extreme poverty than are school-aged children. Child poverty rates are three times higher for Black and Hispanic children than they are for White children, and children of color are least likely to have health insurance (Children's Defense Fund, 2008). This means that a rather large proportion of children may arrive at the doorsteps of their centers and schools with insufficient nutrition for effective learning, untreated chronic medical conditions, and undue stress and anxiety from unsafe living conditions and/or the threat of homelessness. Their language skills may also be inadequate to meet the middle-class expectations of the school curriculum, and their enthusiasm for learning may be dampened by the hardships and distress of not having basic needs met. Early educators encounter a lot of inequity in the lives of children, particularly in urban areas and in states with policies that are particularly unsupportive of children and families.

As the gap between rich and poor widens, early childhood programs tend to be segregated by SES: affluent families send their children to private preschools and primary schools, and families with the lowest incomes are eligible for Head Start. The demographics of public schools are becoming increasingly diverse, with marked differences in quality between low- and high-income neighborhoods. As families from increasingly varied backgrounds move into and across the country, early childhood schools and centers are enrolling children with more diversity in languages and cultures. An additional influence on diversity in early childhood programs is the recent trend toward inclusive early childhood environments where children with a variety of ability levels play and learn together.

The Influence of Inclusion Policies

In the mid-1970s, federal legislation for the first time mandated that children with special needs were entitled to a free public education that was tailored to meet their individual needs. Previously, many children with disabilities stayed at home or went to private schools, and public schools often did not have well-trained special education teachers. This initial special education legislation, the *Education of All Handicapped Children Act* (EAHCA), was passed following a number of civil rights cases addressing the rights of racial minority students.

The EAHCA was quite a landmark, amended in 1986 to include eligible preschool children (ages 3 to 5) and older secondary students (ages 18 to 21) under the federal mandate for special education services. Since the mid-1980s public schools have been providing special education services to eligible students from age 3 until age 21. Special education services, by law, begin two years earlier and end three years later than general education does. The 1986 amendments to the EAHCA also included an optional provision for states to provide special education services to eligible infants and toddlers: 1986 was a banner year for special services to young children with special needs!

In 1991, the name of the special education law was updated to its current *Individuals with Disabilities Education Act* (IDEA), reflecting a national preference for the term "disability" over the use of the outdated "handicapped" label. The EAHCA and IDEA and subsequent amendments have addressed the responsibilities of school districts to eligible students and their families, including a provision for students ages 3 to 21 to be educated in the *least restrictive environment (LRE)*. The big idea of LRE is that students with disabilities receive educational services with their peers and/or in environments that are as close to the general education classroom as possible.

Most recently, the 1997 and 2004 IDEA amendments emphasized the importance of access to the general education curriculum for all students, including those eligible for special education. In 2002, the Elementary and Secondary Education Act (ESEA) was amended under the title No Child Left Behind Act (NCLB). NCLB emphasized accountability to high standards and educational achievement outcomes for all students. The combination of IDEA legislation and

No Child Left Behind legislation during the George W. Bush administration was a powerful force for *inclusion* of students with disabilities and delays in general education settings with their peers. If you teach in the primary grades, it is almost a certainty that you will have children in your classrooms who also receive special education services.

There is no federal legislation requiring school districts to provide public preschool services, unless they are from poor families or have identified disabilities. The only entitlement programs for preschoolers are Head Start and IDEA services for 3–5-year-olds, so most American children start public school in kindergarten at age 5. For this reason, the concept of LRE isn't relevant for preschoolers in special education classrooms, because rarely are there general education classrooms available in the public schools.

The most progressive approaches emphasize *inclusion* of young children with disabilities in community-based preschool programs or in Head Start classrooms. Head Start programs are required to reserve 10% of their enrollment for preschoolers with identified disabilities. Infants and toddlers who receive special education services are required to be served in *natural environments*, meaning at home or in their child-care settings. There are still many self-contained special education preschool classrooms, but you are likely to have the opportunity to care for and educate young children with special needs in community-based child care or preschool settings.

The focus of special education services has shifted progressively over the years from exclusion of students with special needs, to an emphasis on separate programs and individualized instruction within school buildings, and more recently to specialized instruction delivered within general education classrooms, community preschools, homes, and child-care programs. The diversity in U.S. schools has most definitely been enhanced by inclusion of students with a wide range of abilities.

Diversity Issues Related to Gender

The final aspects of diversity to be discussed here relate to gender. During recent decades, research findings have led to mixed conclusions about the influences on and causes of behavioral differences between the sexes. Do girls play in the housekeeping corner whereas boys gravitate to the large blocks because society reinforces such choices or because their biology is sending them preprogrammed messages? Or is it a combination of the two? Definitive answers have yet to be discovered, but it is known that young children are still developing their sense of gender identity as well as their beginning understandings of societal expectations and roles for each sex.

Many younger children are not yet sure what makes them boys or girls, believing that the answer may lie in concrete and visible factors, such as how they dress, their hair styles, or the games they choose to play. In addition, they have an incomplete understanding of biological permanence, sometimes believing that they might change genders as they get older, perhaps even becoming someone else entirely. Parents may not think to explain biological differences to them, or may find the prospect uncomfortable. Thus, young children sometimes take their confusion to school (Derman-Sparks & Olsen Edwards, 2010). Teachers who simply and matter-of-factly

FIGURE 4.2   Children Do Not Always Conform With Efforts by Teachers and Families to Free Them From Traditional Gender Roles.

provide information about gender can set the stage for children to discover their own identities and negotiate societal expectations.

> Janice was a mother who purposely chose a female pediatrician for her children so that they would see the normality of girls growing up to take on a traditionally male career. When her daughter Kelly was 4, Janice was startled to overhear her say to the boy visiting from next door, "Okay. You'll be the doctor and I'll be the nurse. Boys are always doctors and girls are always nurses." On reflection, Janice realized that a medical TV show Kelly liked to watch with her parents reflected the more traditional gender roles in the medical profession, and she came to understand that society's messages could be stronger than the reality of the children's own lives.

We can say that one important goal for any early childhood classroom is "to free children from constraining, stereotypic definitions of gender role so that no aspects of development will be closed off simply because of a child's sex" (Derman-Sparks, 1993, p. 49). At the same time, the example of Janice and her daughter tells us that achieving this goal involves a major commitment of time, effort, and awareness. Once you begin paying attention to gender roles in your classroom, you are likely to hear children say things that are startling reflections of the messages society sends about how boys and girls are supposed to behave, dress, play, talk, and think. In addition, families often have very definite ideas about gender roles that may or may not match the goals you have for children in your classroom.

Diversity in gender identity and gender roles is evident in the variety of young children's family structures. There are single-parent families with just a father or mother, and two-parent families with mother and father, or two same-sex parents. Some families have two working parents; others have a stay-at-home mother or father. Grandparents and other extended family members may all live under one roof and share child care. A very thoughtful article by Burt, Gelnaw, and Lesser (2010) makes the point that children are harmed when their families are not acknowledged and included in early childhood programs. Teachers often unintentionally harm children of gay, lesbian, bisexual, and transgendered families, for example, through unconscious bias and by never using words, reading books, or having pictures in the classroom that show same-sex parents. Families who are invisible are excluded, with a detrimental effect on their children's developing identities and sense of self-worth.

Gender identity is a product of both biological and social/societal factors. Most often children's biology aligns with their gender identity, but not always. One other aspect of gender role and identity that is beginning to be recognized in early childhood settings is captured in the terms *transgender* and *gender variant* or *gender fluid*. Transgender children have an internal gender identity that does not match their anatomical gender: a biological male who identifies as a girl, or vice versa. Gender variance or gender fluidity are terms that describe children whose gender identity is variable, and/or shows aspects of both male and female (Brill & Pepper, 2008).

Being transgender or gender variant is not a choice for young children, shown clearly by young children who identify strongly across biological genders before they have a fully developed concept of what it means socially or biologically to be male/female. Early childhood teachers have a dual role in supporting children's optimal individual development, and supporting parents who may themselves be struggling to understand a complex and confusing aspect of their children's development.

We wrote in Chapter Two about the misperception that teaching young children is easy, perhaps just a form of babysitting. By now it should be becoming increasingly clear that the actuality is much more complex, that the tasks of meeting all children's needs fairly and positively are not easy ones. Yet, it is only in recent years that professionals at all levels have come to realize that the issue of diversity deserves specific and increased attention.

Valuing All Children and Their Families

In 1987, the National Association for the Education of Young Children (NAEYC) published its first edition of *Developmentally Appropriate Practice in Early Childhood Programs* (Bredekamp, 1987) and differentiated between appropriate practice for groups of children at particular stages of development and appropriate practice given an individual child's own context. Cultural differences, in the first edition, were deemed a part of variations among individuals. A decade later, NAEYC published a revised edition, with the realization that the original view did not sufficiently take into consideration the strong influence that culture has on children's development and on what and how they learn.

NAEYC concluded many years ago, and continues to maintain, that ignoring the important influences of culture on the development of young children can lead to many different problems in practice. When the cultural rules of the home and the early childhood program are congruent, the process of learning is eased. However, when the expectations of the cultures of the home and the school or child-care program are different or conflicting, children can be confused or forced to choose which culture to identify with and which to reject (Bredekamp & Copple, 1997/2009).

An important role for all teachers and caregivers, then, is to help youngsters bridge the disparities between home and school or center. Not to do so can be damaging to children, in both great and small ways. Many beginning teachers choose to ignore cultural differences, declaring that they love all children the same. "Few of us have developed tools to address difficult issues such as discrimination and oppression, and likely naively believe that if we respect the individual child, all will be well" (Boutte, 2008, p. 165). The result of this attitude, however, is that the teacher's cultural view tends to be unconsciously imposed on the children, sometimes with an implicit sense of superiority. When teachers convey that their own cultural views are better, the next step may well be children's differences are interpreted as deficits, as illustrated in the following vignette:

> A teacher educator once looked forward to assigning a practicum student to a particular class of 4-year-olds. The majority of the children were learning English as a second language, seemingly a perfect opportunity for this student, who professed an interest in an international teaching career. Just two days into the experience, however, the practicum student began referring to the "language barrier" that was preventing her from teaching anything of value to the children. Her professor discussed with her the fact that the children, although beginners at English, were already proficient in at least one other home language, and some of them—at just 4 years old—already spoke two. This was a feat that the education student had yet to accomplish, as she only spoke English. Nevertheless, the student continued to focus on the "barrier" that kept her from teaching, and soon she began to speak of the children derogatorily, as "English deficient," seeing the barrier as the children's rather than her own.

Continued work with the student on the part of her university supervisor and the classroom teacher eventually led her to new teaching methods and respect for the children's capabilities, but her original attitude is a common one. Perhaps because teachers have an ingrained disposition to fill in gaps of knowledge, they often look for weaknesses rather than strengths in children. A child who brings another culture and another language to class can be evaluated as having a clearly visible set of deficiencies to be fixed. Yet, it is through honoring the child's abilities and strengths while respecting the family's culture that a teacher can best reach the child. As one writer has said, young children:

> deserve to be in programs where it is safe for them to be who they are. ... Children have the right to feel good about themselves, to learn to be courageous, and not to feel like victims. Children are entitled to their cultural heritage and to be proud of it.

> (York, 1991, p. 23)

The NAEYC Code of Ethical Conduct states that "Above all, we shall not harm children. ... This principle has precedence over all others in this Code" (NAEYC, 2005). Burt, Gelnaw, and Lesser (2010) argue that early educators can inadvertently harm children and families by making assumptions based on their own experience and the majority rule, for example that all children have both a mother and father, that all children will grow up to be heterosexual, or that it is better for children to speak English than any other language. Providing children with the respect they deserve requires that teachers and caregivers know something about the cultural similarities and differences their youngsters bring with them each day.

To understand children's backgrounds most fully, teachers and caregivers also need to know something about their own cultures. This can be even more difficult than learning about another's culture, because our own daily lives have a ring of reality and neutrality, making other points of view seem alien, even unreal. Sociologists describe our unquestioned views as taken-for-granted realities. One example that is frequently given refers to the preference of U.S. mainstream culture to look directly in another's eyes when speaking. This is particularly important when coming across as honest is an issue, or a topic of urgency is being discussed. There are, however, some people who find such physical directness inappropriate, some Hispanic and American Indian cultures, for instance. An illustration of the complexity of this issue is the notion, voiced by an American Indian researcher, that looking down to indicate respect began when Indian children were taken to mission boarding schools (Demmert, 2005). Thus, a child from one of these groups might look at his feet out of respect for his teacher just when she is saying, "Look at me when I talk to you!" Each person in this unfortunate interchange is, at this moment, in possession of a taken-for-granted reality that is a disservice to the occasion. However, it is the teacher's responsibility, not the child's, to comprehend this and to move to a better understanding of the cultural complexities that make up a classroom.

One aspect of cultural complexity that should be considered is the fact that there is great variability among individual practices and values within any cultural group. Stereotyping can result from generalizations that all American Indian children will look at their feet while the teacher talks, that all Asian Americans will work hard in school, or that all Anglo-European children are programmed for competitive individualism. Cultural values commonly held by mainstream Americans do include individualism, privacy, equality, informality, wise use of time, achievement, materialism, and directness. Yet, individual Americans, natives and immigrants alike, accept these values at differing levels of intensity. Or, they may fully accept most of the values but completely opt out on one or two (Lynch & Hanson, 2004). One way to begin handling such complexities in our own teaching lives is to take steps toward a better consciousness of the realities we take for granted, to see our own cultures more clearly.

Learning to See Ourselves More Clearly

How we see ourselves and our backgrounds has direct bearing on our views of teaching and learning. The first step in dealing with the cultural complexities of teaching is to become consciously aware of our values and beliefs and the influence of those values and beliefs on our behaviors.

Robin was a first-year teacher being observed by her principal for the first time. For the occasion, she placed the children's chairs in a horseshoe shape and planned a question-and-answer session around a story they were all reading together.

The principal sat quietly in the back, taking occasional notes, until she noticed a disturbing pattern. Robin rarely called on any girls, ignoring their raised hands in favor of answers from the boys. Bit by bit the girls began to wilt visibly, their early enthusiasm soon replaced by looks of boredom or resentment. Eventually, Robin began calling on children in what appeared to be a left-to-right order around the horseshoe. The principal breathed a sigh of relief; the girls would finally get a chance. To her amazement, Robin did go around the room in order, but continued to ignore the girls by jumping right over them to call on the next boy. When the principal later brought this to Robin's attention, she denied the possibility that it had happened until the principal showed her the chart she had made of the experience. Together they discussed solutions, finally settling on the idea that Robin should make a mental checklist as she called on children, consciously alternating boys and girls as much as possible.

It takes continuing efforts toward self-awareness, and sometimes the observations of a colleague or friend, to prepare ourselves well for handling cultural complexity. A good place to start is to reflect on our own cultural backgrounds, particularly in regard to education. Perhaps you come from a family with many educators in it, so that teaching was a natural choice for you. Or, your family may not particularly value education, but you are pressing ahead anyway, because you believe in the career you have chosen. Perhaps your family takes a different view of education entirely, valuing it for training in specific, hands-on trades and not for the more academic approach you are experiencing.

Caroline, an experienced kindergarten teacher, thought she treated all her children with equality and made sure she gave positive feedback and encouragement in appropriate doses to everyone. One day, a friend on vacation from teaching in another state came to visit Caroline's class. She enjoyed her time with Caroline, but she observed a behavior that bothered her and decided it presented issues that should be discussed. Caroline was stunned to hear that she regularly hugged and touched the White and Hispanic children but not the Blacks. In fact, she couldn't quite believe it and spent the next week in some self-observation and soul searching. Finally, she admitted to herself it was true, realized that it was most probably related to her southern upbringing, and immediately went to work changing her behaviors.

Whatever your family's values and beliefs regarding education, and whether you have accepted or rejected those views, you have been shaped by their influence and will take your attitudes with you into the classroom.

At the end of this chapter, in the section Extending Your Learning, there are suggested activities that are intended to help increase your cultural self-awareness. We urge you to try at least one activity. In the meantime, as you have opportunities to work with children, try to observe your own behaviors with English language learners, boys and girls, and with children of different abilities, economic backgrounds, and ethnicities. See if you are drawn to or uncomfortable with one group or another. Do you tend to talk with girls more than boys and engage in physical play more with boys than with girls? Do you avoid physical contact with children whose hygiene is less than ideal, or whose clothing is dirty? Once you identify some of your biases, make specific plans for expanding into new patterns of behavior and thinking, so that all children will feel safe, included, recognized, and satisfied in their interactions with you.

Learning About Others

In addition to increasing our own self-awareness, an important step in serving children well is to learn something about their cultural backgrounds, particularly if their families have recently immigrated or have influential members—grandparents, perhaps—who influence the families' views on education and childrearing. This section provides overviews of several cultures commonly found in U.S. centers and schools at the beginning of the 21st century. It is important to restate, however, that there are degrees and variations in acceptance of and participation in any culture, even by those who have known only one culture from birth. Additionally, cultures evolve over time, ensuring that some elements may take new forms or even disappear. This is especially true following immigration.

Anglo-European Culture

In the United States, the traditional mainstream culture is Anglo-European. Its roots are seen in documents such as the Constitution and the Declaration of Independence that underlie legal decision-making and the rights and privileges that most citizens have come to expect. The culture's roots are also in the nation's mythology of pilgrims seeking religious freedom, patriots fighting their war for independence, and brave families heading west with few possessions but plenty of dreams. Built into this heritage can be found a Puritan work ethic that only permits play once all tasks are done; independent decision-making based on enlightened self-interest; and risk-taking that allows for failure but generally expects success. Few people today undergo the same strenuous challenges of these earlier settlers, but the founders' attitudes can still be found, even in early education settings. The work ethic remains in the requirement that children finish all their work before heading out to recess; independent decision-making occurs when learning choices are made by children at centers rather than by teachers; and risk-taking is valued when creativity is nurtured at the expense of a single standard of success.

Other values (see Althen, 1988; Lynch & Hanson, 2004), most of which can be traced back to the country's early days and the Anglo-European, include:

- *Equality.* American history is replete with the struggle to live up to this value. From freeing Blacks from slavery to providing women with voting rights, from mandating public education for children with disabilities to grappling with ways to make access to higher education more equitable, the vision of equality continues, slowly, to come closer to reality.
- *Focus on the future, belief in progress and change.* When settling their new land, early Anglo-European Americans had few historical frames of reference for what they did; every

decision, every move to a new home site was an act of pioneering. Their descendants carry with them a belief that people are in charge of their own destinies; that progress is almost always possible, given one's own effort and self-confidence; and that change is generally for the good. This value is maintained sometimes in the face of resistance to change, for example in many reoccurring political debates about health care, immigration, education reform, and the role of corporate influence on the political system.

- *Respect for action and achievement, inclination toward materialism.* For people focused on progress, change, and self-determination, hard work is, not surprisingly, a concomitant value. Increasingly, the material rewards for hard work have become a strong emphasis, and the growing materialism that outsiders comment on has become a matter of concern for Anglo-European Americans themselves.

- *Attention to time.* Progress, change, and achievement may come about through hard work, but respect for the clock is seen as an underlying requirement. Value is placed on being on time and on timely efficiency, not only in the work place but in social interactions. Just as it is important to be on the job at the stated starting hour, so it is expected that arrival at a social function won't be much later than the time provided by the hosts' invitation. In the first case, a few minutes early may even be preferred.

- *A preference for informality.* To many outsiders, Anglo-European Americans both at home and abroad may be seen to be rude or lacking in class or culture because of their informality of speech, dress, and interaction style. In recent decades, the respect accorded a new acquaintance by using his or her last name has almost entirely disappeared, even for younger children. Jeans and T-shirts are worn everywhere, even on formal occasions. It is possible that such an increase in informality may, in part, be due to the greater emphasis on equality.

- *Communicating with directness and openness.* Subtlety and indirect statements are almost foreign to Anglo-European Americans. "What you see is what you get" and "telling it like it is" are valued sentiments in most interactions, and communication of feelings often accompanies a sharing of thoughts and ideas. However, in situations such as talking with a business superior or a new acquaintance, typically Anglo-European Americans will be more reticent; moving to the next stage of more open sharing is a sign of increasing friendship.

- *The family.* The nuclear family—parents and children—defines the core concept of family for Anglo-European Americans. Members of the extended family, who may live at great distances, are referred to as relatives. Although parents do take charge, in America children are also accorded a say in decision-making, attaining an early equality not found in many other cultures. The self-determination valued by the larger culture is also manifested within the family, as young adults generally prefer to live outside the home and elderly members also prefer their independence, trying to avoid becoming a burden on the younger generations.

- *Childrearing.* Anglo-European American parents essentially begin training their children to grow up and leave home from the time they are born. Newborns are most likely to sleep in their own beds, often in their own rooms. Solid foods are introduced earlier than in some other cultures, and efforts at self-feeding and independent toileting are encouraged and praised. Youngsters may arrive at school wearing mismatched clothing with various fasteners poorly attended to, not because of parental neglect but because the children have been encouraged to choose their own outfits and to dress themselves. In supermarkets and restaurants, young children may be observed making their own choices of foods.

- *Views of illness and disabilities*. Explanations for disabilities generally follow a scientific model that focuses on specific causes: genetic disorders, accidents, disease, prenatal trauma, and so forth. It is believed by most Anglo-European Americans that better diagnoses, health treatments, education, and living conditions can be of help. The view that the attitudes and behaviors of parents, especially mothers, are responsible for some disabilities, for the most part, has been replaced by the focus on genetic causes for even emotional disorders.

Interactions Between the School or Center and Families

Some cultural customs of Anglo-European Americans are important for teachers to keep in mind (Lynch & Hanson, 2004). These include:

- Equal treatment for everyone, no matter their gender or station in life.
- Freedom of speech on most subjects, although topics related to sex, politics, religion, and physical traits (such as body odor) are typically not discussed in a formal situation.
- Open, warm greetings that often include a handshake (even if the ensuing meeting is expected to be difficult). Making eye contact and looking at each other talking indicates honesty and courtesy.
- Except for shaking hands, an expectation that people do not touch during interactions. Personal space of about an arm's length is most comfortable.
- Meetings and conferences that begin on time, or a brief explanation and possibly an apology if a delay is necessary.
- Parents generally expect to be informed of their children's progress and are less likely than parents in some cultures to defer to the teacher's expertise and superiority. Parents of children with disabilities are often strong advocates of their children's rights and are aware of the teacher's responsibilities.
- Teachers should expect variations in the Anglo-European culture as determined by section of the country, rural or urban lifestyles, and national or religious heritage. (This is good advice for all the cultures discussed in this chapter.)

African-American Culture

Before pilgrims landed in what was to become New England, about 20 Africans arrived in Virginia. Like many of the Whites arriving at the same time, they had been kidnapped and sold, then bound to their masters for a set number of years until they had earned their freedom. Blacks and Whites alike were treated abusively, and at times ran away together or bore children together. Either action was punishable, but a subtle difference in the treatment of the two races set the stage for the imminent move to slavery. In 1640, the Virginia legislature passed a law decreeing that masters should provide firearms to White but not Black servants. The same year, three servants, one Black and two White, ran away and were captured. All three men received 30 lashes, but here the equality of punishment stopped. The White servants were indentured for four more years; the Black servant was indentured for "the time of his Natural life" (Takaki, 1993, p. 56). In other words, he became a slave, one of an increasing number during the 1640s. The spread of slavery throughout the Americas led to the forced emigration of 20 million Africans between the 16th and 19th centuries. Of these, 4 million came to North America.

After the American Revolution, in which Black soldiers from each of the 13 colonies partici-pated, slavery was abolished in the northern states. The Civil War in the 19th century may have freed the rest of the slaves legally, but racism continued and grew alongside the increasing participation by Blacks in all aspects of mainstream life. For example, the Ku Klux Klan was organized in 1866, just before the South Carolina House of Representatives found itself with a Black majority. By 1896, the U.S. Supreme Court determined (in *Plessy v. Ferguson*) that states were free to provide separate but equal institutions, and many states, particularly in the South, seized the opportunity, most notably in regard to schools.

Looking for better opportunities, Blacks began to leave the South, only to arrive at the same time European immigrants were also crowding into northern cities. For the most part, help with education, housing, and employment was provided for the Europeans but not for the African-Americans, who soon settled into city slums. "The impact of prejudice, poverty, and urban ghettos continues to affect many African Americans disproportionately to the present day" (Willis, 1998, p. 169). Yet, by the first half of the 20th century, the exodus of Blacks from the South only grew. Sharecropping in the South was at the whim of floods and insect infestations, and Black farmers found themselves encumbered by increasing debt.

Meanwhile, the influx of Europeans to the North halted during World War I, causing factory managers to send labor recruiters to the South. Widespread institutionalized racism continued in both North and South until World War II, when the military was desegregated, and even until 1954, when the *Plessy v. Ferguson* ruling was replaced by the Supreme Court's *Brown v. Board of Education* decision, which desegregated schools nationwide. In various ways, some of them controversial (e.g., the repeal of affirmative action in some states in the late 1990s), the deinsti-tutionalization of racism continued throughout the remainder of the 20th century. Yet informal or social racism continues. "Negative attitudes, instilled by years of institutionalized breeding of fear and contempt, are still evident" (Willis, 1998, p. 170). According to Derman-Sparks and Olsen Edwards, "In every aspect of society, White children are more likely to have access to resources that support healthy development and future success, such as safe neighborhoods and good schools" (2010, p. 77).

Teachers and caregivers can expect, in their encounters with African-American families, to see both the results of this history of maltreatment and the influences of the Anglo-European mainstream culture described above. Within each family, the extent of these influences will vary, as is the case for any culture and its subsets. The influences and values listed and discussed next reflect an African heritage but also, at times, input from the U.S. mainstream culture as well.

- *Language.* The Africans who came to the United States as slaves brought with them a diversity of languages, although there were commonalities within them. It was generally required of Blacks that they learn English, but their interpretation of it was influenced by their native languages. Generations later, some linguistic patterns from these times remain in the speech of many African Americans.
- Linguists who have studied the speech patterns of African Americans in recent decades have altered their previous belief that this language is substandard English to an understanding that Black English has its own standardized rules. It has been observed that Black English tends to be used more broadly among people of lower socioeconomic status (SES) and selectively, depending on the social situation, by those of higher SES (Dillard, 1972).
- *The family.* From the time of slavery, when family members could be sold individually, to the present day, when single mothers are often the official head of household, the African-American nuclear family has been endangered. In its place has been an extended family model with its roots in African traditions. This heritage has led to a valuing of group effort over private gain. With support from the extended family, however, independence is also valued:

  > This may seem at first to be in conflict with the group-effort ethic, but it actually extends that ethic. It has to do with the empowerment that comes when as many as are able can earn a living, meet their family's basic needs, and have a little bit left over to help others in the extended family who may need temporary assistance.

  (Willis, 1998, p. 183)

  Respect for elders, although eroding in most facets of U.S. society, is historically an African-American value. From Africa came the belief that the oldest members of society are the closest to God; centuries later this idea still leads to the assumption that these are the people who lead prayers in any group setting. Obedience to parents and older siblings has been emphasized more than, for example, the discussions and reasoning often favored by those of Anglo-European heritage.
- *Childrearing.* Guidance from adults has traditionally emphasized discipline and obedience. The African proverb that it takes a village to raise a child is born out in the expectation that extended family and responsible community members will participate in the child's discipline and training. Children are expected to obey the family's rules and treat others with respect as soon as they are old enough to understand. "Although these beliefs are not acted upon by all African Americans because of their life circumstances, they form a core set of beliefs that continue to be valued by many" (Willis, 1998, p. 189).
- *Views of illness and disabilities.* These views can vary from an acceptance of the scientific model described in the Anglo-European section, to a belief in simple bad luck or misfortune, to the belief that a child's disability is the result of sinning on the parents' part.

Interactions Between School or Center and Families

Again we emphasize that it is important not to over-generalize the cultural influences on any one group. Some ideas to think about with that necessary caution, however, include:

- Communication is likely to be "high context," that is, less verbal and more through shared history, intonation, facial expressions, and other body language.
- Emphasis may be placed more on the situation than on time. Thus, it is more important to finish the business of a meeting than to watch the clock.
- Addressing parents and other adults by their last names and titles until invited to use the first name is considered polite. Not to do so indicates disrespect.
- Telling ethnic jokes of any kind should be avoided. African Americans often feel as though the joke would be about them if they were out of the room. (This is good advice for all teachers at all times with all cultures.)
- If an African-American child lives with an extended family, it may be someone other than, or in addition to, a parent who is responsible for home–school communication and who should be invited to conferences and special events.

American Indian Culture

It is estimated that before Europeans began to explore and settle North America, the American Indian population numbered about 5 million. By the 1800s, warfare and infectious diseases brought by White settlers had caused a drop to just about 600,000 people. The great loss of population led to a weakening of tribal alliances, leaving an opening for aggressive European advancement.

From the American Indian point of view, interactions were more or less negative, depending on the motives the outsiders brought with them. For the French, economics was the driving force. Trappers and traders lived with the American Indians, learned from and worked with them, and sometimes married them. The English looked more toward building permanent settlements in their own style. American Indians were at times viewed as impediments to success and were thought of as savages and pagans, scarcely worth noticing unless it became necessary to remove them from the land that the English claimed for their king. The Spanish, like the French, brought economic motives but were swayed more by valuable metals than by furs. In addition, they expended their energies spreading their Roman Catholic faith through the establishment of a system of missions. American Indians became a source of free labor as well as potential Christian converts. Faced with the powerful English and Spanish forces of expansion, the American Indians lost hope for keeping either their land or their cultures, and for the most part, they lost both.

As the United States began to form a nation, then expanded geographically, policies toward American Indian populations fluctuated wildly. Throughout much of the 19th century, negotiations took place by treaty. By the end of the century, tribes were relocated to reservations on lands deemed undesirable for the ever-growing numbers of settlers. "Such forced relocation not only broke the spirit of many once-proud Indian nations, but also destined them to a life of poverty and hopelessness—conditions that continue to haunt American Indians today" (Joe & Malach, 1998, p. 130).

Toward the end of the 19th century, the government decided that individual land ownership would make the American Indians more civilized, more productive, and more American. The reservations were carved up into individual plots under the Dawes Act of 1887, with any leftover land reverting to the government for more settlement.

By the 20th century, fewer than 250,000 American Indians were left in North America. Government policies began to focus ever more on assimilation into the mainstream culture. Children were removed from their families and sent to boarding schools, sometimes forcibly. They were punished for speaking their native languages, sometimes by physical cruelty, and denied ties to their home cultures. In the 1960s and 1970s, a time of upheaval nationally, American Indians across the United States began to demand the return of federal surplus land and the rights given to them by long-dishonored treaties. Such events as the occupation of Alcatraz Island and the takeover of the Bureau of Indian Affairs in Washington, DC, drew attention to the continuing plight of American Indians. Some reforms began to be implemented and included the Indian Health Care Improvement Act of 1976 and the Indian Child Welfare Act of 1978. The former provided extra resources for improving American Indian health both on and off the reservation; the latter gave tribes greater power over placement of children put up for adoption.

Today, children are no longer forced to leave home for boarding schools. They may attend public schools or those provided on their reservations. Too often, reservation schools do not have the resources of local public schools, but children attending public schools have not been treated well. Even when much energy is devoted to making school a welcoming place, parents may be reluctant to participate in any way, recalling all too well the pain of their own experiences.

As you think about interacting with American Indian families, consider the cultural values discussed next. Keep in mind that they will be held to different degrees by people who live on reservations or in urban settings and will be somewhat different from tribe to tribe.

- *Group orientation.* Tribal affiliation is an important aspect of identity. Some American Indian languages do not include a word for *I*. Group consensus is important in decision-making, and everyone involved is permitted to speak. Decisions may not be made on the spot but are deferred until everyone has had time to think things over. Aggressive and competitive individualism are usually rejected; children who develop these qualities from the mainstream culture may be taunted by their peers (Joe & Malach, 1998). Mainstream teachers may mistake the more typical quiet, self-effacing behavior as evidence of passivity or laziness, rather than the thoughtful and respectful demeanor valued by the American Indian culture.

- *Acceptance of events.* Members of the mainstream culture tend to focus on taking charge of, or doing something about, negative events or natural disasters. The American Indian approach tends more toward acceptance of the situation "as part of the nature of life and that one must learn to live with life and accept what comes, both the good and the bad" (Joe & Malach, 1998, pp. 140–141).

- *Self-reliance.* Parent-to-child teaching style occurs largely through modeling and direct telling. As children observe their parents in action, they learn quickly about expectations of the adult world. One cross-cultural study (Miller, cited in Joe & Malach, 1998) showed that whereas White and Black children were expected to do regular chores after they reached age 6, American Indian children did so at less than age 5½. American Indian children learned to dress themselves earlier as well, at 2.8 years old as opposed to almost 4 years old for White and Black children.

- *Time orientation.* Time for many American Indians is a more flexible and fluid concept than for people in the mainstream culture. Keeping to the dictates of the clock is not nearly so important as the activity and interactions underway, for example making sure that a meeting or conference is finished satisfactorily for all parties.

- *Language.* During the years that assimilation was emphasized, tribal languages began to disappear. Today, there is a widespread effort to reclaim nearly dead ancient languages. Some schools, including Head Start centers, begin early to teach children both the native culture and language as well as mainstream culture and English.

- *The family.* The extended family is frequently important for American Indians living on reservations, but the nuclear family is more commonly found in urban areas. In extended families, grandparents or other relatives may take a major role in raising young children if the parents are working. It is important for a teacher or caregiver to understand each family's situation before conferring about the welfare of their child.

- *Childrearing.* The extended family may assign different roles to different members. In some tribes, grandparents may provide spiritual and cultural guidance and uncles may handle discipline (Joe & Malach, 1998).

- Traditionally, American Indian children were not disciplined with corporal punishment. They were generally introduced to this approach during the often-abusive years in boarding schools run by the mainstream culture. Their years away from home kept American Indian children from learning parenting skills either from their own culture or from the mainstream culture, whose homes they rarely observed. There are attempts during this generation to heal the wounds of the past and to return to more traditional ways.

- *Views of illness and disability.* Although American Indian families may accept a scientific explanation and treatment of children's sickness and disabilities, they may also turn to their culture to explain the reasons for the problems as well as for additional treatment ideas. Causes such as witchcraft, spirit loss or intrusion, or spells may be considered important influences. Parents may wish to consult with a tribal healer before or during mainstream treatment (Joe & Malach, 1998). In addition, there may be an emphasis on the role of a child with a disability or delay in the family and community that has little apparent relationship to the characteristics of the disability.

Interactions Between School or Center and Families

Remembering again that acculturation varies across families and situations, a number of suggestions can still be made for school–family interactions based on American Indian history, traditions, and present-day culture (Joe & Malach, 1998; Krogh, 1994):

- Before a conference, ask parents which family members should be included. They may or may not wish to bring others. If several people do come, be sure to address and listen to them all.
- Avoid intimidating family members; listen to their ideas and ask questions rather than lecturing to them. Ask them what they see as their child's special talents and gifts.
- Visit the children's homes or reservation. Be a part of the community from time to time by being knowledgeable about holidays and perhaps participating in special events.
- Respect the family's preference for bicultural or bilingual education for their child.
- Take time to learn about the communication style of the American Indian culture in your area. You may need to become more reserved and quiet during meetings than you typically are, and do more listening than talking (another good piece of general advice).

Latin-American or Latino Culture

Today there is concern in much of the United States about illegal immigrants crossing the border from Mexico, but a century and a half ago the situation was reversed. Then, California, Texas, New Mexico, Arizona, and Colorado belonged to Mexico. But, as one Mexican of the time complained, Americans had "formed for themselves" the idea "that God made the world and them also, therefore what there is in the world belongs to them as sons of God" (Takaki, 1993, pp. 172–173). This view was corroborated by the statements and actions of Americans, from presidents to ordinary citizens, many of whom simply moved illegally into Mexican territory. Americans declared it their *manifest destiny* to control the major portion of the North American continent and, by the end of the Mexican War of the 1830s and 1840s, did just that. Suddenly, the northern half of Mexico belonged to the United States, and the area's residents found themselves with a choice of heading south or remaining as potential U.S. citizens. Most chose to stay and before long found they were facing increasing antagonism toward their language and culture on the part of the growing Anglo-European population. The hunger for ever more land also ensured that eventually even the richest Mexican-Californian landholders were stripped of everything they owned.

Many in the United States today have chosen to forget this past, but those of Mexican heritage have, not surprisingly, retained the history as part of their cultural heritage. Similarly, there is a general tendency in the U.S. to regard most Mexican Americans as immigrants although many can trace their ancestry in the area to the 1700s or earlier.

Although less noticeable than immigrant communities from Mexico, because they have not settled in an easily identifiable area, immigrants from other countries in Central America have also been changing the face of the United States in the past generation. The teacher or caregiver involved with families from the various Latino cultures needs to realize that there are a number of differences among them, just as there are within each of the cultures we discussed previously. It is not only geographical difference that must be taken into account but class differences as well. To a great extent, the Latin-American tradition has included notable separation of the classes. At the top are those who claim Spanish ancestry; far below are the *Mestizo* (mixed), Black, and Native classes. A middle-class immigrant family from Mexico City, for example, might well have more in common with the U.S. mainstream culture than with a U.S.-born Mexican family of low-socioeconomic stat us (Zuniga, 1998). Often, immigrants remain more conscious of their class status than people of the mainstream culture realize.

In the Southeast, particularly in Florida, immigration of Spanish speaking peoples has come primarily from Cuba, the Caribbean island the United States attempted to buy from Spain in the 1850s, then fought over five decades later. Making Cuba a U.S. colony was, at times, on the political agenda but, in the end, it retained its independence.

At the very end of the Spanish-American War, even as the final treaty was being delivered for signature, the United States managed to overtake Puerto Rico and keep it for its own territory. Today, immigration comes from both Cuba and Puerto Rico, but in very different fashions. Because Puerto Ricans have U.S. citizenship, they may travel as they please, usually to find more economically satisfying work, then return home, just as any other citizen might do. Cubans, on the other hand, have arrived as refugees in periodic waves since Fidel Castro's revolutionary takeover in 1959. Because the first wave of refugees came from the educated upper classes, the Cuban story has been one of greater economic success than has generally been true for Puerto Rican and Mexican immigrants. The development of Miami as an international trading center has been, to a great extent, the result of the efforts of Cuban exiles.

Although it is difficult to assign a single set of values to a cultural group with so many variations in its subcultures and such divergent geographical origins, several attributes can be listed for teachers and caregivers to consider (Zuniga, 1998):

- *Machismo and a changing patriarchy.* Traditionally, Latino culture has valued strong leadership on the part of the father. In the past generation, this has been changing, as more women enter the workforce and become more highly educated. The tradition remains in many ways and in many families, however, and it is most courteous to speak to the father first if both parents are present at a conference or meeting.
- *Personalismo.* Warm interpersonal interactions are valued over the task orientation of the mainstream culture. Beginning any encounter with some informal chatting helps establish a good working atmosphere and may go a long way toward establishing trust of the teacher or caregiver.
- *Time.* Interpersonal relationships are more important than retaining an inflexible timetable. It is important to avoid giving parents the feeling that you are impatient or always in a rush, connoting that you don't care about them.
- *Language.* It should not be assumed that Spanish is the first language of all immigrant families. A growing number of them come from areas where indigenous languages are prevalent, and they may not be completely fluent in Spanish.

- Communication is generally high context, making body language and attitude as important as the words spoken. Teachers should take care to communicate in all ways their acceptance and respect.
- *The family.* Although the urban family headed by a single mother is a growing phenomenon, Latino families have maintained a far lower divorce rate than have other cultures, a fact that may well be related to the continuing influence of the Roman Catholic religion. Extended families traditionally have predominated.
- *Childrearing.* In general, children are viewed as the prime reason for marriage and as the validation of it. A relaxed attitude is taken toward early achievement, with more focus on nurturing and indulging a young child. Both physical and emotional closeness prevail among all members. Identity with the family rather than independence is nurtured throughout the child's growing up years. Cooperation rather than individualism is generally valued. In poorer families, children may be expected to pitch in by taking on work roles fairly early. Young children are highly valued and babies often garner the attention of unrelated adults and strangers in public places.
- *Views of illness and disability.* Middle-class, acculturated families may well have adopted the Anglo-European scientific views described previously. Others may bring with them a folk tradition as well as influences from the Latino Catholic church, which also incorporates many folk traditions. Thus, a disability may be seen as a curse from some present evil force. Belief in a punishing God and in the inevitable tragedy of life may lead to an accepting and fatalistic view of a disability or chronic illness.

Interactions Between School or Center and Families

Some suggestions that may be helpful across the various Latino cultures include:

- Always begin interactions with some informal conversation; avoid the temptation to get right down to business.
- Tone of voice and body language are important. Avoid coming across as authoritarian, tough, and harsh.
- Try not to appear hurried and impatient. Let the parents know that you are listening and that you care.
- If both husband and wife are present, speak to the husband first. Unless it becomes apparent that they have adopted a more mainstream family structure, continue to defer to the husband as the family leader.
- Communicate your delight in and affection for their children as a centerpiece of, rather than a sideline to, the discussion.

Asian-American Cultures

The fastest growing ethnic minority group in the United States in recent years has been Asian, with a population of about 3.5 million in 1980 expanding to over 8 million in 2000 (U.S. Census Bureau, 2003). Of the cultural groups discussed in this chapter, those of Asian influence are, perhaps, the most varied. The inability of many Americans to tell Chinese from Japanese or Thais from Vietnamese indicates a need to become more knowledgeable rather than any actual lack of difference between the nationalities. As one Chinese immigrant's son argues, the perception that Asian immigrants are all much the same or, at least, mysterious, "serves to disguise the reality of unique customs, traditions, values, beliefs, and familial systems based on political and religious foundations that are thousands of years old" (Chan, 1998, pp. 252–253). Most pertinent for our purposes, a lack of knowledge may lead a teacher or caregiver to misunderstand the feelings that children's families have toward one another—feelings that may be based on centuries of conflict or friendship.

Over the years, immigration from Asian countries to the United States has been affected by two general influences: changing U.S. immigration policies and difficulties in various Asian countries, such as economic hardship and wars. This section discusses these influences on immigrants from two countries. Further research into the experiences of other peoples will broaden a teacher's ability to work well with families from other cultures as well.

Chinese-American History

Widespread famine, economic depression, and civil wars in mid-19th-century China, coupled with the news of recently discovered gold in California, caused the first major influx of Chinese people to the United States. The plan for most of these men, who came by the tens of thousands, was to mine for three to five years, then return home with enough money to retire on. A very few were able to do just that, and so the legend of *Gam Saan* (Gold Mountain) continued to grow, despite the fact that most of the Chinese did not do well and had to find more menial jobs to survive. Soon, many of them were hired by private companies contracted to extend the national railroad system to the West Coast. The Chinese proved to be excellent workers who cost less than U.S. citizens, a situation almost guaranteed to lead eventually to resentments and disputes.

The result was the Chinese Exclusion Act of 1882, the first federal law that banned an entire nationality from entering the United States. It was not repealed until 1943. The years between found some Chinese returning home but many others remaining to face institutional and violent racism. To avoid deportation, it was generally necessary to change one's status from laborer to businessman. The creation of urban Chinatowns provided some cultural security, safety from racism, and business opportunities, and many of these cities within cities remain today.

Due to a rigid quota system, it was not until 1965, with the passage of the Immigration and Nationality Act Amendments, that a second wave of Chinese could enter the United States. Since preferred status was given to educated, professional, and skilled workers, this second group provided a new stereotype of Asians as overachievers. Their children and grandchildren are still labeled today with the expectation that they all will be the best performers in their classes.

Chinese-American Language

The Chinese are connected by a single written language, but the pronunciation of its pictographic characters varies widely across dialects. Chinese contains many monosyllabic words that are often differentiated by the pitch, or tone, of pronunciation. Word order is different from that of English, and there are no tenses, plural endings, or verb conjugations. Imagine the total reorientation to language that every Chinese immigrant child and parent must undergo when learning English!

Vietnamese-American History

Although Vietnam's northern border touches China, and many of its original inhabitants are thought to have come from southern China, the country's culture and language have evolved quite differently in many ways. China ruled the country for about a thousand years, but beginning in 111 B.C., numerous rebellions led to independence that lasted until the French colonized Vietnam, from 1883 to 1954. During World War II, the Japanese occupied the country and, this time, rebels adopted Communism. After the war, the French tried to regain control but managed only to retake the south while the Communists controlled the north. With the French finally repelled from the south as well, the country was officially divided between North and South, both sides claiming exclusive power over the entire country. By 1960, war was in full swing, with the Soviet Union and China aiding the North and the United States supporting the South.

During the 20 years of the Vietnam War, many South Vietnamese put themselves at risk to aid the U.S. troops. As the South and its U.S. allies lost the war, many South Vietnamese were forced to flee. Over time, more than 1 million became refugees in both Asian and Western countries, primarily in France and in the United States. These ranged from educated professionals to Hmong people from remote mountain areas and to "boat people" who had survived extraordinarily horrific conditions. Immigration policy has been to disperse the Vietnamese throughout the United States rather than permitting "Vietnam-towns" to develop. Thus, in almost any area of the country, teachers and caregivers may encounter second- or even first-generation Vietnamese immigrants.

Vietnamese-American Language

Like Chinese, Vietnamese is tonal, contains many monosyllabic words, and has no plurals, tenses, or verb conjugations. Originally, written Vietnamese was based on the Chinese system but, since World War I, the Roman alphabet, with several additional tone marks, has been adopted.

Shared Values

Although their societies have developed in some differing ways, Chinese and Vietnamese also share values that are similar, with roots that go back thousands of years. Thus, the following cultural traits can generally be applied to both:

- *Family.* The Asian family as the central focus of the individual's life "engenders primary loyalty, obligation, cooperation, interdependence, and reciprocity" (Chan, 1998, p. 292). In Asian cultures, the individual is believed to be today's extension of a family that goes back to the beginning of time. Thus, there is as much thought for the past as for the present. Both the Chinese and the Vietnamese adhere to the ancient Confucian hierarchical system in which the father has primary leadership within the nuclear family but living grandparents are at the top of the extended family.

- *Harmony.* "The keynote of existence is to reconcile divergent forces, principles, and points of view in an effort to maintain harmony. The individual must strive to achieve intrapsychic harmony, interpersonal harmony, and harmony with nature as well as time" (Chan, 1998, p. 293). Asian Americans guided by the tradition of harmony avoid confrontation; demonstrate constraint in verbal, social, and emotional interactions; help others save face by showing respect; and value politeness and tact. A teacher or caregiver with a tendency toward extreme directness should keep these characteristics in mind in order to help interactions with more traditional Asian Americans to succeed.

- *Patience and endurance.* Along with patience and endurance, industriousness and tolerance have provided strength to Vietnamese and other southeast Asians who have lived through subjugation, war, and great loss. For the Chinese, it has been important to persevere quietly, without complaint. For many Asian Americans, it is bad form to share problems with someone such as the teacher. They may even smile and assure everyone that everything is just fine, thus politely sparing others the need to share their pain.

- *Childrearing.* Having children is the cement of marriage, more important than the relationship between husband and wife. During a child's infancy, loving parents are permissive, tolerant, and ready to answer every discomfort. Breast feeding may last two years or longer, but toilet training may begin after just a few months, although it is not coercive. The indulgence of the early years is replaced, once school age is reached, with an expectation of self-discipline, responsibility, and a better understanding of adult mores and roles. Whereas the early years are characterized by guidance from the mother, the father now participates in childrearing as well, and disciplinary expectations are increased.

- *Views of illness and disability.* Families that have recently immigrated may well retain traditional views that conflict with the Anglo-European scientific model. A child's good behavior and success in school are viewed as the family's responsibility. Thus, a child with a behavior disorder or mental retardation can become a source of embarrassment for the family, someone who just needs more support from home. A mother's behavior during pregnancy may be seen as the cause of a disability, including such things as eating taboo foods, engaging in reckless or inappropriate activities, or using tools, particularly scissors or knives.

Interactions Between School or Center and Families
Asian cultures can vary widely, but some suggestions may prove helpful in your interactions:

- In communication, body language is much more subdued than in other cultures, e.g., Anglo-European, African American, and Latino. Speaking with great animation may be overwhelming and turn off useful exchanges. Emotional restraint and general reserve will be received with more comfort.
- Sustained eye-to-eye contact is considered rude and should be avoided.
- Until you know the parents well, avoid asking personal questions about their lives. This even includes asking their opinions on politics, which for many Asian cultures is akin to asking pointed questions in the mainstream culture about religious preference.

Some General Conclusions

There are in the United States today numerous ethnicities, cultures, and nations of origin. It is impossible within the confines of this single chapter to do more than touch on a few. We hope, however, that the descriptions provided here may give the reader two directions for further learning: a better realization that knowledge of child and family background can go far toward positive family interactions and progress in learning; and a better understanding of one's own culture. If your culture was represented in one or more of the descriptions, were there items that surprised you but rang true? Were there some that did not seem quite right? Should others be added? As we delve further into the attributes of our own and others' cultures, we gain appreciation of our common humanity as well as greater skill in providing the most positive atmosphere for the intellectual, emotional, and social growth of all the children entrusted to us.

It is important to learn about and respect other cultures, abilities, and viewpoints; yet doing so is not sufficient to move our society forward. It is also important to realize that biases develop very early in children's lives, thus making it a clear responsibility of early childhood educators to be proactive in their classroom responsibilities.

Being Proactive in the Classroom or Center: An Overview

Early childhood educators have a responsibility to avoid harm and provide an atmosphere that equips young children with tools and strategies to stand up against bias and prejudice, for the benefit of themselves, other adults, young children, and the adults the children will become. There is a large body of information and resources to support teachers in their efforts, most notably:

- *Anti-bias Education for Young Children and Ourselves*, by Louise Derman-Sparks and Julie Olsen Edwards.
- *Roots and Wings: Affirming culture in early childhood programs*, by Stacey York.
- *Teaching and Learning in a Diverse World*, by Patricia Ramsey.

Each of these resources provides philosophical, theoretical, and empirical information, as well as a multitude of practical strategies for addressing diversity in all its forms in early childhood programs. A hallmark of the materials available to support anti-bias and multi-cultural early education is that teachers are supported and encouraged to go beyond knowledge to take action, investigate their own beliefs, challenge existing practices, and make things better for children. Anti-bias education (ABE) has a very ambitious agenda, as illustrated by the four ABE goals:

1. Each child will demonstrate self-awareness, confidence, family pride, and positive social identities.
2. Each child will express comfort and joy with human diversity; accurate language for human differences; and deep, caring human connections.

3. Each child will increasingly recognize unfairness, have language to describe unfairness, and understand that unfairness hurts.

4. Each child will demonstrate empowerment and the skills to act, with others or alone, against prejudice and/or discriminatory actions.

(Derman-Sparks & Olsen Edwards, 2010, p. xx)

Our goal in this chapter has been to provide some introductory considerations for the reader who is beginning to interact with children and families from a variety of backgrounds. We hope that an atmosphere of acceptance, caring, and concern for all children will imbue our readers' teaching practices and that you will adopt the four ABE goals above as your own. As you think about ways to make all children feel welcome and valued, it is essential to have some more specific guidelines to frame your everyday interactions. The following list is adapted from the three books listed above (Derman-Sparks & Olsen Edwards, 2010; Ramsey, 2004; and York, 2003).

Teachers should:

- Recognize the beauty, value, and contribution of each child.
- Provide children with accurate, developmentally appropriate information about race, language, culture, ability, gender anatomy and identity, and social class.
- Encourage young children's openness and interest in others, willingness to include others, and desire to cooperate.
- Promote effective and collaborative relationships with children's families.

Children should:
- Develop positive gender, racial, cultural, class, and individual identities.
- See themselves as part of the larger society, identifying with and relating to members of all groups, as well as with their own family and heritage.
- Learn to respect and appreciate the diverse ways in which other people live.
- Feel pride but not superiority in their racial identity.
- Feel free to ask about their own and others' physical characteristics; about issues of racism, ability, culture, gender; and about current events.
- Experience discussions and activities in early childhood programs that promote engagement with concepts related to diversity and interactions with people from a variety of backgrounds.

Families should:

- Feel welcome and comfortable in the early childhood program.
- Participate as active partners in their young children's educations to the extent they desire.
- Be confident about sharing information and making suggestions about their children and/or the program.
- Expect that their perspectives and opinions will be acknowledged and considered.

Suggestions to teachers for achieving these goals include:

- Post welcoming signs in each home language of the children in your classroom.
- Make anti-bias education a priority every day and include anti-bias updates as a standing feature of newsletters and conferences.
- Learn basic teaching and learning vocabulary in children's home languages.
- Invite visits from local community leaders and participate in community celebrations.
- Use words like "a few," "some," "usually," "sometimes," "many," and "most" to describe family structure, gender concepts, and SES. For example, "Many families have two parents, and some families have just one parent." "Some families have a Mom AND a Dad; sometimes there is a Mom OR a Dad; and sometimes there are two Mommies OR two Daddys." "In many families there are brothers and sisters, and many children are the only one; often children are the only one for a while and then there is a new baby."
- Look carefully at the room's materials for play. Do they respect and reflect the cultures of all your children? Are there chopsticks and a tortilla press in the housekeeping area? Commercial tools for the housekeeping corner, for example, typically reflect middle-class, Anglo-European values.
- Scan all books to see if pictures represent varying ethnicities, ages, family structures, and abilities. Are both genders engaged in nontraditional as well as traditional roles? Are there pictures of same-sex parents, children of ambiguous gender, wheelchairs, eyeglasses, walkers, hearing aids, and so forth?
- Decorate the walls with photographs of people from various cultures, ethnicities, and abilities. Discuss them informally with the children.
- Balance individually oriented activities with cooperative learning experiences.
- Display alphabets, labels, and quotes from different writing systems. Teach a few words or numbers in different languages, particularly those represented by cultures in the classroom.
- Avoid pictures, dolls, and activities that stereotype or misrepresent other cultures: festival clothes presented as though they are worn all the time; historical representations presented as if they were current; teaching about a country of origin to explain about their U.S. descendants (e.g., Japan to learn about Japanese Americans).
- Avoid token studying of ethnic or cultural groups only at high-visibility times (e.g., Blacks for Martin Luther King's birthday, American Indians at Thanksgiving).
- Do not ignore children's discriminatory comments or behavior—they will not go away. Rather, make rules about the treatment of others, then intervene immediately if necessary, just as you do with any misbehavior. Teach about feelings, friendship, respect, citizenship, stereotypes, and differences.
- Listen to your own speech and observe your own interactions. Do you speak with a harsher tone of voice for some children than for others? Do you touch some children less than others? Are you more inclined to take disciplinary action toward some?

In this chapter we have discussed the need for all children and their families to feel welcomed and valued in our classrooms and centers. We described several cultures commonly seen in the

United States today and the ways in which their members might look at their experiences in and out of the classroom environment. We also considered a few practical ways to incorporate a respect for diversity in the classroom or center. Finally, we should point out that given the multi-cultural nature of today's world, diversity is an important issue for all teachers, not just for those who teach in a diverse classroom. All children deserve opportunities to learn about the complex world around them.

EXTENDING YOUR LEARNING

As in the previous chapters, Suggestions 1 and 2 focus on your developing philosophy of teaching and learning.

1. After reading this chapter, do you find that your thinking has changed, or perhaps been solidified, pertaining to diversity issues and your teaching? Reflect on the feelings you had as you read this chapter and what those feelings will mean to your teaching. Add these ideas to your personal philosophy notes.

2. Look over the picture you drew. Now that you have read this chapter, does it appear that there are children who are missing from your classroom? How do you feel about your place-ment in relation to the children and to the physical environment? If you have used colored artwork and avoided stick figures, you should be able to answer these questions. Either redraw as appropriate or add commentary to the back of your picture.

3. Visit a school or center with several languages represented. Interview teachers and observe the ways in which non-English-speaking children are introduced to their new language. Find out how children's needs are met while they are learning to communicate using English.

4. Recall your first introduction to differences in gender, race and ethnicity, ability, and social status. How did you respond to your new knowledge: Was the experience positive, negative, or mixed? Do you have uncomfortable memories of your own actions or of those of others to children who were different in these ways? Have you experienced prejudice or discrimination yourself?

5. Think about the views of your family members concerning differences in gender, race, ability, and economic status. Do you generally accept them? Reject them? Can you explain why?

6. Choose a country about which you know little, one that has children registered in schools and centers in your area. First, do some library research about that country's history, geography, and culture. Then interview two or more parents (or grandparents) from that country about their views of education. Consider how you could adapt your curriculum or methodology to meet their children's needs from the family's cultural point of view while still providing the skills the children will need to survive well in the mainstream culture.

7. Start a file box of ideas for your classroom that incorporate ways to handle diversity issues. You might have a section for each area of the curriculum, another for parents, and another for the environment.

8. During your student-teaching experience, invite all parents to participate and share in class-room activities and outings. Have parents teach songs or read picture books in their native languages.

9. Has your thinking changed, or perhaps been solidified, pertaining to cultural issues and your teaching? Reflect on your feelings as you read this chapter and what they will mean to you in your teaching. Add these ideas to your personal philosophy notes.

10. Take advantage of opportunities to attend and participate in public events sponsored by cultural groups other than your own. Accompany families, if invited, to traditional healers, holiday celebrations, family gatherings. Note the aspects of each event that are familiar and comfortable as well as those that are unfamiliar and uncomfortable for you.

INTERNET RESOURCES

Web sites provide much useful information for educators and we list some here that pertain to the topics covered in this chapter. The addresses of Web sites can also change, however, and new ones are continually added. Thus, this list should be considered as a first step in your acquisition of a larger and ever-changing collection.

Center for Language Minority Education and Research
www.clmer.csulb.edu/

Culturally & Linguistically Appropriate Services Early Childhood Research Institute
http://clas.uiuc.edu

Global Classroom
www.global-classroom.com

The Global Schoolhouse
www.gsh.org

Immigration and Naturalization Service
www.uscis.gov/portal/site/uscis

Multicultural Book Review Homepage
www.isomedia.com/homes/jmele/homepage.html

Multicultural Pavilion
www.edchange.org/multicultural/

National Black Child Development Institute
www.nbcdi.org/

National Latino Children's Institute
www.nlci.org/common/index2.htm

Viet Nam Online Community
www.php.com/

VOCABULARY

Achievement gap. Systematic differences in educational performance across groups of students, usually defined by gender, race/ethnicity, and/or social-economic status (SES).

Affirmative action. Policies that attempt to promote equal opportunity members of minority groups and promote diversity, primarily in the workplace.

High context communication. Communication between people that emphasizes non-verbal signals such as body language.

Indentured servant. A person under contract binding him or her, as a laborer, to another for a given length of time. In the early American colonies, an immigrant so bound.

Institutionalized racism. Differential access to the goods, services, and opportunities of society; inherent limitations of opportunities that disadvantage members of minority racial groups.

Low context communication. Communication between people that emphasizes verbal language at the expense of non-verbal signals.

Manifest Destiny. A U.S. doctrine of the 19th century in which the country's continued territorial expansions was postulated to be obvious and necessary.

Mestizo. A colonial term used to refer to people of mixed European and Amerindian ancestry.

Monolingual. Proficiency in a single language.

(Continued)

Multi-cultural. Containing many cultures. In education, the focus is on appreciating the contributions of all cultures.

Nuclear family. Parents and their children who share living quarters.

Separate but Equal. Until 1954, when overturned by the U.S. Supreme Court, a doctrine that racial segregation in schools and other facilities was constitutional as long as the facilities were about equal for both Blacks and Whites.

SES. Abbreviation for *social economic status*, a descriptor that combines income, education, and occupation into a measure that describes social status.

Taken for granted realities. Elements of a culture that are so embedded as to be invisible to the members of the culture as anything other than realities that are believed to pertain to all humans.

References

Althen, G. (1988). *American ways: A guide for foreigners in the United States.* Yarmouth, ME: Intercultural Press.

Barnett, W. S., & Yarosz, D. J. (2007). Who goes to preschool and why does it matter? *Preschool Policy Brief,* Issue 15. New Brunswick, NJ: National Institute for Early Education Research.

Boutte, G. S. (2008). Beyond the illusion of diversity: How early childhood teachers can promote social justice. *The Social Studies, 99*(4), 165–173.

Bredekamp, S. (Ed.) (1987). *Developmentally appropriate practice in early childhood programs serving children from birth through age 8.* Washington, DC: National Association for the Education of Young Children.

Bredekamp, S., & Copple, C. (Eds.) (1997). *Developmentally appropriate practice in early childhood programs* (2nd ed.). Washington, DC: National Association for the Education of Young Children.

Bredekamp, S., & Copple, C. (Eds.) (2009). *Developmentally appropriate practice in early childhood programs: Serving children from birth to age 8* (3rd ed.). Washington, DC: National Association for the Education of Young Children.

Brill, S., & Pepper, R. (2008). *The transgender child: A handbook for families and professionals.* San Francisco: Cleis Press.

Burkam, D. T., & Lee, V. E. (2002). *Inequity at the starting gate.* Washington, DC: Economic Policy Institute.

Burt, T., Gelnaw, A., & Lesser, L. K. (2010). Do no harm: Creating welcoming and inclusive environments for lesbian, gay, bisexual, and transgender families in early childhood settings. *Young Children, 65*(1).

Chan, S. (1998). Families with Asian roots. In E. Lynch & M. Hanson (Eds.), *Developing cross-cultural competence* (2nd ed.). Baltimore, MD: Paul H. Brookes.

Children's Defense Fund (2008). *The state of America's children 2008: Highlights.* Washington, DC: Author.

Demmert, W. (2005). Personal communication.

Derman-Sparks, L. (1993). *Anti-bias curriculum: Tools for empowering young children.* Washington, DC: National Association for the Education of Young Children.

Derman-Sparks, L., & Olsen Edwards, J. (2010). *Anti-bias education for young children and ourselves.* Washington, DC: National Association for the Education of Young Children.

Dillard, J. (1972). *Black English: Its history and usage in the United States.* New York: Random House.

Joe, J., & Malach, R. (1998). Families with Native American roots. In E. Lynch & M. Hanson (Eds.), *Developing cross-cultural competence* (2nd ed.). Baltimore, MD: Paul H. Brookes.

Krogh, S. (1994). *Educating young children: Infancy to grade three.* New York: McGraw-Hill.

Lynch, E., & Hanson, M. (2004). *Developing cross-cultural competence: A guide for working with young children and their families* (3rd ed.). Baltimore, MD: Paul Brookes Publishing Company.

NAEYC (2005). Position statement. *NAEYC code of ethical conduct and statement of commitment,* rev. ed. Brochure. Washington, DC: Author.

Ramsey, P. (2004). *Teaching and learning in a diverse world: Multicultural education for young children* (3rd ed.). New York: Teachers College Press.

Swiniarski, L., Breitborde, M., & Murphy, J. (1999). *Educating the global village: Including the young child in the world.* Upper Saddle River, NJ: Merrill.

Takaki, R. (1993). *A different mirror.* Boston, MA: Little, Brown.

U.S. Census Bureau (2003). *The foreign-born population: 2000. Census 2000 brief.* U.S. Department of Commerce.

U.S. Department of Education, National Center for Education Statistics, Digest of Education Statistics, 2003.

U.S. Department of Health and Human Services: Commissioner's Office of Research and Evaluation and the Head Start Bureau, Administration on Children, Youth, and Families. (2008). *Dual language learners: What does it take?* Washington, DC: Author.

Willis, W. (1998). Families with African American roots. In E. Lynch & M. Hanson (Eds.), *Developing cross-cultural competence* (2nd ed.). Baltimore, MD: Paul H. Brookes.

York, S. (1991). *Roots and wings: Affirming culture in early childhood programs.* St. Paul, MN: Redleaf Press.

York, S. (2003). *Roots and wings: Affirming culture in early childhood programs* (Revised ed.). St. Paul, MN: Redleaf Press.

Zuniga, M. (1998). Families with Latino roots. In E. Lynch & M. Hanson (Eds.), *Developing cross-cultural competence* (2nd ed.). Baltimore, MD: Paul H. Brookes.

Culture as Framework Versus Ingredient in Early Childhood Education

A Native Hawaiian Perspective

C. Kanoelani Naone and Kathryn Au

An Indigenous Historical Perspective

We use the term *indigenous* to refer to peoples who inhabited an area before it was colonized or annexed, who continue to observe their own cultural practices and values, and who regard themselves as a nation (Castagno & Brayboy, 2008). Native Hawaiians qualify as an indigenous group within the United States because they were the first to inhabit the Hawaiian archipelago, and did so for nearly 2,000 years before the arrival of the British explorer James Cook in 1778; maintained their distinct, non-Western culture in the face of unrelenting efforts to stamp it out; and have long sought recognition by the U.S. government as a nation with a status comparable to that attained by Native American tribes.

Native Hawaiian children of today are descendants of the original Polynesian inhabitants of the Hawaiian Islands. As with other indigenous populations in the U.S. and around the world, Native Hawaiians have experienced tremendous disruptions to their well-being and traditional way of life during more than 200 years of Western contact and colonization (Benham & Heck, 1998; Kame'eleihiwa, 1992). Chief among the tools of colonization has been a system of Western schooling, introduced to the islands by Congregational missionaries from New England, beginning in the 1820s, rooted in Protestant values of discipline and individualism (Nāone, 2008). Reports have long documented the unfortunate effects of conventional Western schooling for many Native Hawaiian children. The poor outcomes of this system are plainly seen at all levels of schooling, beginning with the elementary grades and reaching to the university. Results indicate that, as a group, Native Hawaiian students in the public schools of Hawai'i have reading and math scores below those of students in other groups (Kamehameha Schools Office of Program Evaluation and Planning, 1993). Not surprisingly, rates of college graduation are significantly lower (Hagedorn, Tibbetts, Kanaʻiaupuni, Moon, & Lester, 2004), limiting life opportunities, such as employment in fields requiring advanced education.

A paradox raised by these statistics is that, prior to the advent of Protestant missionary schooling, Native Hawaiians were a technologically and socially advanced society with an education system that allowed for a complex and deep level of knowledge, ranging from food and sustenance in an island environment to all aspects of the arts (Kanahele, 1986). Furthermore, 20 years after Hawaiian became a written language, literacy rates among Native Hawaiian equaled or exceeded those in other societies (Nāone, 2008). In the second half of the nineteenth century, while the missionaries and their descendants used literacy to position Native Hawaiians as inferior heathens, Native Hawaiians were able to appropriate literacy as a tool for their own purposes, namely, cultural preservation and political resistance (Au & Kaomea, 2008).

Culture as Framework

We believe that the solution to improving the educational futures and lives of Native Hawaiian students lies in applying traditional aspects of Native Hawaiian education in the context of the modern world. As implied in our remarks about literacy and Native Hawaiians, we do not believe in retreating to the past, but rather in creating educational pathways where Native Hawaiians may appropriate Western technologies for their own purposes and prosper in a globalized world, while holding firm to their cultural identity as an indigenous people.

Specifically, from the perspective of early childhood education, what can be done to help young Native Hawaiian children prosper in school and later in life? What are the characteristics of a successful early childhood education program with the dual goals of giving children a firm grounding in their own culture, while preparing them for academic success according to Western standards? Our position is not to elevate Native Hawaiian cultural knowledge over Western knowledge, or vice versa. We believe that children can benefit from acquiring both types of knowledge, and that each has its place in Native Hawaiian early childhood education programs. Yet, given the dominance of Western knowledge in schooling in modern Hawaiʻi, we must be aware that our challenge will almost always be to secure a proper place for Native Hawaiian cultural knowledge.

We argue that an early childhood education program capable of reaching these dual goals must utilize Hawaiian culture as its very framework. Such a strategy is a departure from conventional efforts to bring Hawaiian culture into schooling by treating culture as an ingredient. Culture is typically treated as an ingredient in what Banks (1995) has called the contributions and additive approaches to multicultural education. An example of the contributions approach would be to read children a storybook about the life of Kamehameha I (the ruling chief who united the islands under one government). An example of the additive approach would be to add several lessons on the life of Kamehameha I, but without changing the structure of the overall curriculum or classroom, for example, to permit analysis not only of this one great historical figure, but also of other accomplished Hawaiian leaders. As these examples imply, when culture is treated as an ingredient, superficial adjustments are made to the content of the curriculum, absent a reframing of the curriculum or classroom itself.

How do we begin to make Hawaiian culture the framework for an early childhood curriculum or program? The answer is that we must start by building on the foundation of Hawaiian values and the worldview from which these values come. These values can and should inform our decisions about all aspects of a program, from its goals, participants, and location, to its social and academic content, to the nature of interactions between adults and children.

Our position is consistent with those of researchers who have called for culturally responsive schooling for indigenous youth, with a clear emphasis on "sovereignty and self-determination, racism, and indigenous epistemologies" (Castagno & Brayboy, 2008, p. 941). In terms of sovereignty and self-determination, the main idea is for Native Hawaiians to take control of their own destiny by deciding which aspects of Western culture and schooling they should accept, and which they should reject. Nāone (2008) writes, "Ultimately, I say that we have the right, the will and the responsibility to say yes to what we can use and no to the things that threaten us and our people" (p. 3).

With respect to indigenous epistemologies, a key question for the education of Native Hawaiian children is what counts as knowledge that should be taught in school and, therefore, included in the curriculum. Beginning with the introduction of Western schooling, the curriculum for Native Hawaiian children has been based on knowledge valued from a Western or mainstream point of view. In this regard, we must remember that, despite their centuries-long subjugation, indigenous peoples and indigenous knowledge systems have existed for millennia. We do well to focus our energies on creating a new system of education by drawing upon the knowledge of millennia, rather than fighting against the subjugation of past centuries. As Mignolo (2000) argues, "Alternatives to modern epistemology can hardly come from modern (Western) epistemology itself" (p. 9).

Several recent studies point to the benefits to Native Hawaiian students of schooling emphasizing Hawaiian culture and language. Although these studies did not specifically address early childhood education programs, they are indicative of the potential of approaches rooted in Hawaiian culture. In the first study, Warner (1996) highlighted the differences between Native Hawaiian students who attended Hawaiian immersion schools and those who attended mainstream public schools. After the Hawaiian language was brought to the brink of extinction in the early 1980s, a small group of dedicated Native Hawaiian educators and parents established the Hawaiian immersion schools as a state-funded alternative to conventional public schools. In these schools, students receive instruction exclusively in the Hawaiian language until grade 5. When the immersion program was founded in 1987, its core curriculum was to be the same as that in other public schools, with the difference being only in the language of instruction. Over time, however, the curriculum has placed an increasing emphasis on Hawaiian culture, as Native Hawaiian scholars, such as Warner, argued for a curriculum based on Hawaiian epistemology and foundations. Warner (1996) noted of students in Hawaiian immersion schools:

They do not appear to suffer the identity crises of the past three generations. They are not ashamed of being Hawaiian and are not ashamed of speaking their language. They are generally motivated to learn the language, and it appears that they tend to be less alienated from school than their monolingual, ethnic Hawaiian, or part-Hawaiian peers. (p. 10)

Kanaʻiaupuni and Ishibashi (2005) compared the academic achievement and engagement levels of Native Hawaiian students enrolled in Hawaiian-focused charter schools to those of Native Hawaiian students enrolled in mainstream public schools. They found that charter school students achieved higher scores on standardized tests of reading and math achievement at grade 9 than did those enrolled in mainstream public schools. Furthermore, reinforcing the conclusions of Warner (1996), charter school students tended to be more engaged in school and to show significantly higher attendance rates.

One of the few studies to examine possible effects of Hawaiian culture in early childhood settings was conducted by Kanaʻiaupuni (2004). She measured various cultural inputs in early childhood education at 14 public and 15 private preschool sites. The study followed children from preschool through grade 1. Kanaʻiaupuni found that the practice of Hawaiian cultural customs in the home had a beneficial effect on children's development. These practices might include experiential activities, such as hula, fishing, and surfing, and oral, academic, and artistic activities, such as genealogy and music. Specifically, children who knew their given Hawaiian name and had a solid understanding of its meaning scored higher on measures of vocabulary, social skills, and language skills than children who had little or no understanding of their Hawaiian name, or who did not have a Hawaiian name. These preliminary findings offer tantalizing hints of the positive effects that a focus on Hawaiian culture may impart to young, Native Hawaiian children.

Culturally Responsive Instruction for Native Hawaiian Children

Culturally responsive instruction is not a new idea. However, reviews show that almost all of the early research on this approach was conducted in elementary and secondary classrooms (e.g., Osborne, 1996; Au & Kawakami, 1994), with a few studies set in early childhood education settings appearing more recently (Genishi & Goodwin, 2008). Application of the principles of culturally responsive instruction offers the promise of narrowing or closing the gap between the educational achievement of Native Hawaiian students and their mainstream peers at all levels of schooling, including early childhood (Sarsona, Goo, Kawakami, & Au, 2007).

Culturally relevant pedagogy (Ladson-Billings, 1995; Osborne, 1996), culturally responsive teaching (Gay, 2000), and culturally congruent instruction (Au & Kawakami, 1994) are slightly different terms for approaches grounded in the same set of beliefs. One belief is that the purpose of using culturally responsive instruction should be to increase the school success of children of diverse cultural and linguistic backgrounds, so that they can achieve at the same high levels as their mainstream peers. Another belief is that school success is to be achieved by drawing upon children's experiences in the home culture, so that school experiences become meaningful. The idea is to promote children's competence in the heritage culture and language, not just mainstream culture and language. Schooling is reconceptualized as a means of immersing children in the cultural traditions of their people, rather than as a means of separating them from these traditions. Indigenous groups, including Native Hawaiians, often give high priority to the preservation of their language and culture because they have come close to having both intentionally and completely eradicated through colonialism.

From a conceptual point of view, we can outline two different theoretical paths for improving the school achievement of students of diverse cultural and linguistic backgrounds. These two paths are shown in Figure 5.1 (adapted from Au, 2007). Au labels the first path the *direct* or *assimilationist* approach. Advocates of this approach think that early childhood and other educational programs should immerse children of diverse backgrounds in mainstream content and interactional processes from the very beginning. An assimilationist approach is reflected in most early childhood education programs, in which children are taught basic concepts such as colors and numbers, and are socialized according to mainstream norms of behavior. The curriculum is generally limited to knowledge and experiences that children are believed to need so that they can be successful in school, with success being defined in terms of readiness and vocabulary tests, as well as other mainstream criteria, all within the confines of middle-class American values and ideals. Educators who follow an assimilationist approach often are unaware that they are doing so, and may believe simply that there is only one right way to "do school," which is independent of the cultural and linguistic backgrounds of their students. When educators place too great an emphasis on mainstream knowledge and skills, and assess children only in these terms, they can easily fall into the pattern of thinking in terms of deficits, rather than differences. In addition, this ideology is based on the premise that children are not able to learn vast and diverse amounts of knowledge. For example, in the U.S., bilingual education may be denigrated because children are not thought to have the ability to gain command of one language, much less two or more, without becoming confused. This assumption is belied by the millions of young children growing up in other parts of the world who readily learn to speak two, three, or even four languages.

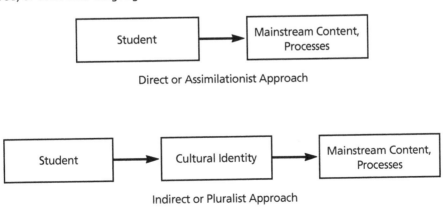

FIGURE 5.1   Two Approaches to Early Childhood Education.

Au labels the second path the *indirect* or *pluralist* approach. This is the path endorsed by advocates of culturally responsive instruction, one that sees children and their families in terms of difference, rather than deficit. Early childhood education programs that follow this second path take the stance of affirming, reinforcing, and building the cultural identity of young children of diverse backgrounds. Educators working in these programs believe that children who have a strong cultural identity, based on a firm grounding in the traditional culture and language of their people, will have a solid foundation upon which to add mainstream knowledge. Children will more readily acquire mainstream knowledge when it can be connected to what they already understand and value. Furthermore, children are educated to become contributing members of the family and community, rather than being alienated from them, and can be active participants in efforts to preserve and perpetuate the language and culture. This second, pluralist path is the one we have chosen to follow with the Keiki Steps curriculum, which seeks to celebrate Native Hawaiian culture.

In keeping with a pluralist path, we must be alert to the assimilationist assumptions frequently underlying efforts to implement conventional, center-based preschools in diverse settings, such as Native Hawaiian communities. Center-based preschools are sometimes regarded as the gold standard, the best solution for preparing young children for success in school and later in life. We urge caution before jumping to this conclusion. Center-based preschools may be the appropriate solution for some families, but, as Sarsona (2004) argues, Native Hawaiian families may not prefer this option. Native Hawaiian families may prefer to have grandparents or other members of the extended family care for the children while the parents are at work. The advantages are that grandparents can pass on traditional knowledge, secure the bonds of family, and give young children richer, more varied experiences than those typically encountered in the classroom. Time with grandparents can be part of the process of integrating children into Native Hawaiian culture, rather than educating them away from it.

Evolution of Keiki Steps

Keiki is one of the common Hawaiian terms for *child*, and Keiki Steps is a parent-participation preschool program for young Native Hawaiian children. From its origins, Keiki Steps has been a grassroots, community-based effort. Keiki Steps came about through the initiative of Michelle Mahuka, a mother of two young children and resident of the Hawaiian homestead community of Nānākuli. In 1998, Mahuka saw a television ad about parent-participation preschool programs (also called play morning programs and, more recently, family–child interaction learning programs), and she decided that she wanted her own children to participate in this kind of program. She called the agency whose name appeared in the ad, only to be informed that there was no parent-participation preschool program serving her rural community. One had been available, but it had closed three years earlier (Roberts, 1993). Mahuka found out that the nearest available program was located in a suburb several miles away, along Farrington Highway. This location did not appeal to Mahuka. She wanted to see if a parent-participation preschool program could be started in Nānākuli, to serve the many families with young children there.

The agency suggested that Mahuka contact Sherlyn Goo, then the executive director of the Institute for Native Pacific Education and Culture (INPEACE), a nonprofit, Native Hawaiian educational services organization (www.inpeace-hawaii.org). Goo heartily endorsed the idea and set about approaching possible funders. In the meantime, Mahuka secured donations from businesses and organizations in the community. Soon after, Goo was approached by parents in the Hawaiian homestead community of Waimānalo who also wanted a parent-participation preschool program for their community. Because funding for the Waimānalo second project fell into place quickly, the first Keiki Steps site began operations there six months before the Keiki Steps site in Nānākuli.

By 2009, Keiki Steps has grown to 13 sites for parent-participation preschools in Native Hawaiian communities, on three of the six main islands in the state of Hawai'i. Keiki Steps to Kindergarten (KSTK), a three-week summer program, was added for the purpose of easing the transition of young children from Keiki Steps into kindergarten. In the summer of 2008, 40 KSTK classrooms at 33 public elementary schools engaged 617 children and their families.

Overview of Keiki Steps Program and Curriculum

As a parent-participation preschool program, Keiki Steps operates four mornings a week, Monday–Thursday, from 7:30 to 11:30 a.m. On two Fridays a month, either a field trip or parent education class is held. Each site can accommodate up to 25 children and their caregivers per session. Elementary schools are the preferred location, because parents or other caregivers can see that the older children arrive safely at their classrooms and then bring the younger children to Keiki Steps. This arrangement significantly contributes to creating seamless transitions from early childhood programs to elementary schools for children and families.

Several major differences may be noted between a Keiki Steps parent-participation preschool and a mainstream center-based preschool, where children are dropped off and picked up. The first is that every child has a teacher present with them at all times, in the sense that the caregiver attends the preschool with the child. One of the goals of Keiki Steps is to help caregivers understand that they are teachers of young children, whether they see themselves in that role or not, and to provide them with support in that role. Although Keiki Steps is called a *parent*-participation program, young children often attend with other family members, such as grandmothers, grandfathers, aunts, and uncles.

A second difference is that Hawaiian culture is weighted equally as a curriculum area, along with literacy, math, science, social studies, and the arts. Keiki Steps has a written curriculum for children from ages 1 through 4, built, in part, on the foundation of Hawai'i's state preschool content standards, and Keiki Steps classrooms are set up just like any other high quality preschool classroom in the U.S., with centers for all aspects of child development. Mainstream curriculum content and best practices are understood and recognized. At the same time, a significant shift has taken place, from treating culture as an ingredient to viewing culture as the framework for the program, in keeping with the concepts discussed earlier in this chapter.

A third difference is that Keiki Steps classrooms use multi-age grouping. While there is a curriculum with activities geared for infants and toddlers, plus a curriculum with activities geared for 3- and 4-year-olds, the children and their teachers—Keiki Steps staff and caregivers—mingle freely. As a result, Keiki Steps classrooms have a warm, inviting feeling, with multiple generations gathered to learn together in the same place.

A final difference between Keiki Steps and conventional early childhood education programs is seen in the comprehensive professional development training program designed for its staff. Nearly all staff members are Native Hawaiian women who reside in the communities served by Keiki Steps, and many are in the workplace for the first time. As a condition of employment, staff members are required to participate in certificate or degree programs to prepare themselves for careers in early childhood education. INPEACE pays for tuition, books, and 4 hours a week of professional development time to support the educational progress of Keiki Steps employees.

Key Hawaiian Values Foundational to the Program

We now discuss key values in Hawaiian culture and traditional education that can be used to frame an early childhood education program. After discussing these values, we will show their application in the Keiki Steps program.

'Ohana and kaiāulu: *'Ohana* is the Hawaiian word for *family*, immediate and extended. In the 'ohana, older siblings care for the younger ones, aunties and uncles care for nieces and nephews, and grandparents and parents all raise children. So seamless are the relationships in 'ohana that the words for niece and nephew did not exist prior to foreign influence; the same words one would use for son and daughter or siblings were used for niece and nephew.

Kaiāulu is the Hawaiian word for *community*, and community is seen as the natural extension of families within Native Hawaiian culture. Native Hawaiians turn to their community for validation, advice, comfort, and safety. They feel responsible to their community, and the community, in turn, accepts responsibility for them. They gain strength from their community, which, in turn, challenges them to become even stronger. Native Hawaiians are vested in the well-being of their community and are called to ensure that every member is held accountable and kept safe.

According to Pukui, Haertig, and Lee (1972), and others (Kamakau, Barrere, Feher, & Pukui, 1991; Kamakau & Hawai'i, 1996), education in the Native Hawaiian tradition was specific to the strengths of the child and performed in a mentoring fashion by kūpuna (*elders*, plural form). Children were encouraged to experience the environment and roam freely until the age of 6 or 7, sometimes older, when they were then selected to be trained in a particular skill (Pukui, Haertig, & Lee, 1972). For example, a child who demonstrated an uncommon memory and strong verbal skills might be watched for some time to determine if indeed that child might become a chanter or story keeper. The kupuna (*elder*, singular form) who was the keeper of that talent, ability, or skill would then accept that child as a student, and the child would become the recipient of the kupuna's specialized knowledge. All children learned to care for the land and serve as stewards of the natural resources around them, but certain children had talents best suited for particular types of environments (such as the ocean or mountains) or work (such as ceremony, reading the natural environment, hula, or combat). In this way, individuals were selected to have a particular skill set passed on to them, based on their strengths and natural talent.

Kūpuna were the teachers, a role for which they were perfectly suited, for several reasons. First, kūpuna possessed the detailed knowledge and expertise that comes as a result of extensive life experience, practicing and testing a particular body of knowledge time and time again over the course of many decades. Secondly, their older bodies, however fit, were not as strong and agile as those of the mākua (*adults*, plural form) who were responsible for raising and harvesting food. In a society where each individual's contribution was needed and valued, it made sense for younger adults, those with stronger bodies, to take on the jobs requiring physical strength and stamina, while the older ones utilized their years of experience and the patience that comes with age. Thirdly, kūpuna, as teachers, perpetuated the value of 'ohana and kaiāulu, where everyone was responsible for the well-being and care of each child. Native Hawaiians have any number of poetical expressions and sayings to express their love and regard for children and the importance of raising children correctly, and children's behavior—proper and improper—is seen as a reflection of the 'ohana. In traditional society, it was important that each child become successful, because the future of the community depended on it. Children were responsible to their elders, and this fostered strong relationships across generations and among community members.

Strengths-based model: Nāone (2008) explains that Native Hawaiians followed a strengths-based model that fostered high levels of self-esteem. As mentioned earlier, individuals were well suited to their roles by both ability and training. They practiced skills necessary for the sustenance, betterment, and very survival of the family and community, and they could be recognized for their expertise and their contributions. It was understood that one did not need to become an expert in all areas, because one could rely on the expertise of others.

Each person had a role and responsibility to family and community that balanced life. The mahi'ai (*farmer*) and family shared the food they grew, the lawai'a (*fisherman*) and family shared their catch from the ocean, the ali'i (*chief*) shared the ability to protect the land base, the 'ōlapa (*hula dancer*) and ho'opa'a (*chanter*) re-enacted and passed on stories so that all would remember the lessons learned generation after generation. The elders from each area of expertise were the teachers of the next generation and remembered for their guidance. Even today, students of traditional hula are taught a particular style of dance according to the teachings that are passed down from each kumu hula (*hula teacher*) to the next, generation after generation. Should they become teachers, they are expected to perpetuate the same style of dance by teaching others to dance and chant following the traditions that were passed on to them.

In the Native Hawaiian system of teaching and learning, young children are given the opportunity to develop and experience the world around them at their own pace. This approach allows children to engage with the environment, both material and interpersonal, in a wide variety of ways, shaped by their own interests and curiosity. When placed in an environment rich in material and human resources, children have many opportunities to build the skills necessary for school and gainful employment. Those experiences include touching, feeling, and exploring a variety of textures (such as sand, dirt, water, and oil), and manipulating objects to learn about cause and effect (such as putting a cap on a bottle, picking leaves or flowers, playing with pots and pans, and pouring water from one size cup to another).

Learning in context: The Native Hawaiian way of learning is not based on lectures and abstract discussions taking place in sterile environments. Instead, learning takes place within the actual cultural context with which the child is expected to engage. Often, the appropriate context is the natural world and great outdoors. Music and hula may well be taught indoors, but, even then, the rhythm and beat of drums and other instruments provides a supportive environment. There is a fundamental and profound assumption that every single cultural activity provides young children with opportunities for learning. Compellingly, the contextualized and exploratory approach to learning favored in Native Hawaiian culture is consistent with the recommendations of experts in brain development (Halfon, Shulman, & Hochstein, 2001).

It is critical to understand the differences between the Hawaiian system of education and the mainstream system prevalent in U.S. classrooms and other Western-dominated locations. Despite the rhetoric of differentiated instruction and the movement toward Response to Intervention (Fuchs, Fuchs, & Vaughn, 2008) in many American classrooms today, all children are expected to learn at the same rate and meet the same end-of-grade expectations for academic achievement. No Child Left Behind (NCLB) (2001), the recent reauthorization of the U.S. Elementary and Secondary Education Act, has exacerbated the push toward normative performance, as measured by large-scale tests. Although educators acknowledge that children develop at different rates in physical, mental, and emotional terms, NCLB fosters the assumption that children can and should progress at the same rate, in terms of academic learning. Obviously, this model does not take account of the child who develops skills in an order other than that specified in the curriculum, who learns at a slower pace, or who has interests and talents beyond those shared by mainstream classmates. In contrast, in the traditional Hawaiian system, children were allowed to mature at their own rate, so late bloomers were not subject to inappropriate expectations that might cause a sense of inadequacy. Children were selected for participation in formal learning when they were developmentally ready, and an age range of several years for the timing of entry into formal learning was accepted and expected.

As implied, depending on their evident abilities and interests, children might be taught by immediate family members, usually grandparents, as well as by kūpuna unrelated by blood. This practice meant that children might be chosen for specialized training in fields beyond those known to immediate family members. The effect was to create closer relationships within the community, as young and old were connected through the bonds of occupation and expertise. Furthermore, everything a child learned had immediate application and practical value to the community, with contributions increasing in magnitude as the child grew older. For example, if a young person had been selected to be a canoe builder, the kupuna teacher might start lessons with planting and caring for the koa tree (a type of acacia, noted for the durability and beauty of its wood) that would ultimately become the canoe. The next step might involve having the youth carry heavy items, to gain the strength necessary to bring a massive koa tree down from the mountains when that time came. Another step might be learning to make carving tools and to carve small items such as bowls, in preparation for the laborious task of shaping an entire canoe. Learning would continue in this fashion until the youth became an expert.

Key to the Native Hawaiian approach was that learning was always initially done with the eyes. An often repeated saying among Native Hawaiians is "E pa'a i ka waha, e hana i ka pepeiao," which advises learners to close their mouths and use their ears. To this day, children are expected to learn by carefully observing their elders' every action, without questioning or interrupting, unless invited to do so. Nāone (2008) recalls, "I can remember watching how to make lei [flower garlands] for what seemed like forever, always waiting in excited anticipation for when I would be ready to make my own."

Once the kupuna judged a young learner to be ready (that is, to have the necessary degree of knowledge, physical skill, patience, and listening ability), the student was assigned a specific task. The learner had to complete the first task successfully before being given another task. New skills were acquired on the basis of skills already mastered, and learners advanced to the next step at their own individual rates.

Tēnā system: Beniamina (personal communication, cited in Nāone, 2008), a *mānaleo* (*native speaker of Hawaiian*) and kupuna from Ni'ihau (a remote, privately owned island, where Hawaiian remains the language of everyday communication) refers to learning in the tēnā system. The literal meaning of *tēnā* is *to command*, *give an order*, or *send on business*. In this system, the child is given a task when the teacher believes that child is ready. If the child completes the task successfully, the child is deemed ready to move on to a more challenging task. If the child does not complete the task successfully, the child is thought not to be ready and to require more time and support for learning. No dire consequences or negative implications are involved; the child will simply be given another chance to complete the same task later on, when better prepared.

Here is an example of how the tēnā system works. A child might be sent down the road to gather palapalai (a lacy fern prized by hula dancers). If the child comes back with a fern other than palapalai (an easy mistake to make, as other ferns may look quite similar), then the child has demonstrated a lack of readiness to identify the proper materials for making a lei. A related task that also requires a discriminating eye would involve the picking of medicinal plants, and the kupuna would know that the child should not yet be sent on such an errand alone.

Where the tēnā system continues to be applied, children show high rates of success in accomplishing tasks, because children have been chosen for learning a particular expertise based on their strengths relevant to that pursuit. Also, kūpuna are adept at watching and assessing children closely, so that children are not tested until the kupuna judges them to be ready to perform well. Children often feel that they are ready much earlier, but with the wisdom gained through years of experience, kūpuna always seem to know when the time is right. With high rates of success and low rates of failure, the tēnā system engenders and preserves passion for life and ensures the perpetuation of a vibrant array of specialized knowledge and skills within Native Hawaiian society. Many of these specialties or cultural practices continue to be perpetuated (for example, featherwork, hula, fishing, and martial arts).

At present, Native Hawaiian families are often given the impression by educators and early childhood providers that the best route is to send their young children to center-based preschools, to be taught by non-family members who are usually outsiders to the community and who may have little knowledge of Hawaiian culture. This route is in marked contrast to the tēnā system, which relies on the values of 'ohana and kaiāulu, and on elders within the family and community who develop close and lasting ties to young children, who customize learning experiences to each child's talents and interests, and who prefer to judge children's efforts on their own merits, rather than in terms of normative expectations.

An Example of Culture as Framework

We believe that Native Hawaiian traditions of learning, including the tēnā system, can and should provide the framework for early childhood education programs for Native Hawaiian communities. We propose dismantling the four walls of the classroom to take education outdoors to the natural environment, where children can become connected to land and place.

In the move from culture as ingredient to culture as framework in Keiki Steps, we built upon a solid foundation by putting 'ohana (*family*) and kaiāulu (*community*) at the very core of the program's philosophy and design. Keiki Steps was enhanced with the advent of Kupu Ola (literally, *to sprout forth life*), an initiative that serves not only the families and children of Keiki Steps, but kindergarten students and their teachers as well. The initiative is being piloted on land at two elementary schools on the Wai'anae coast of the island of O'ahu. The coast is home to the state's largest concentration of Native Hawaiians. In Kupu Ola, parents, caregivers, children, and teachers come together to create and maintain a native plant outdoor classroom. Traditionally, Native Hawaiians followed a moon calendar of 29–30 days to ensure the success of their planting and cultivation. Each day in the cycle has its own name, beginning with *hilo*, the new moon, and centuries of trial and error have produced a system in which fruits, vegetables, medicines, roots, and flowering plants are planted according to the lunar cycle to give each type of plant the opportunity to flourish.

In the design phase, we determine where each type of plant will be located, according to the climate of the area and the practical use of the plant (for example, whether it needs to be easily accessed so its flowers can be picked). The participants learn not only how to plant, but the best conditions for each plant (soil, depth, light, wind, and rain), how to maintain each plant, how to gather the plant materials for cultural use (for example, for medicine, a lei, or an imu [*underground oven*]), and then how to prepare the materials for consumption. Children work at their ability level alongside their parents, grandparents, and teachers. Everyone works together, utilizing the strengths of the group, in order to have the highest level of productivity. For example, the stronger adults dig the holes, the older children carry the plants and potting soil and help put the plants in the hole, and the younger children scoop the dirt into the hole and carry the small rocks. In addition to engaging in the physical activities of planting, all participants hear, learn, and practice the stories and songs of place, including the names of the winds, rains, mountains, and waterways of that particular community, along with traditional chants associated with planting.

The goals of the Kupu Ola initiative are consistent with the Native Hawaiian perspective, which treats children and their learning as inseparable from 'ohana and kaiāulu. Children learn science, math, literacy, and music, as well as traditional Hawaiian knowledge, in the culturally appropriate setting of the outdoor classroom, through hands-on experiences that draw upon all five senses. Parents and caregivers are empowered with cultural knowledge that might otherwise have been suppressed or forgotten. Through participation in Kupu Ola, these adults can have their understandings reinforced or developed, putting them in a stronger position to pass on Hawaiian cultural knowledge to their children and grandchildren. Keeping the flame of Hawaiian tradition burning within families enhances the vitality of the community, as children and adults gain confidence and feel pride in their cultural identity as Native Hawaiians. Finally, native plants, many of them rare and endangered, are preserved to enrich the environment for future generations.

Most important of all from a Native Hawaiian perspective, the Kupu Ola initiative links young children and their families back to the *'āina*, a term that refers to the land and all that sustains the people. Native Hawaiian tradition holds that there is profound knowledge stored in 'āina (Nāone, 2008). In Native Hawaiian tradition, children were taught the names and stories of the places in their home communities, as well as of the places where their ancestors and the ali'i (*chiefs*) came from. Kupu Ola perpetuates these traditions through its outdoor classroom curriculum and is a solid example of utilizing culture as a framework versus ingredient. Field trips will not suffice, because these occasional events keep children in the status of visitors and do not build either the deep knowledge of place or the strong sense of responsibility for place foundational to a Hawaiian worldview. Children must feel their ties to the land on an ongoing, daily basis.

Conclusion

The overarching theme of this chapter is that young children of indigenous backgrounds can benefit from, and, indeed, are entitled to, early childhood education programs that treat culture as framework versus ingredient. It is not enough to infuse culture into education; cultural values and knowledge need to drive how early childhood education is delivered. We argue that treating culture as framework versus ingredient requires a deep rethinking of the assumptions inherent in early childhood education programs designed to serve indigenous groups.

In exploring this theme, we focused on the example of early childhood education for a particular indigenous group, Native Hawaiians. We presented the conceptual basis for culture as framework by reviewing research on culturally responsive instruction, including studies showing the benefits of culturally-focused education for Native Hawaiian students. We outlined the basic elements of a Native Hawaiian perspective toward young children and their learning by referring to two key cultural values: 'ohana (*family*) and kaiāulu (*community*).

We then showed the application of a Hawaiian worldview to a parent-participation preschool program called Keiki Steps. This program is based in Hawaiian communities and run by Native Hawaiian women who reside in these same communities. By moving beyond the confines of the classroom to an outdoor environment, Keiki Steps and the Kupu Ola initiative allow children, parents, caregivers, and teachers to engage together in the creation and maintenance of a cultural garden. As they explore and help in the garden, children are given the opportunity to engage in tasks at their own level and to gain Hawaiian cultural knowledge, as well as mainstream academic knowledge. By building on the foundational concepts of ʻohana, kaiāulu, and ʻāina (land), Keiki Steps strengthens families and prepares children for successful lives within Native Hawaiian communities and beyond. The example of Keiki Steps suggests that culture as framework, versus culture as ingredient, may well serve as a powerful and generative concept in the design of early childhood education programs not only for Native Hawaiians, but for other diverse and indigenous groups as well.

A well known ʻōlelo noʻeau (poetical saying) among Native Hawaiians is "ʻAʻohe pau ka ʻike i ka hālau hoʻokahi" (Pukui, 1983). The literal translation of this saying is, "All knowledge is not taught in the same school," and the meaning is that we can and should learn from many sources. For too long, the knowledge used to formulate educational policies and programs for Native Hawaiians and other indigenous peoples has come from Western, colonial sources. We think the time has now come to build early childhood education efforts for young children of indigenous backgrounds upon the rich cultural traditions that are their heritage.

References

Au, K. (2007). Culturally responsive instruction: Application to multiethnic classrooms. *Pedagogies, 2*(1), 1–18.

Au, K., & Kaomea, J. (2009). Reading comprehension and diversity in historical perspective: Literacy, power, and Native Hawaiians. In S. Israel & G. Duffy (Eds.), *Handbook of research on reading comprehension* (pp. 571–586). New York: Routledge.

Au, K., & Kawakami, A. (1994). Cultural congruence in instruction. In E. Hollins, J. King & W. Hayman (Eds.), *Teaching diverse populations: Formulating a knowledge base* (pp. 5–23). Albany: State University of New York Press.

Banks, J. A. (1995). Multicultural education: Historical development, dimensions, and practice. In J. A. Banks & C. A. M. Banks (Eds.), *Handbook of research on multicultural education* (pp. 3–24). New York: Macmillan.

Benham, M. A., & Heck, R. H. (1998). *Culture and educational policy in Hawaiʻi: The silencing of native voices.* Mahwah NJ: Erlbaum.

Castagno, A., & Brayboy, B. (2008). Culturally responsive schooling for indigenous youth: A review of the literature. *Review of Educational Research, 78*(4), 941–993.

Fuchs, D., Fuchs, L., & Vaughn, S. (Eds.). (2008). *Response to intervention: A framework for reading educators.* Newark DE: International Reading Association.

Gay, G. (2000). *Culturally responsive teaching: Theory, research, and practice.* New York: Teachers College Press.

Genishi, C., & Goodwin, A. L. (Eds.). (2008). *Diversities in early childhood education: Rethinking and doing.* New York: Routledge.

Hagedorn, L., Tibbetts, K., Kana'iaupuni, S., Moon, H., & Lester, J. (2004). Factors contributing to college retention in the Native Hawaiian population. *Research conference on Hawaiian well-being*. Honolulu: Kamehameha Schools.

Halfon, N., Shulman, E., & Hochstein, M. (2001). Brain development in early childhood. In N. Halfon, E. Shulman & M. Hochstein (Eds.), *Building community systems for young children*. Los Angeles CA: UCLA Center for Healthier Children, Families and Communities.

Kamakau, S., Barrere, D., Feher, J., & Pukui, M. (1991). *Tales and traditions of the people of old (Na mo'olelo o ka poe kahiko)*. Honolulu: Bishop Museum Press.

Kamakau, S., & Hawai'i, A. Ō. (1996). *Ke kumu aupuni : Ka mo'olelo Hawai'i no Kamehameha ka na'i aupuni a me kāana aupuni i ho'okumu ai. Honolulu, HI, .* Honolulu: 'Ahahui 'Ōlelo Hawai'i.

Kame'eleihiwa, L. (1992). *Native land and foreign desires*. Honolulu, HI: Bishop Museum Press.

Kamehameha Schools Office of Program Evaluation and Planning. (1993). *Native Hawaiian educational assessment 1993*. Honolulu, HI: Kamehameha Schools Bernice Pauahi Bishop Estate.

Kana'iaupuni, S. (2004). Ola ka inoa (the name lives): Cultural inputs and early education outcomes of Hawaiian children, *Research Conference on Hawaiian Well-being*. Honolulu: Kamehameha Schools.

Kana'iaupuni, S., & Ishibashi, K. (2005). *Hawai'i charter schools: Initial trends and select outcomes for Native Hawaiian students*. Honolulu.

Kanahele, G. H. S. (1986). *Ku kanaka, stand tall: A search for Hawaiian values*. Honolulu HI: University of Hawaii.

Ladson-Billings, G. (1995). Toward a theory of culturally relevant pedagogy. *American Educational Research Journal, 32*(3), 465–491.

Mignolo, W. (2000). *Local histories/global designs: Coloniality, subaltern knowledges, and border thinking*. Princeton NJ: Princeton University Press.

Nāone, C. K. (2008). *The pilina of kanaka and 'aina: Place, language and community as sites of reclamation for Indigenous education—the Hawaiian case*. Unpublished doctoral dissertation, University of Hawai'i, Honolulu.

No Child Left Behind. (2001). *Public Law No. 107–1110, 115 Stat. 1425, 2002*, 2004. Available from http://www.ed.gov/policy/elsec/leg/esea02/beginning/html

Osborne, A. B. (1996). Practice into theory into practice: Culturally relevant pedagogy for students we have marginalized and normalized. *Anthropology & Education Quarterly, 27*(3), 285–314.

Pukui, M. (1983). *'Olelo No'eau: Hawaiian proverbs and poetical sayings*. Honolulu: Bishop Museum Press.

Pukui, M., Haertig, E., & Lee, C. (1972). *Nānā i ke kumu (Look to the source)*. Honolulu: Hui Hānai, an auxiliary of the Queen Lili'uokalani Children's Center.

Roberts, R. N. (1993). Early education as community intervention: Assisting an ethnic minority to be ready for school. *American Journal of Community Psychology 21*(4), 521–535

Sarsona, M. (2004). *Early education choices key to family well-being*. Retrieved July 12, 2005, from http://starbulletin.com/2004/12/02/editorial/commentary.html

Sarsona, M., Goo, S., Kawakami, A., & Au, K. (2008). Equity issues in a parent-participation pre-school program for Native Hawaiian children. In C. Genishi & A. Goodwin (Eds.), *Diversities in early childhood education: Rethinking and doing* (pp. 151–165). New York: Routledge.

Spring, J. (2008). Research on globalization and education. *Review of Educational Research, 78*(2), 330–363.

Warner, S. (1996). *I ola ka 'ōlelo i nā keiki : ka 'apo 'ia 'ana o ka 'ōlelo Hawai'i e nā keiki ma ke Kula Kaiapuni*. Honolulu Department of Hawaiian and Indo-Pacific Languages and Literatures, University of Hawai'i.

Empowering Children Through Gender Diversity

Jeff Daitsman

In the infant room, Ann (1 year; 2 months) takes an interest in the rubber bands I keep on my wrist for my long hair. Concerned that it may be a choking hazard, I start keeping the rubber bands in my pocket when working in that classroom. After that point Ann begins to take an interest in my watch. One day I take the watch off and let her play with it. At first, though she had been excited to put the rubber bands on her wrists under my close supervision, she is hesitant to put the watch on her wrist. She keeps starting to put her hand through the watch that I preset to the smallest size, but then pulling her hand out again. Eventually, though, she does put her hand in and enjoys playing with the watch.

Two months later, Ann is now in the toddler room when I begin sharing some of my memories of her experiences in the infant room, including her fascination with the watch. The moment I take the watch off, Ann's face lights up and she reaches out toward it. After she has played with it and returned it to me, Ann reaches out toward a female teacher's necklaces. I suggest that Ann really likes jewelry, pointing out the similarity between my watch and the other teacher's necklaces. The other teacher then generalizes this statement, saying, "Yes, girls really like jewelry."

As the toddler room is preparing to go outdoors, I inform the children that I will put my hair in a ponytail because it is so hot outside. Missy (3; 2) seems incredulous that I would put my hair in a ponytail since I'm a boy. I tell her, "I'm a boy with long hair." Liam (2; 11) interjects at this point that he's a boy with short hair, and Mario (2; 9) agrees, identifying himself as a boy with short hair as well. Missy points out that Mario's hair is even shorter than Liam's, and she then acknowledges that my hair is longer than hers. The conversation then turns to the hair lengths of the children's family members. Throughout this conversation

Ayiana (2; 6) merely sits by and listens, absorbing the discussion. Two months later, after Missy has moved on to the preschool room, I have my hair tied back while carrying Ayiana when we are outside. Ayiana reaches out and touches my hair, saying, "You're a lady."

As it nears the end of the day in the preschool room Sally (4; 3) is playing with Ayiana's older brother Tanish (4; 3). Sally and Tanish come up to me asking me to help them put on dresses from the housekeeping area. As I help them into their dresses they explain to me that they are having a wedding. After they play with the dresses on for a little while, they come up to me again and inform me that they are two brides and that they are going to get married to each other because they both have babies in their tummies. I then help them stuff baby dolls down their dresses and they tell me that the babies are going to come out at the wedding.

Sally's mother arrives in the midst of this and finds the concept very amusing, though Sally's older brother is not as amused. He glares at Tanish and tells him that boys shouldn't wear dresses. Sally's mother says that if Tanish wants to wear a dress that he can. Tanish smiles and seems unfazed by Sally's brother's comment as Tanish continues to twirl in his dress.

We live in a society in which gendered messages abound. As these three vignettes reveal, such messages can come from a wide variety of sources, including teachers, peers, and family. How a child interprets these messages depends on their individual and cultural background. As teachers, it is our responsibility to help children learn and grow. Learning and growth, however, are not restricted to so-called "academic" domains. If teachers forget this and leave socio-emotional education out of their teaching repertoire, children can come to view stereotypes as being reflective of reality. Shaun Johnson reveals the importance of teachers recognizing that "multiple forms of masculine subjectivities exist apart from the cultural ideal constantly espoused in the media and defended by social norms" (Johnson, 2011, p. 24).

Overpowering the Rapist

Not all men are strong and emotionless; nor are all women nurturing and weak. One day a co-worker of mine came into work badly bruised with a black eye and a distraught look on her face. We spoke before the children arrived, and I learned that she had been attacked in the entrance way to her apartment building by a serial rapist who had been terrorizing her neighborhood. She told me how she fought back and subdued her attacker until police arrived.

While, as a man, I am far less likely to be subjected to such a situation, I nonetheless feel that I would lack the level of agency and strength (some may call it aggression) that my co-worker demonstrated in defending herself. Yet, as a man, I may never have to find out. Social biases place me in a position of privilege in this regard. I will likely never have to deal with the fear of facing someone intent on violating my body in this way. But this is a fear that women live with on a regular basis. According to the U.S. Department of Justice, "the percentage of completed or attempted rape victimization among women in higher educational institutions might climb to between one-fifth and one-quarter" (Fisher, Cullen, & Turner, 2000, p. 10).

The abundance of its occurrence would seem to indicate that rape is not something that is an example of an extreme aspect of society, but rather a deep-seated reflection of the negative impact of dominant views on gender. Despite my co-worker's clear capability in handling herself in this situation, I heard no sense of triumph in her voice as she related the story to me. There was no sense of accomplishment for being the one responsible for putting this man behind bars. There was just the horror of reliving that moment, still so fresh in her mind, in which she had been trapped with a man who wanted nothing more than to use her body as an object.

Nor did this fear dissipate after having related the story. There was a sense of enduring dread that lasted for weeks every time she stepped outside. I recall walking her home on numerous occasions during this period. I couldn't help but consider the irony of the fact that this formidable woman, whom I had no doubt could defend herself much better than I could, felt safer when I escorted her home. It was not about strength, it was about image. In the society in which we live men are viewed as strong and powerful while women are viewed as weak and submissive. Thus, a woman escorted by a man is less likely to be seen as vulnerable than a woman walking alone.

I don't know how she explained her injuries to her students. I doubt that she related the story as she did to me, if she related it at all. After all, how do you explain the concept of rape to a preschooler? Yet it is nonetheless important that our work with young children take into account that we live in a society in which a major subsection of the population can be made to walk in fear. Anti-bias curriculum posits that, "Early childhood educators have a serious responsibility to find ways to prevent and counter the damage before it becomes too deep" (Derman-Sparks & ABC Task Force, 1989, p. 5).

Making Bias Explicit

Often teachers are afraid to use an anti-bias curriculum because they feel that exposing children to concepts of oppression violates the innocence of childhood. But in studying how children develop gender concepts, I have seen that "Denying the existence of stereotyped perceptions succeeds only in perpetuating and manifesting gender-based polarization of children's behavior" (Daitsman, 2011b, p. 11). In order to overcome such polarized behavior, concepts of gender bias need to be made explicit so that children can come to challenge those assumptions and take a more critical view toward stereotypes and discrimination.

The vignettes at the start of the chapter demonstrate a few teachable moments in which such stereotypes can be brought to the level of conscious thought where children and teachers can discuss their preconceived notions and come to an understanding of gender, which is more reflective of reality. As I've previously found, when a child makes a comment such as Ayiana's "You're a lady," it "elicits a good deal of discussion where the children are able to take a closer look at their own biases and form a new framework of understanding the roles of men and women" (Daitsman, 2011a, p. 50).

It is not only children, however, who need to take a closer look at their biases. The female teacher who stated, "Yes, girls really like jewelry," was unconsciously modeling bias for Ann. I have been guilty of this myself at times. Two weeks after the conversation with Missy, I mediated an interaction between Liam and Mario in which I found myself forced to take a closer look at my own unconscious biases. The following is an excerpt from a reflection that I saved under the heading, "How can I prevent gender bias from seeping into my interactions with children?"

> Liam was underneath the climbing structure with the chimes. Any time another child would come near, Liam would tell them, "This is my house." Seeing the reactions of the other children to being rejected, I decided to intervene. When Liam rejected Mario I suggested that maybe Mario was the Daddy in Liam's house. Liam said, "No, I'm the Daddy." I started to suggest that Mario could be the brother when Mario decided to take the role of the Mommy.
>
> It seems all my suggestions were based on the presumption that Mario, as a male, would want to portray a male character. The philosophy that I have promoted with children in the past, that in pretend you can be anything, seems to have eluded me here. I should be more careful when attempting to scaffold children's play that I don't inadvertently promote a gender bias. With Mario as the Mommy, Liam had no qualms with letting him play in his "house."

By engaging in self-reflection, teachers can be more cognizant of moments like this in which their own biases come into play. But self-reflection is only a part of what is necessary to recognize and overcome these moments. It is also important to involve others in such reflection. When teachers are able to examine their own practices in a community of diverse colleagues, certain assumptions are called forth and able to be examined.

For about a year, I facilitated a group known as the Reflective Early Childhood Educators' Social Seminar. When one of the teachers in that group chose to examine the question, "What ways can aggressive play be positively implemented in the classroom?" a former teacher who was on the e-mail list objected to the use of the term "aggressive" as one which she believed had a negative connotation. Unaware that the teacher who had posed the question was female, this former teacher chose to apply a gender value to the term, stating, "Its [sic] a very masculine word and has immediate connotations for meaning in terms of behavior. As a woman, I don't naturally identify what children are doing as aggression. Neither do I identify aggression as a positive life skill. So there's a distinct gender difference already operating" (Gallas, 2009).

This opened up the discussion for an examination of the meaning of the term "aggression" as well as the term "agency" and a comparison of the two. By engaging in this discussion we were able to recognize that, while some of us chose not to attach a value to the term, others of us attached a gender value to it with a negative connotation. Those of us who viewed the term as value-laden had a problem with defining play as aggressive, while those of us who considered that the term could be applied value-free felt more comfortable using it as a descriptive term. As Gallas pointed out, "Your job is not to convince me of the correctness of your position, but rather to consider that there's a different way to look at the play and the word in our culture" (Gallas, 2009). By working together, we were able to recognize that concepts such as aggression and agency can be viewed from multiple perspectives.

A "Liberating Praxis"

Not only is it important for children and teachers to recognize when they themselves have biases that could have an oppressive impact on others in the classroom, but it is also important for children to recognize when such oppression is directed at them and they need to be empowered to resist it. As Paulo Freire puts it, "Problem-posing education, as a humanist and liberating praxis, posits as fundamental that the people subjected to domination must fight for their emancipation" (Freire, 2000, p. 86).

Without resistance, children come to view oppressive relations as part of everyday experience. They become blinded to the inequities inherent in such a system and can become agents of perpetuation of such inequities. Barbara Rogoff points out that "children play actively central roles, along with their elders and other companions, in learning and extending the ways of their communities" (Rogoff, 2003, p. 285). However, Vygotsky indicates that "If the relationships between people undergo a change, then along with them the ideas, standards of behavior, requirements and tastes also change" (Vygotsky, 1994, p. 181). In other words, by changing the social structures that reinforce such oppressive divisions, individuals can come to be transformed as well to relate to each other in a less hostile fashion.

Our role as teachers, then, is to help build in children dispositions with which they can challenge such restrictive social structures. Encouraging inquisitiveness in children needs to include the ability to question the status quo and why society functions the way that it does. One female teacher encouraged her children to question their socially imposed assumptions in an ingenious manner.

Anna De Fina reveals that "While females may wear clothing initially viewed as male, the reverse is highly stigmatized" (De Fina, 2006, p. 21). To help children overcome such stigmatization, when one child in a female teacher's classroom made a biased comment similar to that made by Sally's brother to Tanish in the third opening vignette of this chapter, the teacher pointed out to the children that she herself was wearing what could be considered "boy's clothes" (pants and a shirt). Inspired in part by having heard this story, I have decided to take it upon myself to at times wear "girl's clothes" in the classroom myself.

While I have worn skirts in various contexts outside of the classroom, I had long been hesitant to try it in the classroom for fear of the reaction of parents and administrators. But one year I decided that the day after the local Pride Parade would be a good time to help children like Tanish, who often liked to play dress-up, feel more empowered when they put on dresses from the housekeeping area. After checking with my director, I came into work that day wearing an ankle-length black skirt with flowers on it. I noted the following in my reflections that day:

> As we were transitioning outside, Renate (4; 8) asked me why I was wearing a skirt. I told him that it was because I like to wear skirts when I dance and I was feeling in a dancing mood today. Out in the playground the children from the toddler room were much more curious. Several of them (including Ayiana) felt the texture of the skirt with their hands. One of the boys from the toddler room asked me why I was wearing a skirt, and I told him

the same thing I had told Renate. Unlike Renate and the other preschool room children, however, a single sentence wasn't enough to satisfy their curiosity. When I told them that I liked to wear a skirt when I dance, Zora (1; 11) asked, "Why?"

I responded that I liked the way skirts twirl around me when I spin. I started to spin around. Soon all of the toddler room children who had been gathering around to question me were now all spinning. Zora asked me to spin again, so I obliged her. Mario spun himself so dizzy that he fell on the blacktop. I suggested at this point that maybe we could run instead, and the skirt was forgotten in the joy of the active play as nearly every child from the toddler room ran, flew, and waddled back and forth across the blacktop with me.

Only Tanish ever explicitly asked me at a later date why I only wore the skirt the one time. This reveals to me that Tanish was strongly impacted by the situation and perhaps may have been a contributing factor to his resilience to an older boy telling him that boys can't wear dresses. Zora, too, seemed to have been impacted by the knowledge that I wear skirts at times. Though she never mentioned my wearing of a skirt, in the months following the Pride Parade she did often return to the area in which we had been spinning to show off her own dresses to me before she began spinning around as we had on that day.

Conclusion

While small moments like these are unlikely to change the overall social structures that constrict gendered performances, for the children who take part in them these moments can have a deep and meaningful impact. This can help prepare children for the time when they will be the ones shaping society, helping them to see the importance of being a part of shaping it in a more open and accepting fashion.

By working together to examine our own biases and helping children to overcome theirs, male and female teachers can help pave the way for equitable relations in a future full of possibility. When we help young children to see these possibilities, we are giving them the tools to empower themselves to move forward in creating a world in which bias can be recognized and addressed whenever it may manifest.

References

Daitsman, J. (2011a). The teacher with the beard: A nurturing male helps children overcome bias. In L. W. Watson & C. S. Woods (Eds.), *Go where you belong: Male teachers as cultural workers in the lives of children, families, and communities*. Boston, MA: Sense Publishers.

Daitsman, J. (2011b). Exploring gender identity in early childhood through story dictation and dramatization. *Voices of Practitioners: Teacher research in early childhood education, 14*. Retrieved from http://www.naeyc.org/files/naeyc/file/ Publications/VOP_Daitsman_Final.pdf

De Fina, A. (2006). Group identity, narrative and self-representations. In A. De Fina, D. Schiffrin, & M. Bamberg (Eds.), *Discourse and identity*. New York: Cambridge University Press.

Derman-Sparks, L., & A.B.C. Task Force. (1989). *Anti-bias curriculum: Tools for empowering young children*. Washington, DC: NAEYC.

Fisher, B., Cullen, F., & Turner, M. (2000). *The sexual victimization of college women*. National Institute of Justice. Washington, DC: U.S. Department of Justice, National Institute of Justice and Bureau of Justice Statistics.

Freire, P. (2000). *Pedagogy of the oppressed: 30th anniversary edition*. New York: Continuum International Publishing.

Gallas, K. (2009). Personal communication.

Johnson, S. (2011) A new perspective on the lack of men in education. In L. W. Watson & C. S. Woods (Eds.), *Go where you belong: Male teachers as cultural workers in the lives of children, families, and communities*. Boston, MA: Sense Publishers.

Rogoff, B. (2003). *The cultural nature of human development*. New York: Oxford University Press.

Vygotsky, L. S. (1994). The socialist alteration of man. In R. van der Veer & J. Valsiner (Eds.), *The Vygotsky reader*. Cambridge, MA: Blackwell.

What's on Our Bookshelves?

The Diversity of Children's Literature in Early Childhood Classroom Libraries

Thomas Crisp, Suzanne M. Knezek, and Margaret Quinn

This content analysis explores issues related to representations of diversity in classroom libraries, providing practical solutions for teachers seeking to diversify their classroom book collections.

The world depicted in children's books is overwhelmingly White. It is also a world that is predominantly upper middle class, heterosexual, nondisabled, English-speaking, and male. In short, it may encompass many different worlds, but those worlds share familiar limitations: They are generally normative, limited in scope, and exclusionary of those who fall outside "mainstream" cultural identities. This is not to imply that exemplary books that challenge dominant discourses and normative representations do not exist; remarkable work has been done and is available for young readers. However, in 2016, this much we should be able to agree on: We need to do more—a great deal more. After all, for more than 75 years, librarians, scholars, critics, and creators of children's books have documented, described, and problematized the ongoing lack of diversity in children's literature (see, e.g., Crosby, 1963; Larrick, 1965; Rollins, 1967). Although others have attempted to dismiss, ignore, or justify these disparities, the existence of these issues is overwhelmingly well established and increasingly well documented in the realms of publishing and academic scholarship.

Since 1985, for example, the Cooperative Children's Book Center (CCBC) at the University of Wisconsin–Madison has provided yearly statistics about children's books published by and/or about people who self-identify as members of various "parallel cultures" (a term coined by Hamilton, 1993, p. 363). In their latest report, Horning, Lindgren, Schliesman, and Townsend (2015) stated that across approximately 3,500 books published in 2014 that were received by the CCBC, only around 11%

contained significant content, topics, characters, and/or themes about African or African American, American Indian, Asian/ Pacific or Asian/Pacific American, or Latino or Latino American people. According to the CCBC, the number of multicultural books has remained stagnant for more than 20 years (see, e.g., Horning, 2013). Other researchers have identified similar disparities across these and other cultural identities, including race, religion, socioeconomic status (SES) and class, gender, dis/abilities and developmental differences, and sexual identity (see, e.g., Blaska, 2004; Chaudhri & Teale, 2013; Crisp, 2015).

Recently, a large-scale survey of the publishing and reviewing industries provided much-needed baseline data that contribute to our overall understandings of issues of diversity and representation in the children's literature world (Low, 2016). The survey, conducted by Lee & Low Books, revealed that at all levels measured (e.g., executive, editorial, sales), 77–89% of respondents self-identified as White/Caucasian, 86–91% as straight/heterosexual, and 88–96% as nondisabled. The greatest diversity was found in the area of gender identity, where 59–87% of respondents identified as woman/ciswoman (terms such as *ciswoman* and *cisfemale* are used to describe individuals who self-identify as woman/female and were also assigned that identity at birth), 12–40% as man/cisman (terms such as *cisman* and *cismale* are used to describe individuals who self-identify as man/male and were also assigned that identity at birth), and less than 1–2% of respondents as intersex, gender nonconforming, or transwoman or transman.

It is essential that these industries are diverse, as the cultural identities of those involved in children's book publishing have a direct impact on the types of books created for children. As Reese (2007) noted, much of what we bring to bear on our readings and understandings of children's texts emanates from our own cultural lenses, experiences, and identities. It is fundamentally important that those shaping the creation and dissemination of children's books have the knowledge and cultural intuition needed when working with texts, as it makes it less likely that children's books with problematic, inaccurate, and dishonest treatments continue to make their way into classrooms and the hands of young readers.

Thanks to Lee & Low, the CBCC, and countless others, it is nearly impossible for any of us involved in teacher education, working in educational research and scholarship, and/or who care deeply about children's books to be unaware of the broad-scale issues surrounding diversity in the children's literature world. Further, due to articles and columns in popular media (e.g., C. Myers, 2014; W.D. Myers, 2014), the impact of grassroots organizations such as the #WeNeedDiverseBooks campaign on social media, and blogs such as Reading While White and American Indians in Children's Literature, mainstream cognizance of (and attention to) the lack of diversity in children's books may be greater than ever before.

However, despite progress in our understandings of the factors that influence the availability of diverse children's books, relatively little research has examined the availability of these books in classrooms. As educators with an orientation toward issues of social justice, we are interested in how the available data and increased attention to diversity in children's books have informed the contents of early childhood classroom spaces. We believe that there is a need for data that reveal how teachers, curriculum specialists/designers, media specialists, and others have responded to the lack of diversity in children's books when, for example, they make decisions about which books to make available to their students.

Thus, the purpose of this article is to investigate representations of diversity in books included in early childhood classroom libraries. We hope to contribute to ongoing, critical conversations in the field by providing preliminary baseline data that verify and underscore the need for increased critical attention toward the books selected for inclusion in classroom libraries. Although we direct this article toward classroom teachers, we want to note that in many cases, teachers are limited to using program- or district-mandated books and curricular materials, so the contents of classroom libraries may be entirely beyond their control. Therefore, we suggest that this article is also useful for early childhood program/school leaders and library/media specialists, who may similarly influence both the selection of curricular content and the school culture around issues of diversity and representation. Additionally, we want to be clear from the onset that we do not attempt to provide the level of large-scale statistical data offered by the CCBC and Lee & Low; we hope instead to use our research and findings to provide insights, as well as offer resources and practical suggestions, that all teachers can utilize immediately to assess and improve their own classroom libraries and, by extension, advocate for and enact change that will immediately affect the lives and reading experiences of their students.

Children, Books, and the Value of Classroom Libraries

It seems safe to assume that in the majority of cases, children in early childhood classrooms (e.g., ages 3–5) do not have access to the catalogs of children's publishing houses or even online bookstores such as Powell's Books or Amazon. If they are enrolled in preschool programs, however, they have access to classroom libraries. In these spaces, young children experience (perhaps for the first time) what it means and looks like to have reading options, choice, and varied literary representations. For some young children, the classroom library provides them with their first repeated exposures to a literary canon: In their teacher's books, they will be looking for images of themselves and those they love; they will be learning how to make sense of their lives and experiences, the lives and experiences of others, and the world in which they live (see, e.g., Short, 2012).

Children's literature is utilized in a number of capacities in classrooms, including read-alouds and, possibly, as a way to introduce curricular content (e.g., science, math). Yet, a primary means by which books are made available to young readers is through classroom libraries, and all parties involved in the creation of those spaces have a responsibility to include an array of books that represent the diversity of identities and experiences of the students in our classrooms, as well as people and cultures across the country and around the globe.

There has been extensive research, spanning at least 50 years, underscoring the important role that classroom libraries play in early childhood (i.e., preschool and early elementary) settings (see, e.g., Applebee, Langer, & Mullis, 1988; Fractor, Woodruff, Martinez, & Teale, 1993). Despite the clear indication of the importance of classroom libraries, however, disparities remain in the existence and content of those collections—often along socioeconomic lines. Research by Duke (2000b), for example, suggested that first-grade classrooms serving high-SES populations contained larger selections of books that were more frequently added to or rotated, as well as more opportunity during instruction to use and interact with those books.

Research about the availability of children's texts in classrooms has often centered on the quantity and accessibility of books and other print materials in early elementary classrooms (see, e.g., Duke, 2000b; Jeong, Gaffney, & Choi, 2010; Lee, Lee, Han, & Schickedanz, 2011) with limited attention to preschool classrooms (Guo, Sawyer, Justice, & Kaderavek, 2013). Researchers are generally concerned with the number of texts available in classrooms, the degree to which texts are made available to children, and the time associated with accessibility. Their attention toward diversity of books tends to focus on genre and format, particularly the presence or absence of informational text. For example, in their study of five preschool classrooms, McGill-Franzen, Lanford, and Adams (2002) determined not only that classrooms serving low-SES populations contained fewer accessible books but also that available books were more homogeneous in terms of factors such as complexity level, genre, and subject. Other relevant research has addressed topics such as the nature, quantity, and quality of books used in classroom read-alouds (Pentimonti, Zucker, & Justice, 2011) or the lexical characteristics of books in preschool classrooms (Mesmer, 2016).

Although extant literature has used varied methods and yielded varied findings regarding preschool and early elementary classroom libraries, no published studies to date have examined the books included in classroom libraries as related to the availability and accessibility of multicultural texts. It is that work that we undertake now by sharing what was learned when we collected and analyzed data about the books included in classroom libraries in 21 preschool classrooms in the metropolitan region of Atlanta, Georgia. Because research in this area is limited, it is critical to consider the degree to which preschool classroom libraries, a prominent fixture in many children's lives, are or are not diverse (in every sense of the word).

The classrooms involved in this study were distributed across 11 early childhood sites and generally served low-income, racially diverse (but predominantly African American) populations. They included both Head Start and public pre-K classrooms funded by proceeds from the Georgia Lottery. Nearly all of the teachers in the classrooms studied self-identified as African American females. The mean number of texts per library was 79.1 (standard deviation = 56.74 books), but with a range of 182, the number of books in each classroom library varied drastically (minimum = 18; maximum = 200). The majority of the classroom libraries contained fewer than 50 books at any given time, often with very little book rotation throughout the school year.

At various points during the fall and early winter months of the school year, members of the research team visited individual classrooms and used smartphones to scan the barcodes of all books contained in the classroom library. Data from those scans were automatically uploaded to a private Goodreads account, allowing researchers to catalog each book by classroom in one centralized database. For books that did not have a scannable barcode or were not included in the Goodreads database (e.g., book club editions, books missing dust jackets), team members took photographs of the book covers, Library of Congress information, title pages, and/or other relevant content that would allow us to manually locate and add those books to our database for the appropriate classroom(s). This approach allowed us to locate the specific version of each book in a classroom's library, which was important to our research considering that peritextual elements, words/ narratives, and illustrations can vary from one edition of a book to another.

After data collection was complete, the research team initially utilized instruments created and used previously in studies conducted by the lead author. Grounded in and building on instruments created for similar types of research, these tools, which we describe in more detail throughout this article, have been used successfully with large data sets in past critical content analyses and content analyses of depictions of multicultural or diverse cultural identities in children's literature (Crisp, 2015; Crisp & Hiller, 2011). As a team, we coded the contents of various classroom libraries according to categories focused on religion; SES and class; dis/abilities, developmental differences, and chronic illnesses; sexual identity; gender; and representations of parallel cultures. We additionally coded books according to language, genre and format, and the type of book according to Sims's (1982) categories of melting pot, social conscience, and culturally conscious literature. For the purposes of our research, populations have been identified as diverse or belonging to the multicultural canon as a result of their subordination by dominant groups.

After being trained to use the research instruments, team members involved with the process of coding books independently coded all books in a single classroom library, with each classroom library being coded by multiple team members. Results of this pilot were compared, and subsequent discussions served to resolve discrepancies and standardize approaches to coding. The final instrument was influenced by our time with the books and informed by scholarship written by, among others, Banks (1993), Tatum (1997), and Botelho and Rudman (2009).

Utilizing the final research instrument, the two lead authors independently read and coded every book, compared their results, and resolved any discrepancies in coding by revisiting specific books and reviewing descriptions, definitions, and procedures for data collection in order to resolve differences and reach a consensus (Harry, Sturges, & Klingner, 2005). When classroom libraries were coded with 100% agreement, the results were submitted to a team member charged with collecting and reviewing these submissions for missing data before entering them into SPSS version 22 for statistical analysis. In total, 1,169 books were coded and analyzed; Figure 7.1 provides a visual representation of the total number of books coded for each category of analysis

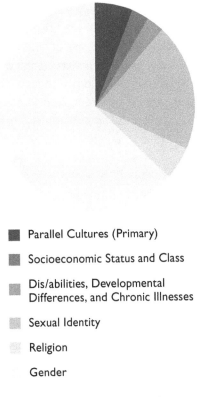

■ Parallel Cultures (Primary)

■ Socioeconomic Status and Class

■ Dis/abilities, Developmental
Differences, and Chronic Illnesses

■ Sexual Identity

■ Religion

■ Gender

FIGURE 7.1   Total Texts Coded as Including Explicit Depictions of Various Cultural Identities (*N* = 1,169)

related to diverse cultural identities. In the following section, we describe our approach to analysis in these (and additional) categories and share findings based on the books included in these 21 classroom libraries.

Depictions and Possibilities: The Search for Diverse Books in Classroom Libraries

When coding books for depictions in many of the categories below (e.g., parallel cultures, gender), we relied exclusively on what was stated explicitly in the book itself. We examined both the primary text and the peritextual content, such as information included on dust jackets, in Library of Congress information, and in author's notes. We divorced ourselves, as much as possible, from interpretations that were based on our own assumptions when determining representations of identity categories. For example, we did not assume that a character depicted wearing a headdress of feathers was supposed to represent an American Indian person. To the contrary, in fact, we know that Native appropriation and "playing Indian" are ongoing issues in children's literature and popular culture.

Finally, when coding books, we followed the lead of several previous researchers (for a more extensive discussion, see Crisp & Hiller, 2011) and generally focused our attention on leading characters (or in the case of nonfiction, leading subjects). We identified the person or people on whom a book is focused or through whom a text is presented for readers and grounded our coding in those representations. Although it is important for readers to see many shades of people in the background of picturebooks (those types of books are accounted for in the Category of Book section), we focused primarily on protagonists and leading figures because of our belief that children need to encounter stories told from the perspective of many different types of characters/subjects.

Examining U.S. Parallel Cultures

For scholars and researchers writing about representations of diversity in children's books, terms such as *parallel populations* and *parallel cultures* are utilized as a way of describing cultural groups that have a history of marginalization in the United States (see, e.g., Bishop, 2003; Hamilton, 1993). In our research, we identified parallel cultures as including populations that exist within the context of the United States and are often included in research and scholarship about diverse or multicultural children's and young adult literature. Although we do not claim that this is an exhaustive list of parallel culture identities, the populations for which we coded were African Americans, American Indians, Asian/Pacific Americans, Latino/a Americans, Middle Eastern Americans, and mixed-race Americans.

In these classroom libraries, only 67 books (5.7%) depicted at least one leading character or subject identified as belonging to a parallel culture—even fewer than the overall percentage of diverse representations reflected in the latest report from the CCBC (11%). As reflected in Figure 7.2, the 67 books in this category comprised a total of 68 representations, with 36 books (53.7%) featuring African Americans, seven (10.4%) featuring American Indians, 10 (14.9%)

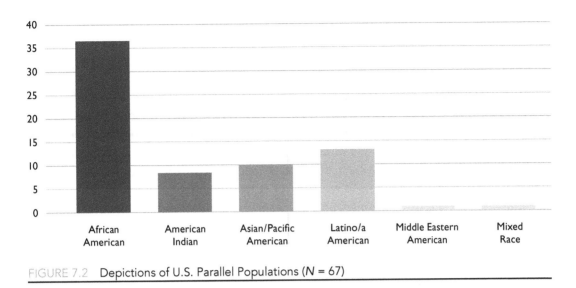

FIGURE 7.2   Depictions of U.S. Parallel Populations (*N* = 67)

featuring Asian/Pacific Americans, 13 (19.4%) featuring Latino/a Americans, and one (1.5%) featuring Middle Eastern Americans. One book (1.5%) depicted a child of mixed race, described as Japanese and Caucasian American; this book is also the only one that explicitly identified a character as Caucasian or White, which should not be interpreted as meaning that this is the only book that depicted Caucasian/White characters. As scholars such as Tatum (1997) have argued, individuals who self-identify as members of dominant cultural groups take their identities for granted, often assuming that there is no need to make them explicit.

It is important to note that because it is beyond the scope of this work, we did not evaluate the representations coded here according to quality of representation (e.g., accuracy of depiction, authenticity), and many of these depictions would be deemed problematic when examined with evaluative criteria for diverse representations. For example, many representations of American Indians were in books that relied on and reinforced stereotypical and historically inaccurate Thanksgiving stories. Overall, 15 (71.4%) of the 21 classroom libraries contained at least one book with content or depictions widely acknowledged as being stereotypical, inaccurate, or otherwise problematic.

We were also interested in the genres and text formats of books that contained depictions of parallel cultures. Utilizing basic genre criteria described by Galda, Sipe, Liang, and Cullinan (2014), we found that the books depicting parallel cultures in these classroom libraries reflected the dominant genres and types of texts published about these populations and that have been problematized by scholars and critics of multicultural literature for decades (see, e.g., Harris, 1997). For example, 85.7% of the books depicting American Indians were either folklore (one) or presented American Indian people exclusively in a historical context (five), and the 60 books depicting African Americans, Asian/Asian Pacific Americans, Latino/a Americans, and Middle Eastern Americans were predominantly contemporary realistic fiction (27 books, or 45%), historical fiction (nine books, or 15%), or nonfiction (seven books, or 11.7%). There were few (if any) books depicting parallel cultures that fit within a literary genre such as science fiction or poetry.

Category of Book

A related, but not identical, area is what we referred to as the category of book. Relying on and extending categories created by Sims (1982), we coded each book as melting pot (presenting a color-blind view of the world and/or depicting people across the rainbow of cultural identities without acknowledging it explicitly), social conscience (written with a social agenda, intended to promote acceptance and harmony, or at least tolerance of different groups), and/or culturally conscious (with a primary goal of speaking to and representing the experiences of underrepresented/marginalized groups). When a book did not fit within any of those categories (e.g., *Chicka Chicka Boom Boom* by Bill Martin Jr. and John Archambault, 1989), we coded it as N/A (not applicable).

Obviously, this type of coding is less straightforward than the coding undertaken for other aspects of this project. The two lead authors, each with more than a dozen years of experience in reading about and researching issues of diversity, representation, and social justice in children's and young adult literature, drew on their knowledge and areas of expertise when cataloging books as melting pot, social conscience, or culturally conscious. In addition, for all books coded as culturally conscious, the authors confirmed their categorizations by locating critiques and analyses from insider experts in the form of published reviews, research reports, and scholarly articles, books, and chapters (see, e.g., Brooks & McNair, 2008; Seale & Slapin, 2005).

Of the 1,169 books analyzed in the study, a total of 438 books (37.5%) were coded as texts that fit within these classifications. As reflected in Figure 7.3, of these 438 books, 263 (60%) were categorized as melting pot books, 145 (33.1%) as social conscience books, and only 30 (6.8%) as culturally conscious literature. This means that of the 1,169 books in 21 class libraries, there were only 30 books (2.6%, or an average of 1.4 books per classroom) coded as being written with a primary goal of speaking to or providing representation of the experiences of underrepresented/ marginalized cultural groups.

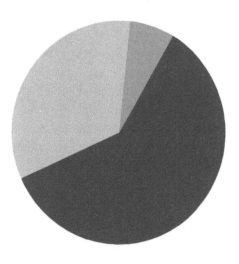

■ Melting Pot

▨ Social Conscience

▨ Culturally Conscious

FIGURE 7.3   Book Category (*N* = 438)

Ses and Class

When analyzing books for depictions of SES and class, we resisted making assumptions about occupations (e.g., waitress, lawyer) or descriptions and depictions of living environments (e.g., cities, suburbs). Instead, we only coded books that explicitly addressed these topics in their depictions and/or themes, such as books that focused on difficulties faced by protagonists when their caregivers could not afford clothing that fit them correctly or whose parents worried about being able to pay bills or purchase groceries. Books were coded as low SES or working class, middle SES or middle class, high SES or upper class, or N/A. As Figure 7.4 indicates, 32 books (2.7%) were coded into these categories, of which 28 (87.5%) were identified as relating to low SES or working class representations, issues, and themes, three (9.4%) as relating to middle SES or middle class, and one (3.1%) as relating to high SES or upper class.

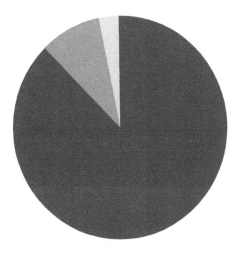

■ Low SES or Working Class

■ Middle SES or Middle Class

High SES or Upper Class

FIGURE 7.4   Depictions of Socioeconomic Status (SES) and Class (*N* = 32)

Dis/Abilities, Developmental Differences, and Chronic Illnesses

Children's literature has a history of depicting people with dis/abilities, developmental differences, and chronic illnesses within an educative frame. Authors frequently write books intended to teach presumably nondisabled readers about some of the problems with which individuals with dis/abilities may be confronted and have to overcome (Tal, 2001).

Only 32 books (2.7%) were coded as depicting leading characters or subjects with dis/abilities, developmental differences, and/or chronic illnesses. As reflected in Figure 7.5, the 32 books in this category comprised a total of 41 different representations. Within those 41 representations, 25 (61%) were coded as being characters with dis/abilities and primarily consisted of characters who wear glasses (visual impairment) or are severely visually impaired or completely without sight, people who are deaf or hard of hearing, or individuals using wheelchairs,

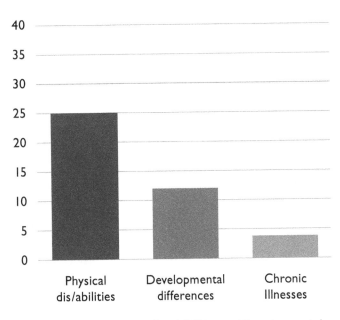

FIGURE 7.5   Depictions of Dis/abilities and Developmental Differences (*N* = 41)

braces, or canes. The 12 depictions (29.3%) of developmental differences are almost exclusively individuals with Down syndrome or autism; one book focused on dwarfism. Finally, the four representations (9.8%) of chronic illnesses were of individuals with either asthma or diabetes.

Sexual Identity

When coding for sexual identity, books coded within the heterosexual category included only representations of characters with romantic and/or sexual attractions toward/ relationships with individuals described in the text (e.g., through gendered pronouns) as members of the opposite sex. Books coded in the lesbian category were those with female characters described as only having romantic and/or sexual attractions toward/relationships with individuals depicted as female. The code gay was used to categorize books with depictions of male characters with romantic and/or sexual attractions toward/relationships with individuals depicted as biological males. The code bisexual was used to categorize books depicting characters of any biological sex described as having romantic and/or sexual attractions toward/relationships with individuals of multiple biological sexes. Any depiction that did not fit within these categories was coded as other (with space to identify the representation), and books that did not include any romantic or sexual attractions/relationships were coded as N/A.

As Figure 7.6 indicates, 217 books (18.6%) were coded as including depictions of various sexual identities. Of those books, all 217 (100%) included depictions of heterosexuality. Although we identified several different books written to inform young readers about the diversity of families and family structures, the invisibility of individuals with nonnormative sexual identities was ultimately reinscribed: Across all 1,169 books, there was only one (0.09%) that included any reference to queer-identified people, devoting one page each to families that include lesbian females or gay males.

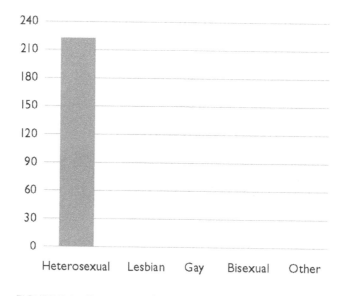

FIGURE 7.6   Depictions of Sexual Identity (*N* = 217)

Religion

With its history of education and didacticism, it is not surprising that religion and religious issues are often present in and a part of children's texts (Wood, 1999). As reflected in Figure 7.7, we coded the books according to any specific religious tradition identified in the text. Based on the world's most prominent religions, we coded books according to the following categories: Christian, Muslim, Hindu, Buddhist, Sikh, Jewish, Baha'i, nonreligious, agnostic, atheist, religious/nonspecific, and other. Books that did not depict religion were coded as N/A.

Across all 1,169 books, only 57 (4.9%) were coded as featuring religion. Of those 57 books, 46 (80.7%) depicted Christianity, three (5.3%) depicted Jewish people, and one (1.8%) depicted Muslims. The remaining books included depictions of religion and religious traditions that were nonspecific (four books, or 7%) or that were categorized as other (three books, or 5%) and highlighted the religious beliefs of the Aztec, Pueblo, or Navajo people.

Gender

The final aspect of cultural diversity for which we coded was gender identity. Although it reinforces binary constructions of language, when coding for gender identity, we relied on normative understandings of gendered nouns (e.g., *girl*, *woman*) and pronouns (e.g., *she*, *he*) to categorize leading characters in books as cisfemale/ciswoman, cismale/cisman, transwoman, transman, ungendered, other, or (in cases in which gender identities were entirely absent) N/A.

As illustrated in Figure 7.8, 691 books (59.1%) were coded as featuring leading characters or subjects. Within these 691 books, we identified 195 (28.2%) that featured leading female/ciswoman characters and 370 (53.5%) that contained male/cisman leading characters. Although 126 books (18.2%) included leading characters who were ungendered, meaning they were not

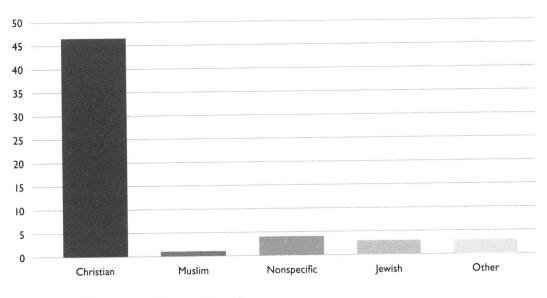

FIGURE 7.7   Depictions of Religion (*N* = 57)

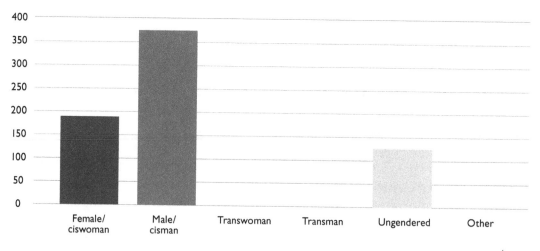

FIGURE 7.8   Depictions of Gender Identity (*N* = 691)

assigned a gender identity (e.g., referred to only in the first or second person, referred to as "the child"), no books were coded as fitting the transwoman, transman, or other categories.

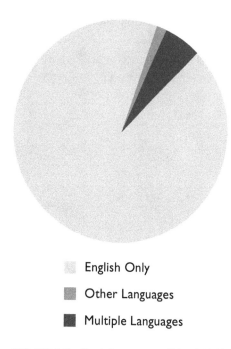

FIGURE 7.9   Book Languages (*N* = 1,170)

Note. The *N* in this figure reflects the fact that some of the 1,170 books were coded within more than one category.

Language

In addition to coding the characters and figures included, all 1,169 books were also coded for representations of language. Books were categorized as containing English only, other language(s) only, or multiple languages. Texts coded within the multiple-languages category included, as examples, everything from texts written equally in both English and Spanish to books written primarily in English but also including one or more words written in another language. As seen in Figure 7.9, 1,065 books (91.1%) in classrooms contained only the English language, and 22 (1.9%) were coded as being written exclusively in other languages (all of which were written in Spanish). Finally, 83 books (7.1%) included multiple languages, such as 49 written in both Spanish and English and five written in Spanish, English, and other languages (Hindi, French, Italian, Japanese, Yiddish, or Hebrew). The remaining books included text written in English alongside a mixture of sign language, Japanese, Chinese, Hebrew, French, Portuguese, Latin, Russian, Vietnamese, Swahili, Igbo, Chamorro, Aramaic, and/or Arabic.

Genre and Format

Finally, although not directly related to depictions of cultural diversity, we would be remiss if we did not include a brief statement about diversity of texts according to the categories of genre and format. Because much of the research about the content of classroom libraries has centered on the lack of informational text in early-grades settings (e.g., Duke, 2000a; Pappas, 1993), we were interested in uncovering whether those findings held true in these contemporary preschool classroom libraries. The work of advocates for increased informational text has been at the forefront of pedagogical conversations for more than a decade now and has resulted in sweeping and substantive changes at the classroom, school, district, and policy levels (see, e.g., the Common Core State Standards), not to mention in the publishing industry, regarding the ways in which children's books are addressed in research and selected for classroom use.

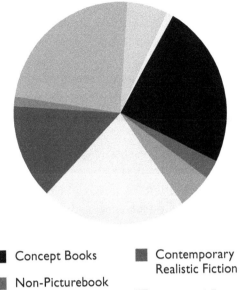

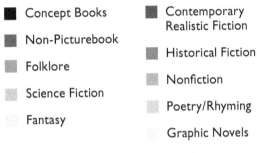

FIGURE 7.10   Book Genres and Formats (N = 1,169)

Relying once more on basic categorizations of genre and text format (e.g., Galda et al., 2014), we coded each book according to the genre(s) and format(s) it represented, with many books coded as belonging to more than one genre and/or format. For example, it was possible for a book to be both poetry and historical fiction or both fantasy and nonfiction. As represented in Figure 7.10, looking across the 1,169 books in these libraries, 65 (5.6%) were coded as folklore, none (0%) as science fiction, 280 (24%) as fantasy, 175 (15%) as contemporary realistic fiction, 18 (1.5%) as historical fiction, and 78 (6.7%) as poetry/ rhyming. Examining text formats, 12 books (1%) were coded as graphic novels and 37 (3.2%) as nonpicturebooks (e.g., anthologies, novels, illustrated storybooks). Instructional books, such as concept books (texts that seek to help children better understand ideas, patterns, relationships, etc.) and nonfiction/informational texts account for 51.5% of all books in early childhood classroom libraries (302 and 300 books, respectively).

Discussion

This study examined the nature of preschool classroom libraries with attention to representations of diverse cultural identities, including parallel cultures; dis/abilities, developmental differences, and chronic illnesses; sexual identities; religion; language; gender; and format/ genre. Results suggest that across all categories explored, books in classroom libraries were lacking in terms of cultural diversity. For example, only 5.7% of these books explicitly depicted people identified as members of parallel cultures, and only 2.6% were coded as culturally conscious literature. Only 2.7% of books in classroom libraries included depictions of class and SES, with the majority of those books focusing on low-SES/working-class people who escape poverty and achieve the American dream. Similarly, another 2.7% of books focus on people with dis/abilities, developmental differences, and chronic illnesses, and the stated purpose of nearly all of these books is to educate presumably nondis abled readers. The greatest diversity was found in representations of gender, but even here, there were nearly double the number of male representations as compared with female, with even fewer ungendered depictions and no representations of transidentified people.

Because of the tenuous relationship between religion and its place in early childhood classrooms, we were not surprised that few books (4.9%) explicitly depicted religion and religious topics or themes. However, child readers are often faced with complexities related to religion and religious beliefs, and we believe that wider representation of various religious beliefs and traditions and further explorations of the ways in which those beliefs shape (and are shaped by) the lives of individuals is essential. We were also not surprised by the absence of books depicting lesbian, gay, and bisexual people: Because sexual identity is often cast as an issue open to debate (as opposed to a category of identity), teachers often try to avoid controversy by excluding these books from their classroom libraries. However, as Levithan (2004) noted, self-identifying as LGBTQ "is a *fact*, and must be defended and represented as a fact. ... Discrimination is not a legitimate point of view" (p. 44).

Our research also revealed little diversity in the languages represented in classroom libraries. Although there are numerous benefits of including multiple languages in early childhood and elementary-grades classrooms, and numerous recommendations for engaging children with such texts (Magruder, Hayslip, Espinosa, & Matera, 2013), few books demonstrating linguistic diversity were available to children in these classrooms. Because of the importance of linguistic diversity, this trend is disappointing for all children, particularly multilanguage users and emerging bilinguals.

Inconsistent with previous research on informational texts in early elementary classrooms (Duke, 2000a), the libraries in this study offered heterogeneity in terms of format/genre, a finding that raised a number of questions for us. Although demand for increased attention on nonfiction books is not new (see, e.g., Meltzer, 1976), in the last two decades, efforts for increased classroom use and presence of nonfiction, specifically informational texts, have been at the forefront of pedagogical conversations about classroom text use. In many ways, the research on informational text by Duke (2000a) parallels the level of influence of Larrick's (1965) work on racial diversity in children's literature: Although neither was the first to make the argument, their scholarship brought these conversations into the mainstream in new ways. We are troubled particularly by one lingering question: Why is it that we seem to have been quick—16 years since Duke's landmark research—to respond to the lack of informational text in classrooms, whereas the lack of cultural diversity in children's books in classrooms is not much different than it was at the time of Larrick's study more than 50 years ago? Although data by the CCBC, Lee & Low, and others may help us generate ideas about why this is a problem on the publishing end, ultimately, we assert that when it comes to classroom libraries, questions about why do not matter: The fact is that although we obviously need more diverse books to be published, quality diverse literature exists already, and there are things that we can be doing right now to improve our classroom libraries.

The research undertaken here contributes to the current literature base in several ways. First, despite being based on a limited number of classrooms and sites in a single metropolitan area, the consistent lack of diversity in books may be indicative of a wider problem facing other classrooms outside the parameters of the study. However, further research is needed to explore classroom libraries on a wider scale. Second, if the preschool libraries investigated are characteristic of average classroom libraries at other levels, this highlights the primary goal of this article and the clearly defined need presented here, that is, to help all teachers and school leaders assess and diversify the contents of their own classroom and school libraries—something many of us can start doing immediately.

It is easy to look at the statistics provided by organizations such as the CCBC and Lee & Low cited at the opening of this article and think to ourselves, That's horrible! It's a huge problem, but that's not my library. My library is pretty good! We believe that the moment we begin to feel comfortable or confident in our collections or start thinking we are doing everything necessary or that can be done to create a library of diverse representations and texts is the moment in which we need to remind ourselves that this type of work is never done: We cannot acquire a set of books and then check "diverse classroom/school library" off our to-do lists. Cultural issues, relationships, languages, and understandings shift and change across time and context, and we need to be evaluating the contents of our libraries on an ongoing basis.

It is also easy to examine the statistics about diverse books and feel overwhelmed or helpless when confronted with the challenge of creating a diverse classroom library. Imagine, however, how different classrooms across the country could be if each of us began creating change at the most local level by examining and diversifying our own classroom libraries. We offer our approach to analyzing preschool classrooms as one model of how this work can be done.

Although we do not expect all teachers to systematically scan the barcodes of their classroom books, we suggest that teachers should begin looking at their classroom libraries through various lenses: What is included in my classroom library when I think about depictions of gender? How does my library look when I think about racial diversity? Who has voice and representation here? Who does not? It is important for school leaders and media/literary specialists to consider the same concerns at a schoolwide level. Considerations should be applied to the written words and illustrations of curricular content, as well as books purchased or selected for school libraries. Of course, we also want to think about the content of depictions: doing our best to ensure that representations are accurate, authentic, nuanced, and wide-ranging. When we inevitably identify gaps in our collections, there are resources that can help us continue creating libraries filled with diverse, high-quality books.

One place to start is by locating book awards that honor diverse books, authors, and illustrators. There are numerous awards for diverse and multicultural books, including several offered through the Association for Library Service to Children. For teachers unsure that a certain type of book award exists, utilizing an online search engine is often a fast and useful way to locate book awards about which we were previously unaware. Although it may seem obvious, there are often multiple awards honoring children's books and/or creators depicting the same population. Spend time exploring award criteria and purpose, the granting agency, and other parameters that can contribute to understandings of the various honors available.

In addition to book awards, a number of professional organizations (e.g., Rethinking Schools, Teaching Tolerance) and blogs (e.g., Latin@s in Kid Lit, American Indians in Children's Literature) exist that are devoted to issues of diversity in schools and children's literature. These websites often serve as hubs where teachers can learn about specific books (both exemplary texts and those that are problematic and should be avoided), delve into larger issues in children's literature, and identify additional resources dedicated to diversity in classrooms and children's books. Many bloggers are also active on social media (e.g., Twitter, Facebook), providing another way to follow trends, engage in current conversations, and explore relevant issues.

There are several ways that teachers can acquire free or low-cost books for their classrooms. At a local level, public libraries (often through "Friends of the Library" sales), independent book-stores, and local chapters of national groups and organizations (e.g., Dolly Parton's Imagination Library) often distribute free books or host book drives to collect new and gently used books for classroom teachers. In many communities, local organizations are dedicated to redistributing new and used children's books (e.g., Bernie's Book Bank in Chicago, Philadelphia Reads Book Bank); find out if your community has a similar organization. Many teachers have found success in creating classroom wish lists on websites such as Amazon and Barnes & Noble and sharing those lists with caregivers, colleagues, and others who can purchase books and have them shipped directly to the teacher.

Crowdsourcing has become a popular means for teachers to obtain funding, and websites such as GoFundMe have created divisions specifically for teachers requesting funding for educational purposes. Other crowdsourcing websites, such as DonorsChoose.org, have been created specifically for K–12 educators. Grants are available that provide funding for classroom and school library book purchases (see, e.g., National Home Library Foundation, Snapdragon Book Foundation) and programs such as First Book, International Book Project, and Kids Need to Read provide free or low-cost books to teachers, schools, and/or educational programs.

We may never be able to say definitively why classroom libraries are not diverse, but we know why it matters: All children deserve to see themselves and the people they love represented (in multiple ways) in the books we bring into our classrooms. As Marley Dias, an African American 11-year-old who launched the #1000BlackGirlBooks drive recently stated, "I was sick of reading about white boys and dogs" (as quoted in Baker, 2016, para. 5). We, as teachers, have an obligation to provide literary images that reflect the diversity of our students, as well as the diversity of the world. We wonder, What would happen if every classroom teacher collected her own data about her classroom library and shared that data with her principal and with caregivers? What could happen locally, nationally, and even globally if we all started taking action in our own classroom libraries *today*?

References

Applebee, A.N., Langer, J.A., & Mullis, I.V.S. (1988). *Who reads best? Factors related to reading achievement in grades 3, 7, and 11* (Report No. 17-R-01). Princeton, NJ: Educational Testing Service.

Baker, B. (2016, January 19). 11-year-old Jersey girl launches #1000BlackGirlBooks [Web log post]. Retrieved from http:// www.phillyvoice.com/11-year-old-jersey-girl-launches-1000blackgirlbooks-book-drive/?platform=hootsuite

Banks, J.A. (1993). Multicultural education: Historical development, dimensions, and practice. *Review of Research in Education, 19,* 3–49.

Bishop, R.S. (2003). Reframing the debate about cultural authenticity. In D.L. Fox & K.G. Short (Eds.), *Stories matter: The complexity of cultural authenticity in children's literature* (pp. 25–37). Urbana, IL: National Council of Teachers of English.

Blaska, J.K. (2004). Children's literature that includes characters with disabilities or illnesses. *Disability Studies Quarterly, 24*(1). Retrieved from http://dsq-sds.org/article/view/854/1029

Botelho, M.J., & Rudman, M.K. (2009). *Critical multicultural analysis of children's literature: Mirrors, windows, and doors.* New York, NY: Routledge.

Brooks, W.M., & McNair, J.C. (Eds.). (2008). *Embracing, evaluating, and examining African American children's and young adult literature.* Lanham, MD: Scarecrow.

Chaudhri, A., & Teale, W.H. (2013). Stories of multiracial experiences in literature for children, ages 9–14. *Children's Literature in Education, 44*(4), 359–376.

Crisp, T. (2015). A content analysis of Orbis Pictus Award-winning nonfiction, 1990–2014. *Language Arts, 92*(4), 241–255.

Crisp, T., & Hiller, B. (2011). "Is this a boy or a girl?": Rethinking sex-role representation in Caldecott Medal-winning picturebooks, 1938–2011. *Children's Literature in Education, 42*(3), 196–212.

Crosby, M.E. (Ed.). (1963). *Reading ladders for human relations* (4th ed.). Washington, DC: American Council on Education.

Duke, N.K. (2000a). 3.6 minutes per day: The scarcity of informational texts in first grade. *Reading Research Quarterly, 35*(2), 202–224.

Duke, N.K. (2000b). For the rich it's richer: Print experiences and environments offered to children in very low- and very high-socioeconomic status first-grade classrooms. *American Educational Research Journal, 37*(2), 441–478.

Fractor, J.S., Woodruff, M.C., Martinez, M.G., & Teale, W.H. (1993). Let's not miss opportunities to promote voluntary reading: Classroom libraries in the elementary school. *The Reading Teacher, 46*(6), 476–484.

Galda, L., Sipe, L.R., Liang, L.A., & Cullinan, B.E. (2014). *Literature and the child* (8th ed.). Belmont, CA: Wadsworth/ Cengage Learning.

Guo, Y., Sawyer, B.E., Justice, L.M., & Kaderavek, J.N. (2013). Quality of the literacy environment in inclusive early childhood special education classrooms. *Journal of Early Intervention, 35*(1), 40–60.

Hamilton, V. (1993). Everything of value: Moral realism in the literature for children. *Journal of Youth Services in Libraries, 6*(4), 363–377.

Harris, V.J. (Ed.). (1997). *Using multiethnic literature in the K–8 classroom*. Lanham, MD: Rowman & Littlefield.

Harry, B., Sturges, K., & Klingner, J. (2005). Qualitative data analysis: Mapping the process. *Educational Researcher, 34*(2), 3–13.

Horning, K.T. (2013, July 11). I see White people [Web log post]. Retrieved from http://ccblogc. blogspot.com/2013/07/i-see-whitepeople.html

Horning, K.T., Lindgren, M.V., Schliesman, M., & Townsend, E.M. (2015). *CCBC Choices 2015*. Madison: Cooperative Children's Book Center, University of Wisconsin–Madison.

Jeong, J., Gaffney, J.S., & Choi, J.-O. (2010). Availability and use of informational texts in second-, third-, and fourth-grade classrooms. *Research in the Teaching of English, 44*(4), 435–456.

Larrick, N. (1965, September 11). The all-White world of children's books. *The Saturday Review*, pp. 63–65, 84–85.

Lee, Y.-J., Lee, J., Han, M., & Schickedanz, J.A. (2011). Comparison of preschoolers' narratives, the classroom book environment, and teacher attitudes toward literacy practices in Korea and the United States. *Early Education and Development, 22*(2), 234–255.

Levithan, D. (2004). Supporting gay teen literature. *School Library Journal, 50*(10), 44–45.

Low, J.T. (2016, January 26). Where is the diversity in publishing? The 2015 Diversity Baseline Survey results [Web log post]. Retrieved from http://blog.leeandlow.com/2016/01/26/where-is-the-diversity-in-publishing-the-2015-diversitybaseline-survey-results/

Magruder, E.S., Hayslip, W.W., Espinosa, L.M., & Matera, C. (2013). Many languages, one teacher: Supporting language and literacy development for preschool dual language learners. *Young Children, 68*(1), 8–12, 15.

McGill-Franzen, A., Lanford, C., & Adams, E. (2002). Learning to be literate: A comparison of five early childhood programs. *Journal of Educational Psychology, 94*(3), 443–464.

Meltzer, M. (1976). Where do all the prizes go? The case for nonfiction. *The Horn Book Magazine, 52*, 17–23.

Mesmer, H.A.E. (2016). Text matters: Exploring the lexical reservoirs of books in preschool rooms. *Early Childhood Research Quarterly, 34*, 67–77.

Myers, C. (2014, March 15). The apartheid of children's literature. *The New York Times*. Retrieved from http://www.nytimes.com/2014/03/16/opinion/sunday/the-apartheid-of-childrensliterature.html?_r=0

Myers, W.D. (2014, March 15). Where are the people of color in children's books? *The New York Times*. Retrieved from http:// www.nytimes.com/2014/03/16/opinion/sunday/where-are-the-people-of-color-in-childrens-books.html

Pappas, C.C. (1993). Is narrative "primary"? Some insights from kindergarteners' pretend readings of stories and information books. *Journal of Reading Behavior, 25*(1), 97–129.

Pentimonti, J.M., Zucker, T.A., & Justice, L.M. (2011). What are preschool teachers reading in their classrooms? *Reading Psychology, 32*(3), 197–236.

Reese, D. (2007). Proceed with caution: Using Native American folktales in the classroom. *Language Arts, 84*(3), 245–256.

Rollins, C.H. (Ed.). (1967). *We build together: A reader's guide to Negro life and literature for elementary and high school use* (3rd ed.). Urbana, IL: National Council of Teachers of English.

Seale, D., & Slapin, B. (Eds.). (2005). *A broken flute: The Native experience in books for children.* New York, NY: AltaMira; Berkeley, CA: Oyate.

Short, K.G. (2012). Story as world making. *Language Arts, 90*(1), 9–17. Sims, R. (1982). *Shadow and substance: Afro-American experience in contemporary children's fiction.* Urbana, IL: National Council of Teachers of English.

Tal, E. (2001). Swimming the mainstream: A discussion of criteria for evaluating children's literature about disabilities. *Bookbird, 39*(1), 30–32.

Tatum, B.D. (1997). *"Why are all the Black kids sitting together in the cafeteria?" and other conversations about race.* New York, NY: Basic.

Wood, N. (1999). Introduction: Children's literature and religion. *Children's Literature Association Quarterly, 24*(1), 1–3.

Children's Literature Cited

Martin, B., Jr., & Archambault, J. (1989). *Chicka chicka boom boom.* (L. Ehlert, Illus.). New York, NY: Simon & Schuster.

Diversity in Preschool Classrooms

The Link Between Diversity and Quality

Jeanne L. Reid and Sharon Lynn Kagan

Abundant data, widely popularized by public information campaigns, have given early childhood education (ECE) a prominent position on the public agenda. But is our society fully capitalizing on the opportunity such attention affords and the significant public investment that comes with it?

Data on what constitutes quality in early childhood education abound, and efforts to address the sustainability of early childhood efforts are gaining momentum, with attention to issues of governance, accountability and capacity development. However, we have not seen similar progress regarding equity within ECE classrooms. Despite concerted efforts to reduce economic inequity among poor children, including the launch of Head Start 50 years ago, issues of racial and socio-economic equity have only been tangentially tackled in programs that segregate children by income, and often in practice, by race, within their preschool classrooms.

> *Quality and equity are inextricably linked.*

To improve child outcomes, policymakers should consider the socioeconomic and racial/ethnic composition of children's classrooms as an important component of preschool quality. In an April 2015 report, *A Better Start: Why Classroom Diversity Matters in Early Education* (NY & Wash. DC, The Century Fdn. & PRRAC), we present the results of a review and analysis of demographic data, current research literature, and national position statements of early childhood organizations. The results indicate that quality and equity are inextricably linked, that programs that are segregated by race/ethnicity and income are rarely of equal quality, and that efforts to make early childhood investments sustainable must take this into account.

The Problem of Inequity in Early Childhood Education

Despite increasing investments in programs for young children, demographic data on early childhood education programs reveal three troubling trends related to equity. First, according to data from the Federal Interagency Forum on Child and Family Statistics, children from low-SES families and Hispanic children are less likely than higher-SES and non-Hispanic children to be enrolled in centerbased early childhood programs. For example, in 2012, only 45.6% of children from families with incomes below the poverty line attended centerbased programs (including pre-K, Head Start and center-based childcare), while among families making at least twice the poverty threshold, enrollment rose to 72%. These data suggest that many children who could most benefit from high-quality preschool are not enrolled.

Second, low-income children are most likely to attend low-quality preschool programs. In 2012–13, for example, more than half a million children in state pre-K programs—41% of nationwide enrollment—attended programs that met fewer than half of the quality benchmarks set by the National Institute for Early Education Research, as reported in their annual report, *The State of Preschool 2013*. The problem is compounded for low-SES families because pre-K programs serving high numbers of children in poverty and racial/ethnic minorities are the most likely to be low quality. Moreover, federal reports on Head Start reveal that overall quality in the programs is uneven, but the level of instructional quality tends to be low.

Third, most children attend public preschool classrooms that are segregated by income and often by race/ethnicity as well. Although overall enrollment in state pre-K programs is remarkably diverse in both family income and race/ethnicity, this diversity in program enrollment does not always translate into diversity *within pre-K classrooms*. Forthcoming research from one of the authors of this article (Jeanne Reid) uses a 2001–04 sample from 11 state pre-K programs, for example, and finds that almost half (47.1%) of the children attended high-minority classrooms (70 to 100% minority) in which, on average, three out of four (75.4%) were poor. Only one-sixth of the children (17.0%) were enrolled in classrooms that were *both* racially diverse and medium- or high-income.

Overall enrollment in Head Start programs is racially and ethnically diverse, though in accord with Head Start policy, far less heterogeneous by family income. By federal law, Head Start programs can enroll up to 10% of its children from families with incomes above the poverty line; programs may also serve up to an additional 35% of children from families with incomes 100 to 130% of the poverty line, as long as the needs of families below poverty has been fully met. Yet the pursuit of diversity is often compromised by pressure to serve the lowest-income children first. In 2012–13, only 7.6% of Head Start children nationwide had family incomes that were at least 100% of the poverty line. Moreover, because many parents prefer neighborhood programs, preschool programs often reflect neighborhood patterns of segregation, a reality that is growing more entrenched.

The Potential of Promoting Diversity to Improve Quality and Equity

The data on preschool classroom diversity matter because the evidence suggests that children who are clustered in high-poverty and high-minority preschool classrooms develop fewer cognitive skills on average than children who may also be low-income and minority, but who attend more diverse classrooms that, on average, are higher SES and lower in minority concentration. For example, a study by Jeanne Reid and Douglas D. Ready of Teachers College, Columbia University, found that children in middle- or high-SES classrooms learned more language and math skills than those in low-SES classrooms, regardless of children's own SES and race/ethnicity and the racial/ethnic composition of their classrooms. Studies in kindergarten and elementary schools support the findings from research at the preschool level.

The process by which preschool composition affects children's learning is complex and not fully clear, but emerging research suggests that interactions among peers are an explanation for how socioeconomically diverse classrooms may promote children's learning. *On average*, low-SES children enter preschool and kindergarten with fewer literacy and math skills than higher-SES children. In preschool, several studies have found that it is beneficial for children to have classmates with relatively high levels of language and math skills, and this is particularly true for children who are less skilled than their classmates; children who are highly skilled tend to be less influenced by the skills of their classmates.

> *To improve child outcomes, policymakers should consider the socioeconomic and racial/ ethnic composition of children's classrooms.*

Peer diversity may also offer important social benefits to all children. Children from a variety of socioeconomic backgrounds and race/ethnicities can learn from peers who are different, and these benefits may be enduring and profound. Exposure to peers from a variety of racial, ethnic and socioeconomic backgrounds can inform emerging social categorizations and prejudices. The friendships that form in diverse classrooms can diminish the social isolation that characterizes children in socioeconomically and racially homogenous neighborhoods, whatever their predominant race or income.

For *A Better Start*, we conducted a content analysis of the central policy/position statements of 14 major national organizations committed to advancing early learning to discern if and how the organizations have addressed this issue of preschool classroom composition. In general, we were unable to find any position statements that specifically called for economic and racial integration within preschool classrooms.

The Recommendations for Building an Excellent, Equitable and Sustainable Preschool System

The research on classroom composition and peer effects in early childhood education suggests that the economic and racial/ethnic segregation of young children limits their learning. Yet much of current preschool policy effectively segregates children by income and often by race/ethnicity. We need to devote concerted attention to classroom composition in the important discourse about what constitutes preschool quality, and how to build an equitable and durable system. Though we recognize the need for broader structural reforms, we offer more immediate recommendations for how to foster diverse preschool classrooms. (For details, see the report, *A Better Start*.)

Build Public and Professional Knowledge
We recommend a coordinated effort to disseminate information regarding classroom diversity in ECE, using diverse sources to reach diverse audiences. Moreover, the government and foundations should support enriching the research base to extend and deepen our knowledge of preschool classroom composition, how it operates in practice, and how it affects subgroups of children, such as those who are learning English as a second language, those of diverse family incomes, those of diverse races/ethnicities, and children with disabilities. In addition, national early childhood organizations should ensure that their policy statements reflect current research and offer guidance to readers and members regarding the effects of classroom integration at the preschool level.

Increase Funding
To support program-level efforts to serve diverse communities, state and/ or federal policymakers should assure that public and private funding streams are adequate to support high-quality preschool programs. For example, the federal government should increase fiscal allocations considerably to allow Head Start providers to use the existing option of enrolling up to 10% of their children from families with incomes above the poverty line without jeopardizing service provision to low-income children.

Consider Location and Subsidize Transportation
Policymakers should consider supporting programs for young children in or near diverse neighborhoods and in or near large employers, such as hospitals, universities and corporations, where employees who are parents of young children may represent diverse backgrounds and may elect to enroll their youngsters in convenient, high-quality programs. At the same time, the predominance of residential segregation requires that policymakers assure that families have access to affordable transportation to diverse programs.

Strengthen Professional Development
To enhance attention to classroom diversity in all ECE teacher preparation efforts, pre-service or in-service, states should support professional development that systematically shares the research on socioeconomic and racial/ethnic diversity to prepare teachers to teach in integrated settings. Higher education and postgraduate education schools should promote enrollment for all prospective teachers in a course on diversity in ECE and assure that student teaching placements include settings where classroom diversity exists.

Support Enrollment and Engagement

Programs need to assure that families know their parenting beliefs and wishes will be respected and embraced in the preschool setting. When families do enroll, administrators and teachers need to engage them as valued members of the preschool community. We call on policymakers and program administrators to support parent outreach and recruitment efforts, and the engagement of parents in their children's preschool experience.

With *A Better Start*, we call attention to the importance of socioeconomic and racial/ethnic diversity within preschool classrooms. Not only is such integration possible, but it is an important (though often neglected) correlate of quality. Taking a stand on quality for *all* children commits our society to the kinds of classroom-level integration that are long overdue, especially for our youngest learners.

Chicano Children's Literature

Using Bilingual Children's Books to Promote Equity in the Classroom

Laura A. Alamillo and Rosie Arenas

Introduction

As a child growing up in California, my parents raised my sisters and me in a traditional Mexican Spanish-speaking home, always acknowledging the American culture that surrounded us, in our neighborhood, our schools, and in our daily lives. It was a combination of these two cultures that determined my identity, knowing that I could switch back and forth between Spanish and English, Mexican and American, while I was in the comforting presence of my family at home on our ranch. However, it was very different at school. I was one of only two dark-skinned, Spanish-speaking students during my elementary school years and there was nothing at my school to validate either my culture nor my identity. (R. Arenas, personal anecdote, 2007)

My parents made a conscious choice to speak to me in Spanish and English. Because of my parent's desire to make me bilingual, I was afforded the opportunity to speak to my grandparents, aunts, and uncles, and later in life I could speak to bilingual children and families. My language and culture were affirmed at home, not at school. I cannot remember reading a book in Spanish at school let alone books with characters who looked like me or my siblings. It was not until my adult years when I began to seek out literature that reflected my experiences as a Chicana. (L. Alamillo, personal anecdote, 2007)

During the past few years, we have heard similar stories from Chicano educators, authors, illustrators, and others about their experiences in school as a bilingual learner placed into settings that neither empowered them nor encouraged them to be proud of their heritage. In the few classrooms that did have literature books those books did not authentically depict the Chicano culture but rather stereotyped it, both in text and in illustrations.

It is because of this lack of authentic bilingual children's books and our own personal experiences that we are committed to promoting equity through the use of literature in the classroom. This article first sets the context by recalling a study conducted by Alamillo (2004) at a California elementary school. That study examined culturally and linguistically responsive pedagogy in the classroom through the use of Chicano children's literature. Both the text and the illustrations found in recent publications and the role they played in the socio-cultural development of children were considered.

The California Context

An analysis of the California context reveals that federal and state educational policy limits the use of bilingual children's literature in the classroom. This lack of inclusion is examined in an elementary classroom in the Bay Area. The focal teacher described here sees a mismatch between what the literature in the prescribed curriculum presents and the cultural and linguistic experiences of the Mexican-descent students in her class.

California public schools are under a tremendous amount of pressure to improve reading and language arts scores. As a result of these pressures, such as the *No Child Left Behind* (NCLB) mandate, schools use scripted reading programs with preselected children's literature. In addition, school-mandated reading programs such as Accelerated Reader[1] have taken the place of authentic forms of children's literature. Because of the lack of alternative forms of children's literature, authentic forms of multicultural children's literature are not commonly used in classrooms.

This situation was noted in Alamillo's 2004 study. It was found that bilingual, Chicano children were not given access to children's literature that connected them to their communities, traditions, and experiences because the teacher was mandated to use the scripted reading program. Specifically, during the 2002-2003 academic year, when the mandated reading program was observed, the focal teacher could not utilize children's books written by Chicano/a writers during reading and language arts time. This teacher expressed concern about not being able to use her selection of bilingual literature, stressing,

> Other books are used during free reading time or when students finish their work. Otherwise, I spend almost two hours per day teaching the program. I have to use the selected literature.

Alamillo (2004) reported that not only did the teacher not have access to authentic forms of bilingual children's literature, but the required literature used in the program did not match the children in the classroom, either culturally nor linguistically.

Alamillo then spent time analyzing the literature used in the mandated reading program over a one-month span. The literature from the program was thoroughly analyzed through a critical lens. This lens allowed Alamillo to investigate how language and culture were represented in the literature. The authors of the literature were investigated with respect to their cultural and language background, connections to the text, and how they portrayed language and culture throughout the theme of the book.

Table 9.1 provides an analysis of the literature in the mandated program. The table was created based on Rudine Sims-Bishop's (1994) criteria for culturally authentic literature. The analysis of the language used in the mandated children's literature revealed that the literature represented Castilian Spanish or a version of Spanish from other Latin American countries. The focal teacher found this mismatch problematic, seeing a disconnect between the Spanish used in the text and the Spanish spoken by her students of Mexican descent.

As shown in the table, the language, racial, and/or ethnic background of the authors and/or illustrators did not match nor represent the Mexican-descent students in the focal classroom. It is important to note here that an author's racial and ethnic background should not be the sole indicator of whether a piece of literature is authentic; however, the racial and ethnic background of the author is a starting point for investigating cultural authenticity.

The majority of the students in this first grade, bilingual classroom were either born in Mexico or were first generation born in the United States. The information revealed in Table 9.1 clearly conflicts with prevailing research on multicultural children's literature since it indicates that an author's language, racial, and ethnic background does matter when children identify and/or relate with a book. These connections are especially important when children of color engage in discussion about a book.

Table 9.1 highlights the limitations of using only pre-selected literature that leaves distinct cultural and linguistic experiences out of the classroom instruction and discussion. What message are we sending Chicano children who are not seeing themselves, their communities, families, experiences, and languages in the text they read in their classrooms? Are we indirectly questioning the validity of their language use, the language use in their homes, and their experiences living in the United States?

Our presentation of these issues at the National Association for Bilingual Education annual conference in 2006 drew interesting feedback from our audience. That audience, comprised mainly of Chicano/a teachers, indicated that they never had the opportunity to read Chicano children's literature in school. Similar to our experiences and those of the authors and illustrators selected in this research, it was not until college that any of us had access to Chicano literature that reflected our language and culture.

Theoretical Background

Children's literature intended for Latinos first appeared in the United States to meet the needs of Spanish language speakers during the late 1960s and early 1970s, but it soon became evident

TABLE 9.1 Mandated Reading Program Children's Literature—First Grade Bilingual Classroom, Books used in Winter 2003

Title	Copyright & Publisher	Author and/or illustrator	Ethnic or cultural heritage of author	Language(s) used
El Amigo Nuevo	1995, Laredo Publishing, US	Maria Puncel & Ulises Wensel	Not Given	Spanish
Gansa Tonta	1992, Fondo de Cultura Economica, Mexico	Ellen Stoll Walsh	Not Given	Spanish
Una Torta de Cumpleanos para Osito	1988, Switzerland	Max Velthuij	Not Given	Translated from English to Spanish by Guillermo Gutierrez
Quiero Un Gato	1989, Ediciones Destino/ Barcelona,Spain	Tony Ross	Not Given	Spanish
El Tesoro Escondido Del Capitan Tifon	1989, Editorial Attontida Buenos Aires, Argentina	Korky Paul & Peter Carter	Not Given	Spanish
La Cama de Plumas de Agata	1996, Santillana, US	Carmen Agra Reedy & Laura Seeley	Not Given	Spanish
El Panuelo de Seda	1993, Mexico	Alma Flor Ada	Cuban	Spanish
Timoteo va a la Escuela	1982, Altea Madrid, Spain	Rose Wells	Not Given	Translated from English into Castilian Spanish
Viva! Una Pinata!	1996, Dutton, US	Elisa Kelvin	Listed as born in Los Angeles	Spanish

that although the literature was in Spanish, it was not representative of the majority of language-minority children in the U.S. While it was typically high quality literature, most of the authors were from Spain and Argentina, thus the form of the Spanish language in which it was written was not appropriate for, nor were the illustrations descriptive of, the children in our U.S. classrooms.

Alamillo (2007) categorizes Chicano children's literature as distinct from Latino children's literature. In order to make the distinction between the two, it is crucial to understand the term Chicano. The term Chicano, grounded in the Chicano Movement of the 1960s, addresses the issues of identity and civil rights. It is a word meant to identify Mexican Americans with their indigenous heritage while at the same time seeking to eliminate racism (Rosales, 1996). So it is fitting that Chicano children's literature today stresses issues of social justice, as did the Chicano movement when it was initiated in order to achieve racial equality in society and higher education.

Therefore, the authors of Chicano literature address topics of social justice, such as immigration, racial discrimination, language prejudice, and other concepts traditionally not found in children's books. This Chicano literature presents issues that call for social action in our society. In addition to addressing issues of social justice, Chicano children's literature presents themes which aim to affirm and validate Chicano experiences in the United States. While these might appear to be similar to issues that other Latinos face, they are unique in the sense that this experience is more connected to the indigenous mother culture.

Since Chicano literature addresses issues of discrimination, it is appropriate to examine the literature in classrooms today in terms of equity. Currently, based on our observations of the literature used in many classrooms, the children's books available in reading programs fail to address either language or cultural diversity. There are some appropriate selections by Chicano authors and illustrators in the anthologies found in classrooms, but the texts and illustrations are edited, condensed, and therefore manipulated to create a false sense of authenticity (Ewing, 2008).

This highlights a matter of equity that is not being addressed. We believe that understanding the distinction between equal education and equity is essential in order to appreciate the importance of using Chicano literature in a culturally and linguistically diverse classroom. Sonia Nieto (2004) differentiates equal education from equity by explaining that equal education means only providing the same resources and opportunities, presented in the same way, for all students.

Similarly, Banks (2007) defines equity in this way:

> *Equity pedagogy* is teaching strategies and classroom environments that help students from diverse racial, ethnic, and cultural groups to attain the knowledge, skills, and attitudes needed to function effectively within and to help create and perpetuate a just, humane, and democratic society. This definition suggests that is not sufficient to help students to learn to read, write, and compute within the dominant canon without questioning its assumptions, paradigms and hegemonic characteristics. (pp. 92–93)

It is important to help students, when they are relating to literature, to become reflective so that they look at all the possibilities while responding to the literature. Furthermore, educators must also consider the skills, talents, and experiences that all students bring to their education (Moll, 2005) as valid starting points for further exploration of how equity is practiced in the classroom through the use of literature. We stress the importance of using culturally responsive children's literature in order to address and assure equity in a multilingual, multicultural classroom.

Using Cultural Knowledge

According to Gay (2000), culturally and linguistically responsive pedagogy involves the use of cultural knowledge, prior experiences, frames of reference, and performance styles of ethnically diverse students to assure that learning encounters are more relevant to and effective for the students. It teaches to and through the strengths of these students. It is culturally validating and affirming. Moll (2004) champions this idea as he identifies these prior experiences as the "funds of knowledge" that students and families possess when encountering new experiences.

This is how we motivate students to become engaged in learning—by empowering them and their families as resources of knowledge that can connect with the educational goals and outcomes of their schools. Banks (2007) has summarized several studies that support the use of culturally responsive pedagogy and concludes that when teachers understood the funds of knowledge their students possess, achievement increases and students are engaged as active learners in their education.

Another key point of culturally responsive pedagogy that Gay (2000) has mentioned is the "frame of reference," which comes from those early or previous experiences that have shaped the students' thoughts and ideas about the world, and specfically the knowledge that they possess of their world. Freire (1983) has called this knowledge, which informs the act of reading based on the frame of reference we each possess, as our way of "reading the world," He believed that the comprehension of a text requires the intersection of text with context.

In this way, students can truly see the author's purpose when juxtaposing it within the reader's frame of reference. By using culturally and linguistically responsive literature in the classroom, teachers are allowing students to experience these books, in both text and illustration, in a manner that allows them to read their world. Flor Ada (2003) states that, "Every child needs to reclaim and revitalize his or her sense of self," and this is what happens when authentic literature is used.

Seeking Authenticity

Authenticity is a term that many times is confused with accuracy. It is not easy for us to view reality from a cultural perspective that differs from our own, and thus we tend to look only at the factual information or at what is familiar to us as readers. However, Mo and Shen (2003) suggest that authenticity is not just accuracy or the avoidance of stereotyping, but that it also involves cultural values and issues and practices that are accepted as norms of the social group (p. 200).

Accuracy is merely reporting a series of facts. But authentic, culturally and linguistically responsive literature goes beyond just knowing about other cultures. In our view it is about authentically depicting one's own reality in children's books, true to one's own identity, reflecting and projecting the reality of humankind through the lens of the reader.

We argue that this type of literature must be looked at in terms of both the text and illustrations, since we are addressing not only literature for young adults but also picture books for children. Galda and Short (1993) agree when they say,

> Since a picture book, by definition, is a book in which both illustrations and printed text are essential to the story, children must be able to 'read' pictures and text to understand the story in its fullest sense. (p. 506)

In seeking to understand stories representing Chicano culture, the notion of insider/outsider perspective comes in to play as well (Fox & Short, 2003). In this article, we frequently mention authors and illustrators who offer insider perspectives on the experiences presented. Authors such as Amada Irma Pérez, Gloria Anzaldúa, and Gary Soto, and illustrators Maya Christina Gonzalez, Simón Silva, and Carmen Lomas Garza, base their children's books on their own personal experiences.

Arenas (2008) stresses:

> The stories that Chicano(a) authors and illustrators tell about their own childhoods, about who they are in this country, in this culture are very similar to our students' lives. As educators using children's books that reflect the Chicano culture of the students in our classrooms we must note that we need to carefully choose books that do this in positive ways. (p. 11)

The authors and illustrators mentioned above offer a unique and authentic perspective on the topics addressed in this article.

Looking at the Text

Chicano children's literature presents themes that represent the heterogeneity within the Chicano community, portraying especially the experiences of living in the United States. As we found from a review of such literature, there are consistent themes in Chicano children's literature, and to explore those themes we will first focus on the language used in the texts.

Initially it is important to note that Chicano writers are presenting authentic portrayals of the language varieties inherent to the Chicano community. For example, in *Chato's Kitchen* (Soto, 1995), Soto portrays a main character, Chorizo, as able to code switch from Spanish to English throughout the story line—"No, de veras, hombres. I'm ok" (p. 4). These authentic depictions of language variety are culturally responsive to language used in Chicano homes (Gay, 2007). The use of literary code switching in Soto's literature validates the bilingualism existing in the homes of Chicano students (Alamillo, 2004).

Literary code switching involves the alternating use of Spanish and English in the text. It is strategic and intentional. Soto grew up in Fresno and refers to his experiences growing up there in his literature, including the language diversity existing in homes. He represents the Chicano experience in Fresno by depicting authentic cultural and language practices in the text of his books. The use of code switching is evident in Soto's work. It is distinct and different from providing direct Spanish translations such as those found in most bilingual children's books.

The use of code switching or Chicano English represents authentic language practices. These hybrid language practices are evident in Chicano children's literature (Gutierrez, Baquedano-Lopez, & Tejeda, 1999). The juxtaposition of English and Spanish is strategic and structured in its use, and can be described as more than code switching. It is a more systematic, strategic, and sense making process among those who share the code (pp. 287–288).

The notion of hybridity is also evident in Chicano children's literature and is found in *Grandma and Me at the Flea/Los Meros, Meros Remateros* by Juan Felipe Herrera (2002):

> I smell toasty hot chocolate and my favorite—scrambled eggs with *nopalitos*, juicy cactus. After breakfast, I help Grandma get ready for the flea market ... I wrap Western pants and shirts into tight *burritos*. Grandma loads the clothes into her van with the sign on the side: *Los Meros, Meros Remateros* Fresno, California. *Vamonos!* I say. (p. 5)

In this passage, Herrera uses Spanish throughout the English text. He made strategic choices in the words he provided in Spanish. Obviously the Spanish use of the words give the passage a certain affect English could not provide.

In *My Diary From Here to There/Mi Diario de Allá Hasta Aquí* (Pérez, 2002) the use of the word *m'ija* is strategic as well:

> Amada *m'ija*, I can see how worried you've been. Don't be scared. Everything will be all right. But how do you know? What will happen to us? I said. He smiled, *M'ija*, I was born in Arizona, in the States. When I was a big kid like you—my *Papá* and *Mamá* moved our family back to Mexico. (p. 11)

The use of the word *m'ija* suggests intense love and affection on the part of the parent. Children can relate to the use of the word *m'ija* by their parents, family members, and teachers who use term of endearment to identify them. There is a direct connection to the home when authors use this word and therefore it validates the home language and culture. The language used in Chicano children's literature represents the linguistic diversity in Chicano homes. Authors who portray this diversity are also portraying authentic language practices.

In the same study by Alamillo (2004), the children expressed connections to the use of hybridity in the text. When asked if they knew someone who spoke like the characters in the book, the majority of the students responded yes, they knew someone who spoke English and Spanish:

TEACHER: *¿Tú conoces a alguien quien habla como los personajes en el libro?* / Do you know someone who speaks like the characters in the book?

STUDENT: *Mi papi.* / My father.

STUDENT: *Mis primos grandes.* / My older cousins.

STUDENT: *Mi amigo Kevin.* / My cousin Kevin.

STUDENT: *Mi abuelita.* / My grandmother.

STUDENT: *Mi hermano.* / My brother. (p. 118)

All of the students interviewed identified someone who was bilingual in their family or used code switching at home. Such literature reflects language as used at home and by various family members. Students identified with the content and the languages presented. Clearly, Chicano children's literature presents authentic portrayals of the Chicano experiences in the United States.

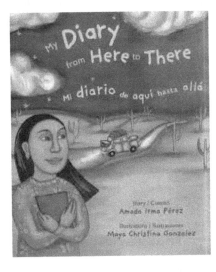

Children are able to associate the languages in the text with the language of the children's book. By identifying someone who code switches at home, the children recognize their own voices as those voices are highlighted in published books by Chicano authors. The authors validate the home language by representing how people actually talk with friends and family.

In reviewing bilingual, Chicano children's books by Juan Felipe Herrera, Gary Soto, Francisco Alarcón, and Gloria Anzaldúa, Alamillo (2004) also found recurring themes throughout the literature. Alamillo began by looking at the language present in the text and then used Barrera and Quiroa (2003) and Sims-Bishop (1994) to identify criteria for looking at authentic children's literature.

Alamillo identified recurring themes such as border crossing, immigration, language, validation, and family relationships in Chicano children's literature. The border crossing theme was distinct from the theme of immigration because the story took place along the border. Anzaldua's (1995) text, *Friends From the Other Side*, takes place along the U.S.-Mexican border and is one example of literature that addresses specific issues unique to the border crossing theme. Chicano children's literature represents experiences in the United States, as contrasted with literature taking place in Mexico. This is significant since many Chicano students may not have prior knowledge of experiences gained from living in Mexico.

In addition to the use of code switching in the text and the culturally relevant themes in the literature, Chicano children's literature also presents illustrations that students can identify with on a personal basis. These culturally relevant themes present images in which Chicano children can see themselves directly. It allows children to identify with the experiences presented and the language used in the text. The literature validates their "funds of knowledge" and directly affirms their unique experiences.

Looking at the Illustrations

The purpose of illustrations in children's picture books is not merely as entertainment but, as Marantz amd Marantz (2000) stress, "But moving beyond the verbal to the visual, we want to look at how the art in picture books may expand children's understanding of others" (p. 13). This is what will initially attract the reader to the book.

So the importance of illustrations, as we look at Chicano children's literature, is for children to be able to view the illustrations as a vehicle to understand not just others, but particularly themselves. It is crucial that time be spent on "reading" the illustrations since they play such an important part in the story being told. The ability to read the images in a book gives meaning to those images (Shulevitz, 1985; Schwarcz & Schwarcz, 1991; Lacy, 1986; Nikolajeva & Scott, 2001; Cope & Kalantzis, 2000; Kress & van Leeuwen, 1996; Unsworth, 2001) and points to the importance of communication via the illustrations of children's books.

Upon examining children's book illustrators, however, we found that very few represent the Chicano way of life we have defined earlier in this article. Rather, most illustrations in books that attempt to depict the Chicano culture, a culture that Gloria Anzaldúa (1987) describes as "borderland cultures," represent the merging of two cultures, forcefully or voluntarily. Such illustrations will not offer the Chicano student anything familiar.

For the purposes of this article, illustrators accurately representing the Chicano culture—George Ancona, Carmen Lomas Garza, Maya Christina Gonzalez, Bobbi Salinas, and Simón Silva—were chosen because they are among a relatively small group of Chicano artists who have had the opportunity to voice their motivation for depicting their culture in children's books.

These are artists and illustrators chosen by publishers to authentically depict the Chicano culture through their renditions of stories told by others about the Chicano experience. These artists look at their work as a way to seek their own identity. As Freire (1970) put it, "Those who authentically commit themselves to the people must re-examine themselves constantly" (p. 61). This re-examination has happened with every book these Chicano artists have illustrated.

We now introduce each of these five illustrators, offering brief descriptions of a few selected books they have illustrated, and describing their views about their work as children's book illustrators.

George Ancona

Children's book illustrator and author-photographer George Ancona, born in Brooklyn, New York, in 1929, describes the process of becoming what he is today as a journey to find himself, his identity, and his roots. To discover what he had *not* learned about his heritage while growing up in the United States, he set out upon a search, and in doing so he realized that there must be many children and young adults with the same questions he had about his home culture.

As he began work on his books, *Pablo Remembers: The Fiesta Day of The Dead* (1993), *Mayeros: A Yucatec Maya Family* (1997), and *The Piñata Maker/El Piñatero* (1994), Ancona was discovering his own identity. He describes this experience in the following words:

> I think this is what I have to share, the joy of discovery. What has happened is that my life really goes into those books, whether it is a photograph or a sketch, but first it is a human experience—my experience relating to people that I'm meeting—that comes first. (personal communication, 2003)

As a Chicano artist, Ancona has been able to depict the culture more authentically now than he could before he had a point of reference to guide him. *Barrio: Jose's Neighborhood* (1998) is about a young boy's neighborhood in the Mission District of San Francisco and his daily experience of being bilingual and bicultural in a community that embraces multiculturalism. *Harvest* (2001) is about the contributions of immigrant families to the food industry and their retention of the home culture while participating in the majority culture. *Fiesta USA* (1995) depicts several cultural celebrations and how they have been adapted and incorporated into neighborhoods in the United States. These are books that authentically depict reality for Chicano children living in the U.S. today.

Ancona's goal of sharing his journey and his discoveries with children reaffirms what Marantz and Marantz (2000) meant when they said, "When children enjoy books because they relate to characters, identify with situations, and understand personalities or behavior, they come to the realization that there are others like themselves." In essence, this is what drove Ancona towards photography. In recoding the reality of his people, he found his own reality.

Carmen Lomas Garza

One of the most original Chicano artists is Carmen Lomas Garza. During the 1950s and 1960s while living and attending school in Texas, Lomas Garza was humiliated and excluded because she spoke Spanish and thus suffered through prejudice and discrimination. By the time she had completed high school she said, "I was confused, depressed, introverted, and quite angry" (Garza, 1994, p. 12). Even so, she continued her education at the university where her artwork was criticized for being, "too political, too primitive, and not universal" (Day, 2003, p. 180).

The Chicano movement of the 1960s helped Lomas Garza find her voice and strength as a Chicana and as an artist. It helped her have pride in her heritage and traditions and she finally felt liberated to be able to paint about her daily life with family and friends. She was one of the first published illustrators to depict the Chicano way of life in her paintings—not only to validate that reality for Chicano children and adults but also to provide a glimpse into the Chicano reality through her detail-rich illustrations.

Lomas Garza's illustrations depicted elements of the Chicano culture that previously had never been addressed in children's books, such as folk healing, miracles, and religious icons and practices. Her books, *Family Pictures/Cuadros de familia* (1990) and *In My Family/En Mi Familia* (1996), represent Lomas Garza's life growing up in the 1950s, and *Magic Windows/Ventanas Mágicas* (1999) celebrates the art of cut paper or *papel picado,* depicting common themes. All of these books portray the Chicano way of life.

As Lomas Garza says,

> We should not fear other cultures, we should embrace them, that's why my art shows the beauty of my people. My art is not for decor. My art is there to touch the soul. (Lomas Garza, 1991)

Maya Christina Gonzalez

Illustrator Maya Christina Gonzalez was surprised at not seeing illustrations that seemed familiar in books she found in her classrooms and in the library when she was growing up. She said,

> As a child I would go looking for my face in my coloring books, in my storybooks, but I never found my round, Chicana face, my long dark hair. So I would go to that blank page in the back or the front of these books and draw my own big face right in where it belonged. (Gonzalez, personal communication, 2000)

Gonzalez has illustrated several books by Chicano authors such as Francisco Alarcón, including his series of four bilingual poetry books about his family and personal experiences, ranging in themes from migrant workers to his joy of discovery in the back yard in *Laughing Tomatoes and Other Spring Poems/Jitomates Risueños y Otros Poemas de Primavera* (1997), *From the Bellybutton of the Moon and Other Summer Poems/Del Ombligo de la Luna y Otros Poemas de Verano* (1997), *Angels Ride Bikes and Other Fall Poems/Los Ángeles Andan en Bicicleta y Otros Poemas Del Otoño* (1998), and *Iguanas in the Snow and Other Winter Poems/Iguanas en la Nieve y Otros Poemas Del Invierno* (2000).

Gonzalez is also the illustrator for Gloria Anzaldúa in *Prietita and La Llorona* (1994), a gentler version of the traditional Mexican folktale depicting La Llorona as a healer; and for Amada Irma Pérez in her three books based on her family memories entitled, *My Very Own Room/Mi Propio Cuartito* (2000) about a little girl who finally gets her own room away from her five little brothers, *My Diary From Here to There/Mi Diario de Aquí Hasta Allá* (2002) tracing the author's journey from Mexico to California, and *Nana's Big Surprise/Nana, ¡Qué Sorpresa!* (2007) about how a grandmother's family helps her overcome grief in a surprising way.

Gonzalez has captured the Chicano spirit in her illustrations by including details that are part of the culture together with her bright palette of colors and lots of big, round, Chicano faces. She also authored her own book about finding color all around her during her childhood in the book, *My Colors, My World/Mis Colores, Mi Mundo*, (2007). She comments,

> We belong everywhere. Our face is important. It is a mark of who we are and where we come from.

Bobbi Salinas

As a Chicana author and illustrator, Bobbi Salinas is committed to encouraging, motivating, and teaching her readers about the possibilities in life given the opportunity. Her books address the topic of equity through storytelling, in both the text and the illustrations. In her book, *The Three Pigs/Los Tres Credos: Nacho, Tito, and Miguel* (1998), Salinas retells the traditional tale while adding some stereotypical cultural details. Then she introduces Miguel, the third little pig. She portrays him as an intellectual working on his computer with an extensive library of multicultural books.

Salinas also wrote and illustrated *Cinderella Latina/La Cenicienta Latina* (2002) in which she sets the fairy tale in the present day Southwest, depicting "Serena" as a young woman who realizes that self-respect, courage, and humor are the keys to making your dreams come true.

As Salinas (1998) states,

> I believe that when educating young people, we must provide them with truth and experiences that help them develop their critical minds. Through clear thinking and feeling, they will have the skills to grow to be literate, to have lives full of options, to be empowered, and to be contributing members of society. (p. 32)

This is her purpose in writing books for and about Chicanos—to empower them to have lives full of options.

Simón Silva

Lastly, artist Simón Silva, who grew up in a migrant farm worker family in the fields of Southern California from the age of eight, discloses humbly,

> I grew up with a certain amount of shame about who I was, and it wasn't until I came to understand and appreciate my culture that I was able to find true purpose for myself and my art. (Silva, 1997)

This did not occur until he attended college and began to learn about his home culture, a culture he was just beginning to embrace.

The illustrations he created for books such as *Gathering The Sun: An Alphabet in Spanish and English* by Alma Flor Ada (1997), a series of poems honoring the people that work in the fields, and *La Mariposa* by Jiménez (1998) about the author's experiences growing up as a migrant farm worker in the Central Valley and coast of California, brought him immediate attention as a

Chicano artist. Having the opportunity to illustrate these books also enabled him to re-discover pride in his own background. Silva states,

> My images are simplistic, powerful, beautiful, and about the Chicano culture … I have used these images—scenes I used to be ashamed of—to empower myself and other Chicanos. (As cited in Dorantes, 2003)

Self-Discovery of Identity

The five artists discussed above are only a few of those who authentically illustrate Chicano children's books. For them, illustration is not only an opportunity to visually portray the author's text, but it is one of self-discovery of their own identity and place in the world.

In other words,

> The illustrators have the same vision, the same hope for the children reading their books—that Latino children see themselves in a positive way so it will make a difference in their lives and the lives of others. (Arenas, 2004, p. 25)

Recommendations

Highlighted here are two distinct ways at looking at Chicano children's literature. Through Alamillo's research we looked at the written text of the literature. The language used in the text should represent the children culturally and linguistically. Based on a study done at a California elementary school, Alamillo (2004) found that the literature used in the mandated Spanish reading program did not represent the Mexican-descent students either culturally or linguistically. Instead, the literature being used portrayed an experience unfamiliar to the children in the classroom.

Through Arenas' studies we then described the importance of also looking at the illustrations in literature. Examining the illustrator's perspectives, Arenas (2004) highlights Chicano illustrators' intentions when illustrating Chicano children's literature and identifies illustrators who intentionally illustrated authentic portrayals of Chicano/Latino characters.

As a result of collaborating in this research on text and illustrations, we have developed qualifying elements to determine the suitability of bilingual children's literature. By reviewing exemplary Chicano children's literature, we have identified examples of those elements in Table 9.2.

The elements used to qualify the selections as exemplary Chicano literature include:

1. *Bilingual Text*—The story is written in English on one page and Spanish on the facing page or English on the top half of the page and Spanish on the bottom half of the page.
2. *Use of Authentic Language*—The language used includes code-switching with Spanish words within the English text, sometimes defining the Spanish word within the English text and other times standing alone.

TABLE 9.2 A Partial Selection of Exemplary Chicano Children's Books with Qualifying Elements

Title	Copyright Date	Author	Illustrator	Qualifying Elements
Gathering the Sun: An Alphabet in Spanish and English	1997	Alma Flor Ada	Simón Silva	• Bilingual book, English text/Spanish text • Based on elements in the lives of migrant farmworkers • Colorful illustrations represent the pride and beauty of the people who work the fields • Chicano perspective
From the Bellybutton of the Moon and other Summer Poems/Del ombigo de la luna y otros poemas de verano	1998	Francisco X. Alarcón	Maya Christina Gonzalez	• Bilingual book, English text/Spanish text • Book three in a series of four seasonal books of poems • Based on Alarcón's memories growing up in southern California • Poems address issues relevant to the Chicano culture and depicts the blending of the traditional culture with the new • Colorful illustrations depict the warmth and joy of Chicano families and children • Chicano perspective
Barrio: Jose's Neighborhood	1998	George Ancona	George Ancona	• Follows the life of a young Chicano living in San Francisco, CA • Uses authentic language with a glossary at the end of the book • Depicts a blending of cultures in school, neighborhood, and cultural events • Photographs represent the daily lives of people and events in the neighborhood • Chicano perspective

(Continued)

TABLE 9.2 *(Continued)*

Title	Copyright Date	Author	Illustrator	Qualifying Elements
Prietita and the Ghost Woman/ Prietita y La Llorona	1995	Gloria Anzaldúa	Maya Christina Gonzalez	• Bilingual book, English text/Spanish text • Uses authentic language • Addresses traditional cultural elements of healing/curanderismo and how it is passed on through generations • Variation of the traditional folktale and depicts La Llorona as a powerful woman spirit • Warm illustrations authentically represent the people and land of the southwest • Chicana perspective
Family Pictures/ Cuadros de Familia	1990	Carmen Lomas Garza	Carmen Lomas Garza	• Bilingual book, English text/Spanish text • Paintings are based on Lomas Garza's memories growing up as a Chicana in Texas depicting the daily life, beliefs, & celebrations • Text is a description of paintings • Chicana perspective
My Colors, My World/Mis colores, mi mundo	2007	Maya Christina Gonzalez	Maya Christina Gonzalez	• Bilingual book, English text/Spanish text • Based on Gonzalez's memories growing up in the desert in California • Text and illustrations depict a search for acceptance and beauty in a child's world • Chicana perspective
Grandma and Me at the Flea/ Los meros meros remateros	2002	Juan Felipe Hererra	Anita DeLucio-Brock	• Bilingual book, English text/Spanish text • Based on Hererra's memories growing up in central California • Uses authentic language • Addresses issues of Chicano culture and value of community • Illustrations authentically represent the "flea market" with goods and people • Chicano perspective

Title	Copyright Date	Author	Illustrator	Qualifying Elements
La Mariposa	1998	Francisco Jiménez	Simón Silva	• Based on Jiménez's memories growing up in a migrant family • Uses authentic language • Depicts a search for identity and acceptance in a new culture while retaining the native culture • Illustrations authentically depict the farmworkers and setting of story • Chicano perspective
My Diary From Here to There/Mi Diario de Aquí Hasta Allá	2002	Amada Irma Pérez	Maya Christina Gonzalez	• Bilingual book, English text/Spanish text • Based on Pérez's memories growing up as a young girl immigrating to the United States • Addresses issues of immigration, leaving a familiar place and relocating to a new country • Illustrations authentically and beautifully represent the people in the story • Chicana perspective
Nana's Big Surprise/Nana, ¡Qué Sorpresa!	2007	Amada Irma Pérez	Maya Christina Gonzalez	• Bilingual book, English text/Spanish text • Addresses issues of death, the grieving process, and healing through a caring family • Illustrations colorfully represent the hope for joy throughout the book, authentically depicting the people and events • Chicana perspective

3. *Authentic Cultural Representations through Text*—The text addresses themes of the Chicano culture in realistic and relevant ways.
4. *Authentic Cultural Representations through Illustrations*—The illustrations use images that are representative of the Chicano culture through the use of visual elements such as color, style, and media.
5. *Insider Perspective*—The author or illustrator portrays the Chicano culture as a reflection of their own perspectives as Chicanos(as).

These elements can be used to critique and select literature, analyze cultural authenticity, and avoid stereotypes. The two of us argue that readers must take into consideration both the text and illustrations when choosing appropriate literature for children. These considerations are crucial when selecting literature for children, since children are heavily influenced by what they read and see.

In addition, authentic portrayals of the Chicano community affirm and validate existing experiences in that community. Chicano children are affirmed when they see true images of their community and read authentic stories of their families. The utilization of such books will help children develop linguistically, cognitively, and academically, and can potentially be used to build awareness between Mexican born children and their U.S. born Mexican peers. The literature can break down stereotypes in the classroom and can be used to build acceptance for all groups.

The literature we describe and advocate is by no means only for Chicano children. Chicano children's literature is multicultural and it should serve as American literature for all students, depicting the lives of Mexican-descent children living in the United States.

Conclusion

As we have shared in our personal anecdotes, the effort to maintain our native language and culture was a conscious decision made by our families and by us as individuals. Our schooling contributed little to this effort. However, in light of the current cultural context in California, we believe that now, more than ever, it is crucial that literature used in the classroom represent the children in the classroom—for two primary reasons.

First, appropriately-selected literature will validate and empower Chicano children by representing them, specifically, as a unique language and cultural group, within the over-arching category of "Latino" students. Chicano children's literature is one tool to begin this process of validation.

Second, the literature used as part of the curriculum should authentically depict the Chicano experience to avoid stereotyping by children outside that culture. Alamillo (2005) sums up the importance of recognizing and learning about the Chicano culture when she says,

> In this case, being Chicano/a is not just a label. It is an identity, an experience.
> It links one to social, political and historical movements. One does not say they

are Chicano/as without thinking of what comes with it: the language, the culture, community and family. It is a way of living. (p. 14)

In a classroom of bilingual, Chicano students, teachers must affirm existing cultural and language practices by using tools such as authentic Chicano children's literature. If appropriately selected and used, this literature will promote equity, drawing upon the funds of knowledge students bring to school and will provide that pathway by which Chicano children will be able to search and authenticate their own identity.

When schools begin to focus on culturally responsive pedagogy that includes validating the students' languages and cultures, then issues of inequity will begin to disappear. Teachers must find a way to go beyond what is mandated and take it one step further by creating a culturally responsive curriculum, which includes using appropriate literature, to address issues of social justice and action.

James Banks describes this process as "to know, to care, and to act" (personal communication, October 11, 2007). Schools must first allow students to care and know about their own issues and then bridge connections to other marginalized communities. The end result is to care enough about all issues and all communities, in order to see the connections and make changes that will be equitable for all children. Chicano children's literature can serve as an important tool in this process. It is not enough to simply use Chicano children's books. We must strive to use authentic literature in a way that will promote equity in the classroom.

Note

1 Accelerated Reader is a guided reading intervention program that promotes independent reading practice, manages student performance by providing students and teachers feedback from quizzes based on books the students read, and closely involves teachers with student reading of text. Only two studies have been conducted on the effectiveness of this program and it was found that Accelerated Reader had no discernible effects on reading fluency, mixed effects on comprehension, and potentially positive effects on general reading achievement.

References

Ada, A. F. (1997). *A magical encounter: Latino children's literature in the classroom.* (2nd ed.). Boston: Pearson Education.

Ada, A. F. (2003). *Gathering the sun: An alphabet in Spanish and English.* New York: Lothrop, Lee & Shepard Books.

Alamillo, L. (2004). Chicano children's student's responses to bilingual children's literature. Unpublished doctoral dissertation, University of California, Berkeley.

Alamillo, L. (2007). Selecting Chicano children's literature in a bilingual classroom: Investigating issues of cultural authenticity and avoiding stereotypes. *Journal of the Association of Mexican American Educators*, Fall.

Alarcón, F. X. (1997). *Laughing tomatoes and other spring poems/Jitomates risueños y otros poemas de primavera*. San Francisco: Children's Book Press.

Alarcón, F. X. (1998). *From the bellybutton of the moon and other summer poems/Del ombligo de la luna y otros poemas de verano*. San Francisco: Children's Book Press.

Alarcón, F. X. (1999). *Angels ride bikes and other fall poems/Los ángeles andan en bicicleta y otros poemas del otoño*. San Francisco: Children's Book Press.

Alarcón, F. X. (2000). *Iguanas in the snow and other winter poems/Iguanas en la nieve y otros poemas del invierno*. San Francisco: Children's Book Press.

Ancona, G. (1993). *Pablo remembers: The fiesta of the Day of the Dead*. New York: Lothrop, Lee & Shepard Books.

Ancona, G. (1994). *The piñata maker/El piñatero*. San Diego, CA: Harcourt Brace & Company.

Ancona, G. (1995). *Fiesta USA*. New York: Lodestar Books.

Ancona, G. (1997). *Mayeros: A Yucatec Maya family*. New York: Lothrop, Lee & Shepard Books.

Ancona, G. (1998). *Barrio: Jose's neighborhood*. San Diego, CA: Harcourt Brace & Company.

Ancona, G. (2001). *Harvest*. Tarrytown, NY: Marshall Cavendish.

Anzaldúa, G. (1987). *Borderlands/La frontera: The new Mestiza*. San Francisco: Aunt Lute Books.

Anzaldúa, G. (1995). *Friends from the other side*. San Francisco: Children's Book Press.

Anzaldúa, G. (1996). *Prietita and the Ghost Woman*. San Francisco: Children's Book Press.

Arenas, R. (2004). Reflections of the spirit: Voices of children's book illustrators of Mexican descent—A participatory study with George Ancona and Felipe Dávalos. Unpublished doctoral dissertation, University of San Francisco.

Arenas, R. (2008). Telling our stories—using Chicano literature for children and young adults as a means of searching for identity and promoting cultural awareness and self-worth. *Journal of the Association of Mexican American Educators*, Fall.

Banks, J. (2007). *Educating citizens in a multicultural society* (2nd ed.). New York: Teachers College Press.

Baquedano-Lopez, P., Alvarez, H., & Gutierrez, K. (2001). Literacy as hybridity: Moving beyond bilingualism in urban classrooms. In J. J. Halcon & M. L. Reyes (Eds.), *The best for our children*. New York: Teachers College Press.

Barrera, R., & Quiroa, R. E. (2003). The use of Spanish in Latino children's literature in English: What makes for cultural authenticity? In D. L. Fox & K. G. Short (Eds.), *Stories matter: The complexity of cultural authenticity in children's literature*. Urbana, IL: The National Council of Teachers of English.

Day, F. A. (1997). *Latina and Latino voices in literature: For children and teenagers*. Portsmouth, NH: Heinemann.

Dorantes, K. (2003). *The art of Simón Silva: A biography*. [Electronic version]. Retreived on June 19, 2004 from http://www.simonsilva.com/indexf.html.

Ewing, T. (2008). Original picturebooks and Houghton Mifflin anthologies: A comparative analysis. Unpublished master's thesis, California State University, Fresno.

Fox, D. L., & Short, K. G. (Eds.). (2003). *Stories matter: The complexity of cultural authenticity in children's literature*. Urbana, IL: The National Council of Teachers of English.

Freire, P. (1970). *Pedagogy of the oppressed*. New York: Continuum.

Freire, P. (1983). The importance of the act of reading. *Journal of Education, 165*, 5–11.

Galda, L., & Short, K. G. (1993). Visual literacy: Exploring art and illustration in children's books. *The Reading Teacher, 46*(6), 506–516.

Garza, C. L. (1990). *Family pictures/Cuadros de familia*. San Francisco: Children's Book Press.

Garza, C. L. (1994). *A piece of my heart/Pedacito de mi corazón*. New York: New Press.

Garza, C. L. (1996). *In my family/En mi familia*. San Francisco: Children's Book Press.

Garza, C. L. (1999). *Magic windows/Ventanas mágicas*. San Francisco: Children's Book Press.

Gay, G. (2000). *Culturally responsive teaching*. New York: Teachers College Press.

Gonzalez, M. C. (2007). *My colors, my world/Mis colores, mi mundo*. San Francisco: Children's Book Press.

Gutierrez, K., Baquedano-Lopez, P., & Tejeda, C. (1999). Rethinking diversity: Hybridity of hybrid language practices in the third space. *Mind, Culture and Activity: An International Journal, 6*(4), 286–303.

Herrera, J. F. (2002). *Grandma and me at the flea/Los meros, meros remateros*. San Francisco, CA: Children's Book Press.

Jiménez, F. (1998). *La mariposa*. Boston: Houghton Mifflin Company.

Kress, G. R., & van Leeuwen, T. (1996). *Reading images: The grammar of visual design*. New York: Routledge.

Lacy, L. E. (1986). *Art and design in children's picture books*. Chicago: American Library Association.

Marantz, S., & Marantz, K. (2000). Picture books peek behind cultural curtains. *Book Links, 9*(3), 13–18.

McLaughlin, M., & DeVoogd, G. L. (2004). *Critical literacy: Enhancing students' comprehension of text*. New York: Scholastic.

Mo, W., & Shen, W. (2003). Accuracy is not enough: The role of cultural values in the authenticity of picture books. In D. L. Fox & K. G. Short (Eds.), *Stories matter: The complexity of cultural authenticity in children's literature*. Urbana, IL: The National Council of Teachers of English.

Moll, L. (2005). *Funds of knowledge*. Mahwah, NJ: Lawrence Erlbaum Associates.

Nieto, Sonia (2004). *Affirming diversity: The sociopolitical context of multicultural education* (4th ed.). Boston: Pearson Education

Nikolajeva, M., & Scott, C. (2000). The dynamics of picturebook communication. *Children's Literature in Education, 31*(4), 225–239.

Pérez, A. I. (2000). *My very own room/Mi propio cuartito*. San Francisco: Children's Book Press.

Perez, A. I. (2002). *My diary from there to here/Mi diario de allá hasta aquí*. San Francisco: Children's Book Press.

Pérez, A. I. (2007). *Nana's big surprise/Nana, ¡Qué sorpresa!* San Francisco: Children's Book Press.

Rosales, F. A. (1996). *Chicano! The history of the Mexican American civil rights movement*. Houston, TX: Arte Público Press.

Salinas, B. (1998). *The three pigs: Los tres credos—Nacho, Tito and Miguel*. Oakland, CA: Piñata Publications.

Salinas, B. (2002). *Cinderella Latina/La cenicienta Latina*. Oakland, CA: Piñata Publications.

Schwarcz, J. H., & Schwarcz, C. (1991). *The picture book comes of age: Looking at childhood through the art of illustration*. Chicago: American Library Association.

Shulevitz, U. (1985). *Writing with pictures: How to write and illustrate children's books*. New York: Watson-Guptill Publications.

Silva, S. (1997). *Small town browny: Cosecha de la vida*. San Bernardino, CA: Arte Cachanilla.

Sims-Bishop, R., & Cai, M. (1994). Multicultural literature for children: Towards a clarification of the concept. In A. Dyson, & C. Genishi (Eds.), *The need for story: Cultural diversity in the classroom and community*. Urbana, IL: The National Council of Teachers of English.

Unsworth, L. (2001). *Teaching multiliteracies across the curriculum: Changing contexts of text and image in classroom practice*. Philadelphia, PA: Open University Press.

Discussion Questions

1. In your own words, define prejudice, racism, and stereotypes.
2. How do stereotypes and prejudice evolve, and how do they impact all cultures?
3. Think about your own culture. What are some of the explicit and implicit elements of your own culture(s)?
4. In your opinion, what does considering cultural identities and differences mean for teaching young children in school?

Activity

Talk with a partner about the possible consequences of learning when teachers do not acknowledge cultural diversity or sufficiently attend to students' cultures.

UNIT III

DIVERSITY AND EXCEPTIONAL CHILDREN

Training Teachers to Promote Pretend Play in Young Children With Disabilities

Erin E. Barton and Mark Wolery

Children with disabilities engage in less object play than children without disabilities (Blasco, Bailey, & Burchinal, 1993); children with autism display fewer play behaviors and less variety in their play with objects (e.g., Jarrold, Boucher, & Smith, 1996; Ungerer & Sigman, 1981). Object play, however, is important for young children with disabilities for a variety of reasons. Object play sets the occasion for social interactions and communication with peers (McConnell, 2002) and provides a context for implementing instruction (Sandall, Hemmeter, Smith, & McLean, 2005), such as activity-based interventions (Pretti-Frontczak & Bricker, 2004), embedded learning opportunities (Sandall & Schwartz, 2002), and response prompting procedures (Wolery, 2001). Also, play with objects may increase engagement in inclusive settings (Lieber, 1993; Morrison, Sainato, Benchaaban, & Endo, 2002) resulting in higher sociometric ratings by peers without disabilities (Strain, 1985).

With typically developing children, object play can take many forms and frequently involves using objects in nonliteral ways. Nonliteral behaviors involve pretense, and play taxonomies refer to these behaviors as a distinct category. However, there are major inconsistencies in the name and response definition of these behaviors across taxonomies. For example, nonliteral behaviors were referred to as pretend play, symbolic play, functional play, or object play. To be precise and consistent, the term *pretense* is used here to refer to only and all nonliteral play behaviors.

In a number of studies (e.g., DiCarlo & Reid, 2004; Jarrold et al., 1996) children with disabilities were taught to engage in pretense behaviors using adult prompts. A review of the literature identified 16 intervention studies on teaching pretend play to children with disabilities (Barton & Wolery, 2008). Five major weaknesses were identified. First, pretense behaviors were measured inconsistently across studies. For example, Lifter, Sulzer-Azaroff, Anderson, & Cowdery (1993) measured only functional play with pretense and denoted assigning absent attributes as pretend play. DiCarlo and Reid did not define the target behaviors with replicable precision (i.e., "a single step action that appeared to imitate a real life situation involving objects that corresponded to the toys used in the action", p. 199). They included a variety of examples, but did not include any non-examples. It is difficult to discern which behaviors were *not included* as pretend play behaviors. Nonliteral play with dolls or with miniature objects was defined as pretend, symbolic, or functional play, depending on the report. For example, walking the doll (Kim, Lombardino, Rothman, & Vinson, 1989), using a banana as a phone (Sherrat, 2002), talking into a miniature phone (DiCarlo & Reid, 2004), bringing an empty cup to mouth (Kasari, Freeman, & Parapella, 2006) were measured as pretend play in the respective studies.

Second, only 3 of 16 studies removed all prompts from the measurement context (Kasari et al., 2006; MacDonald, Clark, Garrigan, & Vangala, 2005; Sherrat, 2002). The use of prompts during measurement limits conclusions about change in pretense behaviors. Behavior cannot be considered acquired, unless it is performed without prompts (i.e., transfer of stimulus control has occurred from the prompts to the toys or objects).

Third, limited measurement of maintenance and generalization of children's pretense behaviors occurred in sessions without adult prompting. For example, 4 of 16 play intervention studies measured generalization. However, only 2 specifically programmed for generalization (Lifter, Ellis, Cannon, & Anderson, 2005; Lifter et al., 1993) and none removed prompts from the generalization sessions. For pretense behaviors to count as generalized pretend play, the behaviors must occur in novel situations in which prompts are not used.

Fourth, in most studies, research staff, rather than classroom teachers, applied the interventions (Barton & Wolery, 2008). Further, only two studies reported the interventionist experience and training. This limits the generality of the pretend play studies.

Fifth, almost no studies measured the fidelity of adults' prompting, including whether the prompts were actually removed. Three of 16 play intervention reports described procedural fidelity (Kasari et al., 2006; Stahmer, 1995; Thorp, Stahmer, & Schreibman, 1995). However, only Kasari et al. met basic standards for procedural fidelity.

A frequently used procedure in this literature was the system of least prompts (Barton & Wolery, 2008). The system of least prompts has been implemented with fidelity in direct instructional arrangements (Doyle, Wolery, Ault, & Gast, 1988) and in play contexts to promote communicative exchanges in young children (Filla, Wolery, & Anthony, 1999). Thus, it was selected for this study. Effective strategies for training teachers to use new interventions include (a) short training sessions with brief procedural manuals (Filla et al., 1999), (b) guided practice and rehearsal (Lifter et al., 2005), (c) video examples (Moore & Fisher, 2007), and (d) verbal and written performance feedback (e.g., Casey & McWilliam, 2008). These components were used to train the teachers to implement the system of least prompts in this study.

This study addresses the methodological weaknesses noted earlier in the literature on teaching children with disabilities to use pretense behaviors. Specifically, children's pretense behaviors were measured and taught using a taxonomy developed from the intervention and assessment literature on pretend play (Barton & Wolery, 2008). Maintenance was measured periodically across the study in probe sessions with the teacher but without prompts. Generalization was measured in two ways: (a) with an adult who was not the child's teacher and who did not use prompts (generalization across adults), and (b) with an untrained set of toys and an adult who was not the child's teacher and did not use prompts (generalization across toys and adults). Classroom teachers were the instructors, rather than research staff, and procedural fidelity data were collected on the teachers' use of the intervention package.

Method

Participants

Teacher Participants
Four female teachers from a university-based inclusive preschool participated. Inclusion criteria for the teachers were (a) minimum of 1 year of classroom experience, (b) no previous instruction on promoting pretense behaviors, and (c) study-eligible children enrolled in their classroom. Each teacher was assigned to a child participant in her classroom. Darcy was a 28-year-old lead teacher with a Bachelors degree in Speech Pathology. She had 6 years of paid experience with children. Amy was a 27-year-old lead teacher with a Master's degree in School Psychology. She had 3 years of paid experience with children. Lucy was a 48-year-old co-teacher in the classroom with Amy. She held a high school diploma with 2 years of college and had 24 years of paid experience with children. Beth was a 24-year-old co-teacher with a Master's degree in Special Education and had 3 years of paid experience with children.

Child Participants
Four preschoolers with disabilities were recruited from the three classrooms of consented teachers. Inclusion criteria for the child participants were (a) a diagnosed disability based on school records; (b) age less than 60 months; (c) minimum mental age of 18 months as measured by the Mullen Scales of Early Learning (MSEL; Mullen, 1995), because children without disabilities begin to engage in pretend play behaviors at about 18 to 24 months (Belsky & Most, 1981; Fein, 1981); (d) consistent school attendance (80% for previous month based on teacher report); (e) ability to participate in a play activity with an adult for 8 min; and (f) less than eight different unprompted play behaviors and no unprompted symbolic behaviors during an adapted version of the Structured Play Assessment (SPA; Ungerer & Sigman, 1981). The last two criteria were measured in a 10-min videotaped play assessment. Table 10.1 shows this data on the children.

TABLE 10.1   Demographic and Assessment Data for Child Participants

Child	Gender	Chrono-logical Age in Months	Mental Age in Months[a]	Disability	Pretest: Structured Play Assessment[b]		Posttest: Structured Play Assessment[b]	
					# Different Unprmpted FPP	# Different Un-prompted Symbolic Behaviors	# Different Un-prompted FPP	# Different Un-prompted Symbolic Behaviors
Daniel	M	43	36	Language delay	2	0	3	18
Anna	F	43	23	Autism	0	0	15	2
Liz	F	50	27	Develop-mental delay	0	0	16	12
Brain	M	30	18	Autism	0	0	Not assessed	Not assessed

Note. FPP = Functional play with pretense.

[a]Mullen Scales of Early Learning. [b]Structured Play Assessment was adapted for this study based on Ungerer & Sigman (1981).

Daniel was a 43-month-old European American male and fraternal twin of Anna. Darcy was his teacher. Daniel had a mental ace of 36 months on the MSEL and was the highest functioning of the four children. He regularly used three- to five-word phrases to express wants and needs and to comment and narrate his play. He received speech and language therapy (SET) from the local school district. He infrequently engaged in social interactions with peers or adults. His teacher described his object play as rigid, repetitive, and restricted to themes involving movie cartoon toys.

Anna was a 43-month-old European American female (twin sister of Daniel) who received a diagnosis of autism at 24 months. Amy was her teacher. Anna had a mental age of 23 months and received special education, SLT, and occupational therapy (OT) from the local school district. She did not initiate conversations, but she was verbally imitative and repeated three- to four-word statements. She did not initiate interactions with peers unless prompted by an adult. Anna rarely played with toys without adult prompting and often was alone in the book or music areas of the classroom turning the pages of books or playing musical instruments.

Liz was a 50-month-old European American female diagnosed with developmental delays. Lucy was her teacher. Liz had a mental age of 27 months and received SLT and OT from the local school district. She was verbal, but often used gestures, signs, and one-word utterances to request preferred items; she rarely initiated conversations or interactions with adults or peers. The majority of Liz's social interactions were responses to adult behaviors. Liz participated in a feeding program each morning during the study. She displayed a few rigid play behaviors, which emulated her feeding program (using a spoon to scrape the inside of a bowl). She rarely elaborated on this play without adult prompting. Liz rarely played independently with toys in the classroom.

Brian was a 30-month-old African American male with a diagnosis of autism. Beth was his teacher. Brian had a mental age of 18 months and received SLT from a local early intervention provider. He exhibited echolalia and unintelligible speech, which he used to request objects and attention from adults. Brian often used vocalizations and gestures to request adult attention or to be picked up. He rarely initiated interactions with peers, except when attempting to retrieve a preferred object. He often ignored peers' initiations. Brian displayed a few rigid and brief play sequences with the housekeeping toys, which replicated mealtime activities (feeding and cleaning). Brian spent the majority of his time during free play at the sensory table (e.g., shaving cream, Jell-O) or rolling vehicles back and forth. Brians caregiver abruptly removed him from school before the study ended.

Settings

The initial teacher training session occurred in the conference room at the school. Additional training sessions were in individual teachers' classrooms. The adapted SPA sessions occurred in a school therapy room. All experimental sessions for children were conducted in each child's classroom. During these sessions, other adults and children participated in the typical classroom routines and activities.

Materials

Five toy sets were used (three for instruction, one for generalization, and one for the adapted SPA) and are shown in Table 10.2. Each set was used with each teacher–child dyad. The toy sets were (a) selected to provide children with opportunities to use pretense behaviors, (b) based on toys available in preschool classrooms, and (c) similar to toys in previous pretend play studies (Lifter et al., 1993; Thorp et al., 1995). Although each toy set contained objects with similar functions (e.g., dolls, spoons), all objects were markedly different in form (e.g., shape, size, color) across toy sets.

Response Definitions and Measurement

Teacher Behaviors

The intervention package included a system of least prompts, contingent imitation, and a system for reinforcement for all children. However, the specific teacher behaviors varied based on the child's response patterns. Seven teacher behaviors were measured in each experimental session for all teachers. *Contingent imitation* was the teacher doing the same behavior (motor or vocal) as the child. A *correct model prompt* was the teacher doing a pretense behavior with a toy and verbally describing the action at least 12 s but not more than 20 s after a previous prompt or pretense behavior. A *model prompt error* was the teacher failing to provide a model within 20 s of the last child pretense behavior, modeling a nonpretense behavior, or providing a correct model after 20 s of the last child pretense behavior. A *correct physical prompt* was the teacher using her hands to guide the child's hands through a pretense behavior within 5 s

TABLE 10.2   Toys by Type of Toy Set

| Instructional Toy Sets | | | Generalization | |
Toy Set 1	Toy Set 2	Toy Set 3	Toy Set	SPA Toy Set
2 baby dolls	doll house	2 adult figures	2 baby dolls	2 baby dolls
2 bottles	adult male figure	2 sponges	2 cloths	doll house
2 sippy cups	adult female figure	4 plates	2 bowls	2 plates
2 sponges	baby figure	4 bowls	2 cups	2 cups
2 plates	cat figure	2 teaspoons	2 sponges	2 sippy cups
2 sheets of paper	dog figure	2 forks	2 large spoons	2 stacking rings
2 bowls	2 bear figures	2 serving spoons	2 trays	1 bottle
2 pieces of ribbon	doll house fence	2 spatulas	2 adult figures	3 wooden rods
2 square blocks	2 doll house chairs	2 ladles	4 animal figures	2 sheets of paper
2 wooden rods	doll house bed		2 square blocks	2 cars
2 small lotion bottles	baby stroller rubber bands 4 toothbrushes 2 sheets of card stock 2 paper coin rollers 2 container lids			2 small telephones 2 brushes 2 sponges 2 square blocks 2 rectangle blocks

SPA = Structured Play Assessment.

of a model prompt that did not result in a pretense behavior. A *physical prompt error* was the teacher failing to deliver a physical prompt within 5 s of a model prompt that did not result in a pretense behavior, using her hands to move a child through a nonpretense behavior, or delivering a physical prompt more than 5 s after a model prompt that did not result in a pretense behavior. A *prompt sequence error* occurred when the teacher delivered a physical prompt before delivering a model prompt. *Missed opportunities* occurred when more than 20 s elapsed without a child pretense behavior and the teacher failed to deliver the prompt sequence. Event sampling was used to record each of these behaviors. Data were collected using a digital video recorder, coded using ProCoderDV (Tapp & Walden, 2000), and analyzed using INTMAN software (Tapp et al., 2006).

For Amy (Anna's teacher), four additional behaviors were measured. *Correct toy presentation* was Amy placing two or three toys in Anna's lap within 12 s but not more than 20 s after the last prompt or last pretense behavior. A *toy presentation error* occurred when Amy failed to place two or three toys in Anna's lap within the time window or only placed one toy in Anna's lap. *Correct picture presentation* occurred when Amy showed Anna a picture depicting a pretense behavior and verbally described the depicted action at least 12 s but not more than 20 s after the last prompt or last pretense behavior. A *picture presentation error* occurred when no picture was shown to Anna within the time window or a picture was presented but Amy failed to label the action. For Lucy, two additional behaviors were measured. A *correct toy choice* was Lucy saying, "Do you want to play with the _____ or the _____?" and holding two toys in front of Liz at least 12 s but not more than 20 s after the last prompt or pretense behavior. A *toy choice error* occurred when Lucy failed to hold two toys in front of Liz or did not ask Liz to make a choice.

Adapted Structured Play Assessment (SPA)

The SPA is used to describe children's optimal play skills (e.g., Mundy, Sigman, Ungerer, & Sherman, 1987; Ungerer & Sigman, 1981). The SPA has six behavior categories and was adapted for this study by dividing functional play into two categories: functional play with and without pretense. Three categories did not indicate pretense: *simple manipulation of one object* was any child movement of a single object (e.g., mouthing a block); *relational manipulation of more than one object* was moving two objects in relation to each other in a nonfunctional way (banging a car on top of a block); and *functional play* was moving an object or moving two objects together in a functional way (closing doors on a tov house, putting puzzles together). Four categories indicated pretense: *functional play with pretense* (FPP) was movement representing a nonliteral action of one or more objects (puts spoon to doll's mouth); *object substitution* (OS) was movement of one object as if it were a different object (putting a block to the doll's mouth as if it were a bottle); *imagining absent objects* (IAO) was a movement implying an object was present although it was not (putting a fist near a doll's mouth to feed without the bottle); and *assigning absent attributes* (AAA) was movements or vocalizations assigning roles, emotions, or attributes (picking up a doll and saying, "crying."). Event sampling was used to count the number of play behaviors across each category. The SPA was used as a pre- and posttest, and pretest scores were used as an inclusion criterion.

Pretense Behaviors

An event recording system was used with child pretense behaviors using three steps. First, each pretense behavior was coded as prompted or unprompted to provide evidence for transfer of stimulus control. Unprompted pretense behaviors were those occurring without a prompt in the previous 5 s. Prompted pretense behaviors were those occurring within 5 s of a teacher prompt. Second, each pretense behavior was coded as same or different. Behaviors were coded as different if they had not occurred previously in the session and as the same if they had occurred previously in the session. Thus, the total number of prompted same, unprompted same, prompted different, and unprompted different pretense behaviors was generated for each session to examine the diversity of pretense behaviors. Third, the pretense behaviors were coded by type: functional play with pretense, object substitution, imagining absent objects, and assigning absent attributes (see Barton & Wolery, 2008) using the same definitions as for the adapted SPA.

In addition, the number of sequences and number of behaviors per sequence were measured with event recording. A sequence consisted of at least two related pretense behaviors occurring within 3 s of each other. For each sequence, the number of pretense behaviors was counted. Finally, each vocalization related to a pretense behavior was recorded. Vocalizations were coded as prompted if they were imitative and occurred less than 5 s after a teacher vocalization and unprompted if they occurred more than 5 s after a teacher vocalization, regardless of whether they were imitative or non-imitative.

Interobserver Agreement (IOA)

A second observer coded at least 20% of the videotaped sessions for each toy set, condition, and child. Because event recording was used, the formula for calculating IOA was the smaller number of one observer divided by the larger number of the other observer and the quotient was multiplied by 100 (Gast, 2010). The IOA data for child pretense behaviors are shown in Table 10.3.

Design and Procedures

This study used a multiple probe design across three toys sets and replicated across four children with disabilities (Gast & Ledford, 2010). The design progressed through the following conditions: (a) initial probe condition measuring each child's behavior with each toy set in sessions with the child's teacher and sessions with a nonteacher adult (generalization across adults) who did not prompt pretense behaviors, (b) initial teacher training session followed by instructional sessions on the first toy set with each child and daily generalization measures with a nonteacher adult who did not prompt pretense behaviors, (c) second probe condition measuring each child's behavior with each toy set in sessions with the child's teacher and sessions with a nonteacher adult (generalization across adults) in which neither used prompts, (d) second teacher training session followed by instructional sessions on the second toy set with each child and generalization measures with a nonteacher adult who did not use prompts, (e) third probe condition identical in procedures to the second probe condition, (f) third teacher training session and instructional sessions on the third toy set and generalization measures as in the second intervention condition, (g) final probe condition identical in procedures to the second and third probe conditions, (h) generalization across toy sets measuring the child's behavior with a new toy set and with the nonteacher adult who did not prompt pretense behaviors, and (i) posttest wirh the SPA in which pretense behaviors were not prompted. The decision to intervene with each subsequent tov set was based on a clear change in level of the child's number of unprompted pretense behaviors.

Initial Probe Condition

These 8-min sessions occurred before teacher training. The investigator told the teachers to play with their child "as they normally would"; they were free to use verbal, model, or physical prompts. Flach toy set was assessed for at least three sessions (nine total sessions).

TABLE 10.3 Percentage of Interobserver Agreement for Teacher and Nonteacher Adult Generalization Sessions by Child Behavior

Participant Behavior	Condition (Sessions With Teacher)		Condition (Generalization Sessions With Nonteacher Adult)	
	Probe Mean (range)	Instructional Mean (range)	Probe Mean (range)	Instructional Mean (range)
Daniel				
Prompted	100	95 (93–100)	100	100
Unprompted	97 (95–98)	95 (93–100)	100	100
Type	93 (85–100)	96 (95–100)	100	99 (91–100)
Same/Differ	96 (88–100)	97 (90–100)	100	91 (80–95)
Sequences	100	100	100	100
Vocalizations	95 (78–100)	96 (83–100)	100	100
Anna				
Prompted	96 (93–100)	94 (80–100)	100	100
Unprompted	98 (93–100)	95 (88–100)	100	96 (80–100)
Type	96 (90–100)	97 (93–100)	100	100
Same/Differ	91 (87–100)	97 (90–100)	93 (89–99)	100
Sequences	100	100	100	100
Vocalizations	100	100	100	90 (82–98)
Liz				
Prompted	87 (78–92)	88 (80–92)	100	100
Unprompted	99 (97–100)	90 (82–95)	95 (94–100)	91 (85–100)
Type	100	89 (82–100)	93 (90–100)	91 (80–100)
Same/Differ	100	88 (77–95)	92 (89–100)	90 (80–100)
Sequences	100	100	100	100
Vocalizations	100	100	100	100
Brian				
Prompted	89 (78–100)	97 (88–100)	100	100
Unprompted	98 (90–100)	95 (85–100)	100	94 (80–100)
Type	97 (88–100)	93 (88–100)	100	91 (84–100)
Same/Differ	100	100	100	91 (82–100)
Sequences	100	100	100	100
Vocalizations	100	100	100	100

Teacher Training

The goals were to train the teachers to (a) use contingent imitation during play, (b) use the system of least prompts with the a specific toy set, (c) discriminate nonpretense from pretense behaviors, and (d) identify examples of four types of pretense (functional play with pretense [FPP], object substitution [OS], imagining absent objects [IAO], and assigning absent attributes [AAA]). Contingent imitation was taught to focus the teacher on the child's current behavior and to elicit the child's attention to the adult behavior (Ingersoll & Shreibman, 2006). Immediately after the initial probe condition, the teachers were given a six-page manual 3 days before the initial 45-min training session. The manual included a rationale for the study, a description of the prompts and prompting procedures, a definition and description of contingent imitation, examples of teacher statements to be used, and examples of pretense behaviors. This session occurred with the teachers as a group at the end of the school day and focused intervention procedures with Toy Set 1. In the first 30 min, the investigator and teachers discussed and reviewed the manual and watched the video. The video included two 10-min segments: (1) the investigator modeling contingent imitation and the prompting sequence with a child, and (2) a child without disabilities engaging in pretense and nonpretense behaviors with the first toy set. The teachers then practiced the prompting sequence with nonparticipant children, and the investigator provided feedback and praise for correct use of the procedures.

Training for the second and third toy sets occurred individually with each teacher after her child completed the second and third probe conditions, respectively. These sessions were shorter (20–30 min) and occurred in the teachers classroom. The investigator reviewed the manual and videos and modeled each of the four types of pretense behaviors with the new toy set. Again, the teacher practiced using the prompting sequence with nonparticipant children, and the investigator provided feedback and praise for correct use of the procedures. In addition, before each child instructional session, the investigator gave the teacher a checklist with at least two examples of each type of pretense behaviors with the current toy set. During the session, the investigator recorded examples of correct use of and errors with the prompting sequence. After each session, the investigator provided verbal and written feedback using a one-page feedback form with space for examples of four pretense behaviors the teachers had prompted and the number of missed opportunities to prompt. The investigator asked teachers to initial that they received the feedback. This feedback form was used for the duration of the study.

Child Instructional Sessions

In the 8-min instructional sessions, the teachers contingently imitated the child, applied the system of least prompts targeting the four types of pretense behaviors (functional play with pretense, object substitution, imagining absent objects, and assigning absent attributes), and praised all pretense behaviors. A system of least prompts was used with three or four levels from least to most intrusive, depending on the child's responses. The first level (independent level) consisted of the presentation of the materials and the verbal statement "let's play" at the beginning of the session. The teacher waited 12 to 20 s while contingently imitating and observing the child; if the child did not do a pretense behavior, the teacher modeled a pretense behavior and labeled the action. The teachers were asked to prompt all four types of pretense behaviors within each session based on the child's behavior or interest. For example, if the child was banging a spoon on the floor, the teacher imitated banging the spoon, waited 12 to 20 s, moved the spoon into a cup, made a stirring motion, and said, "I'm stirring." Or, if the child was not touching any toys, but looking at the sponges, the teacher picked up a sponge, moved it back and forth on the carpet, and said, "It's a fast car!" If the child did not imitate the model or do a pretense behavior within 5 s, the teacher used full physical, hand-over-hand prompts (the controlling prompt) to assist the child in doing a pretense behavior.

Consistent with a system of least prompts, the prompt sequence was adapted based on the child response patterns. For Anna and Liz, prompt levels were added because of low response rates. These levels occurred after the presentation of the toys and before the physical model in the prompting sequence. For Anna, a picture with a written description of the pretense behavior was presented with the model prompt (introduced during Toy Set 1 and included with Toy Set 2). Anna's teacher and parents suggested adding this visual cue, because visuals had been used successfully in teaching her new skills. With Toy Set 3, specific materials were presented to her with a verbal prompt, "Let's play," 12 to 20 s after the presentation of the toy set. For Liz, a choice between two toys was provided after the presentation of the toys, prior to the physical model (with Toy Set 1 only). Daniel consistently resisted hand-over-hand prompting so the controlling prompt was placing the toy in or near his hands.

If the child engaged in a pretense behavior, the teacher delivered descriptive praise (e.g., "Good feeding the baby, Liz"). However, descriptive praise did not function as a reinforcer for pretend play for Anna. Amy reported that edibles functioned as reinforcement for a variety of other skills for Anna; thus, she presented a small edible to Anna after each prompted and unprompted pretense behavior for Toy Sets 1 and 2 except during probe conditions. With Toy Set 3, Amy thinned the delivery of an edible to every other pretense behavior.

Second, Third, and Final Probe Conditions

These 8-min sessions occurred with each teacher-child dyad for at least three sessions wirh each toy set. The procedures were identical to the initial probe condition, except teachers were told to refrain from using the system of least prompts, contingent imitation, or reinforcement (i.e., descriptive praise or an edible) to prompt pretense behaviors. Teachers provided descriptive praise for remaining in the play area.

Unprompted Daily Generalization Probes Across Adults

Generalization of child pretense behaviors was measured in 5-min play sessions with a non-teacher adult prior to the probe and instructional sessions. Two graduate students in special education served in the role of nonteacher adult. The nonteacher adult presented the same toy set used in the instructional sessions, but did not deliver prompts or use contingent imitation. Descriptive praise for sitting (e.g., "I like the way you are sitting") was delivered about every 20 s if the child remained in the specified area. For Anna and Liz, these generalization sessions were conducted intermittently to avoid toy or session satiation. Because of high rates of escape attempts, praise was delivered more often to Brian.

Generalization Probes Across Materials and Adults

One session was conducted per child during the final probe condition. File nonteacher adult used the procedures identical to those of the unprompted daily generalization session with a new toy set (see Table 10.2).

Results

Procedural Fidelity

Three types of procedural fidelity data were assessed. First, each teacher completed a 12-step checklist after each teacher training session. This checklist assessed whether the teacher training sessions were conducted as planned. Data indicated all 12 steps occurred in each training session. Second, the teachers initialed the daily feedback form to verify feedback was delivered. The forms were reviewed, and the teachers initialed 100% of them for each instructional condition. Third, video records of teacher behaviors in probe and instructional sessions were observed directly and coded. A second observer coded at least 20% of the video records for each teacher and condition to measure IOA on the teacher behaviors. IOA was calculated using the smaller divided by the larger method for each teacher behavior. IOA for Darcy's procedural fidelity was 94% (81%–100%) for Toy Set 1 and 100% for Sets 2 and 3; for Amy it was 88% (81%–100%) for Toy Set 1 and 100% for Sets 2 and 3; for Lucy it was 93% (86%–100%) for Toy Set 1, 91% (83%–100%) for Set 2, and 95% (88%–100%) for Set 3; for Beth it was 100% for Toy Set 1 and 92% (90%–100%) for Set 2.

The percentage of correct implementation was calculated for each session by subtracting the number of errors from the total number of prompts and dividing by the total number of prompts. The scores for all sessions were averaged to obtain a mean percentage of correct implementation per toy set. for Darcy, the mean percentage of correct implementation for Toy Set 1 was 88% (range: 69–100) and was 100% for Sets 2 and 3. For Amy, the mean percentage of correct implementation for Toy Set 1 was 84% (range: 67–100), and was 100% for Sets 2 and 3. For Lucy, the mean percentage of correct implementation for Toy Set 1 was 85% (range: 50–100), 94% for Set 2 (range: 83–100), and was 100% for Set 3. For Beth, the mean percentage of correct implementation for Toy Set 1 was 82% (range: 63–100), and 100% for Set 2. Toy Set 3 was not used because Brian withdrew from school unexpectedly. These data indicate the teachers used the intervention package with high fidelity. With each teacher, the lowest percentages of correct implementation occurred with Toy Set 1—indicating the teachers were acquiring the skills needed to use the intervention correctly.

Effects on Pretense Behaviors

Acquisition and Maintenance of Pretense Behaviors

The number of unprompted and prompted pretense behaviors for Daniel, Anna, Liz, and Brian are shown in Figures 10.1 to 10.4, respectively. Total unprompted pretend play included any of the four types of pretense behavior (FPP, OS, IAO, & AAA). Unprompted pretend play increased with the introduction of the intervention; a clear functional relation was established between the intervention package and unprompted pretend play across toy sets and children.

For Daniel, Figure 10.1 shows that his unprompted pretense behaviors were low (less than three behaviors) in each session of each toy set during the initial

> *Unprompted pretend play increased with the introduction of the intervention; a clear functional relation was established between the intervention package and unprompted pretend play across toy sets and children.*

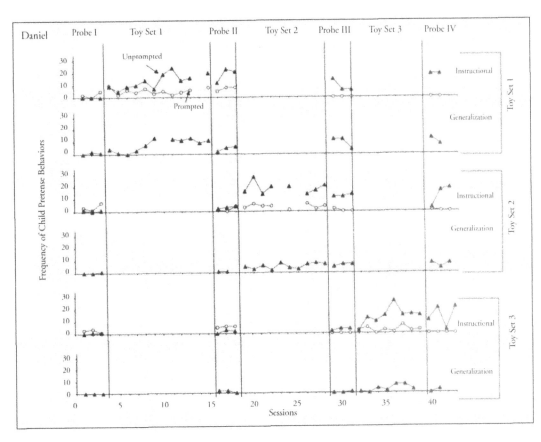

FIGURE 10.1 Frequency of Prompted and Unprompted Pretense Behaviors for Daniel

Notes. Open circles = prompted; closed triangles = unprompted.

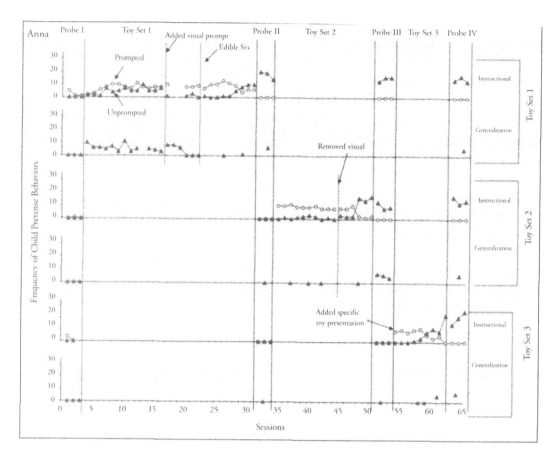

FIGURE 10.2   Frequency of Prompted and Unprompted Pretense Behaviors for Anna

Notes. Open circles = prompted; closed triangles = unprompted.

probe condition. With the intervention for Toy Set 1, his prompted and unprompted pretense behaviors increased with an accelerating trend for unprompted pretense behaviors. In the second probe condition, his unprompted pretense behaviors for Toy Set 1 remained high (mean of 18.7 for the three sessions) and his unprompted pretense behaviors on other sets remained low. This pattern was replicated across the two subsequent toy sets. Thus, for each toy set, the unprompted pretense behaviors were low in probe conditions prior to intervention, increased during intervention, and maintained at high levels in probe conditions after intervention.

For Anna, Figure 10.2 shows that unprompted pretense behaviors were zero in each session of each toy set during the initial probe condition. She had a few prompted pretense behaviors in this condition for each toy set. With the intervention for Toy Set 1, both her prompted and unprompted pretense behaviors increased slightly. With the introduction of the visual prompt (instructional session 14) and the edible reinforcer (instructional session 18), prompted pretense behaviors increased and an accelerating trend is noted for unprompted pretense behaviors toward the end of the condition. In the second probe condition, her unprompted pretense behaviors for Toy Set 1 displayed an immediate and

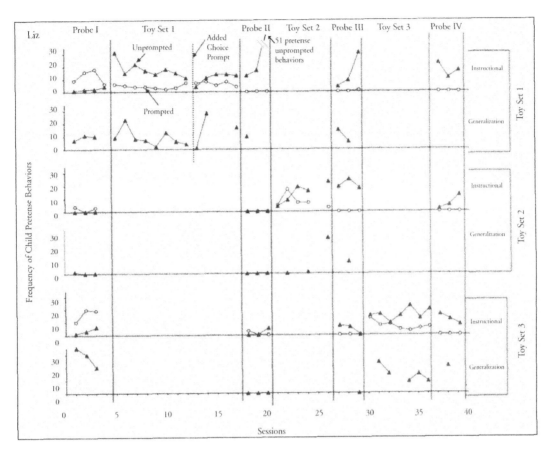

FIGURE 10.3   Frequency of Prompted and Unprompted Pretense Behaviors for Liz

Notes. Open circles = prompted; closed triangles = unprompted.

large increase in level (i.e., mean of 9.3 for the last three instructional sessions and 17.7 for the three probe sessions); unprompted pretense behaviors for Toy Sets 2 and 3 remained at zero. The introduction of the intervention (including the visual prompt and edible reinforcer) for Toy Set 2 resulted in an abrupt increase in prompted pretense behaviors and a gradual increase in unprompted pretense behaviors, with transfer of stimulus control occurring during the last three sessions. The visual prompt was discontinued after the tenth intervention session. During the third probe condition, unprompted pretense behaviors for Toy Set 2 remained high at a level slightly lower than the last three intervention sessions; Toy Set 1 maintained at levels similar to the second probe condition, and Toy Set 3 remained at zero. With the introduction of intervention for Toy Set 3 (including the presentation prompt and edible reinforcement delivered for every other prompted or unprompted pretense behavior), an abrupt increase in prompted pretense and an accelerating trend in the number of unprompted pretense behaviors occurred. In the final probe condition, an accelerating trend in the number of unprompted pretense behaviors occurred with the last data point slightly higher than the last data point during the instructional condition for Toy Set 3. Unprompted

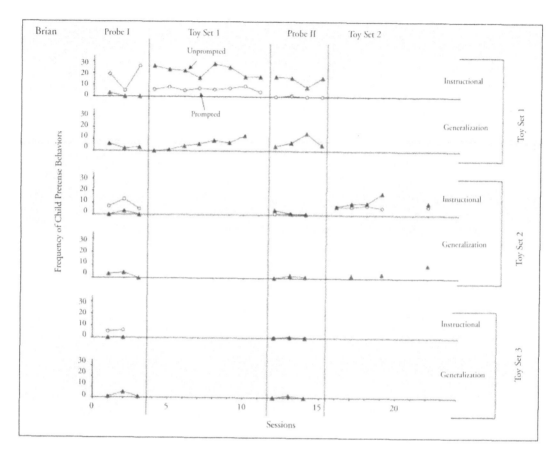

FIGURE 10.4   Frequency of Prompted and Unprompted Pretense Behaviors for Brain

Note. Open circles = prompted; closed triangles = unprompted.

pretense behaviors for Toy Sets 1 and 2 maintained at high levels. Thus, for each toy set, the unprompted pretense behaviors were low in probe conditions prior to intervention, increased during intervention, and maintained at high levels in subsequent probe conditions (without prompts *or* edible rein forcement).

For Liz, Figure 10.3 shows that her unprompted pretense behaviors were low (less than six behaviors) in each session of each toy set during the initial probe condition. She had several prompted pretense behaviors for Toy Sets 1 and 3 (between 10 and 20), and few prompted pretense behaviors for Toy Set 2 (less than five). With the intervention for Toy Set 1, her unprompted pretense behaviors abruptly increased and then had a decelerating trend. With the introduction of the choice, unprompted pretense slightly increased and stabilized around 13 behaviors per session. In the second probe condition, her unprompted pretense behaviors for Toy Set 1 remained high and displayed an accelerating trend (mean of 27). No increase occurred in unprompted pretense behaviors for Joy Sets 2, and a slight increase occurred for Toy Set 3. These remained at zero behaviors for Toy Set 2 and below six behaviors for Toy Set 3. The introduction of intervention for Toy Set 2 (without the choice prompt) resulted in an accelerating trend in the number of unprompted pretense behaviors. In the third probe condition, unprompted pretense behaviors For Toy Set 2 remained high. Toy Set 1 started lower than during the third probe condition and showed an accelerating trend similar to the second probe condition. A slight increase occurred for Toy Set 3, but the number of unprompted pretense behaviors was less than eight. With the introduction of intervention for Toy Set 3, an accelerating trend in the number of unprompted pretense behaviors occurred and then stabilized at a level higher than during the third probe condition. In the final probe condition, the numbers of unprompted pretense behaviors were high across toy sets. Thus, for each toy set, the unprompted pretense behaviors were low in probe conditions prior to intervention, increased during intervention, and maintained during subsequent probe conditions.

For Brian, Figure 10.4 shows that his unprompted pretense behaviors were low for all toy sets in the initial probe condition. He had several prompted pretense behaviors during this condition for Toy Set 1. With the introduction of the intervention with Toy Set 1, unprompted pretense behaviors immediately increased and prompted pretense behaviors had a decelerating trend. In the second probe condition, he had more unprompted pretense with Toy Set 1 than in the first probe condition, but slightly lower than during intervention. Toy Sets 2 and 3 remained low during the second probe condition. With the intervention for Toy Set 2, the unprompted pretense behaviors increased to a higher level than during previous probe sessions. He was absent for several days and returned for one final instructional session before he withdrew from school. His unprompted pretense behaviors for Toy Set 2 were above previous probe conditions and lower than last session of intervention.

Types of Pretense Behaviors
Four types of pretense behaviors were measured (FPP, OS, IAO, and AAA). For each child, the percentage of each type of unprompted pretense behaviors was similar across intervention and generalization sessions within toy sets; the percentages for each type are shown in Table 10.4. Daniel had higher percentages of object substitution behaviors than the other three types with Toy Set 1, more assigning absent attributes behaviors with Toy Set 2, and similar percentages of object substitution and assigning absent attributes behaviors with Toy Set 3. He displayed few unprompted functional play with pretense behaviors across the toy sets. Anna displayed more unprompted functional play with pretense than object substitution with Toy Sets 1 and 3. With Toy Set 2, Anna displayed more unprompted object substitution than functional play with pretense. She displayed no imagining absent objects or assigning absent attributes. Liz and Brian displayed more functional play with pretense than object substitution, imagining absent objects, and assigning absent attributes across the three toy sets.

Diversity of Pretense Behaviors
The intervention was designed to teach children a diverse repertoire of pretense behaviors from four categories rather than specific responses. Within the session, the teachers were free

TABLE 10.4   Percentage of Each Type of Unprompted Pretense Behaviors by Toy Set During Intervention Conditions

Participant Condition	Toy Set 1 Type of Pretense				Toy Set 2 Type of Pretense				Toy Set 3 Type of Pretense			
	FPP	OS	IAO	AAA	FPP	OS	IAO	AAA	FPP	OS	IAO	AAA
Daniel												
Intervention	1	73	20	5	4	34	3	59	8	39	23	30
Generalization	2	79	18	1	2	26	0	72	42	42	16	0
Anna												
Intervention	82	18	0	0	47	53	0	0	78	22	0	0
Generalization	89	11	0	0	0	0	0	0	80	10	0	0
Liz												
Intervention	72	16	0	12	5	55	8	32	74	17	2	7
Generalization	95	2	1	2	0	36	0	64	90	10	0	0
Brian												
Intervention	72	18	5	5	40	24	1	35	—	—	—	—
Generalization	70	25	5	0	53	27	0	20	—	—	—	—

Note. FFP = functional play with pretense; OS = object substitution; IAO = imagining absent attributes; AAA = assigning absent attributes.

to vary the type of pretense they prompted. Thus, the diversity (defined as the number of different pretense behaviors per session) of pretense behaviors was a critical measure. The mean and ranges of the number of different pretense behaviors are shown in Table 10.5 for probe conditions with the teacher and with the non teacher adult (generalization sessions). Teachers did not prompt pretense behaviors during the probe conditions; thus, probe condition data were analyzed because the diversity measure could be influenced by the teachers' prompts during intervention sessions. Three conclusions are noted: (a) the number of different pretense behaviors increased for all children on all toy sets after intervention was applied, (b) the children consistently had more different pretense behaviors with the teacher than with the nonteacher adult, and (c) the effects maintained across probe conditions. In summary, all children learned to engage in a variety of pretense behaviors in each condition and their performance maintained in sessions with teacher prompts removed.

Sequences of Pretense Behaviors

None of the children demonstrated sequences of pretense during the first probe condition. Overall, Daniel, Anna, and Liz displayed less than 10 sequences across subsequent conditions and toy sets. Brian displayed no sequences with Toy Sets 1 or 2. Thus, the intervention did not appear to promote sequences of pretense behaviors.

TABLE 10.5 Number of Different Unprompted Pretense Behaviors by Probe Condition for Teacher and Generalization Sesions Across Toy Sets

Participants Toy Set	Initial Probe Instruct. Mean (range)	Initial Probe Gen. Mean (range)	Second Probe Instruct. Mean (range)	Second Probe Gen. Mean (range)	Third Probe Instruct. Mean (range)	Third Probe Gen. Mean (range)	Final Probe Instruct. Mean (range)	Final Probe Gen. Mean (range)
Daniel								
Toy Set 1	0	.66 (0–1)	7.3 (6–9)	3.33 (2–5)	4.3 (4–5)	3.67 (2–6)	8.0 (7–9)	1.5 (1–2)
Toy Set 2	.67 (0–1)	0	2.0	1.0	8.3 (6–11)	4.0	10.3 (3–18)	4.3 (2–7)
Toy Set 3	.33 (0–1)	0	.67 (0–1)	1.5 (1–2)	2.6 (1–4)	.33 (0–1)	5.0 (1–9)	1 (0–2)
Anna								
Toy Set 1	0	0	6.67 (5–14)	4	7.67 (6–9)	—	7 (6–7)	—
Toy Set 2	0	0	0	0	6	3.33	6	6
Toy Set 3	0	0	0	0	0	0	11 (5–12)	5
Liz								
Toy Set 1	1 (0–2)	4 (2–6)	7 (5–10)	4 (3–5)	5.67 (4–8)	5 (4–5)	10 (6–13)	—
Toy Set 2	0	1.7 (1–3)	0	0	8.67 (6–11)	6	3 (2–4)	—
Toy Set 3	1.3 (1–2)	2.7 (1–4)	1 (0–3)	0	1.67 (0–5)	0	5.67 (5–7)	7
Brain								
Toy Set 1	.33 (0–1)	3 (2–4)	7.67 (4–11)	4.33 (3–7)				
Toy Set 2	0	1.7 (0–3)	1	.67 (0–1)				
Toy Set 3	1.7 (0–4)	0	0	.33 (0–1)				

Note. Dark lines on table show where intervention occurred.

Vocalizations

For all children in all probe conditions of each toy set, no vocalizations occurred prior to instruction on the respective toy sets. For all children during each instructional condition, some vocalizations occurred; however, for all children except Daniel on Toy Sets 1 and 3, some instructional sessions had no vocalizations. Vocalizations occurred for all children in all post-instruction probe conditions, except for Liz on Toy Set 2 (third and fourth probe conditions). All children had fewer vocalizations during generalization sessions than during instructional sessions, and all children had some generalization sessions with no vocalizations.

Generalization Across Adults

Unprompted pretense was measured with a non teacher adult for Toy Sets 1, 2, and 3. For Daniel and Anna (see Figures 10.1 and 10.2) in probe conditions before intervention, the frequencies of unprompted pretense behaviors were low in generalization assessment sessions; in probe conditions after intervention for all toy sets, the frequencies occurred at higher levels than before intervention and maintained across subsequent probe conditions. For Liz, Figure 10.3 shows that in probe conditions before intervention, the frequencies of unprompted pretense behaviors were low in generalization sessions for Toy Sets 1 and 2; in probe conditions after intervention for Loy Set 2, the frequencies occurred at higher levels than before intervention. In the second and third probe conditions, the frequencies of unprompted pretense behaviors were low in generalization assessment sessions for Toy Set 3; in the probe conditions after intervention for Loy Set 3, the frequencies occurred at higher levels than before intervention. For Brian, Figure 10.4 shows that during instruction with Loy Sets 1 and 2, the frequencies of unprompted pretense behaviors in the generalization sessions displayed an accelerating trend at levels higher than before intervention.

For Daniel, Anna, and Liz, the frequencies of unprompted pretense behaviors in daily generalization sessions during instructional conditions tended to be variable and at lower levels than in instructional sessions. With Anna, the frequencies were particularly low. With Brian, there tended to be an accelerating trend of pretense behaviors in generalization sessions, but his withdrawal from school precluded sufficient replications.

Generalization Across Toy Sets

For Daniel, Anna, and Liz, generalization to a new toy set with the nonteacher adult and without prompts for pretense behavior was assessed in an 8-min session during the final probe condition. Daniel engaged in 32 pretense behaviors, with 17 assigning absent attributes and 11 object substitution behaviors. Anna only demonstrated three pretense behaviors—two functional play with pretense and one object substitution behavior. Liz engaged in 31 pretense behaviors, and 26 functional play with pretense behaviors. Daniel had 24 vocalizations, Anna had none, and Liz had one.

Posttest of the SPA

As shown in Table 10.1, on the SPA pretest, Daniel had two different tin prompted functional play with pretense behaviors and no unprompted symbolic behaviors; Anna, Liz, and Brian had no unprompted behaviors in either category. On the posttest, Daniel's number of unprompted functional play with pretense behaviors were essentially the same, but he had 18 symbolic behaviors. Anna increased substantially on functional play with pretense behaviors, and she had two symbolic behaviors. Liz increased substantially in both categories. Brian did not have the posttest because he had withdrawn from school.

Discussion

This study examined the relation between the teachers' use of the system of least prompts and contingent imitation and pretense behaviors of children with disabilities. The effects of the intervention were evaluated on children's acquisition, maintenance, and generalization of the pretense behaviors. A number of measures were used, including the number of prompted and unprompted pretense behaviors during intervention sessions with their teachers; the types, the diversity, and sequences of pretense behaviors; and the use of vocalizations related to pretense behaviors. Six findings are discussed.

First, as shown in Figures 10.1 to 10.4, the intervention was functionally related to an increase in the number of unprompted pretense behaviors across children in the intervention sessions, which maintained across probe conditions when no prompts were used and at lower levels in the generalization-across-adult sessions, again without prompts. The intervention produced consistently higher levels of pretend play across children and toy sets in the intervention sessions and in probe conditions after intervention. The levels of pretense behaviors in the final intervention sessions for all participants were at least three times, and often more than four or five times, the levels prior to instruction. Daniel had means of 0, 3, and 3.25 unprompted pretense behaviors prior to instruction and means of 16.7 17.3, and 14 for the final three instructional sessions across Toys Sets 1, 2, and 3, respectively. Anna displayed no unprompted pretense behaviors prior to instruction and means of 9.5, 15.7 and 14.3 for the final three instructional sessions across Toys Sets 1, 2, and 3, respectively. Liz had means of 1.6, 0, and 4.3 unprompted pretense behaviors prior to instruction and means of 13.7, 19.3, and 18.7 for the final three instructional sessions across Toys Sets 1, 2, and 3, respectively. Brian had means of 1 and 2 unprompted pretense behaviors prior to instruction and means of 19.7 and 12.7 for the final three instructional sessions across Toys Sets 1 and 2, respectively. I hits, substantial transfer of stimulus control occurred from the adult prompts to the materials.

This adds to the literature indicating systematic instructional practices can be embedded into play activities of young children (Filia et al., 1999) and to the growing literature indicating play, including pretend play can be taught systematically (Lifter et al., 2005). Also, this study expands earlier research on using systematic prompting to teach pretend play (DiCarlo & Reid, 2004; Lifter et al., 1993, 2005). For example, DiCarlo and Reid demonstrated children with disabilities acquired increased rates of unprompted pretense with the introduction of a least-to-most prompting hierarchy. In their study, three participants acquired rates of 0.6, 1.0, and .10 unprompted pretense behaviors per min during instructional sessions. They did not report measuring pretend play in contexts without prompts. In the current study, Daniel averaged 1.7, 2.3, and 1.8 unprompted pretense behaviors per min during instructional sessions across the three toy sets respectively. Anna averaged 0.5, 0.5, and 0.8, unprompted pretense behaviors per min across the three toy sets respectively. For Anna, these averages take into account the delayed treatment effects with several initial instructional sessions at zero. Liz averaged 1.9, 1.8, and 2.0, unprompted pretense behaviors per min across the three toy sets respectively. Brian averaged 2.7 unprompted pretense behaviors per min with hoy Set 1, and 1.4 with Toy Set 2, before he was abruptly removed from the school. However, it should be noted DiCarlo and Reid defined pretend play with some ambiguity, making interpretations and comparisons difficult.

In addition, the intervention produced consistently higher levels of pretend play in probe sessions without prompting across all children. For example, the levels of pretense behaviors in the probe conditions following intervention for all participants were at least two times the levels in the probe condition prior to intervention, and in most cases close to three times the level. For Toy Set 1 with Daniel, Toy Sets 1, 2, and 3 with Anna, and Toy Set 2 with Liz, unprompted pretend play went from not occurring prior to intervention to occurring in every session of every probe condition after intervention. These findings are important and significant for advancing the literature. Unlike other studies, the maintenance and generalization of pretend play was measured in repeated probe conditions across toy sets. Only three studies have measured pretend play in context without prompts (Kasari et al., 2006; MacDonald et al., 2005; Sherrat, 2002). Severe methodological flaws limit the interpretation of Sherrat's study.

No other studies measured generalization of pretend play concurrently across adults. The generalization across adults of pretend play was measured during probe and instructional conditions. The children showed increased, yet lower, levels in the generalization-across-adult sessions; this has important implications for both practice and research. The nonteacher adult in this study did not prompt *or* respond to the child's pretense behaviors—suggesting that systematic teaching of pretense behaviors might generalize to settings without a responsive adult. This may have practical value for families. For example, childrens ability to engage independently in pretend play may free up time and reduce demands on caregivers.

Second, the participants demonstrated all four types of pretense behaviors (see Table 10.4) in both intervention and generalization-across-adult sessions, except Anna who did not show assigning absent attributes. Again, in the instructional sessions teachers prompted all four types of pretense, but were free to vary the amount of prompting of each type. The results demonstrate patterns in the types of pretense each child emitted across the toy sets, which is consistent with the pretend play literature. Anna, Liz, and Brian displayed more functional play with pretense than the three substitution behaviors. Conversely, Daniel had higher percentages of object substitution, assigning absent attributes, and imagining absent objects. It is interesting to note that he was the highest functioning (based on mental age and behavioral repertoire) of the four participants. This finding builds on previous research; for example, Lifter et al. (1993) and Lifter et al. (2005) targeted developmentally appropriate play for young children with autism and pervasive development disorders (PDD), respectively. For most children, the targets were functional play with pretense behaviors. Kasari et al. (2006) found that children with autism who participated in a pretend play intervention showed a significant increase in differential unprompted symbolic behaviors (similar to object substitution, assigning absent attributes, and imagining absent objects). However, the overall average play level for the children with autism after treatment was functional play with pretense. Future studies should examine whether a sequence of instruction is more efficient; for example, focusing on functional play with pretense and object substitution and then shifting to assigning absent attributes and imagining absent objects. Perhaps this sequence would produce a more evenly distributed use of the four categories of pretense.

Third, the intervention taught children to exhibit different pretense behaviors during each session, which maintained, at a lower level, in generalization across adult sessions (see Table 10.5). Further, each child emitted pretend play from all four categories (except Anna, see previous discussion). This diversity maintained across toy sets and probe conditions for all children. This finding suggests the participants were acquiring and generalizing a general class of responding that could be characterized as pretend play. This finding argues for engaging in systematic instruction of play, including pretend play, for children who do not display such behaviors. These results are remarkable and significant for advancing the literature on play in young children. Of the three studies measuring pretend play in contexts without prompts, only one measured the diversity of play behaviors (Kasari et al., 2006). Given the decreased levels of diversity of play behaviors in young children with disabilities, particularly children with autism, when compared to children with typical development, the diversity of play behaviors appears to be an important, if not essential goal for play interventions.

Fourth, the number of vocalizations increased across all participants, although not specifically prompted or reinforced. When the teachers applied the system of least prompts, they modeled and physically prompted actions on toys and described the actions being prompted. This suggests that the combined prompt (i.e., action with the verbal description) may have corollary effects of teaching both the action and vocalizations. The finding also raises the question of whether specific vocabulary (e.g., names of toys or actions) could be taught through the verbal descriptions of the actions. Frey (2006) modeled expansions of children's actions on toys and described the actions; this produced an increase in the number and diversity of actions. She did not measure children's vocalizations. A future study should evaluate whether prompting the action without the verbal description also increases children's vocalizations. Also, the effects of describing and not describing the actions with the prompt should be evaluated.

Fifth, the intervention did not change the number of pretense sequences. The prompts were provided for single pretense behaviors rather than for a sequence of behaviors (e.g., feeding a doll with a block, and then putting the doll to bed and covering it with an imaginary blanket). Future studies should evaluate whether adding themes to the play or systematically prompting sequences would increase the number of pretense sequences.

Sixth, children generalized the pretense behaviors to novel toy sets with a nonteacher adult who did not prompt their behaviors. This occurred both with the generalization toy set and on the posttest of the adapted SPA (see Table 10.1). Although earlier studies measured generalization across toys (e.g., Lifter et al., 1993; Stahmer, 1995; Thorp et al., 1995), none did so in play sessions without adult prompting. This study adds to the literature by suggesting generalization will occur in contexts where prompts were not used. However, this finding should be interpreted with caution as the generalization toy set was not measured during the initial probe condition. Future studies should evaluate whether this generalization occurs across other times of the day when an adult is not directly with the child (e.g., free play periods).

Teachers' Use of the Intervention Procedures

A secondary purpose of this study was to evaluate the teachers' acquisition of the intervention procedures (i.e., contingent imitation and system of least prompts). Thus, the study had two levels of independent variables: the teachers' use of the intervention with children, and the investigator's training and feedback to the teachers. Although each teacher received three training sessions staggered across time, the second and third sessions focused on using the previously trained intervention with new materials (toy sets). The current design is weak in terms of drawing conclusions about the existence of a functional relation between the training and the teachers' use of the intervention. However, the measurement of teachers' use of the intervention shows that they used the procedures with fidelity. They made fewer procedural errors as the study progressed across toy sets. Further, the training used in this study is feasible and extends the research on professional development (e.g., didactic training with feedback) to training teachers to use the system of least prompts with pretend play.

It is important to note that although the teachers had at least 3 years of paid experience working with children, they had a variety of formal education backgrounds as is typical in early childhood programs. It is unclear whether the training package would result in less educated or experienced individuals using the intervention with fidelity. Future studies should examine strategies for training less experienced or educated teachers to use systematic procedures for teaching pretend play.

The intervention was complex and the behavioral categories targeted involved subtle discriminations. As a result, the training was designed to be powerful based on the professional development literature (Filla et al., 1999; Moore & Fisher, 2007); it involved a number of components, including a short manual, video examples, focused discussions, practice with nonparticipant children with feedback, a checklist of example behaviors before each intervention session, and feedback after each intervention session. Although each component is a recommended training practice, we cannot identify from this study which (if any) components were responsible for teachers' use of the intervention. Future component analysis studies can identify the active elements, but it is our subjective opinion that the feedback seemed critical.

In addition, future studies should focus on the frequency with which prompts should be used. In this study, teachers were taught to implement a prompt in a window of 12 to 20 s from the last pretense behavior or last prompt. It is unclear whether a larger window (e.g., 30–60 s) would also be effective and easier to implement. This intervention included contingent imitation to focus the teacher's prompting on materials being used by the child with the assumptions that child attention would be maximized and the teacher could teach an additional behavior with the same materials. It is unclear whether these assumptions were met; thus, evaluating the intervention without contingent imitation should be addressed in future studies.

Limitations

This study has a number of limitations. The sessions were all conducted with one teacher and one child in a designated area of the classroom. The nonteacher adult who conducted most of the generalization-across-people sessions was the same individual across the study; thus, she was not a novel adult by the end of the study. Further, the generalization sessions occurred in the same classroom as the intervention sessions. Generalization across settings was not assessed except for the posttest on the adapted SPA. Likewise, generalization across toys only was measured during the final probe condition to avoid toy satiation. However, this limits comparisons to baseline sessions, prior to intervention. Finally, during the intervention sessions, the number of prompts did not necessarily decrease. Teachers continued to prompt the children frequently. This indicated children had opportunities to engage in more pretense behaviors than they did; however, it is unclear how frequently typically developing children with similar toys would use pretense behaviors. Future studies should measure the social validity of these outcomes by comparing to the frequency and types of pretense behaviors exhibited by peers.

Implications for Practice

This study has a number of implications for practice. First, when teachers use the system of least prompts systematically, children may engage in more pretense behaviors of different types, maintain the increased frequency, and generalize it to situations with adults who do not prompt their pretense behaviors. In this study, children were taught to engage in the same behaviors with the same toys as children with typical development. These findings have both functional and practical value for children. For example, this increases the possibility for positive social interactions and communication with peers, provides a context for learning and practicing other skills, and might reduce time spent engaged in maladaptive behaviors. As such, this intervention is recommended for use.

Second, this study provides clear, operationalized categories for pretend play, which were functional for teaching and measuring pretend play. This has important implications for practice and research. Across the pretend play literature, the definition of pretend play was inconsistently and vaguely operationalized, which limits the replication and interpretation of pretend play studies. The taxonomy used in this study can be used in classrooms to measure and teach play and applied in future research.

Third, teachers can be taught to use a complex intervention to promote children's use of pretense behaviors in preschool classrooms. Regardless of their level of education

The taxonomy used in this study can be used in classrooms to measure and teach play and applied in future research.

or experience, all four teachers in this study implemented a system of least prompts with high fidelity across three toy sets. Further, they were responsive to the child's behaviors and used appropriate prompts based on the child's behaviors. This is an important finding because most pretend play studies used trained interventionists rather than teachers, and only two of these studies reported the interventionists' experience or training.

In summary, the results of this study provide promising data regarding the systematic prompting of pretense behaviors by preschool teachers in "real world" inclusive classrooms. Teachers implemented the intervention package with high fidelity, and the children engaged in more unprompted pretense behaviors. Specific, intentional interventions, such as the one described here, are necessary to ensure children with special needs engage in pretense behaviors alongside their peers in inclusive, preschool classrooms.

References

Barton, E. E., & Wolery, M. (2008). Teaching pretend play to children with disabilities: A review of the literature. *Topics in Early Childhood Special Education, 28,* 109–125.

Belsky J., & Most, R. (1981). From exploration to play: A cross sectional study of infant free play behavior. *Developmental Psychology, 17,* 630–639.

Blasco, P. M., Bailey, D. B., & Burchinal, M. A. (1993). Dimensions of mastery in same-age and mixed-age integrated classrooms. *Early Childhood Research Quarterly, 8,* 193–206.

Casey, A. M., & McWilliam, R. A. (2008). Graphical feedback to increase teachers' use of incidental teaching. *Journal of Early Intervention, 30,* 251–268.

DiCarlo, C. F., & Reid, D. H. (2004). Increasing pretend toy play of toddlers with disabilities in an inclusive setting. *Journal of Applied Behavior Analysis, 37,* 197–207.

Doyle, P M., Wolery, M., Ault, M. J., & Gast, D. (1988). System of least prompts: A review of procedural parameters. *Journal of the Association for Persons with Severe Handicaps, 13,* 28–40.

Fein, G. G. (1981). Pretend play in childhood: An integrative review. *Child Development, 52,* 1095–1118.

Filla, A., Wolery, M., & Anthony, L. (1999). Promoting children's conversations during play with adult prompts, *Journal of Early Intervention, 22,* 93–108.

Frey, J. (2006). *Use of play expansions to increase the diversity of object play in young children with disabilities* (Unpublished master's thesis). Peabody College, Vanderbilt University, Nashville, TN.

Gast, D. L. (2010). *Single subject research methodology in behavioral sciences.* New York, NY: Routledge.

Gast, D. L., & Ledford, J. R. (2010). Multiple baseline and multiple probe designs. In D. L. Gast (Ed.), *Single subject research methodology in behavioral sciences* (pp. 276–328). New York, NY: Routledge.

Ingersoll, B., & Shreibman, L. (2006). Teaching reciprocal imitation skills to young children with autism using a naturalistic behavioral approach: Effects on language, pretend play, and joint attention, *Journal of Autism and Developmental Disorders, 36,* 487–505.

Jarrold, C., Boucher, J., & Smith, P. (1996). Generativity deficits in pretend play in autism, *Journal of Developmental Psychology, 14,* 275–300.

Kasari, C., Freeman, S., & Parapella, T. (2006). Joint attention and symbolic play in young children with autism: A randomized controlled intervention study. *Journal of Child Psychology and Psychiatry, 47,* 611–620.

Kim, Y. T, Lombardino, L. J., Rothman, H., & Vinson, B. (1989). Effects of symbolic play intervention with children who have mental retardation. *Mental Retardation, 27,* 159–165.

Lieber, J. (1993). A comparison of social pretend play in young children with and without disabilities. *Early Education and Development, 4,* 148–161.

Lifter, K., Ellis, J., Cannon, B., & Anderson, S. R. (2005). Developmental specificity in targeting and teaching play activities to children with pervasive developmental disorders. *Journal of Early Intervention, 27,* 247–267.

Lifter, K., Sulzer-Azaroff, B., Anderson, S., & Cowdery, G. E. (1993). Teaching play activities to preschool children with disabilities: The importance of developmental considerations, *Journal of Early Intervention, 17,* 139–159.

MacDonald, R., Clark, M., Carrigan, E., & Vangala, M. (2005). Using video modeling to teach pretend play to children with autism. *Behavioral Interventions, 20,* 225–238.

McConnell, S. R. (2002). Interventions to facilitate social interaction for young children with autism: Review of available research and recommendations for educational intervention and future research. *Journal of Autism and. Developmental Disorders, 32,* 351–372.

Moore, J. W., & Fisher, W. W. (2007). The effects of videotape modeling on staff acquisition of functional analysis methodology. *Journal of Applied Behavior Analysis, 40,* 197–202.

Morrison, R. S., Sainato, D. M., Benchaaban, D., & Endo, S. (2002). Increasing play skills of children with autism using activity schedules and correspondence training. *Journal of Early Intervention, 25,* 58–72.

Mundy, P., Sigman, M., Ungerer, J., & Sherman, T. (1987). Nonverbal communication and play correlates of language development in autistic children. *Journal of Autism and Developmental Disorders, 17,* 349–364.

Mullen, E. M. (1995). *Mullen Scales of Early Learning* (AGS ed.). Circle Pines, MN: American Guidance Service.

Pretti-Frontczak, K., & Bricker, D. (2004). *An activity-based approach to early intervention* (3rd ed.). Baltimore, MD: Paul H. Brookes.

Sandall, S., Hemmeter, M. L., Smith, B. J., & McLean, M. E. (2005). *DEC recommended practices: A comprehensive guide for practical application in early intervention early childhood special education.* Longmont, CO: Sopris West.

Sandall, S., & Schwartz, I. S. (2002). *Building blocks for teaching preschoolers with special needs.* Baltimore, MD: Paul H. Brookes.

Sherrat, D. (2002). Developing pretend play in children with autism. *Autism, 6*(2), 169–179.

Stahmer, A. (1995). Teaching symbolic play skills to children with autism using pivotal response training. *Journal of Autism and Developmental Disorders, 25,* 123–141.

Strain, P. S. (1985). Social and non-social determinants of acceptability in handicapped preschool children. *Topics in Early Childhood Special Education, 4,* 47–58.

Tapp, J., Ticha, R., Kryzer, E., Gustafson, M., Gunnar, M. R., & Symons, F. (2006). Comparing observational software with paper and pencil for time-sampled data: A field test of Interval Manager (INTMAN). *Behavior Research Methods, 38,* 165–169.

Tapp, J., & Walden, E (2000). PROCODER: A system for collection and analysis of observational data from videotape. In T. Thompson, D. Felce, & F. J. Symons (Eds.), *Behavioral observation: Technology and applications in developmental disabilities* (pp. 61–70). Baltimore, MD: Paul H. Brookes.

Thorp, D., Stahmer, A., & Schreibman, L. (1995). Effects of socio-dramatic play training on children with autism. *Journal of Autism and Developmental Disorders, 25,* 265–282.

Ungerer, J., & Sigman, M. (1981). Symbolic play and language comprehension in autistic, mentally retarded, and normal children. *Developmental Psychology, 20,* 293–302.

Wolery, M. (2001). Embedding constant time delay in classroom activities. *Young Exceptional Children Monograph, 5,* 81–90.

High-Quality School-Based Pre-K Can Boost Early Learning for Children With Special Needs

Deborah A. Phillips and Mary E. Meloy

Children with special needs have participated in public education alongside their typically developing peers for more than 30 years. Passage of the Education for All Handicapped Children Act of 1975 (EHA; now the Individuals With Disabilities Education Act, IDEA) assured children with disabilities the right to a free and appropriate education. The legislation placed a priority on serving children in the *least restrictive* environment, fueling a nationwide expansion of inclusive public school classrooms. More recently, the explicit inclusion of students with special needs in the accountability provisions of the No Child Left Behind Act of 2001 has reinforced the value placed on inclusive education and added to both the pressures and opportunities that confront school systems as they attempt to provide these children with appropriate and effective instruction (Lordeman & Jones, 2010; Wakeman, Browder, Meier, & McColl, 2007).

The 1986 reauthorization of EHA provided strong financial incentives to states to provide public education for all eligible 3- to 5-year-old children who met criteria for *developmental delay* by 1991–1992, signaling an important shift towards preventive approaches to special education (Farran, 2000; Krauss & Hauser-Cram, 1992). The hope was that early intervention would result in lower special education costs over the school years. During the ensuing decade, the number of 3- to 5-year-olds receiving special education services grew by almost 50% (U.S. Department of Education, Office of Special Education and Rehabilitative Services, 2005), reaching 706,242 children (5.82% of the preschool population) in 2006 (Blackorby et al., 2010). One third of these preschoolers received all of their special education in early childhood environments with peers without disabilities, including Head Start, child care, and pre-K settings (U.S. Department of Education, 2006).

These trends have been accompanied by a very active debate regarding the most appropriate settings, activities, and focus and intensity of services for advancing the development of this young cohort (Administration for Children and Families, 1995; Bailey, Me William, Buysse, & Wesley, 1998; Guralnick, 2001; Kochanek & Buka, 1999; Wolery & Bailey, 2002). The growth in reliance on inclusive early education settings, in particular, has directed empirical attention to examining the role that high-quality early education programs can play in fostering school readiness for these children (Carlson et al., 2009; Hebbeler et al., 2007; Holahan & Costenbader, 2000). In fact, early childhood education has long been viewed as an important strategy for enhancing the later academic success of young children, especially those who are vulnerable as a result of environmental or biological circumstances (Shonkoff & Meisels, 2000). Extensive reviews of the relevant literature for children with disabilities have consistently concluded that early education programs can positively influence school participation and outcomes for this population (Dunst, Snyder, & Mankinen, 1989; Farran, 2000; Guralnick, 1998), although strong research designs are rare and efforts to identify more and less effective approaches to early intervention have remained elusive. It is, nevertheless, well documented that low-income children who participate in high-quality early education programs experience reductions in special education placements once they enter school (Campbell & Ramey, 1995; Conyers, Reynolds, & Ou, 2003; Redden, Ramey, Ramey, Forness & Brezausek, 2003; Schweinhart, Barnes, & Weikart, 1993).

However, the landscape of early childhood education has undergone dramatic changes in the last decade as a result of widespread expansions in state pre-K education (Barnett et al., 2010). These programs have added a prominent option to the array of early intervention programs for young children with special needs, yet their potential to foster the early learning and development of children with special needs remains an unaddressed question. Barnett and colleagues (2010) estimated that in the 2009–2010 school year, 425,388 3- and 4-year-olds with special needs were in state pre-K classrooms (both school-based and mixed delivery systems) with typically developing peers—comprising approximately 5.1% of the total preschool-age population.

Of particular interest are the growing number of school-based pre-K classrooms, in light of prior evidence that effective "transition" or kindergarten entry strategies significantly improve the school success of children with special needs and that children are more likely to receive transition services if they attend pre-K and kindergarten in the same school (Carlson et al., 2009; Schulting, Malone, & Dodge, 2005). Wolery and colleagues (Wolery, Holcombe, Brookfield et al., 1993; Wolery, Holcombe, Venn et al., 1993) have reported that close to three quarters of public school pre-K programs include children with disabilities. The pressing question is whether school-based pre-K offers these children a head start towards successful elementary school performance, as it does for other children (Gormley, Phillips, & Gayer, 2008; Gormley, Phillips, Newmark, Welti, & Adelstein, 2011), or whether it constitutes an early start to learning disparities that distinguish many of these children from their typically developing classmates as they move through school (U.S. Department of Education, National Center for Education Statistics, 2007).

This study was designed to address this question. Specifically, we utilized a quasi-experimental design (regression discontinuity) to compare the kindergarten achievement test scores of children with individualized education programs (IEPs) who had attended the school-based pre-K in Tulsa, Oklahoma (as 4-year-olds) to the pre-K achievement test scores of children with IEPs who were about to begin the program the following school year. We further compared the kindergarten test scores of the pre-K enrollees with special needs to those of their classmates without IEPs. The Oklahoma pre-K program has received national attention because, as one of a handful of programs with universal eligibility, it reaches a higher percentage of 4-year-olds (71%) than any other program in the nation (Barnett et al., 2010). The pre-K program is not only universal in its eligibility; it is fully inclusive in its approach to special education. It also offers relatively high-quality educational opportunities to the enrolled children compared to other pre-K programs around the country (Phillips, Gormley, & Lowen-stein, 2009), and thus offers an important opportunity to examine whetner high-quality, school-based pre-K can serve as an effective early intervention program in fostering school readiness among children with special needs.

There are reasons to be both hopeful and concerned about the role of school-based pre-K programs in the education of children with special needs. On the one hand, pre-K programs share features with early intervention programs that appear to be effective in supporting the development of young children with special needs. For example, the developmental benefits of high-quality early intervention services appear to derive, in part, from their child-focus and reliance on structured, carefully sequenced curricula (Graham & Bryant, 1993; Guralnick, 1998; Odom & Diamond, 1998; Shonkoff & Hauser-Cram, 1987), features that are central to school-based pre-K education. In their comprehensive analysis of services provided for young children with special needs in Montgomery County, Maryland, Markowitz, Hebbeler, Larson, Cooper, and Edmisten (1991) found that children who received services in classroom settings made larger gains on the Battelle Developmental Inventory (Newborg, 2004) than did children who received services in home-based or therapeutic settings—a result that has been replicated (Schwartz, Carta, & Grant, 1996). Moreover, although research findings on inclusion are mixed (see Guralnick, 1997; Odom & Diamond, 1998), the weight of the evidence seems to suggest that inclusion is beneficial for children with mild disabilities, and may support social development to an even greater extent than academic skills (Bailey et al., 1998; Holahan & Costenbader, 2000; Odom et al., 2004). Many school-based pre-K programs (including Tulsa's program) rely heavily, if not exclusively, on inclusive classrooms to serve young children with special needs (Smith, Kleiner, Parsad, & Farris, 2003).

As a case in point, evidence on Head Start, for which federal guidelines require inclusion of children with special needs, has documented the program's effectiveness in promoting the development of these children, albeit modestly (Conyers et al., 2003; Gietzen & Vermeersch, 1980). Indeed, recent evidence from the National Head Start Impact Study revealed that children with special needs who enrolled in Head Start as 3-year-olds had made significant gains in math and social-emotional development at the end of first grade relative to their peers who did not attend Head Start (U.S. Department of Health and Human Services, Administration for Children and Families, 2010). Children without special needs who attended the program did not realize these gains. Whether these findings generalize to school-based pre-K programs, however, remains to be seen.

On the other hand, it is widely recognized that inclusion does not guarantee quality services (Buysse, Wesley, Bryant, & Gardner, 1999; Division for Early Childhood, 2007), and that, although necessary, high quality alone does not appear to maximize the learning and development of children with special needs in early education settings (Guralnick, 2001; Odom et al., 2004). In addition, teachers in early childhood inclusive programs, including state pre-K programs, are typically not trained in special education, nor are special education professionals routinely available to these programs (Buysse, Wesley, Keyes, & Bailey, 1996; McDonnell, Brownell, & Wolery, 1997; Whitebook et al., 2004; Wolery & Wilbers, 1994). Finally, close family involvement and support, along with deliberate orchestration of the array of supports and services needed by children with disabilities, are core tenets of service delivery for these children (Bruder, 2005; Dunst & Trivette, 1997; Guralnick, 1997, 1998, 2005a, 2005b). Yet school-based teachers and administrators do not typically view these kinds of activities as central responsibilities.

This study assessed the impact of Tulsa's high-quality, inclusive school-based pre-K program on the school readiness of children with special needs. We addressed two questions:

1. Does enrollment in Tulsa's pre-K program foster school readiness among children with special needs? We hypothesized that children with special needs who attended the pre-K program would perform at significantly higher levels on tests of preliteracy and pre-math skills at kindergarten entry when compared to children with special needs who had not yet experienced the pre-K program.

2. Does the Tulsa pre-K program have comparable impacts on children with and without special needs? Given the documented quality of the program, and its emphasis on structured instruction and inclusion—factors that have been linked to successful programs for children with special needs—we hypothesized that the effect of the program would be comparable for children with and without special needs.

Methods

Participants

Participants in this study were kindergarten and pre-K children enrolled in the Tulsa, Oklahoma, school-based pre-K program during the 2005–2006 and 2006–2007 school years, respectively. After obtaining institutional review board approval, those who enrolled during the 2005–2006 school year (the treatment group, referred to as *alumni*) were tested as they were entering kindergarten. Those who enrolled during 2006–2007 (the comparison group, referred to as *entrants*) were tested as they were entering pre-K. The combined sample of 3,048 participants included 312 children with special needs (129 entrants and 183 alumni) and 2,752 typically developing children (1,367 entrants and 1,385 alumni).

We included typically developing children in the study sample to compare the effect of pre-K participation for children with and without special needs. The majority of both groups were in full-day programs (88.4% and 83.1%, respectively) and there were no differences between the two groups on full day status. All pre-K classrooms in Tulsa maintain a child: teacher ratio of 10:1 and a maximum classroom size of 20. Two teachers are assigned to each classroom. All lead teachers must have a bachelor's degree and an early childhood teaching certification. These teachers are paid the same wage scale as K-12 teachers in the Tulsa Public School system. Assistant teachers do not have any specific education or training requirements.

Special needs status was determined using administrative data records that identified children who had an IEP in place. The administrative data records also provided the date of the initial IEP meeting, disability code(s), and the level of classroom inclusion the child experienced (full inclusion, inclusion with pull-out for special services, and noninclusive). Children were considered to have special needs for the purpose of this study if the date of their initial IEP meeting occurred prior to the end of their kindergarten year. Selection of the end of kindergarten as our cut-off was guided by feedback from the Tulsa Public School system indicating that children who are granted IEPs during kindergarten are not substantively different (in terms of the presence or severity of disability) from children who are given IEPs during the pre-K year (A. McKenzie, personal communication, September 8, 2008), perhaps because of the similar school-based setting and personnel of pre-K and kindergarten in Tulsa. Nevertheless, in light of evidence that type, severity, and complexity of special needs predict timing of identification (Palfrey, Singer, Walker, & Butler, 1987) and that disabilities such as speech or language impairments or autism tend to be identified earlier than others (Guarino, Buddin, Pham, & Cho, 2007), we examined whether the children identified as having special needs before or during pre-K differed from those identified in kindergarten. The results revealed that children who received their IEPs in kindergarten and those who received them earlier did not differ in their disability code(s) or achievement test scores, and sensitivity checks confirmed that our substantive results do not differ when children who received IEPs in kindergarten are removed from the sample.

A total of 312 children from the larger Tulsa Public Schools (TPS) pre-K sample had been designated *special needs* (had IEPs in place) by the end of kindergarten. Of those children, 250 children or 80% were in full-inclusion pre-K classrooms, 46 children or 14.5% were in full inclusion classrooms with periodic removal for special services (e.g. speech therapy sessions), and the remaining 16 children or 5.5% were in other, noninclusive, pre-K classroom settings. Only children in full inclusion and full inclusion with removal for special services classrooms—124 entrants and 172 alumni, for a total sample of 296 children—were included in the analyses. Children in other classroom settings were dropped to ensure that estimates reflected the effects of the "typical pre-K experience" on children with special needs and could be compared to the experience of typically developing children in the program. There were no major differences in the demographic characteristics or disability codes of the 16 children who were dropped from the sample and those who remained.

Our final sample *(N = 296)* consisted of 94 children (31.8%) whose special needs were identified prior to entering the pre-K program, 147 children (42.9%) who were identified during pre-K, and 55 children (18.6%) who were identified during kindergarten. The majority of the children in this sample (289 or 97.5%) were primarily categorized as having a developmental delay. In Tulsa, this category is utilized as a catch-all for young children with mild to moderate needs who are not achieving at the level of their peers, but for whom future developmental status is uncertain (A. McKenzie, personal communication, September 8, 2008). Of the children who were categorized as having a developmental delay, 121 were assigned no other disability code. The majority of these children (168) were, however, assigned a secondary disability code as follows: 156 with speech impairments, 14 with learning disabilities, one with autism, one with other health impairments, and one with hearing impairments. The remaining seven children were not coded as experiencing developmental delays—but were categorized as having speech impairments only (six) or speech impairments and mental retardation (one). Thus, the sample of children with special needs in this study, although heterogeneous, consisted predominantly of those with mild and moderate delays who may or may not continue to receive services in elementary school and beyond.

Of the 296 children with special needs included in the sample, 68.6% were male, 38.5% were white, 40.5% were black, 8.9% were Hispanic, and 11.8% were Native American. In terms of mothers education, 16.8% of mothers of children with special needs had not completed high school, 24.9% had graduated high school, 47.4% had completed an associate's degree or attended some college, and 11.0% had completed a bachelor's degree or higher. Finally, 64.5% of children with special needs qualified for free lunch, 10.5% qualified for reduced-price lunch, and 25% paid full-price lunch; 5.1% were English language learners; 56.1% lived with their biological father; and 50.5% had internet access in the home.

The 2,752 typically developing children in this study had not been identified as developmentally delayed or otherwise in need of special services (IEP status) by the end of their kindergarten year. Of the typically developing children (both entrants and alumni), 49.6% were male, 32.8% were White, 34.2% were Black, 22.2% were Hispanic, 9.4% were Native American, and the remaining were Asian. In addition, 19.1% of these children's mothers had not completed high school, 27.4% had graduated high school, 39.7% had completed an associate's degree or attended some college, and 13.9% had completed a bachelor's degree or higher. Finally, 63.6% of typically developing children qualified for free lunch, 12.4% qualified for reduced-price lunch, and 24% paid full-price lunch; 15.5% were English language learners; 62.5% lived with their biological father; and 51.9% had Internet access in the home.

Measures and Procedure

The data used in this study are from student tests and parent surveys administered in August 2006 in Tulsa, Oklahoma, as well as administrative data records from the TPS system accessed in June 2008. Children were tested on their pre-academic skills using the Woodcock-Johnson Tests of Achievement III (WJ III; Woodcock, McGrew, & Mather, 2001), a nationally normed, widely used assessment tool that has been used extensively with racially and socioeconomically mixed samples, and with children with special needs (Chase-Lansdale et al., 2003; Henry, Gordon, & Rickman, 2006; Puma et al., 2005). Three subtests of the WJ III were selected to reflect age-appropriate preacademic skills: Letter-Word Identification, Spelling, and Applied Problems. The Letter-Word Identification subtest measures prereading and reading skills. It requires children to identify letters that appear in large type and to pronounce words correctly (the child is not required to know the meaning of any particular word). The Spelling subtest measures prewriting and spelling skills. It measures skills such as drawing lines and tracing letters and requires the child to produce uppercase and lowercase letters and to spell simple words correctly. The Applied Problems subtest measures early math reasoning and problem-solving abilities. It requires the child to analyze and solve math problems, performing relatively simple calculations.

These subtests are appropriate for relatively young children, including preschoolers (Mather & Woodcock, 2001), and have been used in other studies with this age group (Chase-Lansdale et al., 2003; Henry et al., 2006; Puma et al., 2005). Barbara Wendling, a nationally recognized expert on the WJ III and a highly experienced trainer, trained teachers to administer the three tests at one of two training sessions held in Tulsa in late August 2006. Teachers administered the WJ III subtests during the first week of school (designated as a testing week for TPS, prior to the start of classes). Teachers administered all tests in English unless the child being tested was designated a bilingual student, in which case the child was also given a Spanish version of the test, the Batería III Woodcock-Muñoz (Woodcock, Muñoz-Sandoval, McGrew, & Mather, 2005). Only the English-language test scores are analyzed in this article.

We collected data on individual child and parent characteristics via surveys that were completed by the parents while their child was being tested. Parents were asked the child's race and gender, the mothers highest level of education, if the father lived at home with the child, and whether the family had Internet access in the home. We measured family socioeconomic status via an income proxy. Schools reported the lunch status of all children, which provided three levels (i.e., free lunch, reduced-price lunch, full-price lunch). Standard cut-offs for lunch status are determined by the U.S. Department of Agricultures National School Lunch Program and correspond to 130% of the federal poverty level (FPL) for free lunch, 185% of the FPL for reduced-price lunch, and above 185% of the FPL for full-price lunch.

Data Analysis
Selection bias is the key difficulty in assessing the effects of any voluntary program, regardless of the population it serves. Children whose parents enroll them in a voluntary pre-K program, for example, may differ in important ways from children whose parents do not enroll them. To the extent that these differences are measurable, their influence can be controlled. However, if some of these differences (e.g., children's intelligence or motivation and parental attitudes) are not measured, then any direct group comparison will be biased, as will the estimated effects of participation in the program. In effect, differences between enrolled and not-enrolled children that are ascribed to the pre-K program may actually be partially attributable to these types of preexisting sample differences.

Regression-Discontinuity Design
To reduce selection bias, we utilized a regression discontinuity (RD) design to estimate the direct impact of pre-K participation on children with special needs and typically developing children, respectively, and to determine whether a differential effect of participation existed for the two subsamples. This approach builds on previous work with the TPS data (Gormley et al., 2008;

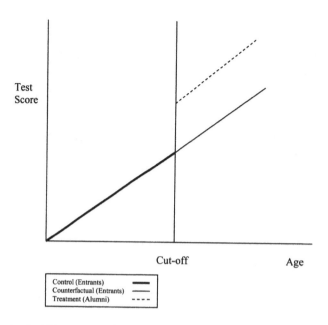

FIGURE 11.1   Hypothetical Illustration of Regression Discontinuity Design

Gormley & Gayer, 2005; Gormley, Gayer, Phillips, & Dawson 2005), others' work evaluating pre-K for typically developing children (Barnett, Lamy, & Jung, 2005), and evaluations of language/reading interventions for developmentally at-risk children (Tuckwiller, Pullen, & Coyne, 2010; Vaughn, Wanzek, Murray, Scammacca, & Linan, 2009).

RD substantially reduced selection bias by creating a treatment group that consisted of children who attended the pre-K program in the 2005–2006 school year and a comparison group that consisted of children who were about to begin the pre-K program at the beginning of the 2006–2007 school year. TPS enforces a strict cutoff date for pre-K eligibility (September 1) that is identical to the cut-off date for kindergarten eligibility. This means that students who were born on or before September 1, 2001, were eligible to participate in the pre-K program for the 2005–2006 school year but students who were born after that date were not eligible to participate until the following year. This strict birthday qualification creates a situation where assignment into the pre-K treatment group is based solely on the cut-off variable, in this case age, which is unrelated to the selection process. The associated inability of researchers or parents to manipulate a given child's assignment into the treatment or comparison group increases confidence that treatment estimates are unbiased (Imbens & Lemieux, 2008; Lee & Lemieux, 2010).

Figure 11.1 provides a hypothetical illustration of this design. The dotted line to the right of the cut-off date shows hypothetical test scores of the treatment group and the bold solid line to the left of the cut-off date shows hypothetical test scores of the comparison group. The key challenge in estimating the effect of TPS pre-K is to estimate the counterfactual or test-score outcomes for treated children had they not been treated. The solid line to the right of the cut-off date depicts the counterfactual. The regression discontinuity design assumes that the counterfactual is continuous at the cut-off date, so any jump in estimated test scores for the treated children relative to the counterfactual can be attributed to their participation in the pre-K program.

The underlying assumption that supports using this analytic design to assess the impact of the pre-K program is that a child who just made the pre-K entrance cut-off date and a child who just missed the cut-off date should have similar characteristics (both measurable and immeasurable), except that one child has already received the treatment (Tulsa pre-K) and the other has not. We tested this assumption for measurable characteristics using the entire sample of children with special needs (reflected in a 12-month window in age around the cut-off date). As Table 11.1 indicates, there were no statistically significant differences between the children who had experienced pre-K and were entering kindergarten (the treatment group) and the children who were just entering pre-K (the comparison group) for gender, ethnicity, resident father status, Internet access, or free lunch status. There were, however, differences between the two groups for mothers education level. Specifically, the comparison group had more highly educated mothers.

TABLE 11.1 Demographic Characteristics of Pre-K Students With Special Needs: Alumni Versus Entrants

	Comparison			Treatment			
Variable	M	SE	N	M	SE	N	Difference
Special needs ID before pre-K	0.290	0.041	124	0.337	0.036	172	−.047
Special needs ID during pre-K	0.516	0.045	124	0.483	0.038	172	.033
Special needs ID during kindergarten	0.194	0.035	124	0.180	0.029	172	.013
Female	0.339	0.043	124	0.297	0.035	172	.042
Black	0.395	0.044	124	0.413	0.038	172	−.018
White	0.355	0.043	124	0.407	0.038	172	−.052
Hispanic	0.097	0.027	124	0.081	0.021	172	.015
Native American	0.145	0.032	124	0.099	0.023	172	.046
Lunch status							
Paid	0.008	0.008	124	0.000	0.000	172	.008
Reduced	0.298	0.041	124	0.215	0.031	172	.083
Free	0.081	0.025	124	0.122	0.025	172	−.041
Maternal education							
No high school diploma	0.621	0.044	124	0.663	0.036	172	−.042
High school diploma/GED	0.137	0.031	124	0.273	0.044	172	−.168***
Some college/associate's degree	0.274	0.039	124	0.261	0.031	172	.013
Bachelor's degree or higher	0.508	0.045	124	0.349	0.035	172	.159***
Resident father status	0.500	0.045	124	0.535	0.038	172	−.035
Internet access in the home	0.476	0.045	124	0.436	0.038	172	.040

*$p < 0.10$. **$p < 0.05$. ***$p < 0.01$.

Inadequate sample size prevented tests to confirm whether imbalances diminish and the treatment effect remains for the children with special needs as the window (age in months) around the cut-off variable narrows. However, narrowing the window around the cut-off date for the larger sample of typically developing children in this study and the entire sample of children (with and without special needs) who attended the pre-K program (Gormley & Gayer, 2005; Gormley et al., 2005; Gormley, 2011) confirmed that for these populations, imbalances diminished and test score differences remained.

We are confident that the imbalances in the sample of children with special needs do not reflect a manipulation of children's assignment into the treatment or comparison group. Rather, they reflect a policy-induced loss of children with special needs whose mothers were poorly educated from the comparison group. The implications of these imbalances for the interpretation of the magnitude of pre-K program impacts for children with special needs are discussed later in this article. However, these imbalances do not affect the validity of utilizing RD in this study because they are not correlated with the cut-off date.

Analytic Approach

The primary goal of this study was to estimate the effect of pre-K program participation for children with special needs. To do this, we ran a series of Ordinary Least Squares (OLS) regressions on the subsample of children with special needs, including both entrants to (N = 124) and alumni of (N = 172) the pre-K program. The initial model utilized a dichotomous variable (treatment) which captured whether the student was born on or before September 1, 2001, and represents treatment status equal to 1 for students who participated in the pre-K program in 2005–2006 and equal to zero for students who participated in the Tulsa pre-K program in 2006–2007, child's age (qualify) measured as the difference in days between the student's date of birth and September 1, 2001, and an interaction term for child's age by treatment. Covariates added to this model included race, gender, free lunch eligibility, maternal education, whether the child lived with his or her biological father, and whether the child had Internet access at home. Although, theoretically, the covariates should be uncorrelated with the treatment variable and are therefore unnecessary inclusions in the model if the underlying assumptions of the regression discontinuity design hold, we included them here to increase the precision of the estimated treatment effect.

After estimating the effect of pre-K participation on the preacademic skills of children with special needs, we compared the impact of participation on children with special needs to that of their typically developing peers. To accomplish this, we ran a similar series of OLS regressions on the combined sample of special needs and typically developing children (N = 3,048). This series of regressions utilized a fully interacted model, which included students' special needs status; an interaction variable capturing the relative effect of treatment for students with special needs; and interaction terms for all of the covariates with special needs status.

We implemented multiple imputation as a strategy to address the prevalence of missing data, particularly with regards to demographic variables that relied on parental survey report (Rubin, 1996), using the ice program in Stata (version 10.0) to create five imputed data sets that were then combined to produce estimates of the missing data values (Royston, 2004, 2005a, 2005b). In this study, missing values for gender, ethnicity, maternal education level (passively imputed), resident father status, and Internet access, were imputed. Missing values for WJ III test scores (outcome variables) and free lunch status were not imputed. Children with missing values for either the outcome variable or for free lunch eligibility were dropped from the analyses. In each of the models, approximately half of the children who were dropped were missing WJ III test scores; the majority of these children failed to show up to school on the day they were being tested. Tests of the sensitivity of the estimates to different methods of dealing with missing data indicated that findings were robust.

Results

Impact of Pre-K for Children With Special Needs
Table 11.2 presents tests of the hypothesis that children with identified special needs benefited from their enrollment in the pre-K program. Of the 296 entrants and alumni with special needs,

TABLE 11.2   Effect of Pre-K on Raw Test Scores: Children With Special Needs

Variable	Letter-Word Identification		Spelling		Applied Problems	
	b	SE	b	SE	b	SE
Treatment	3.433***	1.109	3.049***	0.728	1.295	1.347
Age in days	0.004	0.003	0.004	0.002	0.006	0.004
Age in days × treatment	0.002	0.005	−0.002	0.004	0.009*	0.006
Female	0.329	0.632	1.105***	0.413	1.006	0.739
Black	−1.468**	0.607	−0.781	0.505	−2.451**	0.828
Hispanic	0.272	1.112	0.105	0.678	−2.373*	1.366
Native American	0.062	0.765	−0.390	0.602	−1.283	1.106
Asian	8.599***	0.999	1.160**	0.586	4.333***	1.223
Reduced-price lunch	−0.446	1.033	−0.187***	0.781	−0.328	1.195
Free lunch	−0.505	0.844	−0.142	0.577	−0.704	0.967
Maternal education						
No high school diploma	−0.528	0.916	−0.446	0.580	1.594	1.118
Some college/ associate's degree	1.263*	0.737	0.734	0.857	2.067**	0.828
Bachelor's degree or higher	3.338*	1.859	1.016	0.857	2.132	1.508
Lives with father	0.357	0.709	0.728*	0.412	0.261	0.861
Internet access in home	1.445**	0.667	0.232	0.514	1.417*	0.837
Constant	3.333***	1.233	3.375***	0.839	6.428***	1.725
Number of observations	252		243		250	

*$p < 0.10$. **$p < 0.05$. ***$p < 0.01$.

252 were included in the analysis for the WJ III Letter-Word Identification subtest, 243 were included in the analysis for the Spelling subtest, and 250 were included in the analysis for the Applied Problems subtest due to missing values (for test scores or free lunch eligibility). We calculated effect sizes by dividing the estimated treatment effect by the standard deviation of the comparison group. Children with special needs who had participated in the pre-K program had significantly higher Letter-Word Identification raw test scores (b = 3.433, SE = 1.109, p < 0.001) and Spelling raw test scores (b = 3.049, SE = 0.728, p < 0.001) than children who had selected into the program but had not yet experienced it, after controlling for age and other demographic variables. These results indicate test score impacts of 3.433 points (a 1.093 effect size) for the Letter-Word scores and test score impacts of 3.049 points (a 1.155 effect size) for the Spelling scores. There were no differences between the two groups on the Applied Problems raw test scores (b = 1.295, SE = 1.347, p > 0.10). Figures 11.2 and 11.3 provide graphical depictions (scatterplots) of the RD findings. In both figures, the jump in test scores at the cutoff date represents the impact of the pre-K program on test scores, which we have estimated here.

Comparing Pre-K Impact for Children With and Without Special Needs

Table 11.3 presents a direct comparison of the effect of pre-K program participation on typically developing children and children with special needs for all three WJ III subtests (see Table 11.4 for full regression results). Due to missing values for the outcome variables or free lunch eligibility, 2,746 of the complete sample of entrants and alumni (N = 3,048) were included in the analysis

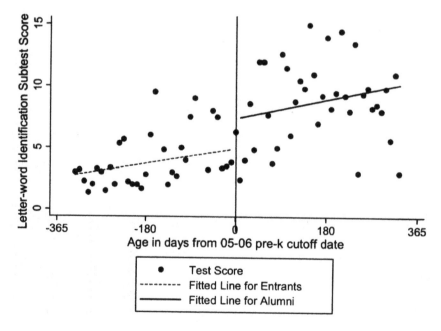

FIGURE 11.2   Scatterplot of Regression Discontinuity for Letter-Word Identification Subtest

Note. Each data point represents the average test score for groups of children born within a 10-day window.

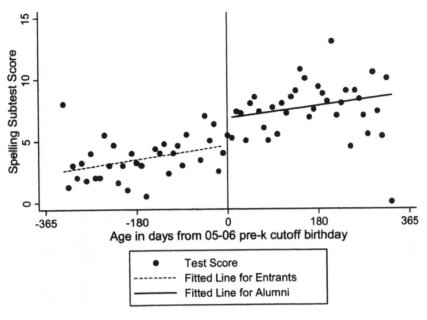

FIGURE 11.3   Scatterplot of Regression Discontinuity for Spelling Subtest

Note. Each data point represents the average test score for groups of children born within a 10-day window.

for the Letter-Word Identification sub test, 2,641 were included in the analysis for the Spelling subtest, and 2,724 were included in the analysis for the Applied Problems subtest. There were no significant differences in the effect of program participation on the test scores of children with and without special needs for any of the subtests.

Figure 11.4 illustrates the test-score gains associated with pre-K participation for children with special needs and typically developing children, converted into age equivalence scores in

TABLE 11.3   Comparison of the Effect of Pre-K on Raw Test Scores of Typically Developing Children and Children With Special Needs

Variable	Typically Developing		Special Needs		Difference (Treatment by Special Needs Status)	
	b	SE	b	SE	b	SE
Letter-Word Identification	3.736***	0.350	3.433***	2.209	−0.303	1.137
Spelling	2.121***	0.224	3.049***	0.728	0.928	0.758
Applied Problems	2.000***	0.335	1.295	1.347	−0.705	1.365

*p < 0.10. **p < 0.05. ***p < 0.01.

TABLE 11.4   Regression Results

Variable	Letter-Word Identification		Spelling		Applied Problems	
	b	SE	b	SE	b	SE
Treated	3.735***	0.351	2.121***	0.224	2.000***	0.335
Special education status	−2.490**	1.254	−2.255***	0.864	−5.512***	1.718
Special education status × treated	−0.303	1.137	0.928	0.758	−0.705	1.365
Qualify age in days	0.007***	0.001	0.008***	0.001	0.012***	0.001
Qualify × cut-off	0.001***	0.002	−0.001	0.001	0.003*	0.002
Special ed status × qualify age in days	−0.004	0.003	−0.005**	0.002	−0.007	0.004
Special ed status × qualify × cut-off	0.003	0.005	−0.000	0.004	0.014**	0.006
Reduced-price lunch	−1.224***	0.337	−0.376***	0.336	−1.094***	0.295
Free lunch	−1.164***	0.251	−0.562**	0.163	−1.189***	0.239
Black	−0.043	0.218	−0.367**	0.147	−2.179***	0.222
Hispanic	−1.436***	0.243	−0.178	0.159	−3.395***	0.263
Native American	−0.252	0.305	0.090	0.187	−0.387	0.288
Asian	−0.134	0.585	0.552	0.467	−2.996***	0.637
Female	0.838***	0.164	1.108***	0.106	0.536***	0.166
Lives with father	0.157	0.184	0.227*	0.133	0.049	0.222
Internet access in home	1.064***	0.207	0.544***	0.149	0.938***	0.222
Mother's education (ME)						
No high school	−0.326	0.252	−0.390*	0.200	−0.801***	0.266
Some college	0.664***	0.208	0.297**	0.146	0.667***	0.230
College grad and up	1.804***	0.354	1.086***	0.213	2.104***	0.317
Reduced price lunch × special ed status	−0.778	1.065	0.190	0.786	0.767	1.201
Free lunch × special ed status	−1.135***	0.888	0.420	0.163	0.485	0.970
Black × special ed status	−1.424**	0.632	−0.415*	0.512	0.272	0.222
Hispanic × special ed status	1.708	1.110	0.283	0.681	1.022	1.356
Native American × special ed status	0.315	0.807	−0.479	0.617	−0.896	1.113
Asian × special ed status	8.734***	1.147	0.608	0.738	7.329***	1.357
Female	−0.510	0.636	−0.003	0.416	0.470	0.738
Lives with father × special ed status	0.200	0.733	0.501	0.413	0.213	0.897

Internet access in home × special ed status	0.381	0.653	−0.312	0.556	0.479	0.814
ME: No high school × special ed status	0.203	0.953	−0.055	0.625	2.395**	0.266
ME: Some college × special ed status	0.599	0.744	0.437	0.513	1.400*	0.841
ME: College grad and up × special ed status	1.534	1.840	−0.070	0.861	0.029	1.498
Constant	5.823***	0.380	5.630***	0.276	11.940***	0.418
Observations		2746		2641		2724

$*p < 0.10.$ $**p < 0.05.$ $***p < 0.01.$

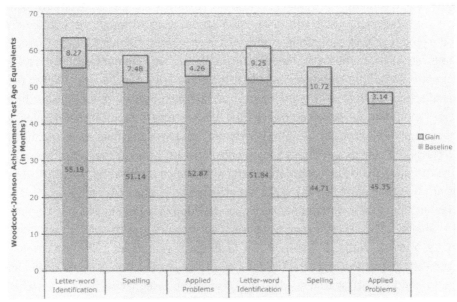

FIGURE 11.4   Tuba Pre-K Program Impacts in Monthly Equivalents for Typically Developing Children and Children With Special Needs

months. It is important to note that for WJ III the relationship of test-score points to months gained is non-linear. Children with special needs, who scored lower than children without special needs on all three subtests prior to pre-K participation, demonstrated larger age equivalence gains despite comparable gains in terms of raw test score points for the two groups.

Discussion

This study represents the first effort to look at the effects of school-based pre-K education on the school readiness of children with special needs. It addressed the question of whether school-based pre-K offers young children with special needs, operationalized by IEPs, a head start towards successful elementary school performance or whether it fails to advance the early learning of these children. The results are cause for optimism. School-based pre-K education, as experienced in Tulsa, supported the early learning of children with special needs, as hypothesized. Indeed, the impact of pre-K on the achievement test scores of the children with IEPs was not statistically different from the impact of pre-K on the scores of their typically developing classmates.

The program appears to have its largest effects on the Letter-Word Identification subtest, which assesses prereading abilities, and the Spelling subtest, which assesses prewriting skills, for children with special needs. The Applied Problems subtest of early math reasoning and problem-solving abilities did not exhibit significant differences between the children with special needs who had and had not yet attended the pre-K program. This pattern of results also characterized the complete sample of children—those with and without special needs—who attended the Tulsa pre-K program during the 2005–2006 school year, although the Applied Problems subtest did produce significant group differences in this larger sample (Gormley et al., 2008).

The relatively greater impact of the program on literacy than on numeracy skills may reflect the differential amount of classroom time that the Tulsa pre-K teachers devoted to these two domains of school readiness. To gain a better understanding of practices inside the school-based pre-K programs, we deployed highly trained observers to monitor the morning sessions of all classrooms (Phillips et al., 2009). On average, the pre-K teachers allocated 33% of their morning classroom time to preliteracy and writing activities, whereas they allocated only 17% of their time to math activities. In addition, emerging evidence is revealing that early math skills, perhaps more so than early literacy skills, are affected by young children's executive function capacities, including their working memory and attention (Espy et al., 2004; Li-Grining, Raver, & Smith-Donald, 2010). These capacities pose special challenges to children with disabilities (Gathercole, Alloway, Willis, & Adams, 2006; Liebman & Goodman, 1995), which may render typical premath instruction less effective than preliteracy instruction in fostering kindergarten readiness for children with special needs. It may also be the case that young children with special needs require more individualized math instruction than their peers without special needs, and than was provided in Tulsa pre-K classrooms.

Not only did pre-K attendance bolster the school readiness of the children with special needs, but its impacts were comparable to those for the typically developing children. The effect sizes for the children with special needs were 1.093 and 1.155 for the Letter-Word Identification and Spelling tests, respectively. These effect sizes exceed those reported for other state-funded pre-K programs, which range from .17 to .68 (Wong, Cook, Barnett, & Jung, 2008), with data reported for complete samples that likely include some children with special needs but consist predominantly of typically developing children. Moreover, although the children with special needs scored lower on each of the WJ III subtests than the children without special needs both prior to and after attending pre-K, as expected, their test gains expressed in monthly equivalents were quite large for both the Letter-Word Identification and Spelling subtests. Indeed, as compared to the children with special needs who had not yet experienced pre-K, those with pre-K experience gained over 9 months on the Letter-Word test and close to 11 months on the Spelling test. Although gains on the Applied Problems subtest were not significant for the children with special needs, it is notable that their scores on this test of pre-math skills placed them over 3 months ahead of children with special needs who had not yet attended the program. Nevertheless, in light of the importance of early mathematics concepts for children's continued academic success (Duncan et al., 2007), efforts to improve mathematics instruction within the context of inclusive programs that serve children with special needs are critical.

There is reason to believe that these results may actually represent a conservative estimate of the impact of pre-K on the school readiness of children with special needs. The comparison group of children with special needs, who were just entering the pre-K program, as compared to the treatment children, had more highly educated mothers. These differences in maternal education appear to be the direct result of an administrative initiative within TPS to funnel all children with special needs, regardless of socioeconomic status, into the local Head Start program and away from the public pre-K program (A. McKenzie, personal communication, September 8, 2008). Highly educated mothers may have resisted the placement of their children with special needs into Head Start, thus creating the observed higher maternal education level, on average, in the TPS pre-K comparison group than the treatment group and resulting in a conservative estimate of the treatment effect. Indeed, analyses designed to test this hypothesis (available from authors upon request) confirmed that impacts presented here are conservative.

Although the current study did not examine the specific features of the Tulsa pre-K program that might account for its positive impacts on the early learning of children with special needs, it is noteworthy that, in prior analyses, the TPS pre-K classrooms scored higher on classroom quality on a range of indicators as compared to a multistate sample of school-based pre-K programs (Phillips et al., 2009). Quality of early educational environments clearly matters for children with special needs, as it does for all children (Conyers et al., 2003). More specifically, these indicators included observational assessments of time management, reliance on instructional techniques that maximize students' engagement and foster higher order thinking skills, and providing feedback that expands understanding. These classroom features have been associated with children's early learning in previous studies (Howes et al., 2008; Mashburn et al., 2008). Tulsa pre-K teachers also devoted more classroom time, relative to pre-K teachers in other states, to literacy and math instruction.

In light of evidence within the special education literature that children with special needs benefit from well-organized, structured, and sequenced instruction, as well as from intensive exposure to learning materials (Guralnick, 1998; Hill, Brooks-Gunn, & Waldfogel, 2003), these features of Tulsa pre-K are strong candidates for future efforts to identify the predictors of the gains demonstrated by the children with special needs in these classrooms. Tulsa's almost exclusive reliance on inclusion, combined with the relatively high quality of instruction provided, may also contribute to the promising results (Bailey et al., 1998; Holahan & Costenbader, 2000; Odom et al., in press), although, we were not able to compare inclusive and noninclusive classrooms in this study. A relatively new literature examining peer effects in pre-K classrooms may also be pertinent in the context of Tulsa's reliance on inclusive classrooms. Henry and Rickman (2007) found that the ability levels of children's peers within preschool classrooms were directly related to the variation in children's cognitive, prereading, and expressive language skills at kindergarten entry. Although peer effects have not been examined for children with special needs, it is plausible that they may operate in a similar fashion within integrated classrooms.

Full-day preschool attendance generates higher rates of developmental progress for children with special needs than does half-day attendance (Holahan & Costenbader, 2000); the fact that close to 90% of the children with special needs in the Tulsa pre-K program attended for a full day may also play a role in the gains made by these children. Finally, in addition to the evidence of high-quality instruction described above, it is notable that every pre-K teacher in the Tulsa pre-K program had a bachelor's degree, was early-childhood certified (although not necessarily certified in special education), and was paid on the wage scale for public school teachers, suggesting a relatively well-educated early childhood teacher workforce that focused classroom time on instruction.

Although these factors may account for the strong progress towards school readiness made by the children with special needs who attended the Tulsa pre-K program, they also limit the generalizability of the findings. The findings are also specific to pre-K that is both universal and inclusive. Other limitations concern an inability to examine variation in outcomes associated with specific subgroups within the population of children with special needs defined either by disability code or severity of disability, or by variation in family characteristics or environmental risk, due to both lack of information and the small sample size. Indeed, our findings should be viewed as generalizable only to young children with relatively mild to moderate disabilities. The enormous heterogeneity in both biological and environmental causes of disability, and its contribution to variability in response to early intervention, is an extremely pressing issue that this work cannot inform (Guralnick, 2005a).

Unfortunately, we lacked information on other services received by the children in this study, which may have contributed to their progress beyond the benefits of the pre-K program, as well as on the family circumstances of the children in our study. The developmental systems approach (Guralnick, 2005b, 2011) highlights the important contribution of the family in fostering the development of children with special needs. However, absent family-level data, we are unable to ascertain how family dynamics in either the comparison or treatment group may have contributed to our results.

Yet the current results document that the TPS pre-K program is efficacious in preparing young children with a range of mild to moderate special needs for the demands of elementary school. In light of the rapid growth in special education enrollments within state pre-K programs, many of which rely at least in part on school- based classrooms, these are very promising results. Concerns that the needs of these children will be neglected in the context of pre-K programs that are not designed specifically with children with special needs in mind, or that state pre-K may even contribute to disparities in learning that emerge during the school years for these children, would appear to be largely unfounded when the quality of early education is high and when pre-K education is tightly integrated into the elementary education system. The challenge for the future is one of ensuring that this is not a unique pattern of results. This entails deciphering the "active ingredients" of the Tulsa program for children with special needs and taking the necessary steps to translate this information into programs across the nation that meet the needs of young children with early delays and disabilities.

References

Administration for Children and Families. (1995). *Passages to inclusion: Creating systems of care for all children. Monograph for state, territorial and tribal child care administrators*. Washington, DC: Administration for Children, Youth, and Families. (ERIC Document Reproduction Service No. ED406819)

Bailey, D. B., McWilliam, R. A., Buysse, V., & Wesley, P. W. (1998). Inclusion in the context of competing values in early childhood education. *Early Childhood Research Quarterly, 13*, 27–47. http://dx.doi.org/10.1016/S0885-2006(99)80024-6

Barnett, W. S., Epstein, D. J., Carolan, M. E., Fitzgerald, J., Ackerman, D. J., & Friedman, A. H. (2010). *The state of preschool 2010*. New Brunswick, NJ: Rutgers University, National Institute for Early Education Research.

Barnett, W. S., Lamy, C., & Jung, K. (2005). *The effects of state pre kindergarten programs on young children's school readiness in five states*. New Brunswick, NJ: Rutgers University, National Institute for Early Education Research.

Blackorby, J., Schiller, E., Mallik, S., Hebbeler, K., Huang, T., Javits, H., ... Williamson, C. (2010). *Patterns in the identification of and outcomes for children and youth with disabilities* (NCEE 2010–4005). Washington, DC: U.S. Department of Education National Center for Education Evaluation and Regional Assistance.

Bruder, M. B. (2005). Service coordination and integration in a developmental systems approach to early intervention. In G. J. Guralnick (Ed.), *A developmental systems approach to early intervention: National and international perspectives* (pp. 29–58). Baltimore, MD: Brookes.

Buysse, V., Wesley, P. W., Bryant, D., & Gardner, D. (1999). Quality of early childhood programs in inclusive and noninclusive settings. *Exceptional Children, 65*, 301–314.

Buysse, V., Wesley, P. W., Keyes, L., & Bailey, D. (1996). Assessing the comfort zone of childcare teachers in serving young children with disabilities. *Journal of Early Intervention, 20*, 209–210. http://dx.doi.org/10.1177/105381519602000301

Campbell, F. A., & Ramey, C. T. (1995). Cognitive and school outcomes for high-risk African-American students at midlife adolescence: Positive effects of early intervention. *American Educational Research Journal, 32*, 743–772. http://dx.doi.org/10.3102/00028312032004743

Carlson, E., Daley, T., Bitterman, A., Heinzen, H., Keller, B., Markowitz, J., & Riley, J. (2009). *Early school transitions and the social behavior of children with disabilities: Selected findings from the Pre-Elementary Education Longitudinal Study*. Washington, DC: National Center for Special Education Research.

Chase-Lansdale, L., Moffitt, R., Lohman, B., Cherlin, A., Coley, R., Pittman, L., ... Votruba-Drzal (2003). Mothers' transitions from welfare to work and the well being of preschoolers and adolescents, *Science, 299*, 1548–1552. http://dx.doi.org/10.1126/science.1076921

Conyers, L. M., Reynolds, A. J., & Ou, S-R. (2003). The effect of early childhood intervention and subsequent special education services: Findings from the Chicago Parent-Child Centers. *Educational Evaluation and Policy Analysis, 25,* 75–95. http://dx.doi.org/10.3102/01623737025001075

Division for Early Childhood, Council for Exceptional Children. (2007). *Promoting positive outcomes for children with disabilities: Recommendations for curriculum, assessment, and program evaluation.* Missoula, MT: Author.

Duncan, G. J. Dowsett, C. J. Claessens, A. Magnuson, K. Huston, A. C., Klebanov, P., ... Brooks-Gunn, J. (2007). School readiness and later achievement. *Developmental Psychology, 43,* 1428–1446. http://dx.doi.org/10.1037/0012-1649.43.6.1428

Dunst, C. J., Snyder, S. W., & Mankinen, M. (1989). Efficacy of early intervention. In M. C. Wang, M. C. Reynolds, & G. H. Walber (Eds.), *Handbook of special education: Research and practice—Low incidence conditions* (pp. 259–294). New York, NY: Pergamon.

Dunst, C. J., & Trivette, C. M. (1997). Early intervention with young at-risk children and their families. In R. Ammerman & M. Hersen (Eds.), *Handbook of prevention and treatment with children and adolescents: Intervention in the real world* (pp. 157–180). New York, NY: Wiley.

Espy, K., McDiarmid, M. M., Cwik, M. F., Stalets, M., Hamby, A., & Stern, T. E. (2004). The contribution of executive functions to emergent mathematic skills in preschool children. *Developmental Neuropsychology, 26,* 465–486. http://dx.doi.org/10.1207/s15326942dn2601_6

Farran, D. (2000). Another decade of intervention for children who are low-income and disabled: What do we know now? In J. Shonkoff & S. Meisels (Eds.), *Handbook of early intervention* (2nd ed.). New York, NY: Cambridge University Press.

Gathercole, S. E., Alloway, T. P., Willis, C., & Adams, A. (2006). Working memory in children with reading disabilities. *Journal of Experimental Child Psychology, 93,* 265–281. http://dx.doi.org/10.1016/j.jecp.2005.08.003

Gietzen, D., & Vermeersch, J. A. (1980). Health status and school achievement of children from Head Start and free school lunch programs. *Public Health Report, 95,* 362–368.

Gormley, W. (2011, January). *Regression discontinuity: A view from Tulsa.* Presentation at the Workshop on Regression Discontinuity Methods in Prekindergarten Evaluations, Cambridge, MA.

Gormley, W., & Gayer, T. (2005). Promoting school readiness in Oklahoma: An Evaluation of Tulsa's pre-K program. *Journal of Human Resources, 40,* 533–558.

Gormley, W, Gayer, T., Phillips, D., & Dawson, B. (2005). The effects of universal pre-K on cognitive development. *Developmental Psychology, 41,* 872–884. http://dx.doi.org/10.1037/0012-1649.41.6.872

Gormley, W., Phillips, D., & Gayer, T. (2008). Preschool programs can boost school readiness. *Science, 320,* 1723–1724. http://dx.doi.org/10.1126/science.1156019

Gormley, W., Phillips, D., Newmark, K., Welti, K., & Adelstein, S. (2011). Social-emotional effects of early childhood education programs in Tulsa. *Child Development, 82,* 2095–2109. http://dx.doi.org/10.1111/j.1467-8624.2011.01648.x

Graham, M. A., & Bryant, D. M. (1993). Characteristics of quality, effective service delivery systems for children with special needs. In D. M. Bryant & M. A. Graham (Eds.), *Implementing early intervention: From research to effective practice* (pp. 233–252). New York, NY: Guilford.

Guarino, C., Buddin, R., Pham, C., & Cho, M. (2007). *Working paper: Characteristics associated with the early identification of children with special needs in California* (WR-439-EDU). Pittsburgh, PA: RAND Education.

Guralnick, M. J. (1997). Second-generation research in the field of early intervention. In M. Guralnick (Ed.), *The effectiveness of early intervention* (pp. 3–23). Baltimore, MD: Brookes.

Guralnick, M. J. (1998). Effectiveness of early intervention for vulnerable children: A developmental perspective. *American Journal of Mental Retardation, 102,* 319–345. http://dx.doi.org/10.1352/0895-8017(1998)102<0319:EOEIFV>2.0.CO;2

Guralnick, M. J. (2001). Social competence with peers and early childhood inclusion. In M. J. Guralnick (Ed.), *Early childhood inclusion: Focus on change* (pp. 3–35). Baltimore, MD: Brookes.

Guralnick, M.J. (2005a). Early intervention for children with intellectual disabilities: Current knowledge and future prospects. *Journal of Applied Research in Intellectual Disabilities, 18,* 313–324. http://dx.doi.org/10.1111/j.1468-3148.2005.00270.x

Guralnick, M.J. (Ed.). (2005b). *A developmental systems approach to early intervention: National and international perspectives.* Baltimore, MD: Brookes.

Guralnick, M.J. (2011). Why early intervention works: A systems perspective. *Infants and Young Children, 24,* 6–28. http://dx.doi.org/10.1097/IYC.0b013e3182002cfe

Hebbeler, K., Spiker, D., Bailey, D., Scarborough, A., Mallik, S., Simeonsson, ... Nelson, L. (2007). *Early intervention for infants and toddlers with disabilities and their families: Participants, services and outcomes, Final report of the National Early Intervention Longitudinal Study.* Menlo Park, CA: SRI International.

Henry, G., Gordon, C. S., & Rickman, D. K. (2006). Early education policy alternatives: Comparing quality and outcomes of Head Start and state prekindergarten. *Educational Evaluation and Policy Analysis, 28,* 77–97. http://dx.doi.org/10.1002/pam.20158

Henry, G. T., & Rickman, D. K. (2007). Do peers influence children's skills development in preschool? *Economics of Education Review, 26,* 100–112. http://dx.doi.org/10.1016/j.econedurev.2005.09.006

Hill, J. L., Brooks-Gunn, J., & Waldfogel, J. (2003). Sustained effects of high participation in an early intervention for low-birth-weight premature infants. *Developmental Psychology, 39,* 730–744. http://dx.doi.org/10.1037/0012-1649.39.4.730

Holahan, A., & Costenbader, V. (2000). A comparison of developmental gains for preschool children with disabilities in inclusive and self-contained classrooms. *Topics in Early Childhood Special Education, 20,* 224–236. http://dx.doi.org/10.1177/027112140002000403

Howes, C., Burchinal, M., Pianta, R., Bryant, D., Early, D., Clifford, R., & Barbarin, O. (2008). Ready to learn? Children's pre-academic achievement in pre-Kindergarten programs. *Early Childhood Research Quarterly, 23,* 27–50. http://dx.doi.org/10.1016/j.ecresq.2007.05.002

Imbens, G. W., & Lemieux, T. (2008). Regression discontinuity designs: A guide to practice. *Journal of Econometrics, 142,* 615–635. http://dx.doi.org/10.1016/j.jeconom.2007.05.001

Kochanek, T. T., & Buka, S. L. (1999). Influential factors in inclusive versus non-indusive placement for preschool children with disabilities. *Early Education & Development, 10,* 191–208. http://dx.doi.org/10.1207/s15566935eed1002_5

Krauss, M. W., & Hauser-Cram, P. (1992). Two generations of family research in early intervention. In M. Guralnick (Ed.), *The effectiveness of early intervention* (pp. 611–624). Baltimore, MD: Brookes.

Lee, D. S., & Lemieux, T. (2010). Regression discontinuity designs in economics. *Journal of Econometric Literature, 48,* 281–355. http://dx.doi.org/10.1257/jel.48.2.281

Li-Grining, C. P., Raver, C. C., & Smith-Donald, R. (2010). *School readiness and academic competence during preschool: Evidence from CSRP.* Unpublished manuscript, Loyola University Chicago, Illinois.

Liebman, J. L., & Goodman, J. E (1995). Learning in early intervention programs: The generalization and maintenance of IEP objectives. *Early Education and Development, 6,* 127–143. http://dx.doi.org/10.1207/s15566935eed0602_2

Lordeman, A., & Jones, N. L. (2010). *The Individuals with Disabilities Education Act (IDEA): Interactions with selected provisions of the No Child Left Behind Act (NCLB)* (Congressional Research Service, No. 7-5700, RL32913). Washington, DC: U.S. Government Printing Office.

Markowitz, J. B., Hebbeler, K., Larson, J. C., Cooper, J. A., & Edmisten, P. (1991). Using value-added analysis to examine short-term effects of early intervention. *Journal of Early Intervention, 15,* 377–389. http://dx.doi.org/10.1177/105381519101500406

Mashburn, A. J., Pianta, R. C., Hamre, B. K., Downer, J. T., Barbarin, O., Bryant, D., ... Howes, C. (2008). Measures of classroom quality in prekindergarten and children's development of academic, language, and social skills. *Child Development, 79,* 732–749. http://dx.doi.org/10.1111/j.1467-8624.2008.01154.x

Mather, N., & Woodcock, R. (2001). *Examiner's manual, Woodcock–Johnson Achievement Test-III.* Chicago, IL: Riverside.

McDonnell, A. P., Brownell, K., & Wolery, M. (1997). Teaching experience and specialist support: A survey of preschool teachers employed in programs accredited by NAEYC. *Topics in Early Childhood Special Education, 17,* 263–285. http://dx.doi.org/10.1177/027112149701700303

Newborg, J. (2004). *Battelle Developmental Inventory,* Second Edition. Rolling Meadows, IL: Riverside Publishing.

Odom, S. L., & Diamond, K. E. (1998). Inclusion of young children with special needs in early childhood education: The research base. *Early Childhood Research Quarterly, 13,* 3–25. http://dx.doi.org/10.1016/S0885-2006(99)80023-4

Odom, S. L., Pungello, E. P., & Gardner-Neblett, N. (Eds.). (In press). *Implications of Developmental Health Science for Infant/Toddler Care and Poverty.* The Guilford Press.

Odom, S. L., Vitztum, J., Wolery, R., Lieber, J., Sandall, S., Hanson, M. J., ... Horn, E. (2004). Preschool inclusion in the United States: A review of research from an ecological systems perspective. *Journal of Research on Special Educational Needs, 4,* 17–49. http://dx.doi.org/10.1111/J.1471-3802.2004.00016.x

Palfrey, J. S., Singer, J. D., Walker, D.K., & Butler, J. A. (1987) Early identification of children's special needs: A study in five metropolitan communities. *Journal of Pediatrics, 111,* 651–659. http://dx.doi.org/10.1016/S0022-3476(87)80238-X

Phillips, D. A., Gormley, W., & Lowenstein, A. (2009). Inside the pre-kindergarten door: Classroom climate and instructional time allocation in Tulsa's pre-K programs. *Early Childhood Research Quarterly, 24,* 213–228. http://dx.doi.org/10.1016/j.ecresq.2009.05.002

Puma, M., Bell, S., Cook, R., Heid, C., Lopez, M., Zill, N., … Bernstein, H. (2005, May). *Head Start impact study: First year findings*. Washington, DC: U.S. Department of Health and Human Services, Administration for Children and Families.

Redden, S. C., Ramey, S. L., Ramey, C. T., Forness, S. R., & Brezausek, C. M. (2003). Special education placements among former Head Start children: A descriptive multi-site study. *Education & Treatment of Children, 26,* 1–21.

Royston, P. (2004). Multiple imputation of missing values. *The Stata Journal, 4,* 227–241.

Royston, P. (2005a). Multiple imputation of missing values: Update. *The Stata Journal, 5,* 1–14.

Royston, P. (2005b). Multiple imputation of missing values: Update of ice. *The Stata Journal, 5,* 527–536.

Rubin, D. B. (1996) Multiple imputation after 18+ years (With discussion). *Journal of the American Statistical Association, 91,* 473–489. http://dx.doi.org/10.2307/2291635

Schulting, A. B., Malone, P. S., & Dodge, K. A. (2005). The effect of school-based kindergarten transition policies and practices on child academic outcomes. *Developmental Psychology, 41,* 860–871. http://dx.doi.org/10.1037/0012-1649.41.6.860

Schwartz, I. S., Carta, J. J., & Grant, S. (1996). Examining the use of recommended language intervention practices in early childhood special education classrooms. *Topics in Early Childhood Special Education, 16,* 251–272. http://dx.doi.org/10.1177/027112149601600208

Schweinhart, L. J., Barnes, H. V., & Weikart, D. P. (1993). *Significant benefits: The High/Scope Perry Preschool study through age 15*. Ypsilanti, MI: High/Scope.

Shonkoff, J. P., & Hauser-Cram, P. (1987). Early intervention for disabled infants and their families: A quantitative analysis. *Pediatrics, 80,* 650–658.

Shonkoff, J. P., & Meisels, S. J. (2000). *Handbook of early childhood intervention*. New York, NY: Cambridge University Press.

Smith, T., Kleiner, A., Parsad, B., & Farris, E. (2003) *Prekindergarten in U.S. public schools: 2000–2001*. Washington, DC: Department of Education, National Center for Education Statistics.

Tuckwiller, E. D., Pullen, P. C., & Coyne, M. D. (2010). The use of the regression discontinuity design in tiered intervention research: A pilot study exploring vocabulary instruction for at-risk kindergartners. *Learning Disabilities Research & Practice, 25,* 137–150. http://dx.doi.org/10.1111/j.1540-5826.2010.00311.x

U.S. Department of Education. (2006). *Twenty-eighth annual report to Congress on the implementation of the Individuals with Disabilities Education Act*. Washington, DC: Author. Retrieved from http://www2.ed.gov/about/reports/annual/osep/2006/parts-b-c/index.html

U.S. Department of Education, National Center for Education Statistics. (2007). *The nation's report card*. Retrieved from http://nces.ed.gov/nationsreportcard/

U.S. Department of Education, Office of Special Education and Rehabilitative Services, Office of Special Education Programs. (2005, April). *Twenty-fifth annual report to Congress on the implementation of the Individuals with Disabilities Education Act, Vol. 1*. Washington, DC: Author.

U.S. Department of Health and Human Services, Administration *for Children* and Families (2010, January). *Head Start impact study. Final report.* Washington, DC: Author.

Vaughn, S., Wanzek, J., Murray, C. S., Scammacca, N., & Linan, S. (2009). Response to early reading intervention: Examining higher and lower responders. *Exceptional Children, 75,* 165–183.

Wakeman, S. Y., Browder, D. M., Meier, I., & McColl, A. (2007). The implications of No Child Left Behind for students with developmental disabilities. *Mental Retardation and Developmental Disabilities Research Reviews, 13,* 143–150. http://dx.doi.org/10.1002/mrdd.20147

Whitebook, M., Phillips, D., Bellm, D., Crowell, N., Alamzaraz, M., & Jo, J. Y. (2004). *Two years in early care and education: A community portrait of quality and workforce stability.* Berkeley, CA: Center for the Study of Child Care Employment.

Wolery, M., & Bailey, D. B. (2002). Early childhood special education research. *Journal of Early Intervention, 25,* 88–99. http://dx.doi.org/10.1177/105381510202500204

Wolery, M., Holcombe, A., Brookfield, J., Huffman, K., Schroeder, C., Martin, C. G., ... Fleming, L. A. (1993). The extent and nature of preschool main-streaming: A survey of general early educators. *The Journal of Special Education, 27,* 222–234. http://dx.doi.org/10.1177/002246699302700205

Wolery, M., Holcombe, A., Venn, M. L., Brookfield, J., Huffman, K., Schroeder, C., ... Fleming, L. A. (1993). Preschool mainstreaming: Current status and relevant issues. *Young Children, 49*(1), 78–84.

Wolery, M., & Wilbers, J. S. (1994). *Including children with special needs in early childhood programs.* Washington, DC: National Association for the Education of Young Children.

Wong, V. C., Cook, T. D., Barnett, W. S., & Jung, K. (2008). An effectiveness-based evaluation of five state pre-kindergarten programs. *Journal of Policy Analysis and Management, 27,* 122–154. http://dx.doi.org/10.1002/pam.20310

Woodcock, R. W, McGrew, K. S., & Mather, N. (2001). *Woodcock-Johnson III NU tests of achievement.* Rolling Meadows, IL: Riverside.

Woodcock, R. W., Muñoz-Sandoval, A. F., McGrew, K. S., & Mather, N. (2005). *Batería III Woodcock-Muñoz.* Rolling Meadows, IL: Riverside.

Predictors of Change in Eligibility Status Among Preschoolers in Special Education

Tamara C. Daley and Elaine Carlson

The process for obtaining special education services is well specified within the regulations of the Individuals With Disabilities Education Act (IDEA, 2004). In contrast, there are no clearly defined federal criteria regarding the process by which a child leaves special education. If districts rely on federal law for guidance, regulation 300.534 (c)(1) of IDEA 2004 states simply that "a public agency must evaluate a child with a disability in accordance with Sections 300.532 and 300.533 before determining that the child is no longer a child with a disability"; Sections 300.532 and 300.533 outline evaluation procedures. The only available research on the topic among very young children suggests that as many as 50% of preschool programs do not have written specifications for exit criteria (Thurlow, Ysseldyke, & Weiss, 1988). Leaving special education has historically been considered rare (Finn, Rotherham, & Hokanson, 2000), and data on declassification have been collected by the Office of Special Education Programs (OSEP) only since 1993–1994 and only for students ages 14 and older.

Despite the vagaries associated with exiting special education, many young children *do* receive services and support for a period of time and then stop. Data from Washington and Colorado showed that one sixth to one third of children graduating from preschool were placed in general education programs with no support (Edgar, McNulty, Gaetz, & Maddox, 1984). Stile, LeCrone, and Ames (1991) reported the same outcome for 1 in 10 children from 74 school districts in New Mexico. Among children receiving preschool special education services in two North Carolina counties, 28% were no longer receiving services upon entry into elementary school (Wong, 1997).

Longitudinal analyses have produced similar findings. Thirty-two percent of preschoolers who were classified as having speech impairments in a Maryland county exited special education during a 4-year period. Even among children identified with two or more disabilities, 11% left special education by the first year of elementary school (Markowitz & Bridges-Cline, 1991). Higher rates were observed in a more recent study of children who were enrolled in preschool special education in Utah; approximately 50% of children were no longer receiving services 2 years after their initial enrollment in the study (Innocenti, 2005).

We know relatively little about the factors that are associated with leaving special education, but given that the regulations of IDEA frame the process of declassification in terms of eligibility determination, we can turn to this body of research as background. Within the special education literature, there is a longstanding and ongoing criticism of classification and eligibility practices, stemming from seminal works such as Nicholas Hobbs' *Issues in the Classification of Children* (1975). Certain disability categories have particularly come under fire for being social constructions; for example, the emergence of the learning disability category was seen as a way for children of middle-class, white families to receive services without being stigmatized (Sleeter, 1986). More recently, critics have asserted that Asperger's syndrome is used for eligibility purposes when it often reflects normal variations in personality (Molloy & Vasil, 2002). In short, many researchers have identified theoretical flaws with any system that lacks "reliability, coverage, logical consistency, utility, and acceptability to users" (Cromwell, Blashfield, & Strauss, 1975, p. 22), all of which are limitations critics have raised of the categorical eligibility system under IDEA.

A comprehensive review of the criticisms of current IDEA eligibility practices, which abound in the literature, is beyond the scope of this article, but a few examples are illustrative. Racial and ethnic disproportionality in special education placement has been identified as a problem for decades; two panels convened by the National Academy of Sciences, in 1982 and 2002, addressed this issue at a national level (Donovan & Cross, 2002; Heller, Holtzman, & Messick, 1982). In part because of these panels, IDEA now includes specific activities that are aimed at providing support to districts with evidence of significant disproportionality. Consistent with this, recent work (e.g., Skiba, Poloni-Staudinger, Gallini, Simmons, & Feggins-Azziz, 2006) notes that longstanding differences in classification based on race and ethnicity are still present, with African American children more likely to be classified as having mental retardation and emotional disturbance than non-African American children. Of note, however, Hibel, Farkas, and Morgan (2006) found that African American, Hispanic, and Asian students were much *less* likely to be placed into special education programs and that attending schools with lower average performance, being female, and lacking academic readiness also decreased a student's chance of entering special education.

Several researchers have demonstrated powerful district-level influences on classification. For example, using functional profiles, Singer, Palfrey, Butler, and Walker (1989) showed that classification of children, particularly those with the labels of emotional disturbance and mental retardation, varied based on district of residence. Similarly, researchers have demonstrated that low-achieving students in general education are functionally similar to many students identified as having learning disabilities (Ysseldyke et al., 1983). Even using the most current data available from OSEP, it is clear that there is wide variability and overlap in criteria and definitions across districts and states, particularly for some disability categories (Hallahan et al., 2007).

Past research has examined declassification in the context of some of these same factors, although to a more limited degree. Several studies have confirmed that children who exit special education have higher academic and intellectual functioning than those who remain eligible (Carlson, 1997; Halgren & Clarizio, 1993; Innocenti, 2005; Ysseldyke & Bielinski, 2002). Across age groups, children identified as having speech or language impairments and learning disabilities were the most likely to leave special education (Carlson; Carlson & Parshall, 1996; Halgren & Clarizio; Innocenti; Walker et al., 1988; Wong, 1997). Nevertheless, a small percentage of children (2%–4%) declassified in a recent study of elementary-age children were previously identified as having autism, mental retardation, and multiple disabilities (SRI International, 2005).

Although child functioning is a logical predictor of declassification, certain demographic factors have also been linked with declassification. Higher incomes were associated with greater declassification among school-age children (Carlson, 1997; SRI International, 2005) and with more frequent checks on progress among preschoolers (Markowitz & Bridges-Cline, 1991); children of lower income families across a range of ages were more likely than those in higher income families to be reclassified into different disability categories (Halgren & Clarizio, 1993).

With respect to race, declassification was reported to be more likely among White children than among African American or Hispanic children in school-age samples (Carlson, 1997) and less likely for African American children within the category of speech impairment (Walker et al., 1988). Some demographic factors, such as gender, have not previously been linked to declassification (Carlson; Carlson & Parshall, 1996).

We are not aware of any studies that have examined important process variables, such as parent involvement or school outreach, in relation to declassification. Two studies examined parent satisfaction as it relates to change in disability category and change in programming. Parents of school-age children who left special education were slightly more likely to report being very satisfied with their child s school than parents of students who continued receiving services (SRI International, 2005); Halgren and Clarizio (1993) found no such association between parent satisfaction and declassification.

Ideally, characteristics of a child's district and school would not play a central role in determining changes in eligibility status. But a New York study found that suburban preschool programs had the highest percentage of preschool children declassified, and New York City programs had the lowest percentage (MAGI Educational Services, Inc., 2003). In contrast, a comparison in North Carolina found that preschoolers from an urban county were more likely to leave special education than those from a rural county (Wong, 1997). Other factors, such as size of the special education program and district wealth, have not previously been examined.

As referenced earlier, past research has documented numerous flaws in the predominant system of eligibility determination for children in the United States, which at best might be characterized as inconsistent (Ysseldyke, 2001; Ysseldyke et al., 1983). A smaller body of past research has examined the opposite process, declassification, with mixed and limited findings. Therefore, the central question of this study can be stated as follows: Is the process of declassification one that is logical and predictable from relevant child factors or, in contrast, is it one that varies according to demographic or district-level characteristics?

This study includes a range of independent variables to explore this question. As noted ealier, some of these have previously been examined in the literature (child academic skills, gender, race/ethnicity, and disability category; transition status; household income; metropolitan status; and parent satisfaction), whereas others have not (district size, preschool special education enrollment, and wealth; parent involvement; and school/program outreach). We also address some limitations of past studies of preschool special education status. Specifically, they have either sampled all students in one district or a sample of students from a set of districts within a state, and many of the studies of preschoolers are more than 2 decades old. In this study, we use a large, nationally representative sample of children ages 3 through 5 and eligible for special education services during the 2003–2004 school year to examine declassification after 2 years. This study represents an opportunity to extend the literature on declassification by filling gaps in what we know and providing current data for a preschool-age population.

Method

Design and Sample

The PEELS, sponsored by the National Center for Special Education Research in the U.S. Department of Education, is following a nationally representative sample of 3,104 children from a population of approximately 670,000 children who were receiving special education services in 2004, when they were 3 through 5 years old. PEELS used a two-stage sample design: In the first stage, a national sample of local education agencies (LEAs) was selected. In the second stage, a sample of preschoolers with disabilities was selected from lists of eligible children provided by the participating LEAs.

The PEELS data collection includes parent/guardian interviews, teacher questionnaires, direct assessments of the children, and questionnaires sent to children's programs, schools, districts, and states. Instruments were designed to capture information on the characteristics of children receiving preschool special education, the services they receive, their transitions from early intervention to preschool and from preschool to elementary school, and their educational performance. (Data from an early childhood program director, elementary school principal, and state education agency questionnaire were not used in this analysis.)

Children were recruited into PEELS as 3-, 4-, and 5-year-olds. All participating 3-year-olds were newly enrolled in special education during the recruitment period; participating 4- and 5-year-olds included children both newly enrolled in special education during the recruitment period and those who had already been identified as eligible for services. Because the PEELS sample was selected by age, not by grade, some of the children were in kindergarten; others were in preschool, day care, or at home. The children may or may not have received early intervention services from birth to age 3 through Part C of IDEA.

Eligibility criteria for study participation were: (a) there was an English- or Spanish-speaking adult or an adult who used signed communication in the household or, alternatively, could respond to questions using a telephone relay service or interpreter for the hearing impaired;

(b) this was the family's first child sampled for PEELS; and (c) the sampled child's family resided in the participating school district at the time of enrollment in PEELS. Eighty-eight percent of the families were found eligible for the study, and 80% of those eligible agreed to participate.

The data presented have been weighted to generate national estimates. Different weights were used, depending on the sources of data. These weights adjust the child base weights to account for nonresponse on specific data collections in specific waves or groups of waves. (For a more detailed description of family recruitment, sampling, and weighting procedures, see Markowitz et al., 2006, at www.peels.org.)

Measures

Outcome Variable: Special Education Eligibility Status

At the time they were recruited into PEELS, all children had an active individualized education program (IEP) or individualized family service plan (IFSP). At each point of data collection, teachers reported whether the child had either an IEP or IFSP. If those data were missing for the relevant year, teacher reports from the following year were used to determine changes in the child's IEP status. Teachers were routinely asked whether the child received special education services during the previous year. If data on IEP status were still unavailable from both these sources, parent response was used. Because of the large-scale nature of the study, independent confirmation of eligibility status was not available. The primary declassification variable used in this study identifies children declassified by the 2005–2006 school year, with declassification occurring either between 2003–2004 and 2004–2005, or between 2004–2005 and 2005–2006. A small group of children (5.8%) discontinued special education services prior to 2003–2004 data collection. These children were excluded from the analyses presented here. In addition, children who changed from one disability classification to another (for example, from developmental delay to mental retardation) were not considered declassified, because they continued to receive services under IDEA.

Control Variable: Preschool Status

The transition from preschool to kindergarten is a time when special education eligibility may receive particular scrutiny, with an inclination among some educators and administrators to give the child a chance in general education (Edgar, Heggelund, & Fischer, 1988). Therefore, as a control variable in the multivariate model, we have included whether the child remained in preschool from 2003–2004 to 2005–2006. This variable was based on teacher report.

Demographic and Household Characteristics

Demographic and family characteristics, such as child gender, race/ethnicity, and household income, were obtained through the parent interview. For this analysis, race/ethnicity was derived from a series of questions and recoded into three categories: Hispanic and of any race, Black or African American only (not Hispanic), and White only (not Hispanic). Children from other racial groups were excluded from analyses by race because the samples were too small to produce reliable results.

District Characteristics

Information about district wealth, metropolitan status, and size of the district's preschool special education program was taken from the Quality Education Data (QED) district file, which was used as the PEELS district sampling frame. PEELS uses the same cut points as the QED. District poverty was defined as a percentage of the district's children falling below the federal government poverty guidelines, where *high wealth* was 0% to 12%, *medium wealth* was 13% to 34%, *low wealth* was 35% to 40%, and *very low wealth* was more than 40%.

Metropolitan status was defined by the designations of the U.S. Department of Education's National Center for Education Statistics (NCES), as applied by QED, and was classified as *urban, suburban,* and *rural.*

District preschool special education enrollment size (for children ages 3 through 5 years) was categorized as *small* if the district had 41 or fewer children enrolled, *medium* if it had between 42 and 117 children enrolled, *large* if it had 118 to 390 children enrolled, and *very large* if the district had 391 or more children enrolled.

Overall district size was obtained through the LEA questionnaire and was based on total district enrollment. Based on cutoffs used in the NCES Common Core of Data, the districts were categorized as *small* if they had 300 to 2,500 students, *medium* if they had 2,501 to 10,000 students, *large* if they had 10,001 to 25,000 students, and *very large* if they had more than 25,000 students.

Disability Category

Information on children's primary disability category was obtained from their teachers or service providers. If those data were missing, disability information was obtained from enrollment forms submitted by district personnel. Because of the small sample sizes for some disability categories, a *low-incidence* category was created; it included deaf/blindness, deafness, hearing impairment, traumatic brain injury, visual impairment, and other disabilities that were specified on the teacher questionnaire or enrollment form. Therefore, in this study, primary disability is grouped into nine categories: autism, developmental delay, emotional disturbance/behavior disorder, learning disability, mental retardation, orthopedic impairment, other health impairment, speech or language impairment, and low-incidence disabilities.

School/Program Outreach, Parent Involvement, and Parent Satisfaction

Three scales on school/program outreach, parent involvement, and parent satisfaction were developed using questions from the parent interview and were created using Master's partial credit model of scaling (Master's, 1982). This model provides estimates of item locations or calibrations along a common measurement continuum. Unidimensionality along the construct was determined by goodness-of-fit statistics. These infit statistics compare each child's observed response pattern to his or her expected response pattern for each specific overall score. The expected value of the mean square INFIT (MNSQ) is 1.00. Deviation above 1.00 indicates potential departures from unidimensionality; values less than 1.00 flag potential violations of local independence. A reasonable criterion value for goodness-of-fit for non-high-stakes measures is between 0.7 and 1.3 (Wright & Linacre, 1994). For all three measures, the INFIT (MNSQ) statistic was well within the acceptable bounds.

The school/program outreach scale reflected parent interview responses for three variables: the frequency of personal notes, notices, and phone calls from the school. The INFIT (MNSQ) statistic for this scale was 0.92.

The parent involvement scale included 11 items from the parent interview related to participation in school and classroom activities (e.g., attending a school meeting or a class event, a parent-teacher conference, or planning groups; volunteering in the classroom; helping with field trips; and fundraising); involvement in the IEP process (e.g., attending the meeting, involvement in generating goals, and parent satisfaction about their involvement in determining IEP goals); and the number of other parents from the child's program with whom the respondent spoke. The INFIT (MNSQ) statistic for this scale was 0.98.

The parent satisfaction scale comprised 17 variables, covering respondent satisfaction with the child's program/school and teachers; communication with staff; availability, quality, and amount of services received; feelings toward special education professionals, in general, and feelings toward the professionals who worked with their child, in particular; and satisfaction with the child's IEP goals. The INFIT (MNSQ) statistic for this scale was 0.97.

Functioning, Behavior, and Emerging Literacy Skills

Parents provided information about the severity of their child's disability, a six-component variable based on the framework of the ABILITIES Index (Bailey, Simeonsson, Buysse, & Smith, 1993) and consisting of cognition, communication, overall health and limitations that were due to health, regulation of activity level, regulation of attention, and understanding of language. Using the PEELS sample, validity of an abbreviated index was also established through significant correlations with age at which children began receiving special education or therapy service ($r = .22$), the teacher-reported amount of modification to curriculum materials ($r = .42$), and with the number of services the child received in the school ($r = .37$). The PEELS ABILITIES Index also significantly differentiated between children who took alternate and regular assessments in PEELS (Daley, Simeonsson, & Carlson, 2008).

Teachers provided information on children's problem behavior using a standardized rating scale, the Preschool and Kindergarten Behavior Scales, Second Edition (PKBS-2; Merrell, 2002). The Problem Behaviors composite comprises Externalizing and Internalizing Problems subscales. The composite score is converted to a standard score, which is based on a distribution with a mean of 100 and a standard deviation of 15. This scale has Cronbach alpha coefficients of .93 to .95 and 3-week test-retest reliability from .70 to .78 for the two subscales (Merrell).

A direct one-on-one assessment was used to obtain information on the preacademic skills of preschoolers in the sample. More than 400 assessors in participating LEAs were employed and trained to administer the one-on-one assessment. These assessors included school psychologists, teachers, administrators, and other individuals experienced in administering standardized assessments to young children with disabilities. In this report, we use data from two emerging literacy assessments, the Woodcock-Johnson III Letter–Word Identification subtest (Woodcock,

McGrew, & Mather, 2001) and a psychometrically shortened version of the Peabody Picture Vocabulary Test-III (PPVT-III; Dunn & Dunn, 1997).

The Letter—Word Identification test measures the child's word identification skills. Initial items require the child to identify letters that appear in large type, and the remaining items require the child to pronounce words correctly. The standard scale score used in the Letter—Word Identification has a mean of 100 and a standard deviation of 15 (Woodcock et al., 2001). Test developers reported a 1-year test-retest correlation of .92 for children ages 4 to 7 (McGrew & Woodcock, 2001).

The PPVT-III is a measure of receptive vocabulary. The standard administration of the PPVT-III involves the assessor showing the child four pictures on a single page then asking the child to point to the picture that matches a word the assessor speaks aloud. PEELS uses a psychometrically adapted and shortened version of the PPVT-III. With the shortened version, all children are presented a core set of 14 items. If their performance on the core set of items is extremely low or high, they are administered an easier basal set of items (for children who get all or most of the core items incorrect) or a harder ceiling set of items (for children who get all or most of the core items correct) to determine their basic or extended level of performance. The Item Response Theory (IRT) true-score for the items in the core item set was used to determine basal and ceiling decision rules appropriate for the PEELS target population. The IRT true-score is a model-based estimate of the number right raw score. Raw scores on the core item set were used to determine whether a child would actually receive either the additional basal or ceiling item set. The IRT estimate of test reliability for a population having distribution parameters equal to those of the PEELS latent ability distribution is $r = .78$. The sample-based IRT reliability obtained from ability estimates and standard errors of measurement in PEELS is $r = .86$.

Because the PEELS adapted version of the PPVT and the full PPVT have a common subset of items, it was possible to apply a linear transformation to the proficiencies of the PEELS assessment so that proficiencies were comparable to the national norming sample. Therefore, the PPVT short forms yield the same expected score values as the full PPVT, making use of the publisher's norms appropriate. The standard version of the PPVT-III has high alternate form reliability for the standardized scores (.88 to .96). Test-retest reliability coefficients were in the .90s (Dunn & Dunn, 1997). Children's scores on the various parts of the test were transformed into a single score and placed on a standardized scale with a mean of 100 and a standard deviation of 15.

The PPVT and Woodcock-Johnson III Letter—Word Identification subtest were selected because they were administered to the largest number of children in the sample (some measures were administered only to older or younger children). If the child could not follow simple directions, had a visual impairment that would interfere with test administration, or began the direct assessment but could not meaningfully participate because of a disability, an alternate assessment, the Adaptive Behavior Assessment System-II (ABAS-II; Harrison & Oakland, 2003) was used. Coefficient alpha reliabilities for the ABAS-II subtests on the teacher and day-care provider forms ranged from .72 to .97, with higher reliabilities for composite domain scores ($r = .92$ to .97). Test-retest reliabilities for periods of 2 days to 6 weeks ranged from .66 to .98, depending on age level and subtest. Approximately 100 students included in the analyses reported in this study had an alternate assessment; these children are included in all univariate analyses except for those involving the two literacy measures from the standard assessment battery.

Analysis

Logistic regression is a technique that is similar to multiple regression but is used with binomially distributed dependent variables—in this case, whether the child was declassified. To identify predictors of change in eligibility status, we conducted a series of univariate logistic regressions, with each individual predictor entered and with change in eligibility status as the dependent variable. We then conducted a multivariate logistic regression with all the individual predictors together. Logistic regression generates an odds ratio, which is a statistic that can provide information on the likelihood of a particular outcome. The adjusted odds ratio generated from the multivariate logistic regression represents, for each level of the independent variable, the increased probability that children were declassified relative to other levels of that variable. The odds ratio can be interpreted as a useful predictor of the outcome when the 95% confidence interval around the odds ratio does not include the value 1.0. Conversely, if the value of 1.0 is included in the 95% confidence interval, the results suggest that there are no significant differences in the probability of a given outcome for the two groups (i.e., the subgroup in question and the reference group).

In data preparation and analysis, imputation was conducted for selected items on the child assessment data, teacher questionnaire data, and parent interview data. In general, the item missing rate was quite low, mostly less than 10%. Different methods of imputation were used depending on the nature of missing data and available information for imputation. The methods included hot-deck imputation, regression, external data source, and deterministic or derivation method, based on the internal consistency principle of interrelated variables. In some cases, a postulated value was imputed after analyzing missing patterns.

The data presented here are population estimates statistically weighted to represent all children ages 3 through 5 receiving special education services. Analyses were conducted using WesVar Version 4.2 (Westat, 2002) and PROC SURVEY-LOGISTIC in SAS to account for the complex probability sampling used in PEELS.

Results

Between winter/spring of school year 2003–2004 and winter/spring of school year 2004–2005, 16% of preschoolers with disabilities had their special education services discontinued. Of those children who were receiving services in 2004–2005, once again, 16% were no longer receiving special education services 1 year later.

Univariate Prediction of Change in Eligibility Status

Table 12.1 presents frequencies for all predictors, and Table 12.2 presents the univariate odds ratios for each predictor as it relates to declassification.

TABLE 12.1   Sample Characteristics and Percentage of PEELS Subsample Who Were Declassified From 2003–2004 Through 2005–2006

	Children Declassified	
	Unweighted	Weighted
Variable (Total unweighted N)	N	% (SE)
Gender		
Female (N = 915)	163	31.0 (3.0)
Male (N = 2,188)	341	24.0 (1.7)
Household income		
More than $40,000 (N = 1,353)	275	28.3 (1.9)
$20,001–$40,000 (N = 842)	133	25.2 (2.1)
$20,000 or less (N = 791)	96	22.1 (3.9)
Ethnicity		
White (N = 1,875)	353	27.2 (2.1)
Hispanic (N = 643)	75	16.9 (4.3)
African American (N = 319)	25	20.1 (2.4)
Disability category		
Speech or language impairment (N = 1,562)	369	36.7 (2.1)
Autism (N = 188)	6	2.9 (1.9)
Developmental delay (N = 806)	96	20.5 (2.4)
Emotional disturbance (N = 44)	6	38.7 (15.8)
Learning disability (N = 73)	2	3.1 (2.8)
Mental retardation (N = 86)	0	0
Orthopedic impairment (N = 43)	3	6.7 (4.6)
Other health impairment (N = 56)	1	5.6 (3.2)
Low-incidence disability (N = 150	15	12.5 (3.9)
District wealth		
High (N = 631)	156	27.1 (2.3)
Medium (N = 554)	124	24.2 (2.7)
Low (N = 518)	155	29.6 (4.5)
Very low (N = 302)	69	20.8 (2.2)
District size		
Very large (N = 763)	100	19.7 (2.0)
Large (N = 448)	73	24.7 (4.5)
Medium (N = 1,014)	171	27.5 (3.0)
Small (N = 526)	109	36.8 (4.2)
District size of special ed program		
Very large (N = 402)	83	19.3 (1.7)
Large (N = 560)	131	23.9 (4.1)
Medium (N = 489)	112	23.8 (3.2)
Small (N= 554)	178	36.3 (3.0)
Metropolitan status		
Urban (N = 549)	130	21.4 (2.1)
Suburban (N = 1,047)	259	26.0 (1.8)
Rural (N = 409)	115	34.3 (5.5)

Note. Percentages describe a nationally representative weighted sample. Ns vary because of missing data.

TABLE 12.2   Unadjusted Odds Ratios (OR) and Adjusted Odds Ratios (AOR) for Children Declassified From 2003–2004 Through 2005–2006

	Children Declassified	
Predictor Variable	**Univariate OR (95% CI)**	**Multivariate AOR (95% CI)**
Control variable:	—	
Remained in preschool		1.00
Did not remain in preschool	—	.460 (.183, 1.16)
Gender		
Female	1.00	1.00
Male	.706 (.518, .961)*	.603 (.369, .985)*
Household income		
More than $40,000	1.00	1.00
$20,001–$40,000	.850 (.610, 1.18)	.763 (.436, 1.33)
$20,000 or less	.716 (.486, 1.06)	1.12 (.603, 2.08)
Disability category		
Speech or language impairment	1.00	1.00
Autism	.053 (.020, .141)***	.083 (.013, .554)**
Developmental delay	.446 (.317, .628)***	.809 (.482, 1.36)
Emotional disturbance	1.09 (.261, 4.53)	.108 (.014, .822)*
Learning disability	.056 (.011, .270)**	<.001 (<.001, <.001)
Mental retardation	<.001 (<.001, <.001)***	<.001 (< .001, < .001)***
Orthopedic impairment	.123 (.029, .522)**	.158 (.029, .874)*
Other health impairment	.102 (.013, 765)*	<.001 (< .001, < .001)***
Low–incidence disability	.245 (.116, .519)**	.076 (.024, 244)***
Ethnicity		
White	1.00	1.00
Hispanic	.674 (.455, 1.000)*	1.12 (.597, 2.11)
African American	.542 (.303, .970)*	1.37 (.606, 3.11)
District wealth		
High	1.00	1.00
Medium	.856 (.590, 1.242)	.634 (.311, 1.29)
Low	1.13 (.776, 1.64)	2.35 (1.21, 4.56)*
Very low	.708 (.459, 1.09)	1.86 (.796, 4.36)
District size		
Very large	1.00	1.00
Large	1.33 (.822, 2.16)	.649 (.228, 1.85)
Medium	1.54 (1.03, 2.29)*	.739 (.266, 2.06)
Small	2.37 (1.54, 3.64)***	.689 (.210, 2.26)

(Continued)

TABLE 12.2 (*Continued*)

Predictor Variable	Children Declassified	
	Univariate OR (95% CI)	Multivariate AOR (95% CI)
District size of special ed program		
Very large	1.00	1.00
Large	1.31 (.857, 2.00)	1.63 (.615, 4.34)
Medium	1.30 (.824, 2.06)	3.02 (.964, 9.49)
Small	2.38 (1.59, 3.57)***	5.21 (1.54, 17.61)*
Metropolitan status		
Rural	1.00	1.00
Suburban	.673 (.462, .980)*	.987 (.488, 2.00)
Urban	.521 (.344, 790)**	.973 (.412, 2.30)
Family/teacher		
Parent involvement	1.16 (.988, 1.37)	.987 (.783, 1.25)
School/program outreach	.848 (.741, .971)*	1.05 (.826, 1.32)
Parent satisfaction	1.15 (1.00, 1.32)*	.972 (.773, 1.22)
Child ability/functioning		
Problem behaviors	.961 (.950, .972)***	.983 (.967, .999)*
Child severity	.818 (.779, .859)***	.894 (.827, .967)**
PPVT	1.05 (1.04, 1.06)***	1.03 (1.01, 1.05)**
Letter–Word Identification	1.02 (1.01, 1.03)***	1.01 (.996, 1.02)

PPVT = Peabody Picture Vocabulary Test.

*p < .05. **p < .01. *** p < .0001.

Demographic and Household Characteristics

By 2005–2006, 31% of girls and 24% of boys were declassified; the odds of declassification for girls were 1.41 times as high as the odds were for boys. Income was not significantly associated with declassification, but there was an effect for race/ethnicity. Children who were White were more likely than African American or Hispanic children co be declassified; 27% of White children, 20% of African American children, and 17% of Hispanic children left special education by 2005–2006.

Disability Category

Certain disability groups had a greater percentage of children declassified than others. By 2005–2006, 37% of children with a speech or language impairment and 21% of those with a developmental delay were declassified. Thirty-nine percent of children identified as having an emotional disturbance were also declassified. Despite the high percentage of children in the emotional disturbance group who were declassified, this group represents only 1.1% of the sample and therefore only 1.4% of the total children declassified by 2005–2006 (see Table 12.3). In contrast, children with a speech or language impairment constitute 50% of preschoolers with disabilities and approximately 70% of all preschoolers who were declassified. Every disability category except mental retardation had one or more children declassified.

District Characteristics

The probability of declassification was relatively evenly distributed across districts based on wealth, with high-, medium-, low-, and very low-wealth districts each declassifying between 21% and 30% of children. In contrast to district wealth, both overall district size and district preschool special education enrollment were significantly associated with declassification. Approximately 37% of children from small districts and 20% from very large districts were declassified, and, in fact, total district size was a significant predictor of declassification. Likewise, compared to districts with large and very large preschool special education programs, those with small programs were more likely to declassify students; the odds of declassification for children from districts with small preschool special education programs was twice that of children from districts with very large programs. Last, children from rural areas were significantly more likely to be declassified than those from suburban and rural areas (34%, 26%, and 21%, respectively). All odds ratios are presented in Table 12.2.

School/Program Outreach, Parent Involvement, and Parent Satisfaction

Univariate logistic regressions showed lower odds of declassification for children whose parents reported more frequent program/school outreach, in the form of personal notes, notices, and phone calls. Higher levels of parent satisfaction were associated with greater likelihood of declassification; there was no significant effect for parent involvement.

Ability and Functioning

Comparisons of children's ability and functioning revealed significant baseline (2003–2004) differences between children subsequently declassified by 2005–2006 and those who continued to receive services under IDEA; and, across all measures, higher scores (or better functioning) were a significant predictor of declassification. Children who were declassified had standardized scores that were two thirds of a standard deviation higher on the baseline measure of the PPVT and four tenths of a standard deviation higher on the baseline Letter–Word Identification than children who continued to receive special education services. Teacher report of having fewer behavior problems and parent report of less severe impairment were also positively associated with declassification.

Multivariate Prediction of Change in Eligibility Status

As described earlier, a number of demographic, district, and family/teacher characteristics as well as child performance were predictors of declassification, when examined individually. In

TABLE 12.3 Percentage of all Children Declassified From 2003–2004 Through 2005–2006 Who Were From Each Disability Category

Disability Category	Children Declassified Weighted % (SE)
Speech or language impairment (n = 369)	72.5 (3.7)
Autism (n = 6)	.64 (.39)
Developmental delay (n = 96)	21.6 (2.9)
Emotional disturbance (n = 6)	1.4 (.94)
Learning disability (n = 2)	.26 (.21)
Mental retardation (n = 0)	0
Orthopedic impairment (n = 3)	.53 (.36)
Other health impairment (n = 1)	.54 (.30)
Low-incidence disability (n =15)	2.5 (.74)

Table 12.2, we present the adjusted odds ratios (AORs) for 2-year declassification to illustrate how selected factors relate to change in eligibility status when examined together.

When accounting for all other factors, several demographic and district characteristics remained significant. The odds of declassification for girls were about 1.7 times as high as the odds for boys (p = .0433). The size of the preschool special education program also remained significant. The odds of declassification for children from districts with small preschool special education programs was more than five times as high (p = .0079) as the odds for children from districts with very large programs.

District wealth became a significant predictor in the multivariate analysis, although it was not significant in the univariate analysis. No significant differences were observed between high- and medium-wealth districts. The odds of declassification for children from low-wealth districts, however, were about twice as high as those for children from high-wealth districts (p = .0113) and 3.8 times as high as for children from medium-wealth districts (p < .0001); the odds of declassification for children from low-wealth districts was also nearly twice as high as for children from very low-wealth districts (p = .0027).

Disability category was strongly related to declassification. After controlling for all other variables, the odds of declassification for children categorized as having speech or language impairments were approximately 6 times as high as for children with orthopedic impairments, 8 times as high as for children with emotional disturbance, and more than 12 times as high as for children with autism and low-incidence disabilities. The number of children with learning disabilities and other health impairments was too small to make interpretation of the logistic regression reliable.

Of the four variables that reflect children's ability and functioning, three were significant predictors of declassification for children by 2005–2006. The odds of declassification were significantly higher for children with less severe disabilities, and better performance on the PPVT was also significantly associated with declassification. The odds of declassification were lower for children with more severe behavior problems.

A number of variables that were significantly associated with declassification in the univariate analyses did not reach statistical significance in the multivariate model. These included race/ethnicity, metropolitan status, district size, school/program outreach, parent satisfaction, and Letter–Word Identification scores. In addition, household income and parent involvement were not significant predictors of declassification in either the univariate or multivariate analyses.

Discussion

This study examined whether exiting special education—declassification—can be predicted from factors that logically reflect children's abilities and functioning, given that receipt of services is intended for those who need it most. Of determining which children *enter* special education, Hibel and his colleagues (2006) asked:

> What if, independent of the student's ability to learn, special education placement is affected by characteristics such as the child's social class background, race/ethnicity, or gender? What if such placement varies according to the social context of the school, or of the family within the school? (p. 3)

In this study, one goal was to address the question raised by Hibel and his colleagues with respect to who *leaves* special education. Our regression models included factors representing both ability and functioning and those such as social class background, race/ethnicity, gender, and district characteristics, which we believe should be unrelated to declassification.

Our results suggest some positive news: children's problem behaviors, severity of impairment, and cognitive functioning were all significant predictors of declassification and in the expected direction. This finding is consistent with past research (e.g., Halgren & Clarizio, 1993: Ysseldyke & Bielinski, 2002) and suggests that some of the variance in declassification can be accounted for by children's performance on measures closely aligned with special education eligibility.

In addition, the troubling effect of some factors, such as metropolitan status and race/ethnicity, disappeared once other variables were controlled. This finding is encouraging for those looking for greater objectivity in the special education eligibility process, given the long history of overrepresentation of African American children in certain disability categories. The finding may be considered in conjunction with recent data from Hibel and colleagues (2006) that suggest overrepresentation of African American children has waned. One explanation for a shift—if such a shift is indeed occurring—may be a greater emphasis on identifying and rectifying disproportionality; starting with IDEA 1997, states have been required to collect data to determine if significant disproportionality on the basis of race is occurring.

The less encouraging results, however, are that some factors unrelated to a child's individual needs continued to show an effect, even when more proximal measures of children's abilities were included. Most notably, the odds of declassification were greater for children from low-wealth districts than from high-wealth districts and those districts with smaller preschool special education programs compared to larger ones. One explanation for this finding could be that low-wealth districts and those serving fewer children in special education are more sensitive to the economics of special education and therefore must be more careful in selecting which children receive services. Districts with fewer special education students and lower wealth may have limited service options; an administrator may exit a child with lesser needs to serve a child with greater needs. Or, if a child needs a service that is unavailable, an administrator may choose to formally exit a child from special education rather than risk non-compliance, although both these actions are clearly inconsistent with the mandate of IDEA. At least historically, this may have been the case; Thurlow, Lehr, and Ysseldyke (1987) found that 24% of surveyed preschool programs based exit decisions on staffing availability.

A more positive interpretation is that districts with fewer young children in special education may have greater familiarity with each individual child and a more flexible infrastructure. In this situation, an administrator could make a well- planned choice to provide support for children at the margins of eligibility by working more informally with teachers rather than through an IEP. Whatever the reason for this finding, the association between district factors and declassification deserves further examination from a policy equity perspective and is also important in the context of both accountability and program improvement. However, it should be noted that the relationship between district wealth and declassification was not a wholly linear one; children from low-wealth districts were also more likely to be declassified than children from very low-wealth districts. We do not have a straightforward explanation for this finding, but one possibility is that the smaller number of students from very low-wealth districts (approximately half the number as from low wealth, medium, and high wealth) may have contributed to unreliability of the estimate in this case.

Our study found that, once other factors were controlled, school outreach, parent involvement, and parent satisfaction did not predict declassification. It is possible that our parent measures were not sensitive enough to detect the influence parents may have on this process or that, despite its intuitive appeal, these are not powerful factors in declassification once more proximal indicators of child functioning are considered.

We cannot make any definitive statements about whether a 16% annual declassification rate is too high, too low, or just right. Likewise, we cannot say whether declassification was appropriate for any individual child in the sample. Some children may leave special education because it is their parent's choice to remove them, whether recommended by the school or not. In a recent report of declassification among school-age children, 5% of students left special education because either the parent did not want their child to be in the program or the child did not want to be in the program (SRI International, 2005).

There is reason to believe that a subgroup of children declassified from special education may need services at a later time. Carlson and Parshall (1996) found 11% of children who exited special education in Michigan had teachers who felt the students still needed services, and ultimately, 4% of the students who left special education were found to be eligible again within 3 years. Similarly, Ysseldyke and Bielinski (2002) found that 16% of children who moved to general education after fourth grade returned to special education after fifth grade and noted that more than 6,100 students in their sample changed special education status at least twice over a 5-year period. Of course, it is possible that it was appropriate to both leave and return for some of these children. Therefore, although our data show that children who are declassified, as a group, were performing better on standardized measures and teacher rating scales than children who remained in special education, it may take a number of years to determine whether they continue to perform well without special education support.

This study had several limitations. First, teacher report formed the primary source of data on classification status. Clearly, independent confirmation through school records would have been preferable, but, because of the large-scale nature of the study, such data collection was not conducted. Second, although PEELS is a nationally repre-

> *Some children may leave special education because it is their parent's choice to remove them, whether recommended by the school or not.*

sentative sample, and the data presented here can be generalized to all preschoolers receiving special education services in the United States in 2003–2004, the conclusions drawn may not apply to older children declassified from special education, because preschoolers, as a group, have less severe impairments than their school-age peers; approximately 75% of preschoolers in special education were categorized as either having a speech or language impairment or a developmental delay.

In sum, this study provided an examination of declassification over a 2-year period and found the percentage of preschoolers leaving special education each year to be in the range of previous estimates. In contrast to past research, our results demonstrated relationships between declassification and a number of independent variables, including child gender, the number of preschoolers with disabilities served within a district, and district wealth. If these factors do indeed influence declassification decisions, then children may lose vital support and be placed at risk for school failure (Thurlow et al., 1988). Districts should be aware of this potential when reevaluating children. The controlled data collection and use of multiple data sources across time in the PEELS sample offers some of the strongest evidence to date of the complexity of declassification decisions, and suggests a need for more explicit criteria to assist administrators in the process. If such criteria can be developed, they will provide a degree of standardization that ensures the appropriate children are receiving services. Such criteria can also ensure that the process of declassification remains an individualized one, as intended under the regulations of IDEA.

References

Bailey, D. B., Simeonsson, R. J., Buysse, V., & Smith, T. (1993). Reliability of an index of child characteristics. *Developmental Medicine and Child Neurology, 35,* 806–815.

Carlson, E. (1997). Outcomes for students declassified from special education. *Dissertation Abstracts International, 58,* 4231. (UMI No. 9815240)

Carlson, E., & Parshall, L. (1996). Academic, social, and behavioral adjustment for students declassified from special education. *Exceptional Children, 63,* 89–100.

Cromwell, R. L., Blashfield, R. K., & Strauss, J. S. (1975). Criteria for classification systems. In N. Hobbs (Ed.), *Issues in the classification of children* (pp. 4–25). San Francisco: Jossey-Bass.

Daley, T. C., Simeonsson, R. J., & Carlson, E. (2008). Constructing a measure of severity of disability in a national sample of preschoolers with disabilities. *Disability and Rehabilitation.* 1–15.

Donovan, M. S., & Cross, C. T. (Eds.). (2002). *Minority children in special and gifted education.* Washington, DC: National Academies Press.

Dunn, L. M., & Dunn, L. M. (1997). *Peabody Picture Vocabulary Test* (3rd ed.). Circle Pines, MN: American Guidance Services.

Edgar, E., Heggelund, M., & Fischer, M. (1988). A longitudinal study of graduates of special education preschools: Educational placement after preschool. *Topics in Early Childhood Special Education, 8,* 61–74.

Edgar, E., McNulty, B., Gaetz, J., & Maddox, M. (1984). Educational placement of graduates of preschool programs for handicapped children. *Topics in Early Childhood Special Education, 4,* 19–29.

Finn, C. E., Rotherham, A. J., & Hokanson, C. R. (Eds.). (2000). *Rethinking special education for a new century.* Washington DC: Thomas B. Fordham Foundation and the Progressive Policy Institute.

Halgren, D. P., & Clarizio, H. F. (1993). Categorical and programming changes in special education services. *Exceptional Children, 59,* 547–555.

Hallahan, D. P., Keller, C. E., Martinez, E. A., Byrd, E. S., Gelman, J. A., & Fan, X. (2007). How variable are interstate prevalence rates of learning disabilities and other special education categories? A longitudinal comparison. *Exceptional Children, 73,* 136–146.

Harrison, J., & Oakland, T. (2003). *Adaptive Behavior Assessment System* (2nd ed.). San Antonio, TX: The Psychological Corporation.

Heller, K. A., Holtzman, W. H., & Messick, S. (Eds.). (1982). *Placing children in special education: A strategy for equity.* Washington, DC: National Academies Press.

Hibel, J., Farkas, G., & Morgan, P. (2006). *Who is placed into special education?* (Working Paper No. 0605). University Park: Pennsylvania State University Population Institute.

Hobbs, N. (Ed.). (1975). *Issues in the classification of children.* San Francisco: Jossey-Bass.

Individuals With Disabilities Education Act Amendments of 2004 (IDEA). U.S.C. §§1400 *et seq* (2004).

Innocenti, M. S. (2005). *Classification status of children once enrolled in early intervention programs.* Report submitted to the Utah State Office of Education, Salt Lake City.

MAGI Educational Services, Inc. (2003). *Program quality and its effect on the placement of preschool education children in school-age programs. Special Education Quality Indicator Study.* The University of the State of New York. Retrieved March 9, 2006, from http://www.vesid.nysed.gov/specialed/publications/preschool/researchbul/bulletin.pdf

Markowitz, J., & Bridges-Cline, F. (November, 1991). *A six-year study of children enrolled in special education under the age of five years.* Rockville, MD: Montgomery County Public Schools.

Markowitz, J., Carlson, E., Frey, W., Riley, J., Shimshak, A., Heinzen, H., et al. (2006). *Preschoolers with disabilities: Characteristics, services and results. Wave 1 overview report from the Pre-Elementary Education Longitudinal Study (PEELS).* Retrieved December 1, 2007, from the PEELS Web site: www.peels.org

Masters, G. N. (1982). A Rasch model for partial credit scoring. *Psychometrika, 47*(2), 149–174.

McGrew, K. S., & Woodcock, R. W. (2001). *Technical manual. Woodcock-Johnson III.* Itasca, IL: Riverside.

Merrell, K. W. (2002). *Preschool and kindergarten behavior scales* (2nd ed.). Austin, TX: Pro-ed.

Molloy, H., & Vasil, L. (2002). The social construction of Asperger syndrome: The pathologising of difference? *Disability & Society, 17,* 659–669.

Singer, J. D., Palfrey, J. S., Butler, J. A., & Walker, D. K. (1989). Variation in special education classification across school districts: How does where you live affect what you are labeled? *American Educational Research Journal, 26,* 261–281.

Skiba, R. J., Poloni-Staudinger, L., Gallini, S., Simmons, A. B., & Feggins-Azziz, L. R. (2006). Disparate access: The disproportionality of African American students with disabilities across educational environments. *Exceptional Children, 72,* 411–424.

Sleeter, C. E. (1986). Learning disabilities: The social construction of a special education category. *Exceptional Children, 53,* 46–54.

SRI International. (2005). *Declassification—Students who leave special education.* A Special Topic Report from the Special Education Elementary Longitudinal Study (SRI Project No. P10656). Menlo Park, CA: Author.

Stile, S. W., LeCrone, J., & Ames, M. (1991). *Post-preschool placement of young students with developmental disabilities exiting public special education preschool programs, Final Report.* (Report No. 1 EC 300500). Santa Fe: New Mexico Department of Education, Special Education Unit. (ERIC Document Reproduction Service No. ED 334754)

Thurlow, M. L., Lehr, C. A., & Ysseldyke, J. E. (1987). Exit criteria in early childhood programs for handicapped children. *Journal of the Division for Early Childhood, 11,* 118–123.

Thurlow, M. L., Ysseldyke, J. E., & Weiss, J. A. (1988). Early childhood special education exit decisions: How are they made? How are they evaluated? *Journal of the Division for Early Childhood, 12,* 253–262.

Walker, D., Singer, J., Palfrey, J., Orza, M., Wenger, M., & Butler, J. (1988). Who leaves and who stays in special education: A 2-year follow-up study. *Exceptional Children, 54,* 393–402.

Westat. (2002). WesVar Version 4.2. Rockville, MD: Author.

Wong, M. M. (1997). Patterns of special education placement for preschool and school-age children. *Dissertation Abstracts International, 58,* 4616. (UMI No. 9819362)

Woodcock, R. W., McGrew, K. S., & Mather, N. (2001). *Woodcock-Johnson III Tests of Achievement.* Itasca, IL: Riverside.

Wright, B. D., & Linacre, J. M. (1994). Reasonable mean-square fit values. *Rasch Measurement Transactions, 8,* 370.

Ysseldyke, J., & Bielinski, J. (2002). Effect of different methods of reporting and reclassification on trends in test scores for students with disabilities. *Exceptional Children, 68,* 189–200.

Ysseldyke, J. E. (2001). Reflections on a research career: Generalizations from 25 years of research on assessment and instructional decision making. *Exceptional Children, 67,* 295–309.

Ysseldyke, J. E., Thurlow, M., Graden, J., Wesson, C., Algozzine, B., & Deno, S. (1983). Generalizations from five years of research on assessment and decision making: The University of Minnesota Institute. *Exceptional Education Quarterly, 4,* 75–93.

Early Childhood Teachers' Use of Specific Praise Statements With Young Children at Risk for Behavioral Disorders

Elizabeth Kirby Fullerton, Maureen A. Conroy, and Vivian I. Correa

Researchers suggest that behavior problems often begin prior to children entering kindergarten (Campbell, 1995; Campbell & Ewing, 1989). Estimates of young children with serious problem behaviors fall within the range of 10% to 15% (Campbell, 1995; Webster-Stratton, 1997). Furthermore, the early onset of behavior problems appears to remain stable over time, thereby influencing future success (Campbell & Ewing, 1989; Stormont, 2002). Behavior problems are linked to negative school outcomes, such as grade retention and special education placement (Burchinal, Peisner-Feinberg, Pianta, & Howes, 2002; Hamre & Pianta, 2001), and they may eventually lead to school failure (Patterson, Reid, & Eddy, 2002). Without early intervention, these behaviors may develop into a lasting disabling condition that could become resistant to future interventions (Marchant, Young, & West, 2004).

Early childhood teachers identify children's problem behaviors as one of the most challenging aspects of their job (Campbell, 1995). In addition, researchers have suggested that early childhood teachers often react negatively (e.g., increased restrictions, punitive care) to children who demonstrate problem behaviors (Barnett & Boocock, 1998; Scott-Little & Holloway, 1992). As a result, teachers' interactions with these children tend to be less positive than their interactions with children who do not demonstrate problematic behavior (Raver & Knitzer, 2002). Unfortunately, this negative interaction pattern can lead to fewer learning opportunities (Raver & Knitzer, 2002) and less engagement in classroom activities, resulting in missed opportunities for learning critical school readiness skills (Howes & Smith, 1995;

Raver & Knitzer, 2002; Webster-Stratton, 2000). Given the serious and chronic implications of the early onset of behavior problems in young children, there is a critical need to design and implement effective interventions that teachers in early childhood programs can use to address children's behavioral deficits.

Historically, various forms of teacher attention have been investigated as an effective intervention for ameliorating problem behaviors (e.g., see Baer & Sherman, 1964; Buell, Stoddard, Harris, & Baer, 1968; Hart & Risley, 1995). For many years, teachers and other professionals have been trained to use various forms of attention, such as contingent uses of praise, physical contact, and proximity to increase the occurrence of appropriate behaviors (e.g., on-task behavior, task performance). These studies have assessed the effects of the contingent delivery of attention by itself (e.g., Gable & Shores, 1980) and in conjunction with other interventions such as extinction (e.g., Hall, Lund, & Jackson, 1968; Madsen, Becker, & Thomas, 1968), teacher feedback (e.g., Heider, 1979), and the delivery of tangible reinforcers (e.g., Browder, Hines, McCarthy, & Fees, 1984). Although many researchers suggest that teacher attention can be used as a reinforcer to increase appropriate behavior, relatively little is known about the characteristics of teacher attention that contribute to its reinforcing value.

Teachers' use of specific praise statements is one type of attention strategy that has been found to effectively address problem behavior in elementary classrooms (e.g., see Brophy, 1981; Martens, Hiralall, & Bradley, 1997; Sutherland, Wehby, & Copeland, 2000; Sutherland & Wehby, 2001; Stormont, 2002). In particular, praise has been used to increase appropriate behaviors such as on-task behavior and compliance (Brophy, 1981; Sutherland et al., 2000). By providing praise contingently following the display of appropriate behaviors, children who find praise reinforcing will be more likely to engage in these behaviors in the future (Freeland, 2003). For example, Sutherland and colleagues (2000) examined the effects of teacher praise on the on-task behaviors of 9 elementary-aged students diagnosed as emotional/behavior disordered (EBD) served in a self-contained classroom. Specifically, Sutherland and colleagues taught the classroom teacher to implement behavior-specific praise statements during a teacher-directed activity (i.e., social skills training). Following training, they found the teacher's rate of praise increased, which resulted in an increase in the students' on-task behavior.

In a similar study, Sutherland and Wehby (2001) examined the use of increased rates of teacher praise on correct academic responses of students diagnosed as EBD. Twenty elementary school teachers (Grades K–8) and 216 students diagnosed with EBD (aged 5–15 years) were included in this study. Teachers were randomly assigned to one of two groups (experimental vs. control). Teachers in the experimental group were taught to increase their rates of praise through the use of a selfmonitoring and recording strategy. They found that the use of praise increased for teachers in the experimental group in comparison with the control group. In addition, the number of correct academic responses of students whose teachers were part of the experimental group increased in comparison with the control group teachers and students. They also determined that the teachers' use of reprimands in the experimental group decreased in comparison with the control group.

Martens and colleagues (1997) examined the effects of increased teacher praise on the appropriate behaviors of two 6-year-old boys diagnosed with EBD. In this study, the researchers and teacher targeted two replacement behaviors for each target child. The classroom teacher selected a daily target for delivering of praise contingent on the display of each behavior during a selected activity. Following implementation of intervention, the results indicated that there was an increase in the teachers' use of praise statements and in the children's targeted replacement behaviors.

Although positive outcomes have been associated with teachers' use of praise as an isolated intervention strategy with students with EBD (Brophy, 1981; Cameron & Pierce, 1994, Good & Grouws, 1977), the majority of the research has been conducted with older students and degreed teachers. With younger children at risk for EBD, praise has often been incorporated as a component of intervention packages (e.g., Hemmeter, Fox, Jack, & Broyles, 2007; Stormont, Lewis, & Beckner, 2005; Walker et al., 1997; Webster-Stratton, 1997). Only recently have we begun to see research that begins to investigate the use of isolated strategies. For example, a recent study by Stormont, Smith, and Lewis (2007) examined the relationship between the use of teacher praise and precorrection in Head Start classrooms. These results indicated that when used in combination, praise and precorrection reduced problem behaviors in young children engaged in a small-group activity. Although the results were promising, Stormont and colleagues did not investigate the relative effectiveness of each of these strategies, such as the use of specific praise, as the sole intervention. In addition to examining the relative effectiveness of isolated components of intervention, the examination of the generalization of these behaviors across settings is another research avenue that has not been emphasized.

Although the investigation of specific instructional strategies is an important area of research, the delivery of instruction to teachers when acquiring these skills is also relevant. Research indicates that behavioral consultation with teachers that includes direct training procedures involving modeling, rehearsal, and feedback leads to higher intervention fidelity (Casey & McWilliam, 2008; Lewis & Newcomer, 2002; Mortenson & Witt, 1998, Sterling-Turner, Watson, & Moore, 2002).

With the high prevalence rate of young children demonstrating serious problem behaviors, a logical extension of the current literature is to conduct further research and examine the effectiveness and generalization of isolated components of interventions, such as the use of specific praise, to determine the instructional variables that may contribute to and maintain behavior change in young children. Therefore, the purpose of this study was threefold: (a) to investigate the effectiveness of training using behavioral consultation designed to increase early childhood teachers' use of specific praise statements to address problem behaviors demonstrated by young children at risk for emotional/behavioral disorders, (b) to examine the effects of teachers' use of specific praise statements on the appropriate and problem behaviors of these young children at risk for EBD, and (c) to examine the generalization of teacher and child behaviors across activities.

Method

Participants and Setting

Four early childhood teachers and 4 children served as participants in this study (see *Table 13.1*). Teacher participants were selected based on the following criteria: (a) taught in an early childhood

TABLE 13.1   Participant Characteristics

Dyed	Teacher Education	Teacher Years of Experience	Child Age	BDI-S Results	CBCL Results	Teacher-Reported Behaviors of Concern
1	AA	4	2–11	Pass	Clinical attention/ aggressive behavior	Noncompliance
2	AS	12	3–8	Pass	Clinical attention	Noncompliance
3	AA	6	4–3	Pass	Clinically emotionally, anxious/depressed, withdrawn	Noncompliance, aggression, disruption
4	AA	13	3–10	Pass	Clinical attention	Noncompliance, aggression

classroom with at least one child who demonstrated problem behaviors that interfered with engagement in classroom activities, (b) had a strong work attendance, and (c) provided informed consent. The 4 teachers who participated in the study each had an associate of arts (AA) degree with an average of 9 years of teaching experience (range of 4 to 13 years). Two of the teachers were African American and 2 were Caucasian. Three teachers were female and 1 was male.

Children participants were selected based on nomination by their participating teachers and also met the following criteria for inclusion: (a) demonstration of problem behavior that interfered with engagement in classroom activities, (b) typical development as defined as a score within the normal range on the Battelle Developmental Inventory Screening (BDI-S; Newborg, 2005) to rule out developmental delays, (c) between that ages of 2 and 5 years, and (d) informed consent provided by guardians. The children participants were all boys and ranged in age from 2 years 11 months to 4 years and 3 months at the beginning of the study (see *Table 13.1*). Three of the children were Caucasian, and 1 was African American. Children 1, 2, and 3 lived at home with both parents, whereas child 4 lived primarily with his mother and visited his father once a week. Children 1, 2, and 4 had one sibling, whereas child 3 was an only child. Children 3 and 4 had grandmothers who were actively involved in their care (e.g., picking them up from school, often keeping them overnight and on weekends).

When asked by the primary investigator, the teachers' primary concern for each target child was noncompliance. In addition, according to the teachers, parents were concerned about their child's behavior at home and in school. Following selection of child participants, teachers completed the Caregiver-Teacher Report Form (CTRF; Achenbach, 1992). As indicated by teacher report, each child participant demonstrated clinical levels in subcategories of the CTRF (Achenbach, 1992). Children 1, 2, and 4 demonstrated increased rates of attention problems. Child 1 also demonstrated increased levels of aggression, and child 3 demonstrated increased levels of emotional reactiveness as well as anxious and withdrawn behavior. His preferred activity was sitting on a bench in the classroom library with his blanket, waiting for his parents or grandmother to pick him up.

This study was conducted with teachers in four different classroom settings within two university-based early childhood centers. All classrooms were set up as typical early childhood classrooms and included learning centers such as a book area, a housekeeping area, a manipulative area, an art area, and a gross motor play and outdoor area. On a typical day, classroom 1 had 27 children and 3 teachers, classroom 2 had 40 children and 4 teachers, and classroom 3 and 4 each had 24 children and 2 teachers. Teacher training occurred within the classroom during times when no children were present. Teachers' implementation of intervention (providing the child with specific praise) occurred during a transition activity selected by the teacher as a time when the target child engaged in elevated rates of problem behavior. Given the dynamic nature of an early childhood classroom, the transition activities included, but were not limited to, (a) moving from a self-directed small-group activity such as working in blocks to a teacher- directed large-group activity (circle time), (b) moving from teacher-directed small-group activity such as name-writing practice with shaving cream to a teacher-directed large-group activity (circle time), and (c) moving from a teacher-directed large-group activity (circle time) to small-group teacher-directed activity (working with alphabet blocks). The primary investigator chose the generalization activity and selected a second transition time that occurred daily within the classroom. The transition activities during generalization included (a) outside play to inside, (b) teacher-directed activity to clean up, and (c) from snack to quiet reading. Although the primary investigator videotaped during these times, there was no formal instruction or feedback provided to the teachers.

Response Definitions and Data Collection

Teacher Measures

Teachers' use of specific and nonspecific praise statements served as the primary dependent variables for this study. Teachers' use of specific praise was defined as positive declarative statements specifically directed to the target child that describes the child's behavior (e.g., "You did a nice job washing your hands"). Nonspecific praise statements were defined as positive declarative statements specifically directed to the target child that do not describe the child's behavior (e.g., "Way to go!"). The frequency of the teacher's use of specific and nonspecific praise statements was measured during each observation session, which lasted approximately 5 min. Following each session, the first author viewed the videotapes, and the type of teacher praise statement (specific vs. nonspecific) was coded. Following coding, the frequency of specific and nonspecific praise statements was converted to responses per minute by dividing the frequency of each type of praise statement by the total number of minutes observed (i.e., 5 min). To control for the potential effects of reactivity to the video camera as well as the presence of the video camera by the children and teachers, the investigator videotaped the targeted activity prior to the investigation for a minimum of 1 week.

Child Measures

In addition to measuring teachers' use of specific praise statements, the investigator observed and coded the following child participants' behaviors: engagement and compliance. Engagement was defined as participating in an activity, interacting with peers and teachers, or looking at or using materials in an appropriate manner (McBride & Schwartz, 2003). Compliance was defined as completing an instruction or beginning to follow the instruction within 5 s after the teacher request had been given. These targeted child behaviors were observed and coded from the same videotaped sessions that displayed the teacher's use of praise statements. To measure child engagement, a 6-s partial interval recording system was used. The 5-min session was divided into fifty 6-s intervals, and engagement was coded if the child was engaged at anytime during the 6-s interval. Following the observation, the percentage of intervals engaged was calculated by recording the total number of intervals in which engagement occurred divided by the total number of intervals observed. Compliance was coded based on the number of teacher requests that occurred during each session and converted into a percentage. To illustrate, the primary investigator first recorded the occurrence of a teacher directive toward the target child. Following a teacher directive, the observer recorded whether the target child complied with the request. The percentage of times the target child complied with a teacher request was calculated by counting the total number of times the target child complied and dividing that number by the total number of teacher requests directed toward the target child.

Interobserver Agreement
Interobserver agreement (IOA) was scored by an independent data collector on an average of 38% (range = 33%–47%) of the sessions across all participants. During all phases of the study, IOA was calculated for teacher praise statements (specific and nonspecific) by computing a frequency ratio (Kazdin, 1982). The IOA on engagement and compliance was calculated on occurrence only using the following formula: Agreements/(Agreements + Disagreements) × 100 (Kazdin, 1982). The IOA across all behaviors, participants, and phases averaged 93.6% (range = 84%–100%).

Experimental Procedures and Design
This study was conducted across three phases: preexperimental, baseline, and training/ intervention/generalization. A single-subject multiple-baseline design across 2 participants, replicated by 2 participants (Kazdin, 1982; Kennedy, 2005) was used to evaluate the effects of intervention due to the applied and practical nature of this study (i.e., across sites and severity of child behaviors). Although a multiple-baseline design across 4 participants may be a preferred design based on experimental control and replicability, we believe this study demonstrated experimental control and generalizability through the replication across participants both within and across experiments (Kennedy, 2005). Data were collected during the baseline and intervention/generalization phases for each teacher-child dyad.

Preexperimental
Prior to beginning the study, the primary investigator met with each of the teacher participants to obtain consent and identify possible target children who met criteria for the study. Following this meeting, the primary investigator observed all of the target children across several sessions during a transition activity to confirm that their problem behaviors interfered with their ability

to participate in the activity as indicated by the teachers. In addition, during this phase, the primary investigator completed the BDI-S (Newborg, 2005) with each target child. At the same time, the classroom teachers completed the Child Behavior Checklist-Teacher Report Form (Achenbach, 1992) on each of the target children. The preexperimental phase also served as a habituation period to decrease the potential effects of reactivity of observations on the teachers and children. During this time, the primary investigator entered the room with the handheld camera that was to be used in all phases of the investigation. After a few initial queries regarding the camera, the children went about their day "business as usual."

Once teacher and child participants were identified, the investigator and teachers identified a transition activity in which the target children demonstrated problem behaviors and that occurred at a regular interval each day to target for intervention. As described in *Table 13.2*, the transition activity for the teacher-child dyads 1 and 2 was cleanup from a small-group activity

TABLE 13.2   Child/Teacher Behaviors Prior to Intervention

	Transition Activity	Behavioral Expectations	Child Behavior Observed	Teacher Response to Child Behavior	Child Outcome
Dyed 1	Small group to circle time	1. Put away all materials 2. Proceed to circle	Running from area to area, throwing materials, proceeding to circle without putting away materials	Ignore, threaten without follow-up, time out	Proceed to circle without putting away materials
Dyed 2	Small group to circle time	1. Put away all materials 2. Proceed to circle 3. Sit on assigned square	Continuing to play, proceeding to circle without cleanup, sitting in others' square	Providing a warning without follow-up, time out raised voice	Proceed to time out, did not participate or joined circle sitting in any square
Dyed 3	Small to time teacher-directed literacy activity	1. Sit quietly until called to new activity 2. Proceed directly to teacher-chosen activity	Leaving circle before name is called or not leaving when name is called, going to another class area or the unassigned activity	Ignore problem behavior, provide redirection	Escaped teacher-chosen activity
Dyed 4	Cleanup to circle time	1. Put away all materials 2. Proceed to circle	Leaving center without cleaning up, continue playing	Ignore problem behavior, time out or redirection	Went to circle without putting away materials

and transition to a circle time activity. The transition activity for teacher-child dyad 3 was transition from circle time to a teacher- directed literacy activity, and for teacher-child dyad 4, the transition activity was cleanup after free play and transition to circle time.

Baseline

During the baseline phase, the teacher and child behaviors were observed during the targeted transition activities. Baseline sessions occurred within the classroom during the transition activity without any additional materials provided by the investigator or change to the teachers' routine. Teachers were instructed to conduct business as usual, which included responding to problem behaviors demonstrated by the child as they would typically respond. Each session was videotaped for 5 min for a minimum of three sessions per week until a stable baseline occurred.

During baseline, data were gathered on both the teacher and child behaviors (as described above). For teacher-child dyads 1 and 2, baseline data began on the same day. Collection of baseline data continued with teacher-child dyad 1 until a stable three-point trend in the teacher's use of praise occurred. At that point, the training in use of specific praise statements was conducted with the teacher in dyad 1, and baseline data continued to be collected for dyad 2. When a consistent increasing trend was observed in teacher 1's use of specific praise and a consistent trend in baseline data was observed for teacher 2, the training was conducted with teacher 2. These procedures were repeated for teacher-child dyads 3 and 4.

Training/Intervention/Generalization

Following the establishment of a stable baseline, each teacher received an individual training session by the investigator in the use of specific praise. Training sessions lasted an average of 1.5 hr. The training took place in a quiet room with only the investigator and the teacher present. The teacher had a training booklet developed by the investigator. The content of each training session included the following: (a) a definition of appropriate and problem behaviors demonstrated by the target child, (b) an explanation of how to use specific praise statements to increase appropriate behavior and decrease problem behavior, and (c) examples of specific and nonspecific praise statements. Two verbal checks of the teacher's understanding of specific praise statements were conducted for a criterion of 80% accuracy. In each verbal check, the teacher listened to 10 praise statements (specific and nonspecific) and recorded whether the statement was specific or nonspecific praise. Following instruction in the use of specific praise statements, the investigator and the teacher viewed videotapes from the baseline phase of the study. The teacher was asked to identify situations in which he or she might have used a specific praise statement to encourage the target child's appropriate behavior. Following the viewing of videotapes, the teacher developed five specific praise statements that could be used to encourage the target child to engage in appropriate behavior. The investigator then made five 3 × 5 laminated cards with the teacher-selected specific praise statements on them and gave these cards to the teacher to use during the intervention phase. The teacher posted the cards in a location that could be viewed during the transition time. Examples of the praise statements can be found in *Table 13.3.*

TABLE 13.3   Specific Praise Statements

Training examples of specific praise statements	(1) You did an awesome job putting the doll clothes away. (2) You were a nice friend when you gave a hug. (3) I am so happy that you held my hand when we walked outside.
Teacher-developed examples of examples of specific praise statements	(1) Wow, you did a great job finding your square and sitting down. (2) I am so proud of the way you put all the cars in the bin. (3) You were a good friend helping Sam find a book.

During training, the teacher was encouraged to ask questions and share information. Following each section of the intervention training session, a treatment integrity checklist was completed by the primary investigator and the target teacher to ensure that all training steps were completed. The investigator used the teacher training procedures previously described to conduct all training sessions with the teachers. The training for the first teacher (dyad 1) lasted 2 hr. The teacher completed both written checks with 100% accuracy. Following training, the teacher was able to give examples of five specific praise statements that she could use during the targeted transition activity. The training for the second teacher (dyad 2) lasted 1 hr 45 min. The teacher completed both written checks with 100% accuracy. Following training, the teacher was able to give examples of four specific praise statements that could be used during the target activity. The investigator provided a fifth statement. The training for the third teacher (dyad 3) lasted 1 hr 30 min. The teacher completed written check 1 with 100% accuracy and written check 2 with 90% accuracy. Following training, the third teacher was able to provide examples of five specific praise statements that could be used during the targeted activity. The training for the fourth teacher (dyad 4) lasted 1 hr. The teacher completed both checks with 100% accuracy. Following training, the teacher was able to give examples of five specific praise statements that could be used during the targeted activity. At the end of each training session, the teacher and the primary investigator completed a treatment fidelity checklist to ensure that all training steps were completed as outlined. The findings indicated that each of the training steps was completed 100% of the time for all 4 teachers.

The session was conducted 1 day prior to implementation of the intervention phase (i.e., teacher's use of specific praise statements) in the classroom. Immediately following completion of the training, the teacher was instructed to post the specific praise statement cards in a location that was easy to view to serve as a visual reminder for using the specific praise statements during the targeted transition activity. Following each session during the intervention phase, the investigator provided feedback to the teacher by providing a written note or e-mail to the teacher to briefly review the teacher's use of specific praise statements during the session and provide encouragement for the use of specific praise statements. For example, the investigator provided handwritten notes or notes via e-mail to the teachers such as, "You did a good job using specific praise today! During the transition time, you gave five specific praise statements." If the teacher's use of specific praise statements did not increase, a note was written such as, "I know the class is very busy, please try to remember to provide specific praise statements to

John whenever he uses appropriate behavior." Child behaviors were also observed and recorded during the entire intervention phase to measure the potential effects of the teacher's increased use of specific praise statements on the appropriate and problem behavior.

Generalization probes during the baseline and intervention phases of the investigation were conducted to determine if the teachers' use of specific praise statements and any changes in the children's behavior generalized to a second transition activity in the classroom. They were taken at least twice during the baseline phase and every third session during the intervention phase for all participants. During the generalization probes, the same observation and data collection procedures as previously described for the baseline and intervention phases were followed.

Results

Treatment Integrity
Both teacher and child participants' data were graphed and visually analyzed. The trend of the data in baseline and intervention, the magnitude of difference between baseline and intervention, and data stability and overlap across baseline and intervention were analyzed. In addition, the mean level differences across conditions were compared.

Teacher-Child Dyad 1

Teacher Behavior
As seen in *Figure 13.1*, the rate of specific praise statements for the teacher in dyad 1 stabilized at a rate of 0.0/min during baseline, whereas the rate of nonspecific praise statements in baseline occurred at a slightly higher and more variable rate. Following the training, the rate of specific praise statements used by teacher in dyad 1 dramatically increased, with an overall range from 1.0/min to 2.26/min with a mean of 2.00/min. The magnitude of change in the rate of specific praise statements from baseline to intervention was 0.0/min during baseline to 2.22/min during intervention, and there was an overall positive mean level change of 1.70/min. There was little difference (mean difference = 0.13/min) between baseline and intervention in the rate of nonspecific praise, which ranged from 0.0/min to 0.42/min during intervention, with a mean of 0.20/min.

Child Behavior
As seen in *Figure 13.2*, for the child in dyad 1, the percentage compliant responses were relatively low during the baseline condition. However, once the intervention phase was implemented and the teacher's use of specific praise statements increased, the child in dyad 1 demonstrated a significant increase in the percentage of complaint responses. Compliance increased from baseline (44%) to intervention (100%). This represents an increase of 52% in the mean percentage of compliant responses from baseline to intervention. The percentage of compliant responses during intervention ranged from 62% to 100%, with a mean of 87.72%.

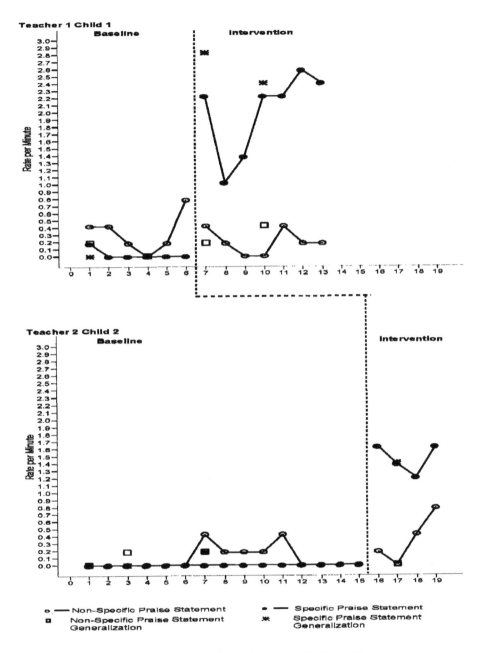

FIGURE 13.1 Teachers' Use of Specific and Nonspecific Praise Statements.

As seen in *Figure 13.3,* the engagement demonstrated by the child in dyad 1 was highly variable during baseline. Following the implementation of intervention, the percentage of time engaged increased and stabilized. During intervention, the mean percentage of time the child in dyad 1 was engaged was 92%, which represents a positive change over a mean of 37% in baseline. The magnitude of difference in engagement from baseline to intervention was 68% to 100%, respectively.

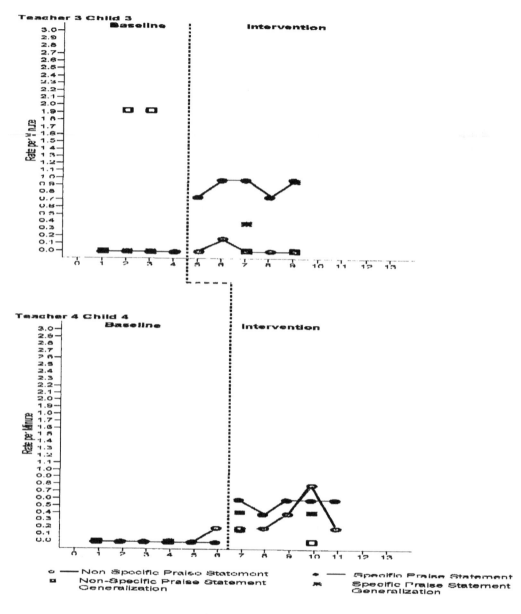

FIGURE 13.1 (Continued).

Teacher-Child Dyad 2

Teacher Behavior

During baseline, both specific and nonspecific praise statements occurred at very low rates by the teacher in dyad 2. Following training and the initiation of intervention, the teacher's rate of specific praise statements increased, ranging from 1.20/min to 1.62/min, with a mean level of 1.46/min (see *Figure 13.1*). The magnitude of change in the rate of specific praise statements from baseline

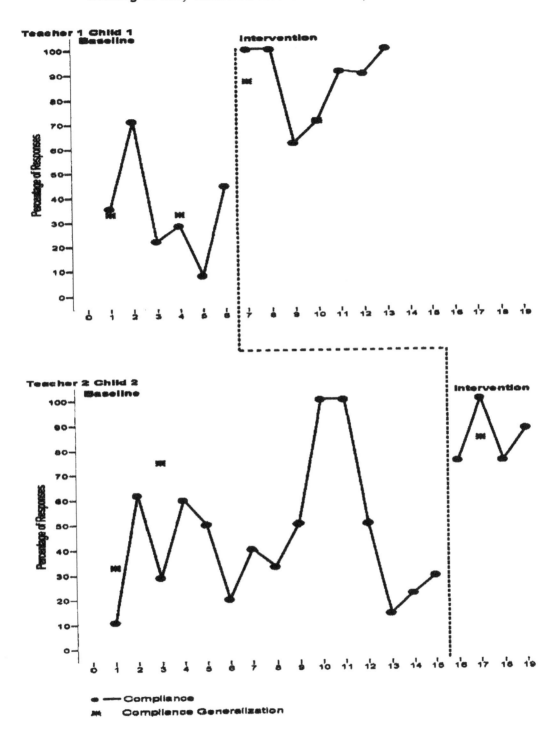

FIGURE 13.2   Child Compliance.

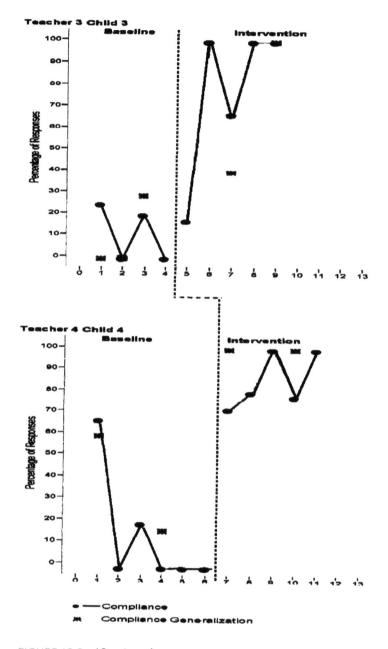

FIGURE 13.2   (Continued).

to intervention was 0.0/min at baseline to 1.62/min in intervention, with an overall positive mean change of 1.44/min. There was a slight difference (mean of 0.25/min) in the rate of nonspecific praise between baseline and intervention, which ranged from 0.0/min to 0.78/min during intervention (mean = 0.35/min). The magnitude of change from baseline to intervention in the teacher's rate of nonspecific praise statements was 0.0/min during baseline to 0.18/min during intervention.

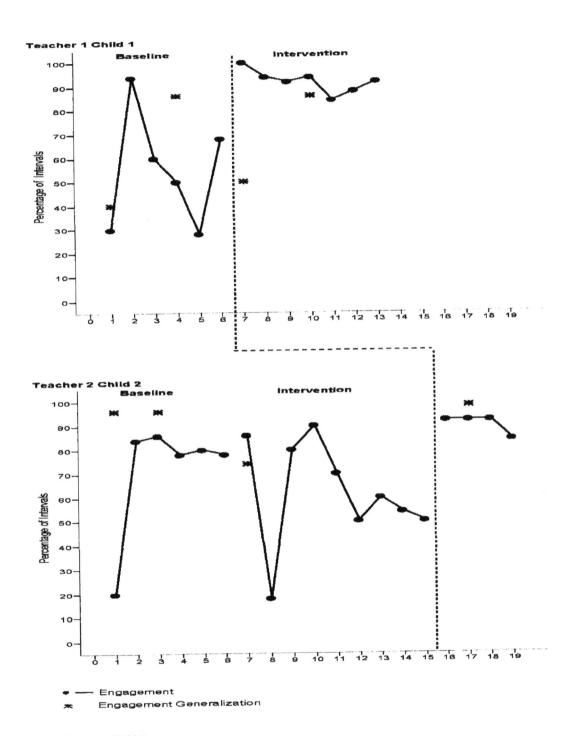

FIGURE 13.3   Child Engagement.

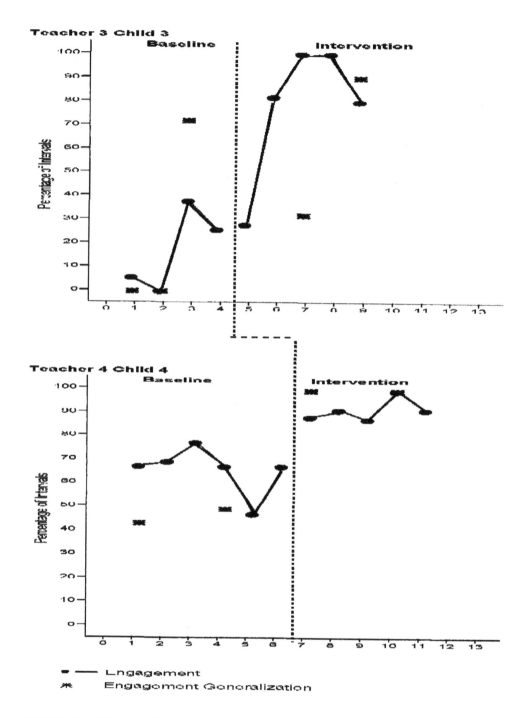

FIGURE 13.3 (Continued).

Child Behavior

As seen in *Figure 13.2*, the percentage of compliant responses displayed by the child in dyad 2 was extremely variable and relatively low during the baseline condition, ranging from 0% to 11%. Once the intervention was implemented, compliance increased dramatically and stabilized, ranging from 75% to 100% with a mean of 84.5%. The magnitude of change in compliance from baseline to intervention was from 29% during baseline to 75% during intervention.

Child 2's engagement occurred at a relatively high percentage of intervals during the baseline condition but was also variable. Following implementation of intervention, engagement increased and stabilized, with a mean of 90% during intervention (see *Figure 13.3*). This represents a positive change of 24.4% in the overall mean percentage of engagement from baseline to intervention. The magnitude of change in engagement from baseline to intervention was 50% to 92%, respectively.

Teacher-Child Dyad 3

Teacher Behavior

The teacher's rate of specific praise statements significantly increased from baseline to intervention, which ranged from 0.78/min to 1.02/min, with a mean level of 0.92/min (see *Figure 13.1*). The magnitude of change in the teacher's rate of specific praise statements from baseline to intervention was from 0.0/min during base-line to 0.78/min during intervention. There was little overall difference (mean = 0.04/min) between baseline and intervention in the teacher's rate of nonspecific praise statements, which ranged from 0.0/min to 0.18/min during intervention. The magnitude of change from baseline to intervention in the rate of nonspecific praise statements was 0.0/min during baseline to 0.04/min during intervention.

Child Behavior

Child 3's compliant responses increased during intervention in comparison with baseline levels (ranging from 17% to 100%, with a mean of 76.8% during intervention). The percentage of time the child was engaged during intervention was 95.5%, which indicated a substantial increase over baseline levels (see *Figure 13.3*). This represents a positive change in the mean of 53.5% from baseline to intervention.

Teacher-Child Dyad 4

Teacher Behavior

The teacher's rate of specific praise statements increased during the intervention condition, ranging from 0.40/min to 0.60/min, with a mean level of 0.60/min. From baseline to intervention, the magnitude of change in the teacher's rate of specific praise statements was from 0.0/min during baseline to 0.6/min during intervention, with an overall positive mean change of 0.6/min. There was also a change between baseline and intervention in the overall rate of nonspecific praise statements, which ranged from 0.19/min to 0.80/min during intervention, with a mean of 0.35/min.

Child Behavior

As seen in *Figure 13.2*, compliant responses demonstrated by the child in dyad 4 during intervention increased, with a range of 72% to 100% and a mean of 86%. Although the child demonstrated relatively high levels of engagement *during baseline*, the percentage of time he was engaged during the intervention phase was 92.25%, which represents a positive change in the mean percentage of engagement during baseline, which was 25.5% (see *Figure 13.3*). The magnitude of change in engagement from baseline to intervention was 68% during baseline to 89% during intervention. The represents a small but notable change.

Generalization

Teacher-Child Dyad 1

Transition from outside play to inside was selected as the generalization setting for dyad 1. Generalization probes were collected twice during baseline and twice during the intervention phases of the study. The data gathered during these probes were similar to findings in the intervention setting. The teacher's rate of specific praise statements increased in the generalization setting following implementation of intervention (see *Figure 13.1*). The rate of specific praise statements during the intervention phase in the generalization setting was 2.82/min and 2.4/min (mean = 2.61/min). Her rate of nonspecific praise statements in the generalization setting during the intervention phase was 0.18/min and 0.42/min (mean = 0.30/min). The percentage of compliant responses demonstrated by the child in dyad 1 in the generalization setting during the intervention phase was 87% and 71%, with a mean level of 79% (see *Figure 13.2*). The percentage of time engaged in the generalization setting during the intervention phase was 50% and 80%, with a mean level of 68% (see *Figure 13.3*). This was an increase of 5% from baseline to intervention.

Teacher-Child Dyad 2

Transition from outside play to inside play was selected as the generalization setting for teacher-child dyad 2. Because of time and logistical constraints, generalization probes occurred 3 times during baseline and only once during intervention. Similar to the findings in the intervention setting, the teacher's rate of specific praise statements increased in the generalization setting to a rate of 1.40/min during the intervention phase (see *Figure 13.1*). This represents an increase of 1.40/min in the generalization setting from baseline to intervention. Her rate of nonspecific praise statements during the intervention phase in the generalization setting occurred at a rate of 0.0/min. This represents a decrease of 0.01/min. The percentage of compliant responses in this setting was 86% (see *Figure 13.2*). When compared with the mean, this represents an increase of 30% from baseline to intervention in the generalization phase. The percentage of time the child in dyad 3 was engaged in the generalization setting during the intervention phase was 98% (see *Figure 13.3*). This is an increase of 9.4% compared with the mean from baseline to intervention.

Teacher-Child Dyad 3

Transition from a teacher-directed literacy activity to cleanup was selected as the generalization setting for teacher-child dyad 3. Generalization probes were collected twice during baseline and twice during intervention. Similar to findings in the intervention setting, the teacher's rate of specific praise statements increased in the generalization setting following implementation of intervention (see *Figure 13.1*). During the intervention phase, the teacher's rate of specific praise statements in the generalization setting was 0.42/min for each observation, with a mean increase of 0.42/min from baseline to intervention. Her use of nonspecific praise in generalization remained at 0.0/min for both sessions. The percentage of compliant responses in the generalization setting was 40% and 100%, with mean level of compliance of 60% (see *Figure 13.2*). This represents an increase of 60% during generalization from baseline to intervention. The percentage of time engaged in the generalization setting during the intervention phase was 32% and 88%, with mean level of 60% of time engaged (see *Figure 13.3*). This is an increase of 60% from baseline to intervention.

Teacher-Child Dyad 4

Transition from snack to quiet reading was selected as the generalization setting for teacher-child dyad 4. Generalization probes were collected twice during baseline and twice during intervention. Similar to findings during the intervention setting, the teacher's rate of specific praise statements increased in the generalization setting following intervention (see *Figure 13.1*). The teacher's rate of specific praise statements during both generalization probes was 0.42/min. This represents an increase in the mean from baseline to intervention of 0.42/min. His use of nonspecific praise statements was 0.18/min and 0.00/min (mean = 0.09/min) in the generalization setting during the intervention phase. The percentage of compliant responses was 100% for both generalization probes during intervention (see *Figure 13.2*). This represents an increase of 61.5% in generalization from baseline to intervention. The percentage of time engaged in the generalization setting during the intervention phase was 100% for both probes (see *Figure 13.3*). This is an increase of 53% of time engaged from baseline to intervention.

Social Validity

Following the completion of the investigation, teachers completed a social validity questionnaire to obtain information regarding their satisfaction with the intervention. Specifically, the teachers completed four questions using a 5-point Likert-type scale. The questions addressed the usefulness and the effectiveness of the intervention. The results indicated that teachers in dyads 1 and 2 found the training to be *somewhat time-consuming,* whereas the teachers in dyads 3 and 4 indicated that the training was *not at all time-consuming,* the range of responses was 1 to 3, with a mean of 1.75. Three teachers (dyads 1, 3, and 4) indicated that the intervention was *very helpful* to the classroom, whereas the teacher in dyad 2 indicated that it was *helpful;* the range of responses was 4 to 5, with a mean of 4.75. All of the teachers noted that the intervention had a *positive effect on increasing the children's appropriate behaviors.* All 4 teachers responded with a rating of 4. Finally, 3 teachers indicated that they were *very likely* to use the intervention in the future, whereas the teacher in dyad 2 indicated that she was *likely* to use it in the future; the range of responses was 4 to 5, with a mean of 4.75.

Discussion

This investigation examined early childhood teachers' use of specific praise statements following training and the collateral effects of an increased rate of specific praise statements on young children's appropriate and problem behaviors. In addition, generalization of changes in teacher and child behaviors was probed across activities.

In general, all 4 teachers increased their rate of specific praise statements following training with no additional coaching sessions required. Although all participants received the same training, the teacher in dyad 4 demonstrated a notably lower rate of specific praise in comparison with the teachers in dyads 1, 2, and 3. This may be because the child in dyad 4 had the lowest rate of problem behavior and therefore a lower level of specific praise was required. As the teachers' specific praise statements increased, the target children's compliance and engagement increased. Finally, although only a limited number of probes were conducted and the results should be viewed with caution, preliminary findings indicated that teacher and child behaviors generalized to a second transition activity. Although a number of positive findings emerged, this study had several limitations that affect the findings. Therefore, the results should be viewed with caution. First, the number of participants was small and limits the overall generality of the findings. The target children in the study demonstrated significant problem behaviors but did not have established disabilities. Therefore, the generalization of findings to children with developmental disabilities, including cognitive and language delays, is unknown. The teacher participants had many years of experience (4–13 years) and relatively high levels of education (minimum of AA degrees) not typically found in early childhood settings. Therefore, it is not known if similar results could be replicated with teachers who have less experience and education. Next, the study took place within two National Association for the Education and Young Children-accredited, university-based childcare centers. Similar results might not have been found in less optimal educational settings (i.e., childcare centers without accreditation). Thus, the generality of the findings of this study may be limited in relation to participants with other characteristics across other settings.

In addition to limitations regarding the generality of findings, several methodological limitations occurred. First, the primary investigator of the study conducted the training for the 4 participating teachers and served as the primary data collector. Although this is a limitation of the study, high levels of IOA were independently obtained. Second, because of the small number of generalization probes obtained, it is difficult to make conclusive statements regarding the generalization findings. Therefore, the generalization data should be viewed cautiously. In addition, for the children in dyads 1 and 2, the training and intervention for the teachers in the use of increased praise statements was introduced when compliance was exhibiting an upward trend. This threatens the internal validity of the study. Noteworthy, however, is the overall mean change as well as the magnitude of change of the child participants' compliance from baseline to intervention levels, therefore suggesting that the intervention was a likely factor for increasing their behavior. Finally, the use of partial-interval recording to examine child participants' engagement may have overestimated their levels of engagement. In future research, measuring the precise duration of engagement or use of momentary time sampling may provide a more representative sample.

Despite these limitations, the findings from the current study support previous research on the use of specific praise statements as an efficient and effective intervention (Dobrinski, 2004, Stormont et al., 2007). Furthermore, as with the current investigation, previous research has suggested that allowing teachers to choose the child and the behaviors to praise will increase the likelihood that the teacher will use the strategy with the target child (Wills, 2002). Finally, the use of modeling, practice, and feedback to train teachers to use specific praise with children exhibiting problem behavior has been demonstrated as an effective strategy in previous research (Freeland, 2003). The current study used similar strategies and demonstrated similar findings.

The present study extended the outcomes of previous research in elementary school settings by focusing on training early childhood teachers to implement specific praise as an intervention strategy and evaluating the generalization of teachers' use of specific praise statements. In addition, this study isolated specific praise statements as the only intervention. Focusing on specific praise as the primary intervention, the results suggest that specific praise can be used alone and is likely to be an effective and efficient intervention strategy. As with past studies, it has been shown that intervention packages that include specific praise statements have a positive impact on increasing appropriate behavior and decreasing problem behavior in young children. In addition, this study provided evidence that specific praise statements are likely to generalize across settings. In this study, although the focus was on training teachers to implement the use of specific praise statements successfully, following the implementation of the intervention there was an increase in children's appropriate behavior (compliance) and an increase in their engagement in the classroom activities. The current study adds to both research and practice in the use of specific praise statements by demonstrating that these statements may be effective in increasing appropriate behavior in young children enrolled in child care centers and emphasizes the importance of providing teachers with effective training and intervention strategies. Similar to research on the use of universal supports to create positive classroom environments, this study also suggests that using specific behavioral consultation strategies (e.g., training and feedback) is an effective means for training early childhood teachers.

Future research should focus on addressing several of the limitations of the current study. First, research has not been conducted on the effects of specific praise statements on young children with atypical development enrolled in childcare centers. In addition, research should focus on whether the teacher's use of specific praise statements generalized to other children in the class. Finally, future researchers may want to investigate maintenance of the intervention over time. In particular, researchers may want to examine whether teachers continue to use specific praise statements with children over time and, if so, the effects of this strategy on their classroom behaviors.

In conclusion, this study presents data indicating that teachers in early childhood settings can be taught to increase their levels of specific praise statements and that when specific praise statements are used, high-risk children's problem behavior decreases and appropriate behaviors increase. Although there are several methodological limitations, these findings have important implications for practice. Specific praise is a relatively simple and underused instructional strategy that teachers can easily implement. If used correctly and consistently, specific praise can have a significant impact on children's behavior and may lead to positive interactions between teachers and their children, thus changing the reciprocal nature of these interactions from coercive to positive and increasing the positive atmosphere of the classroom (Patterson et al., 2002).

References

Achenbach, T. M. (1992). *Manual for the Child Behavior Checklist/2–3 and 1992 profile*. Burlington, VT: University of Vermont Department of Psychiatry.

Baer, D. M., & Sherman, J. A. (1964). Reinforcement control of generalization imitation in young children *Journal of Experimental Child Psychology, 1*, 37–49.

Barnett, W. S., & Boocock, S. S. (1998). *Early care and education for children in poverty*. Albany, NY: SUNY Press.

Brophy, J. (1981). Teacher praise: A functional analysis *Review of Educational Research, 51*(1), 5–32.

Browder, D. M., Hines, C., McCarthy, L. J., & Fees, J. (1984). A treatment package for increasing sight word recognition for use in daily living skills *Education and Training of the Mentally Retarded, 19,* 191–200.

Buell, J., Stoddard, P., Harris, F. R., & Baer, D. M. (1968). Collateral social development accompanying reinforcement of outdoor play in a preschool child *Journal of Applied Behavior Analysis, 1,* 167–173.

Burchinal, M. R., Peisner-Feinberg, E., Pianta, R., & Howes, C. (2002). Development of academic skills from preschool through second grade: Family and classroom predictors of developmental trajectories *Journal of School Psychology, 40,* 415–436.

Cameron, J., & Pierce, W. D. (1994). Reinforcement, reward and intrinsic motivation: A meta-analysis *Review of Educational Research, 64,* 363–423.

Campbell, S. B. (1995). Behavior problems in preschool children: A review of recent research *Journal of Child Psychology and Psychiatry, 36*(1), 113–149.

Campbell, S. B., & Ewing, L. J. (1989). Follow-up of hard to manage preschoolers: Adjustment at age 9 and predictors of continuing symptoms *Journal of Child Psychology and Psychiatry, 36*(1), 871–889.

Casey, A. M., & McWilliam, R. A. (2008). Graphical feedback to increase teachers' use of incidental teaching *Journal of Early Intervention, 30,* 251–268.

Dobrinski, D. (2004). The effects of behavior specific praise used as a delayed directive on the on-task behavior *of* elementary students *ProQuest Dissertations and Theses*, AAT3134988.

Freeland, J. T. (2003). Analyzing the effects of direct behavioral consultation on teachers: Generalization of skills across settings *Dissertation Abstracts International, 63*(10-A).

Gable, R. A., & Shores, R. E. (1980). Comparison of procedures for promoting reading proficiency of two children with behavioral and learning disorders *Behavioral Disorders, 5,* 102–107.

Good, T. L, & Grouws, D. A. (1977). Teaching effects: A process-product study in fourth-grade mathematics classrooms *Journal of Teacher Education, 28,* 49–54.

Hall, R. V., Lund, D., & Jackson, D. (1968). Effects of teacher attention on study behavior *Journal of Applied Behavior Analysis, 7,* 1–12.

Hamre, B. K., & Pianta, R. C. (2001). Early teacher-child relationships and the trajectory of children's school outcomes through grade eight *Child Development, 72,* 625–625.

Hart, B., & Risley, T. R. (1995). *Meaningful differences.* Baltimore, MD: Paul H. Brooks.

Hemmeter, M. L., Fox, L., Jack, S., & Broyles, L. (2007). A program-wide model of positive behavior support in early childhood settings *Journal of Early Intervention, 29,* 337–355.

Heider, J. P. (1979). Time with the psychologist as a reinforcement for work completion *School Psychology Review, 8,* 335–338.

Howes, C., & Smith, E. W. (1995). Relations among childcare quality, teacher behavior, children's play activities, emotional security, and cognitive activity in children *Early Childhood Research Quarterly, 10,* 381–404.

Kazdin, A. E. (1982). *Single-case research designs: Methods for clinical and applied settings.* New York: Oxford University Press.

Kennedy, C. (2005). Single-Case Design for Educational Research. Boston, MA: Pearson.

Lewis, T. J., & Newcomer, L. L. (2002). Examining the efficacy of school-based consultation: Recommendations for improving outcomes *Child & Family Behavior Therapy, 24,* 165–181.

Madsen, C. H., Jr. Becker, W. C., & Thomas, D. R. (1968). Rules, praise, and ignoring: Elements of elementary classroom control *Journal of Applied Behavior Analysis, 1,* 139–150.

Marchant, M., Young, R. K., & West, R. P. (2004). The effects of parental teaching on compliance behavior of children *Psychology in the School, 47,* 337–350.

Martens, B. K., Hiralall, A. S., & Bradley, T. A. (1997). A note to teacher; improving student behavior through goal setting and feedback *School Psychology Quarterly, 12*(1), 33–41.

McBride, B. J., & Schwartz, I. S. (2003). Effects of teaching early interventionists to use discrete trials during ongoing classroom activities *Topics in Early Childhood Special Education, 23*(1), 5–17.

Mortenson, B. P., & Witt, J. C. (1998). The use of weekly performance feedback to increase teacher implementation of a preferral academic intervention *School Psychology Review, 27, 613–627.*

Newborg, J. (2005). *Battelle developmental inventory, 2nd edition, screening test item test book.* Itasca, IL: Riverside Publishing.

Patterson, G. R., Reid, J. B., & Eddy, M. J. (2002). A brief history of the Oregon model. In J. B. Reid, G. R. Patterson, & J. Snyder (Eds.), *Antisocial behavior in children and adolescents* (pp. 3–21). American Psychological Association: Washington, DC.

Raver, C. C., & Knitzer, J. (2002). *Ready to enter: What research tells policymakers about strategies to promote social and emotional school readiness among three and four year olds.* New York: National Center for Children in Poverty.

Scott-Little, M. C., & Holloway, S. D. (1992). Child care providers' reasoning about misbehaviors: Relation to classroom control strategies and professional training *Early Childhood Research Quarterly, 7,* 595–606.

Sterling-Turner, H. E., Watson, T. S., & Moore, J. W. (2002). The effects of direct training and treatment integrity on treatment outcomes in school consultation *School Psychology Quarterly, 17,* 47–77.

Stormont, M. (2002). Externalizing behavior problems in young children: Contributing factors and early intervention *Psychology in the Schools, 3*(9), 127–138.

Stormont, M., Lewis, T. J., & Beckner, B. (2005). Developmentally continuous positive behavior support systems: Applying key features in preschool settings *Teaching Exceptional Children, 37,* 42–48.

Stormont, M., Smith, S., & Lewis, T. (2007). Teacher Implementation of precorrections and praise statements in Head Start classrooms as a component of program-wide systems of positive-behavior support. *Journal of Behavior Education, 6*(3), 280–290.

Sutherland, K. S., & Wehby, J. H. (2001). The effect of self-evaluation on teaching behavior in classrooms for students with emotional and behavioral disorders *Journal of Special Education, 35,* 161–171.

Sutherland, K. S., Wehby, J. H., & Copeland, S. R. (2000). Effect on varying rates of behavior-specific praise on the on-task behavior of students with EBD *Journal of Emotional & Behavioral Disorders, 8*(1), 2–9.

Walker, H. M., Stiller, B., Golly, A., Kavanagh, K., Severson, H. H., & Feil, E. J. (1997). *First step to success (preschool edition).* Fredrick, CO: Sopris West Educational Services.

Webster-Stratton, C. (1997). Early intervention for families of preschool children with conduct problems. In M. J. Gurlanick (Ed.), *The effectiveness of early intervention* (pp. 429–454). Baltimore, MD: Paul H. Brookes.

Webster-Stratton, C. (2000). *The incredible years training series.* Washington, D.C.: Office of Juvenile Justice and Delinquency Prevention.

Wills, H. P. (2002). *A praise game to improve both teacher and student behaviors.* Ann Arbor, MI: ProQuest Dissertations and Theses AA3054003.

Discussion Questions

1. What are effective ways of teaching young children to accept peers with exceptionalities?
2. As educators, can you think of some ways to minimize discrimination in the classroom and school in general?
3. What are your experiences with linguistic diversity, and why is language an important element of culture?
4. How can teachers challenge the stereotypes and prejudices that some students hold about minority groups?
5. What are your reactions to the field of disability studies?
6. What are the challenges of labeling groups of students in school? In your opinion are there any sensitive or professional ways that educators can use labels as a part of their work, or should we not use labels?

Activity

Talk to a partner about the ways that labels can be both helpful and harmful.

UNIT IV

IMMIGRANTS, REFUGEES, AND CHILDHOOD EDUCATION

Immigration and Diversity

Sarah Sifers, Julene Nolan, and Daniel Houlihan

The United States has been a nation of immigrants since the first colonizers arrived from Europe in the late 1600s. In fact, only about 2% of North Americans are descendants of Native North Americans; the remaining 98% are immigrants themselves or descendants of people who migrated to this country (Centers for Disease Control and Prevention [CDC], 2014). In 2012 alone, more than a million people obtained legal permanent residence in the United States, with the largest groups coming from Asian and Latin countries (United States Department of Homeland Security [USDHS], 2013). The population of first-generation immigrants continues to grow rapidly, and it is estimated that by 2050 more than half of children in schools will be from immigrant or diverse households (Hernandez, Denton, Macartney, & Blanchard, 2012).

One commonly held belief is that immigrant children burden the social systems (health, education, welfare) of the United States because they come to this country without language fluency, social supports, or wealth. However, the truth is that recent immigrants demonstrate positive outcomes similar to peers born in this country. Unfortunately, the same is not true for second- and third-generation immigrants. Even though these families have had time to **assimilate** into the dominant culture, they generally demonstrate poorer outcomes in terms of social behavior than recent immigrant families (Coll & Marks, 2012). This phenomenon is called the **immigrant paradox**.

To understand the research regarding immigration and cultural identity development, it is first important to understand how this type of research is conducted. Unlike experimental research, in which it is both ethical and possible to manipulate variables (for example, giving different strengths of drugs or using different behavioral interventions to find out what works best), research that is conducted on groups of people to study culture is called **ethnographic** research. In ethnographic research, it is not possible to assign participants to particular cultural groups. This means that the researcher observes and records events in naturally occurring cultural groups as a means to study cultural practices. When comparisons are made between different cultures, researchers are engaging in **cross-cultural research**. When choosing individuals within a culture to study, it is important that researchers choose people who are more like the average person within that community, so researchers must ensure that they use **representative samples**. This means that they must choose people who represent the overall culture best, and this is achieved by using a random sample that represents the total population in terms of different characteristics like age, gender, geographic location, sexual orientation, religion, socioeconomic status (SES), occupation, and so on. This provides a better chance that the phenomenon being studied reflects the natural occurrence of the same phenomenon in the whole population. For example, if a scientist was studying religious practices of a certain cultural group, she would want to ensure that the sample she studies includes males, females, young, middle-aged, old, rich, middle income, poor, and so on, so that she could learn something that is generalizable to the entire population within that cultural group.

This chapter will explore cultural diversity and immigration in the United States, and how being an immigrant affects adolescent development within psychological and social dimensions. It will examine the microsystems and exosystems of these adolescents and the research around cultural identity development.

Psychological Dimensions

Race or ethnicity is one dimension of diversity; however, a person can represent diversity in several different ways. For example, an Asian-American female who is gender nonconforming, works in law enforcement, and has a learning disability is considered diverse on many axes, depending upon the community in which she lives and works. Even people who represent the majority culture within their race and ethnicity may be diverse in their religious belief, their ability, their sexual orientation, their SES, and so on. Because the world is diverse on so many levels and increasingly becoming globalized, it is important to teach adolescents to recognize and respect diversity in their world.

One of the obstacles that diverse adolescents face is **discrimination**, or unfair treatment based on personal characteristics (e.g., race, gender, SES, ability, religious affiliation, age, appearance, culture, et cetera). When a person or group of people are discriminated against, they face unfair challenges in some or many aspects of their lives. This is made more complex and harder to combat when discrimination is institutionalized. **Institutional discrimination** occurs when the rules and common practices of organizations treat individuals or groups unfairly. One example is when a company uses hiring practices that unfairly eliminate certain candidates. For example, jobs, especially higher-level and higher-paying jobs, may not be widely publicized. The hiring practices might favor a certain group by only considering those people who are recommended by current employees or who have had certain job or educational opportunities that are usually only afforded by those from high-SES families (e.g., requiring an Ivy League education).

Institutional discrimination is a form of **modern racism**, in which racism is more covert and difficult to identify, but nevertheless is present and harmful. Discrimination keeps certain groups of people in low power positions in society. This is called **marginalization**. Adolescents are marginalized in society when people who have more power and influence act in a way that makes adolescents feel unimportant, inconsequential, and invisible. Many theorists believe that marginalization is responsible for aggression and violence in communities, as people act out to express anger and frustration for being treated as insignificant.

Immigrant and diverse families are at more risk for these obstacles when their culture, language, and race are different from the dominant culture of a community. Overall, immigrants are more likely to be victimized and less likely to report victimization (Koo, Peguero, & Shekarkhar, 2012; Peguero, 2009). Discrimination not only affects a person's opportunity and access to resources, it also negatively affects the psychological well-being of immigrants and diverse adolescents (see, for example, Cristini, Scacchi, Perkins, Santinello, & Vieno, 2011; Huynh & Fuligni, 2010). While discrimination and marginalization have a detrimental effect on psychological outcomes, recent research on protective factors for positive psychological development has indicated that ethnic identity development is an important buffer against the negative effects of discrimination and marginalization that ethnically diverse and immigrant adolescents face (Smith & Silva, 2011).

Ethnicity refers to cultural heritage shared among a group. It is based on common ancestors and mutual experiences. **Culture** refers to norms and practices that define a group of people who share a common identity. Culture is tied to emotion, and when others engage in behaviors that offend or violate someone's cultural practices, it can cause intense reactions. A person's cultural beliefs are subject to change based on individual experience. For example, as adolescents grow and learn more about their own cultural practices, they might find some are no longer useful or no longer in alignment with their beliefs. This might be the case in a family that was raised with very traditional roles for men and women. An individual adolescent might come to reject these rolls and change their own cultural practices as they become adults.

Adolescence is a time for identity development, and this can become more difficult for immigrant and diverse individuals depending upon available social supports and exposure to adverse situations. **Ethnic identity** refers to recognizing and claiming the cultural heritage and norms and practices of a person's ethnic group. This is much more easily achieved when one's practices are not very different than those of the dominant culture, or when there is support available. Research indicates that ethnic identity development is related to self-esteem and psychological well-being in people of color, so fostering this development is very important (Smith & Silva, 2011).

Many of the early theories developed to address identity development in immigrant or diverse adolescent populations have focused on pathology within the individual or family, and ignored the effects of discrimination and stereotype (Poston, 1990). Additionally, early **cultural assimilation models** identified how immigrants changed as they sought to abandon their own cultural practices and customs, and become more like the majority culture. These models made the assumption that assimilation was what helped immigrants become well-adjusted within the majority culture. However, they are criticized for being too narrow in their scope and for attributing difficult outcomes to individual failure to become more like the dominant culture.

If adolescents are a minority in a population, they may assimilate into the majority culture by rejecting those customs that represent their culture of origin and taking on norms of the majority. Immigrants who arrived in the early 1900s tended to value this approach and, in fact, it often resulted in better academic and economic outcomes. However, recent research demonstrates that adolescents who take this route suffer poorer psychological outcomes in terms of depression and anxiety.

Another approach is to **acculturate**, which means accepting the norms of the majority culture while maintaining one's own personal culture and integrating the two identities. This is a more popular approach and results in good academic and psychological outcomes, but it must be supported within the community. A third approach is the *alternation model*, in which adolescents change the way they present themselves depending on which group they are near. Adolescents who alternate how they present themselves often engage in **code switching**, which means they change the way they speak, words they use, tone, volume, and inflection depending upon their audience. This approach is associated with poor achievement and poor psychological outcomes.

One aspect of ethnic identity formation that has been overlooked in the past is **bicultural identity** development. This describes a situation in which adolescents strongly identify with two cultures, generally representing those of their parents and the mainstream culture. Increasingly, adolescents area able to identify with more than one culture as the world becomes more globalized and interracial marriage becomes commonplace. Early cultural assimilation models are criticized because they did not account for bicultural identity. Research suggests that adolescents who examine their cultural heritage and are able to create an identity that integrates their heritage with the dominant culture are better adjusted than those who feel pressure to assimilate or alternate their identity.

Cognitive Factors

People use **stereotypes** to categorize and understand the environment. Getting to know and form an opinion about every person we encounter is impossible, so humans simplify this process by assuming people that share one characteristic likely share other characteristics. People learn about characteristics associated with particular cultural groups based on experience, observation, or information they have been exposed to indirectly (e.g., heard from others or in the media). Stereotypes can harm people when we use negative information we have come to believe about a certain group of people and attribute those characteristics to an individual who we believe comes from the same cultural or ethnic group. Furthermore, they overlook the fact that within-group differences are greater than between-group differences. That is, there is more diversity within any cultural group than there are differences between that cultural group and another cultural group.

Stereotype threat is a term coined by Steele and Aronson (1995) that describes a situation in which a person is at risk of confirming a negative stereotype based on identifying their ethnicity. It refers to a series of studies in which African American students who took standardized tests performed worse when they had to identify their race prior to taking the test. The theory is that the pressure to try to disprove negative stereotypes about one's group results in anxiety that leads to poorer performance. A caution is issued by Steele and Aronson that over-interpreting this data can lead policy makers, parents, and educators to attribute the achievement gap to stereotype threat and not consider other factors like opportunity, access to education, SES, and so on. (Steele & Aronson, 2004).

Psychodynamic Factors

Psychodynamic psychology views identity development as a complex and evolving process that is caused by internal conflict and results in either identity achievement or identity diffusion. Freud's conceptualization of identity lends itself to the immigrant and diverse adolescent experience because the goal in psychoanalytic development is to become the person you want to be, whether or not that person conforms to the expectations of others (Ruth, 2012). Psychodynamic psychology views constructs like identity formation and worldview as a result of internal processes. This is not to say that external forces have no impact, but rather that people processes what happens to them in the external world by internally managing these events, and two people process and react to the same events (for example discrimination or marginalization) differently depending upon the strength and development of their defense mechanisms.

One way to understand internal processes experienced by diverse and immigrant adolescents is by understanding the differences in worldview of different cultures. For example, time orientation differs across cultures, in that some cultures view time as a valuable and limited commodity that is too easily spent and too easily wasted. Other cultures view time as an endless commodity that is always in ample supply. If a person from a time-limited worldview has an interaction with a person from a time-endless worldview, one may inadvertently insult the other by not meeting cultural expectations, for instance being late to a meeting. This may make the time-limited person feel disrespected and the time-endless person feel confused and view the other as nervous and anxious or overly critical.

Cultures also differ in their orientation to prescribed social structure. For example, people from a culture that values concrete and defined social structure would never bypass the hierarchy in an organization for help or instruction. Rather, they would only seek guidance from their immediate supervisor. In another culture, seeking to impress the highest-ranking person within an organization may be valued and seen as demonstrating leadership skills. These types of cultural differences can be a significant problem for immigrant adolescents as they must learn not only the concrete skills (language, housing, money, et cetera) of their new culture, but also the intangible differences. Other areas in which attitudes and expectations differ according to culture may include: personal space; importance of self versus the whole community; orientation toward past, present, or future; value of tradition versus innovation; importance of family; orientation toward work and achievement; conformity versus individuality; and orientation toward risk taking.

Psychodynamic theory attributes negative outcomes experienced by immigrants, such as anxiety, depression, or suicide, to the challenge of developing a new identity and having insufficient defense mechanisms to deal with all of the losses that are inherent to migrating to a new country. In adolescent immigrants, the natural process of separation from parents and developing a more individual identity is interrupted because often they must rely on parents for support in navigating the new environment. Negative outcomes for immigrant adolescents are attributed to this disruption of natural development (Sharabany & Israeli, 2008).

Social Dimensions

While understanding the internal experiences of diverse and immigrant adolescents is important, it is equally important to understand the social environment, because it is within the social environment that concerned adults can help struggling adolescents. One issue that affects diverse and immigrant adolescents as well as members of the dominant culture is **ethnocentrism**, or viewing others' culture through the lens of one's own culture and judging other culture negatively. This is a form of *in-group bias*, which means favoring one's own group. When adolescents have strong negative reactions to customs that are different from their own, they may come to negatively stereotype people from other cultures. Education is the best way to combat ethnocentrism.

The United States is a **pluralistic society** in that as a whole it is **integrated** in terms of diversity. That means that many different races, ethnicities, nationalities, and heritages are represented within the population of the United States. However, even in diverse cities, it is common for there to be pockets of homogeneous groups based on race or culture. For example, when new immigrants come to a city, they often find housing in areas that are already populated by immigrants from the same country. This may be because relatives or friends have connected them to this area, because benevolent groups who sponsor refugees have secured housing in one central location, or for a host of other reasons. Given that adolescents' experiences are greatly affected by their surroundings, microsystems and exosystems impact diverse and immigrant adolescent development.

Microsystem Factors

Family, peers, neighborhood, teachers, school, job, faith community, cultural group, and other aspects of an adolescent's microsystem have a large impact on their development. According to the immigration paradox, adolescents who were born in the country of migration to immigrant parents demonstrate worse outcomes in terms of drug and alcohol use, mental illness, educational achievement, and sexual behavior than adolescents who are themselves immigrants (Raffaelli, Kang, & Guarini, 2012). Why would this be so? One explanation is the **cultural integration hypothesis**, which states that those who migrate to another country do so on purpose and must overcome many obstacles, both in their country of origin and in the new country, to achieve immigration. They self-select for these challenges and their mindset, grit, and determination help them succeed. Subsequent descendants of these immigrants do not make the choice for themselves and may become mired in the difficulties associated with being a minority without the resources to effectively cope with the challenges (Marks, Ejesi, & Garcia Coll, 2014).

Other factors that have been identified to put second and subsequent generations at risk include loosening of family ties, more sedentary lifestyles, peer engagement in risky behaviors, and earlier exposure to sexual activity with more partners. However, research comparing recent immigrant outcomes to second and later generation outcomes is criticized because influences on these populations may be vastly different. It is also criticized for investigating risks rather than resilience factors, and focusing on negative outcomes for second and subsequent generation immigrant families (Garcia Coll et al., 1996). It would be more useful to study the same group over time to see if developmental changes occur, and what factors influence these changes both within the individual and among adolescents in the same demographic group. One such longitudinal study of 332 adolescents who are first- or second-generation immigrants demonstrated that internalizing problems decline significantly in secondary school; however, stress associated with acculturation predicted internalizing problems (Sirin, Ryce, Gupta, & Rogers-Sirin, 2013).

Effective prevention and intervention has focused on the microsystems of diverse and immigrant adolescents. In fact, in one study of 277,000 teens, teachers were demonstrated to be an important factor in helping them feel connected to the school community (Chiu, Pong, Mori, & Chow, 2012). Another study of nearly 10,000 immigrant adolescents found that involvement in school sports was a protective factor against negative outcomes, but only for third-generation immigrants and beyond. First- and second-generation immigrants were not helped by school sports involvement and in many instances were more vulnerable to victimization (Peguero, 2013). This information should help to inform programming in schools to assist these adolescents, as well as educate the school population as a whole. Overall, the best approach to support diverse and immigrant adolescents is through programming in the school, in the community, in the neighborhood, and with families.

Much attention has recently been paid to second-generation immigrant adolescents and young adults who seek to join radical and terrorist groups, or who commit atrocities in their adopted country. While there is little research on these individuals, theorists claim that these young people feel isolated and marginalized by society. They feel disillusioned by Western culture, democracy, and wealth-seeking behavior. In their search for purpose, identity formation, and community connectedness, they turn to radicalization to feel passionate about something and to belong to a community that has a concrete purpose. Joining these groups makes them feel powerful and important (Atran, 2010; Bizina, Northfield, & Gray, 2014).

However, these individuals are not significantly different from their peers who do not become radicalized. They do not come from highly religious families or low-SES environments, nor do they experience more discrimination than their peers. Rather, the common theme seems to be a search for meaning, identity, and belongingness, as well as access through social media to powerful images, charismatic leaders, and messages of injustice and moral outrage related to Western values (Atran, 2010; Bizina et al., 2014). Microsystems are becoming more involved in these issues as they seek to engage youth on a local level to help them better channel some of these feelings as they navigate these identity formation years.

Exosystem Factors

Exosystems influence adolescents indirectly by impacting those organizations or people within the microsystems. They can also work to develop supports for immigrant and diverse adolescents. For example, the parents' workplace may offer immigrant services that help families settle in an area and obtain access to resources. While immigration laws would be a way to impact many adolescents, immigration reform policy has been hung up within the political process for decades. The media plays a role in portraying immigrants and diverse adolescents in certain ways that may make it difficult for adolescents to feel good about themselves and hopeful for their future.

School districts may help by implementing district-wide social-emotional learning to help all students understand emotional intelligence and nonverbal communication, as well as develop self-awareness, self-management, social awareness, relationship skills, and responsible decision-making skills. The current approach to social-emotional development presents an illogical paradox. For example, when students do not know how to read, they are taught reading skills. When students do not know how to do math, they are taught math skills. But when students do not know how to behave, they are punished. This is ineffective and puts many students at risk, including those students with low social-emotional skills and those with whom they interact.

Many districts have implemented zero-tolerance policies regarding weapons, violence, and drugs. These policies mandate suspension and expulsion for any infraction of these rules, with the aim of keeping students safe. Unfortunately, zero-tolerance policies have been demonstrated ineffective and ultimately harmful to the students they are trying to support. Prohibiting a student who does not have social-emotional skills from attending schools ultimately makes everyone less safe, as outside of school they are often not monitored and they often socialize with criminals and other at-risk youth. Suspension and expulsion is wholly ineffective in reforming students. In fact, a single suspension increases the probability that a student will drop out of school at age 16.

Children of Illegal Immigrants

The gridlock within the U.S. government regarding immigration reform has created a situation in which there is a growing population of undocumented children and families. An estimated 1.7 million children are living in this country illegally through no fault of their own (Suarez-Orozco, 2010). Most immigrant adolescents are Latino or Asian, with a recent influx of youth from the Middle East, Africa, and Eastern Europe. While most adolescent immigrants were born in this country and thus are U.S. citizens, 5 million of them have one or more parents who are in this country illegally. There is little research on the effect that citizenship status has on developing adolescents, or what role having illegal parents or being an illegal immigrant might have on the immigrant paradox (Marks et al., 2014).

Conclusion

Historically, the United States has been a nation of immigrants, and that trend is not projected to change. In fact, by 2050 more than half of the population will be from diverse or immigrant families. Immigrant and diverse youth face especially difficult hurdles in navigating develop-ment during adolescence, and risk for negative outcomes seems to increase with second- and third-generation immigrants. Combating these negative outcomes can be accomplished through microsystems and exosystems working together to program prevention and intervention for these youth. Adolescence is a critical juncture and time of identity development, and theorists believe that when immigrant adolescents feel marginalized and disillusion with the "American Dream," they are vulnerable to negative outcomes.

Critical Thinking Question

In what ways does your worldview differ from other people your age? From your parents? From your younger relatives? How has it changed since you left high school?

Key Terms

Acculturation—Accepting the norms of the majority culture while maintaining one's own culture and integrating the two identities

Assimilate—To change cultural practices to become more like the dominant culture

Bicultural identity—Identifying equally with two cultural groups

Code switching—Changing the way one speaks, the words one uses, tone, volume, and inflection depending upon the audience

Cross-cultural research—The study of similarities and differences across cultures

Cultural assimilation model—Identifies how immigrants change as they seek to abandon their own cultural practices and customs and become more like the majority culture, assuming that assimilation helps immigrants become well-adjusted within the majority culture

Cultural integration hypothesis—States that those who migrate to another country do so on purpose and must overcome many obstacles, for which they self-select, both in their country of origin and in the new country, to achieve immigration; their mindset, grit, and determi-nation help them to succeed, although subsequent descendants of these immigrants do not make the choice for themselves and may become mired in the difficulties associated with being a minority

Culture—Norms and practices that define a group of people who have a shared identity

Discrimination—Unfair treatment based on personal characteristics (e.g., race, gender, SES, ability, religious affiliation, age, appearance, culture)

Ethnic identity—Recognizing and claiming the cultural heritage and norms and practices of one's ethnic group

Ethnicity—Cultural heritage shared among a group based on common ancestors and mutual experiences

Ethnocentrism—The belief that one's own culture is correct and using the norms and practices of one's culture to negatively judge other cultures

Ethnographic study—Research that is conducted on groups of people to study culture, wherein researchers observe and record events as a means to learn about a group

Immigrant paradox—The phenomenon in which second- and third-generation descendants of immigrants tend to have increasingly poor social, emotional, behavioral, and economic outcomes than their immigrant ancestors

In-group bias—Favoring one's own group

Institutional discrimination—when the rules and common practices of organizations treat individuals or groups unfairly.

Integration—The coming together of different groups to develop a single, more diverse group

Marginalization—Discrimination that keeps certain groups of people in low-power positions in society

Modern racism—A situation in which racism is more covert and difficult to identify, but still present and harmful, including institutional racism

Pluralistic society model—A society that is well-integrated in terms of diversity

Representative sample—A research technique in which subjects who represent the overall culture are chosen to be studied by using a random sample that represents the total population in terms of different characteristics like age, gender, SES, occupation, and so on, to provide a better chance that the phenomenon being studied reflects the natural occurrence of the same phenomenon in the whole population, rather than a single group that is investigated

Stereotype—A mechanism for categorizing and understanding the environment by making assumptions about people based on group membership

Stereotype threat—When a person is at risk of confirming a negative stereotype based on having to identify their ethnicity

Additional Resources

National Association of Secondary School Principals http://www.nasponline.org/resources/principals/Immigrant_FamiliesJan10_NASSP.pdf

National Association of School Psychologists http://www.nasponline.org/publications/cq/39/5/understandingtheplight.aspx

U.S. Committee for Refugees and Immigrants http://www.refugees.org/resources/for-refugees--immigrants/family-strengthening-resources/

Terrorism Research Initiative http://www.terrorismanalysts.com/pt/index.php/pot/article/view/35/html

UK Office for Security and Counter-Terrorism https://www.gov.uk/government/uploads/system/uploads/attachment_data/file/116723/occ98.pdf

References

Atran, S. (2010). Who becomes a terrorist today? *Perspectives on Terrorism, 2*(5), 3–10.

Bizina, M., Northfield, V. T., & Gray, D. H. (2014). Radicalization of youth as a growing concern for counter-terrorism policy. *Global Security Studies, 5*(1), 72–79.

Centers for Disease Control and Prevention. (2014). *American Indian and Alaska native populations.* Retrieved from http://www.cdc.gov/minorityhealth/populations/REMP/aian.html

Chiu, M. M., Pong, S. L., Mori, I., & Chow, B. W. Y. (2012). Immigrant students' emotional and cognitive engagement at school: A multilevel analysis of students in 41 countries. *Journal of Youth and Adolescence, 41*, 1409–1425.

Cristini, F., Scacchi, L., Perkins, D. D., Santinello, M., & Vieno, A. (2011). The influence of discrimination on immigrant adolescents' depressive symptoms: What buffers its detrimental effects? *Psychosocial Intervention, 20*, 243–253.

Coll, C. G. E., & Marks, A. K. E. (2012). *The immigrant paradox in children and adolescents: Is becoming American a developmental risk?* Washington, DC: American Psychological Association.

Garcia Coll, C., Lamberty, G., Jenkins, R., McAdoo, H., Crnic, K., & Wasik, B. (1996). An integrative model for the study of developmental competencies in minority children. *Child Development, 67*, 1891–1914.

Hernandez, D. J., Denton, N. A., Macartney, S. & Blanchard, V. L. (2012). Children in immigrant families: Demography, policy, and evidence for the immigrant paradox. In C. Coll and A. Marks (Eds.), *The immigrant paradox in children and adolescents: Is becoming American a developmental risk?* (pp. 17–36). Washington, DC: American Psychological Association.

Huynh, V. W., & Fuligni, A. J. (2010). Discrimination hurts: The academic, psychological, and physical well-being of adolescents. *Journal of Research on Adolescence, 20*, 916–941.

Koo, D. J., Peguero, A. A., & Shekarkhar, Z. (2012). Gender, immigration, and school victimization. *Victims & Offenders, 7*, 77–96.

Marks, A. K., Ejesi, K., & Garcia Coll, C. (2014). Understanding the US immigrant paradox in childhood and adolescence. *Child Development Perspectives, 8*(2), 59–64.

Peguero, A. A. (2009). Victimizing the children of immigrants: Latino and Asian American student victimization. *Youth and Society, 41*, 186–208.

Peguero, A. A. (2013). An adolescent victimization immigrant paradox? School-based routines, lifestyles, and victimization across immigration generations. *Journal of Youth and Adolescence, 42*, 1759–1773.

Poston, W. C. (1990). The biracial identity development model: A needed addition. *Journal of Counseling & Development, 69*, 152–155.

Raffaelli, M., Kang, H. & Guarini, T. (2012). Exploring the immigrant paradox in adolescent sexuality: An ecological perspective. In C. Coll and A. Marks (Eds.), *The Immigrant Paradox in Children and Adolescents: Is becoming American a Developmental Risk?* (pp. 109–134). Washington, DC: American Psychological Society.

Ruth, R. (2012). Contemporary psychodynamic perspectives on multiple minority identities. In R. Nettles & R. Balter (Eds.), *Multiple minority identities: Applications for practice, research, and training* (pp. 163–184). New York, NY: Springer.

Sharabany, R., & Israeli, E. (2008). The dual process of adolescent immigration and relocation: From country to country and from childhood to adolescence—its reflection in psychodynamic psychotherapy. *The Psychoanalytic Study of the Child, 63,* 137–162.

Sirin, S. R., Ryce, P., Gupta, T., & Rogers-Sirin, L. (2013). The role of acculturative stress on mental health symptoms for immigrant adolescents: A longitudinal investigation. *Developmental Psychology, 49,* 736–748.

Smith, T. B., & Silva, L. (2011). Ethnic identity and personal well-being of people of color: A meta-analysis. *Journal of Counseling Psychology, 58,* 42–60.

Steele, C. M., & Aronson, J. (1995). Stereotype threat and the intellectual test performance of African Americans. *Journal of Personality and Social Psychology, 69,* 797–811.

Steele, C. M., & Aronson, J. A. (2004). Stereotype threat does not live by Steele and Aronson (1995) alone. *American Psychologist, 59*(1), 47–48. doi:10.1037/0003-066X.59.1.47

Suarez-Orozco, C. (2010). *In the best interest of our children: Examining our immigration enforcement policy.* Ad-hoc hearing of the U.S. House of Representatives, July 15. Washington, DC: American Psychological Association.

United States Department of Homeland Security. (2013). *Yearbook of immigration statistics: 2012.* Washington, DC: U.S. Department of Homeland Security, Office of Immigration Statistics.

Development of Tolerance and Respect for Diversity in Children in the Context of Immigration

Oscar Barbarin, Micaela Mercado, and Dari Jigjidsuren

Introduction

America has a long history as a nation of immigrants. It has been a haven for immigrants seeking a more prosperous life. Immigration is an issue that often surfaces in public debates especially those surrounding electoral politics during periods of economic downturns. This discussion is often exacerbated by political demagoguery, which plays on citizens' suspicion, hostility, and fear of encroachment by newcomers. The social divisions reflected in public commentary are strong and the debates are partisan and shrill. Unfortunately these debates legitimize and encourage expressions of pejorative views about immigrants who are seen as a source of terror and a social threat to national culture and way of life. At many different points in our modern history, the discourse on immigration ignores the important contributions made by immigrants and inflames emotions against those who are different.

Discrimination Against Immigrants

In the case of the US, the dream of prosperity and freedom which motivates new arrivals to American shores is often supplanted by the harsh reality of stinging poverty, economic exploitation, social isolation, and ethnic/racial prejudices. This process of social denigration is becoming more pronounced as the waves of white immigrants from Europe gives way to successive waves of brown, black, and yellow immigrants from Latin America, Africa, and Asia. The fact that these immigrants are not WASPs (White Anglo-Saxon Protestants) makes them even more vulnerable to negative stereotyping.

Because recent waves of immigrants also differ in ethnicity, culture, and religion, they may be viewed as soldiers in the cultural wars, which are viewed by some as a threat to national unity and the cultural legacy of the US as an Anglo-Saxon Christian Englishspeaking society. Such an outcome is not necessary. Differences need not be responded to with stereotyping but they often are. In truth, diversity does present challenges but it can also enrich. Peaceful coexistence is possible if divergent groups can come to understand and respect differences and even more so if cultural diversity is viewed as a source of strength and not division. What can be done to increase the likelihood that the people who make up this country will be more likely to view diversity as an asset than a liability?

Respect for Diversity in Young Children

To reach a more optimal state in which diversity strengthens rather than divides a society, it is necessary to foster tolerance and nurture respect for diversity. In building respect for diversity, as in many things, starting early in life may be advantageous. Subtle forms of intolerance and lack of respect for diversity that occur early in life take many forms. In the relationships between immigrant and non-immigrant children there may occur a vigorous trading of disparaging comments, social rejection, exclusion from play, and prejudiced attitudes about those who are different. At any age allaying fears of, reducing conflict with, and nurturing acceptance of those who are different is easier said than done. These are arguably more likely to be achieved if we lay a foundation of mutual respect among children before attitudes become hardened and behavior habitual and intractable. The early manifestations of intolerance may present opportunities for parents, teachers, and caregivers to intervene in ways that plant the seeds of tolerance, open children to more positive attitudes toward those who are different and create a climate in which stigmatizing behavior is less likely to occur. To do this effectively requires an understanding of the processes underlying the development of tolerance on one hand and of the conditions that give rise to negative attitudes, stigmatizing behavior, and social rejection on the other hand. These are complex processes and for that reason it may be helpful to seek guidance from developmental theory empirical research about promising theories and empirical research that illuminate how children develop attitudes and behaviors that reflect tolerance for those who are different and respect for cultural diversity.

Research specifically on development of a non-stigmatizing approach to social difference *and a valuing of cultural diversity* is limited. However, these notions fit conceptually within a larger class of pro-social behaviors on which there is a considerable body of research from which insights might be gleaned. Because this work explores the developmental processes involved in the acquisition of prosocial attitudes and behavior, it can illuminate the processes of and the factors that can be useful to parents and teachers in nurturing prosocial behavior in their offspring and students. Even though not much empirical work has been done directly on development of tolerance and respect for diversity it is possible to extend conclusions from research on the broader class of prosocial behaviors to which it belongs. The evolution of tolerance and respect for diversity is best illuminated by drawing on insights

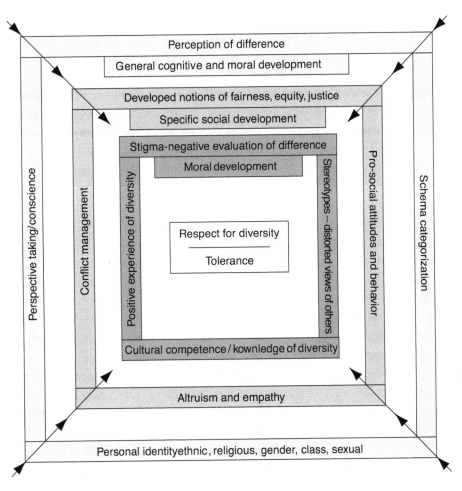

FIGURE 15.1   Nomological Network of Tolerance and Respect of Diversity.

about the formation of prosocial attitudes and behaviors. Figure 15.1 illustrates how DTRD is positioned within a larger framework of social development. It arranges the relevant constructs in a series of three bands surrounding the core constructs of interest, DTRD. The three bands, (1) general cognitive and moral development; (2) specific social developmental processes; and (3) social awareness, identity, and cultural competence are arranged in the order of their conceptual proximity to the core construct of DTRD. The inner or closest band surrounding the core constructs includes the closely related processes of social awareness (e.g., see Selman, 2003; Turiel, 2002), social identity (e.g., see Bem, 1983; Hughes, 2003) and cultural competence (e.g., Rogoff, 2003). Cultural competence is an outcome of children's experiences with diversity and their abilities to negotiate differences. For our purposes identity incorporates ethnic, family, cultural, religious, gender, sexual, and class identity. These are all important features used in defining the self and determining our primary associations. Development of personal identity and social awareness are closely aligned with the development of tolerance and respect for diversity and are best understood as analogues. The content of the view of self, the affiliations that one makes, the allegiances that one develops to an in-group have implications for how one regards and treats the out-groups. This band captures cognitive and social processes implicated in how self and others are perceived, experienced, evaluated, and responded to, especially those who are different. It includes opposing processes, some of which are positively related to diversity and tolerance (e.g. cultural competence) and others are inversely related (e.g. bias, stigma, stereotyping, discrimination). Although less directly related to respect for diversity and tolerance, the two outer rings are nonetheless implicated in their development. The second or middle band includes constructs, which can be grouped under the rubric of *specific* social-developmental *processes*. These are related, but not as closely to the core constructs.

These specific social processes include dispositions toward altruism, empathy, and non-aggressive conflict management. For example, by encouraging prosocial and moral reasoning, children are better able to consider issues of fairness and understand how social systems contribute to inequities (Spears-Brown & Bigler, 2005). These exemplify generally humane approaches to life that may under-gird or serve as a foundation for tolerance and respect but is not co-terminus with them. When one occurs or develops the other is usually present. The third or outer band represents basic cognitive and social developmental processes, which serve as a foundation for processes represented in the two inner bands. This includes research on basic developmental processes such as the development of schema, the capacity for categorization and discrimination, perspective taking, conscience and moral reasoning.

By positioning DTRD conceptually within a broad class of prosocial behaviors it is possible to benefit from an extensive body of theory and empirical work to understand the developmental processes which give rise to tolerance and respect for diversity. Using this body of work, we can explore questions about children's capacity to discern social differences, their proclivity to interpret those differences positively or negatively, and the ability of adults to influence those attitudes. Answers to the core questions we have about parent and teacher socialization of tolerance and respect for diversity in preschool children can be mined from the body of work identified as analogues of diversity and tolerance, on the humanistic behaviors that underlie diversity and tolerance, on identity formation, and on basic processes involved in moral and social development. A review of this literature provides at least partial answers to the following questions:

- To what extent can children detect, perceive and understand differences that exist between groups such as those stemming from culture, religion, race, ethnicity, gender, sexual orientation, socioeconomic status and national origin?
- What is the prevalence and valence of children's attitudes about those who are different, and how do they change over time?
- What factors shape how young children evaluate and respond to those differences?
- Can adult caregivers, particularly parents and teachers, influence the valence of children's attitudes and responses to differences?

Development of Tolerance and Respect for Diversity in Early Childhood

Capacity to Detect Differences

The ability to detect or notice difference is fundamental to the formation of social attitudes about others. The research literature offers an unambiguous answer to questions about young children's ability to discern social differences. For example, awareness of gender differences emerges early in life. By the age of two most children are able to make gender distinctions and accurately label male and female (Campbell, Shirley, & Caygill, 2002). The ability of a child to make these distinctions appears to be based on body type, hair (Intons-Peterson, 1988), and facial features (Quinn, Yahr, Kuhn, Slater, & Pascalis, 2000). By preschool age, children perceive and are well aware of a range of other differences such as those based on skin color, ethnicity, race, language, religion, etc. Using habituation tasks, Katz (2003) found that even at preverbal stages children will attend to novel race cues after seeing same-race faces. Additionally, at 6 months of age, gender cues are salient within same-race faces. Detection of race and gender has been observed in young children's self-identification and is reflected in their social inter-actions. From 18–30 months there is a linear increase in children's ability to self-label and sort dolls and pictures based on race and gender when prompted. At 36–72 months, White children begin to show same-race peer preference while Black children are more likely to make more cross-race friendships (Katz, 2003). Thus this study suggests the development of racial bias at even very young ages, at least for White children.

It is not a far stretch to suggest that this bias may appear in the interaction of immigrant and non-immigrant children. When immigrant and non-immigrant preschool children are placed in close proximity and where repeated social interactions are possible children come to note ways in which they are similar and different from one another. These differences may take the form of dress, language, physical features, behavioral habits, and preferred foods. At the outset it should be noted that discrimination and perception of differences are not inherently bad and to the contrary may be ethologically adaptive and functionally necessary especially in risky envi-ronments. The ability to detect differences and discriminate between those who are similar and familiar from those who are different and strange is harmless *in se*. However, much is determined by the meaning attributed to these differences. Similarity and familiarity may be linked to a higher probability of nurture and safety, just as difference and unfamiliarity may be associated with the higher probability of harm such as from predators. In this way recognizing difference is part of a biologically driven developmental pathway that may be linked to species survival.

Children's Evaluation of Differences

When the ability to detect differences is combined with growing personal identity, interesting consequences emerge. In many cases, children show an explicit preference for the familiar, for characteristics associated with self and the persons the child cares about, especially family. Although even male children show a preference for female faces (arguably because of greater familiarity and attachment to female caregivers), young children often display a preference for and have more favorable attitudes toward persons who are like them on some salient dimension. This proclivity to the familiar establishes a fertile ground for negative evaluations of those who are different. Thus, early stages of childhood have great potentials for ethnocentrism and strong preferences for in-groups (persons like themselves) versus out-groups (persons different in some way from themselves). The possible link between strong identity with one's own group and intolerance of other groups, poses a significant problem for adults who must care for mixed groups that consist for example of immigrant and non-immigrant children.

How much should caregivers nurture and encourage in young children a strong identification with their own ethnic, racial, national or religious groups if it means that non-immigrant children will develop negative views of immigrant children or that immigrant children will be conflicted about assimilating into their new setting? With the significant pressures among immigrants to assimilate, there may be ambivalence about how much to retain an affiliation with the country from which the family emigrated and its people. Among first-generation immigrants the pressure from immigrant parents to assimilate may be great. The age of the immigrant child may impact the nature of those strains. The push to assimilate may be especially strong in the absence of a critical mass of persons with the same language and background. Young children who have not yet mastered their parents' native language and who must learn English may face stiff pressure to forsake the home language and thereby lose an important tie to the parent's culture. Those who choose to promote affiliation and group loyalty, that is a fierce attachment in line with their own group, exploit the natural proclivity and preference children have for their own group over others. This process for same group identification arises from instincts for self protection and need for affiliation. As a consequence of good experiences such as affection, attachment to a maternal figure, as well as likeness to ethnic, cultural and racial characteristics, the child associates their group with safety, comfort and support. Disdain, dislike, and avoidance of strangers, specifically those who are different from the child's in-group, are a parallel process because it is associated with the absence of succor. This reaction may be a reflex, that it is truly unnecessary for survival. One can exist without the other. Viewing one's own group favorably does not necessarily have to trigger avoidance or hatred. It should be possible to nurture attachment to familiar figures without the need to foster suspicion or denigration of out-group members. Fortunately, extreme ethnocentrism and preference for the in-group over the out-group wanes as children mature and gain experience and familiarity with those who are different. Positive experiences with diverse populations may facilitate the decline of ethnocentrism. Although many families and early care environments espouse a color-blind approach to child socialization, research evidence suggests that children become aware of differences and develop negative attitudes toward those who are different far earlier than many adults recognize or acknowledge. Understanding how tolerance and respect for diversity evolve and develop in children is particularly important as America becomes racially, ethnically, and socially diverse.

DTRD and Social Development

Some theorists have proffered a natural human propensity to categorize people, to discriminate and to join groups based on similarity (Katz, 2003). If this position is correct, there is a need to understand more about how these attitudes are formed and how parents and teachers might explicitly socialize children to be prosocial in attitudes and behaviors. Specifically, we need a better understanding of the specific behaviors and processes between children and adults that promote tolerance and respect for diversity.

Since children are able to discriminate among categories of people earlier than once believed and given that differences based on race, gender, and ethnicity at some point become salient and attached to negative valences, the implications for how parents encourage tolerance and respect for diversity should be explored. Although there are many psychological theories that indicate how attitudes develop and how adults come to be biased, very few address how some children develop racist attitudes and others do not.

By extending research of prosocial development and applying them to DTRD, a discernible developmental progression from infancy to adolescence may be explored. In infancy, representations of secure attachment, as an internalized state, are associated with prosocial attitudes and behaviors. By inference, children are more likely to exhibit tolerance and respect diversity. However, it is unlikely that secure attachments by themselves guarantee tolerance. It is in toddlerhood where children's development of a sense of empathy and concern for others provides a less egoistic and firmer foundation on which to build attitudes of tolerance and respect for diversity. This underscores the importance of the need for caregivers to emphasize moments (i.e., behaviors displayed by the child) that may occur within the home or in the context of early childhood programs. Later in middle childhood, children have better defined consciences and a surer moral compass. This established conscience and refined sense of justice provide a durable and resilient basis for tolerance. As sociocognitive competencies related to perspective taking, empathy, and conscience develop and strengthen, the child's capacity to exhibit tolerance and respect for diversity inevitably strengthens.

The relationship between child and adult caregiver is important to the ability to redirect the child's stereotypical thinking or discriminatory behavior. Attachment literature indicates that only when the attachment relationship reflects a secure and responsive one, will children be open to moral socialization messages. Current research assumes that children are motivated to adopt and internalize messages of anti-bias from teachers. However, research indicates that children may actively form racial stereotypes that are opposite that of their authority figures (Bigler, 1999). Second, researchers may also want to include environmental influences such as the media and neighborhood factors (i.e., role models) in future models of the development of anti-biased (or biased) behaviors. Current research assumes that children are passive absorbers of information (Bigler, 1999). However, because of research from the friendship literature, we have indications that children assume some of the stereotypes of society, as reflected in their gendered and racial nature in choice of friendships. Highly biased children are more likely to have same race and same gender peers as friends (Katz, 2003). Finally, future research should include more data on the transactional nature of notions of discrimination and prejudice among child only groupings. Some talk about race and gender occurs outside of the classroom among peer groups. In a study of third- and fourth-grade students' conversations about race, it was found that when low-prejudiced peers were matched with high-prejudiced peers, high-prejudiced peers were less likely to make biased statements. The decrease in bias was significantly related to low-prejudiced peers' positive statements and examples about Blacks and references to cross-race (Black and White) similarities (Aboud & Fenwick, 1999). As a consequence, it is important to understand the mechanisms of how activist children may be used to revise the stereotypes of their peers.

Summary of the Research

The principles extracted from research on prosocial development that may be applicable to the development of prosocial attitudes and respect for diversity include the following:

1. Emotions play a central role in children's prosocial behavior and development.
2. Children who are more easily aroused and who form empathic responses to the emotional distress of others are more likely to display prosocial behavior. By extension these children are more likely to show tolerance and respect for diversity.
3. Relationships are important in the early development of prosocial behavior. Children who have stronger and more secure attachments to adult caretakers are more likely to exhibit prosocial behavior.
4. The social-cognitive processing skills that are critical to prosocial behavior develop and increase with age. These social cognitive skills include the ability to detect differences and empathy.
5. Motivations for prosocial behavior change with age. In infancy and toddlerhood, prosocial behavior is motivated by concern for self and personal distress. Self-oriented hedonism as a motivation for prosocial behavior is manifested in compliance with social norms to help, tolerate, or respect diversity mostly to gain rewards, avoid punishment, or personal distress experienced when someone else is hurt. This is not true during early childhood. In preschool the child moves away from self-oriented hedonism. At this stage the child does not feel distress over the suffering of another and is not motivated to help as a way of relieving personal distress. Instead the child is able to anticipate that one day he might be in the same situation and need help. Thus, a child's empathic behavior is motivated by the need for social approval and by the expectation of reciprocity. Beyond early and middle childhood, children internalize abstract norms and come to view help, tolerance, and respect for diversity as values.
6. Motivation for prosocial behavior parallels and perhaps is driven by social cognitive development. This involves increases of social cognitive skills in the following domains:
   - detecting or *discriminating differences* among people;
   - forming and maintaining securely *attached relationships*;
   - understanding and decoding others' *emotions*;
   - evaluating others behaviors against some *moral code or standard*.

It is the social norms established early in childhood that are predictive of prosocial behavior and willingness to help others. Secure attachment representations, notions of fairness and equity, the development of empathic and guilt responses, and the development of a moral conscience are indicative of altruistic responses. It may be assumed that the social norms regarding how children are taught to respond favorably to racial, gender, ethnic, social, and religious differences include similar variables.

Adult Contributions to DTRD in Children

Figure 15.2 models the different modalities through which adults influence children's development of tolerance and respect for diversity. These modalities include attached relationships, open-minded attitudes, nurturing practices and prosocial modeling.

Our current understanding of parent and teacher contribution to DTRD arises from the quality of the adult–child relationship. Strong attachments, social support, emotional closeness, and adult sensitivity and responsiveness to children's needs promote positive behaviors. When adults display emotionally supportive relationships and respond sensitively to children, children reciprocate the behaviors. For this reason the efficacy of adult practices and implicit adult modeling is contingent on the quality of the adult–child relationship. Accordingly, adult practices such as intentional instruction, use of conversations and literature for socialization of identity and promotion of cooperative learning are all more effective when the adult and child have a strong emotional bond. A similar relation has been demonstrated for the effectiveness of adults as models. To the extent that adults are esteemed and liked by children, their behavior and attitudes are more likely to be emulated by children. And this way, adult practices and modeling can shape and encourage DTRD. Adult behavior and attitudes are likely to be moderated by historical context, attitudes and values that parents have developed about identity, race, religion, sexual orientation, and personal experiences with diversity. To the extent that adults develop open attitudes, judge experiences with diverse populations as positive, and hold cultural values that favor acceptance of difference, the social context can be a

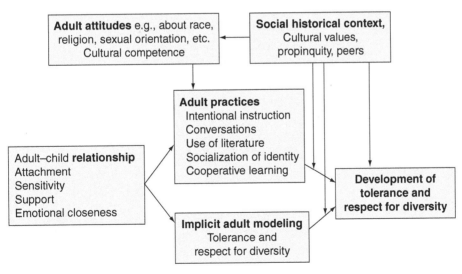

FIGURE 15.2   Parent and Teacher Influences on the Development of Tolerance and Respect for Diversity.

positive influence on adult practices and modeling and in turn provides a propitious spawning ground for DTRD.

Promotion of DTRD by Adult Caregivers

- Adults display a variety of behaviors that children learn to internalize as they develop and build relationships. Parents who display high levels of sensitivity, display relaxed firmness, engage in mutual negotiation of conflict with their child, and make efforts to be emotional available and responsive are closely linked to a child's ability to resolve conflict without aggression.
- Adults who converse and practice scaffolding discourse styles contribute to better language-skill development in children.
- Adults who reason, demonstrate warmth, provide guidance, positive reinforcement, model prosocial behavior, and give their child a chance to perform prosocial behaviors are more likely to have altruistic children.
- Adults may help children establish social norms that are predictive of altruistic behavior such as turn-taking, sharing, cooperating, and helping others in visible distress.
- Adults may impart prosocial behavior such as positive conflict management through modeling as well as promoting discussion and conversation.
- Adults should focus children's judgment of others on internal rather than external attributes.
- In schools, adults may provide children with empathy training activities to increase supportive behavior, helpfulness, cooperativeness, and concern for others and decrease aggressive behavior.

As suggested above, research on moral and prosocial development provides a rich base of knowledge on which to draw inferences about DTRD. This body of work has pointed to the important care giving roles of parents and teachers; relationship interactions such as secure attachment behaviors; the child's cognitive development and ability to detect differences; the critical role of emotional arousal and responses; the shifting basis of prosocial motivation from egoistic of avoidance of punishment to reciprocity and justice; and the development of a range of socio-cognitive competencies such as empathy, social comparisons, conscience and altruism.

Programs to Promote DTRD in Schools and Community Settings

Several curricula and model programs have been developed to promote tolerance and respect for diversity. *Anti-Bias Education* (ABE) (Derman-Sparks, 1989) promulgated by the National Association for the Education of Young Children is one of several anti-bias curricula developed to promote acceptance of diversity. Another example of ABE can be found in the work of Kinderwelt, an organization based in Berlin, Germany. It has developed outreach training projects that seek to address discrimination and bias that immigrant children often face in German preschools. As a group, anti-bias curricula and programs are committed to the educational equality of a diversity of children, and they tend to be more comprehensive in nature by addressing cultural diversity, gender differences, and differences in physical ability (Derman-Sparks, 1989). The principal goal of the Derman-Sparks ABE program is to foster in young children the following outcomes: (1) a firm and positive self concept and group identity, (2) empathy for others, and (3) critical thinking about and the courage to confront bias wherever they see it.

Implementation of anti-bias education (ABE) requires that every aspect of the child's experience at school be rethought and possibly changed from the material aspects and resources of the environment (toys, books, art materials, and center options), to events, stories, and social relations (Derman-Sparks, 1993). By design, ABE is committed to thoughtful and responsive answers to children's questions about difference. To do this well teachers must be involved in a reflective process about the past and current impact of discrimination in society, how personal biases are acted out, how to adjust teaching styles to accommodated differences, and how to address cultural conflict when it arises in the classroom (Derman-Sparks, 1993). Because, self-awareness is a critical first step in the recognition of and positive response to difference, ABE aims to help children recognize that their thoughts, beliefs, characteristics and needs are not the same as others. Because the capacity for self-categorization as belonging to a social group can lead to invidious in-group versus out-group comparisons, nurturance of positive self-concept and group identity must also be balanced by the notions that no child or group is superior to or has the right to be privileged over another (Derman-Sparks, 1993). Such positive self-awareness is not surprisingly associated with peer acceptance (Ramsey & Myers, 1990).

Empathic concern for others is essential to the development of prosocial behavior in young children. Empathy is important because it engenders an appreciation of similarities and differences among people. Even in infancy children will respond empathetically to the cries of other infants. Comparisons of classrooms using ABE and classrooms that did not implement any type of multicultural curriculum revealed that children in ABE classrooms were able to identify more positive attributes about racial minorities than were children in classrooms devoid of a multicultural agenda (Perkins & Mebert, 2005). Moreover, children who acquire multiple classification skills (ability to classify people along multiple characteristics i.e., gender, race, occupation) through teacher implementation of anti-bias curriculum, have better memory for counterstereotypic information (Bigler & Liben, 1992).

Biases, disparaging attitudes and stigmatizing behavior arise from errors in perception and information reprocessing. ABE curricula often cover historical facts and cultural practices to demonstrate what is common in a group but at the same time underscores the existence of within group differences (Sardo-Brown & Hershey, 1995). When children learn about group differences they are helped to question the negative connotations society attaches to some differences. Fostering critical-thinking skills about bias may help children to see the subtle nuances in social situations and help them to internalize moral standards. In classrooms that use teachable moments to discuss racial and gender biases and that employ curricula devoted that address and counter ethnic biases, children are more likely to classify individuals on characteristics other than race (Bernstein Zimmerman, Schindler, Werner-Wilson, & Vosburg, 2000).

However, children's encoding of non-stereotyped information has to be monitored and activities must be continual in order to enhance their development of counterstereotypic information (Bigler & Liben, 1993). Finally, although the goal of interventions is the elimination of racially biased responding, however, to date most interventions only report very small reductions in children's racial bias (Bigler, 1999).

The Morningside Center for Teaching Social Responsibility (www.MorningsideCenter.Org) in New York City has developed an approach to DTRD to give emphasis to conflict resolution and intercultural understanding. These approaches are embodied in two programs: "Resolving Conflict Creatively" and the "4 Rs" (reading, writing, respect, and resolution). Both programs have at their core the teaching of children skills in resolving conflicts without resorting to violence, valuing diversity, especially cultural differences, countering bias and confronting prejudice. The program involves classroom coaching for teachers, peer mediation of conflict as well as training for school administrators and parents. The 4 Rs program integrates conflict resolution into the classroom curriculum for language arts in kindergarten through fifth grade. For example, high-quality children's literature is selected and used to raise issues that may be potentially divisive, and discussed among students. As a part of the program students are engaged in talking, writing and role-playing on universal themes of relationships, community, identity, and conflict. The goal of the discussion is to build skills and understanding in areas such as listening, community building, cooperation, negotiation, celebrating differences, and countering bias.

Another example is the *Al-Bustan Seeds of Culture* (www.albustanseeds.org) a nonprofit organization based in Philadelphia, Pennsylvania. Like ABE and the Morningside Center it attempts to promote DTRD but is more narrowly focused on issues that intersect with Arab American populations. Specifically it attempts to promote understanding of language and culture of the Arab world and respect within the diverse community of Arab-Americans. The program offers children and youth an opportunity to develop new language skills and appreciate Arabic culture. Al-Bustan encourages dialogue, tolerance, and a celebration of diversity.

In contrast to the Al-Bustan Seeds of Culture is the *Early Childhood Equity Initiative* (www.teachingforchange.org/DC_Projects/ECEI/ecei.html). This is a more broadly focused effort of Teaching for Change to develop leaders in early childhood education, in the metro DC area and nationwide, with an understanding of the theory and practice that helps create culturally responsive environments for young children. By working with teachers, daycare providers and parents of preschool aged children can collaborate to identify and promote anti-bias education goals for young children.

Concluding Remarks

Researchers have come to recognize the integral role of the early childhood experience for children's social and cognitive development. Over the past few decades, as more women have entered the workforce, more children have entered childcare at even earlier ages. These children come from families that represent a diverse array of ethnic, cultural, socioeconomic, and religious backgrounds. As a result, today's childcare environment may represent a diversity that may not have existed at any time point in history. Childcare classrooms reflect the diversity of American families and represent an important microcosm to be studied.

Even in early childhood, children must learn to negotiate difference reflected in larger society. Although young children's expressions may not have the same deliberate, affective tenor of adults', it is important to reduce these biases to foster positive self-identities for all children (Banks, 1995). Social and emotional competencies have been linked to positive academic outcomes for children. Thus, the study of curriculum that helps to promote a positive, anti-biased classroom environment is integral to an equal and just education for all children. Parents also play an important role for their children through guidance and modeling behaviors. As children exit childhood and enter the world of adolescence and adulthood, it is inevitable that their new relationships and interactions with others will be highly dependent on their ability to accept norms, values, and standards different from their own.

References

Aboud, F., & Fenwick, V. (1999). Exploring and evaluating school-based interventions to reduce prejudice. *Journal of Social Issues, 55*(4), 767–785.

Aksan, N., & Kochanska, G. (2004). Links between systems of inhibition from infancy to preschool years. *Child Development, 75*(5), 1477–1490.

Banks, C., & Banks, J. (1995). Equity pedagogy: An essential component of multicultural education. *Theory into Practice, 34*(3), 152–158.

Berlin, L.J., & Cassidy, J. (1999). Relations among relationships: Contributions from attachment theory and research. In J. Cassidy & P.R. Shaver (Eds.), *Handbook of attachment: Theory, research and clinical applications* (pp. 688–712). New York: Guilford Press.

Bernstein, J., Zimmerman, Schindler, T., Werner-Wilson, Ronald, J. & Vosburg, J. (2000). Preschool children's classification skills and a multicultural education intervention to promote acceptance of ethnic diversity. *Journal of Research in Childhood Education, 14*(2), 181–192.

Bigler, R. (1999). The use of multicultural curricula and materials to counter racism in children. *Journal of Social Issues, 55*(4), 687–705.

Bigler, R., & Liben, L. (1992). Cognitive mechanisms in children's gender stereotyping: Theoretical and educational implications of a cognitive-based intervention. *Child Development, 63*(6), 1351–1363.

Bigler, R., & Liben, L. (1993). A cognitive-developmental approach to racial stereotyping and reconstructive memory in Euro-American children. *Child Development, 64*(5), 1507–1518.

Campbell, A., Shirley, L., & Caygill, L. (2002). Sex-typed preferences in three domains: Do 2-year-olds need cognitive variables? *British Journal of Developmental Psychology, 18*, 479–498.

Charlesworth, R. (1998). Developmentally appropriate practice is for everyone. *Childhood Education, 74*(5), 274–282.

Derman-Sparks, L. (1989). *The antibias curriculum.* Washington, DC: National Association for the Education of Young Children.

Derman-Sparks, L. (1993). Empowering children to create a caring culture in a world of differences. *Childhood Education, 70*(2), 66–71.

Intons-Peterson, M. (1988). *Children's concepts of gender.* Norwood, NJ: Ablex.

Jones, E., & Derman-Sparks, L. (1992). Meeting the challenge of diversity. *Young Children, 47*(2), 12–18.

Katz, P.A. (2003) Racists or tolerant multiculturalists? How do they begin? *American Psychologist, 58*(11), 897–909.

Maccoby, E. (1992). The role of parents in the socialization of children: A historical overview. *Developmental Psychology, 28*(6), 1006–1017.

Perkins, D., & Mebert, C. (2005). Efficacy of multicultural education for preschool children. *Journal of Cross-Cultural Psychology, 36*(4), 497–512.

Quinn, P.C., Yahr, J., Kuhn, A., Slater, A., & Pascalis, O. (2000). Representation of the gender of human faces by infants: A preference for female. *Perception, 31*, 1109–1121.

Ramsey, P., & Myers, L. (1990). Salience of race in young children's cognitive, affective, and behavioral responses to social environments. *Journal of Applied Developmental Psychology, 11*(1), 49–67.

Sardo-Brown, D., & Hershey, M. (1995). Training of intermediate level teachers on how to develop and implement integrated multi-cultural lesson plan: Assessment of attitudes. *Journal of Instructional Psychology, 22*(3), 259–277.

Spears-Brown, C., & Bigler, R. (2005). Children's perceptions of discrimination: A developmental model. *Child Development, 76*(3), 533–553.

Steelman, L., Assel, M., Swank, P., Smith, K., & Landry, S. (2002). Early maternal warm responsiveness as a predictor of child social skills: Direct and indirect paths of influence over time. *Journal of Applied Developmental Psychology, 23*(2), 135–156.

Stephan, W., & Finlay, K. (1999). The role of empathy in improving intergroup relations. *Journal of Social Issues, 55*(4), 729–743.

Thompson, R. (1999). Early attachment and later development. In J. Cassidy & P.R. Shaver (Eds.), *Handbook of attachment: Theory, research and clinical applications* (pp. 265–286). New York: Guilford Press.

Walker, L., & Taylor, J. (1991). Family interactions and the development of moral reasoning. *Child Development, 62*(2), 264–283.

Zahn-Waxler, C., Radke-Yarrow, M., Wagner, E., & Chapman, M. (1992). Development of concern for others. *Developmental Psychology, 28*(1), 126–136.

Connecting World Religions and Children's Literature

Connie R. Green and Sandra Brenneman Oldendorf

The Storytelling Tradition

Faith groups are bound together by their myths, legends, and shared history, with storytelling at the very heart of human and religious experience (Gangi, 2004). Storytelling has always been a way of conveying beliefs of the world's religions through the oral tradition. The Buddha, Jesus, Muhammad, Abraham, and Nanak (Sikhism) were all storytellers. From the earliest times, indigenous peoples passed on their creation myths and explanations of natural phenomenon to the next generation. As more formalized religions evolved, legends, parables, and proverbs provided followers with an understanding of religious principles and metaphors for daily living. In modern times religious narratives offer a framework for faith, provide examples of ethical living, build awareness of human responsibilities, and connect followers with the sacred.

The term myth is often used in different ways. Kate Baestrup writes,

> For anyone to get at truths that lie beyond fact, we must create myths. I don't mean we have to tell lies. The story we tell can be wholly fictional or the story can be true. If it illustrates the organizing principles by which we understand the world and live in it, the story is a myth in the scholarly sense. (Baestrup, 2007, p. 127)

Myths may explain aspects of nature or the worldview and ideals of a culture and are often believed to contain sacred truths. The word myth derives from the Greek word, mythos, which means speech, thought, or story. While religious stories and myths are found in all major religions (and many smaller ones), we will address Native American spirituality, Buddhism, and Judaism in this chapter as examples of the storytelling tradition.

Storytelling within Native American Spirituality

Native American children's author Joseph Bruchac states:

> More now than ever before, we need the gift of stories which instruct and delight, explain and sustain. Such stories lead us ... to an understanding of who we are and what our place is in the natural world. They help us find respect for ourselves and respect for the earth. They lead us toward the rising sun each dawn, the story of the gift of life. (Bruchac, 1996, p. 81)

Native American storytellers believe that stories are dynamic and should be treated with respect as living things, not as cultural artifacts. In traditional Native American cultures, children were rarely punished for misbehavior; instead adults told stories to redirect and teach about proper behavior. "That's the purpose of storytelling: teaching people who they are so they can become all they are meant to be" (Bruchac, p. 75). According to Bruchac, the spirit of American Indian identity has survived most powerfully through stories.

Within Native American cultures, the sacred and the mundane are not separated. Stories can be prayers or methods of healing and should never be taken lightly; stories strengthen inner spirituality. The Cree language contains the word "achimoona," which means "sacred stories that come from within." The Micmac people refer to the "great man inside," a spiritual being within each person's heart that provides guidance, if one pays attention (Bruchac, 1996).

Storytelling within Buddhism

Within the Buddhist tradition, the Jataka fables are possibly the oldest and largest collection of folk tales in the world (Conover, 2005). These tales originated in Asian culture and blended with Buddhist teachings as the religion spread throughout southern Asia. Eventually the Jataka tales were accepted as Buddhist scripture, with the animal or human hero being viewed as "the Buddha in a former life, working his way towards enlightenment" (Conover, 2005, p. viii).

Though the Buddha did not write any of his teachings, his message was conveyed through conversation, discourse, and storytelling. After Buddha's death, monks and storytellers continued to tell his stories and eventually write them. Tales from the Theravada Buddhist tradition clarify Buddhism's wisdom and compassion for life and convey the concept of karma (originally a Hindu concept), or consequences of one's actions. Within the Mahayanic tradition Zen sutras (sermons or lessons of The Buddha), stories, sayings, and other teachings have been preserved for over 1,000 years (Conover, 2005).

Storytelling within Judaism

Wherever Jews have lived throughout history, they have told stories to pass on their beliefs and traditions to their children. In the early years of Judaism, folk preachers known as *maggidim* recounted parables and tales in their messages. Both the Talmud (commentary on sacred scripture) and Midrash (interpretations of scripture written by rabbis) contain many stories.

Hasidism is a movement within Judaism that is rich in the storytelling tradition. The practice of storytelling is considered a *mitzvah,* a divine commandment (Buxbaum, 1994). Within Hasidism, stories are of utmost importance because they inspire people to "practice and fulfill the teaching of the Torah and the teaching of the rebbes (rabbis or religious leaders)" (p. 72).

Several Hebrew sayings confirm the importance of stories. One saying is, "The story of the deed is greater than the doer." This means that the stories may motivate others to act in a similar fashion. Another familiar saying is that "God loves stories." Some believe that when Jews are telling holy stories, God sits beside them and listens. Many Jews believe that God is a storyteller, as well, for he is said to have given the stories in the Torah directly to Moses. Within Judaism storytelling is seen as a sacred practice, bringing people closer to God.

The contemporary Hasidic storyteller Rabbi Shlomo Carlebach has said,

> The difference between teaching and a story is that in the first we are asking to
> learn something we do not know. But in the story we are asking to be made holy, to
> be made new, like a child, like a tzaddik (righteous person). We are saying, "Please
> tell me! Let me know what I am." (personal communication, cited in Buxbaum,
> 1994, p. 73).

Through stories about one's own religion and other religions, students can learn about themselves and similarities between their own beliefs and the beliefs of others. They can learn that similar themes infuse the stories of people from around the world and throughout time. The concept of self-knowledge and the perennial battle of good and evil forces are conveyed in the writing of Newbery-award winner Madeleine L'Engle', whose novels are influenced by both science and Christianity. A tribute to L'Engle in the *Journal of Children's Literature* ("In Memoriam," 2007) includes the following quotation, "Why does anybody tell a story? It does indeed have something to do with faith—faith that the universe has meaning, that our little human lives are not irrelevant, that what we choose or say or do matters; matters cosmically" (p. 78).

Value of Children's Literature

When children read and discuss religious stories and informational texts they begin to comprehend the multiplicity of faiths in our world. By reading books, viewing films, listening to music, watching dramatic presentations, and listening to story tellers, children can strengthen their understanding of their own convictions, as well as develop tolerance and appreciation for the beliefs of others. Books that address religious diversity can be found in all genres of children's literature, which are described below.

Children's literature is a familiar medium to teachers and provides an inviting way to teach about the important dimension of religious diversity. It is one medium through which students can acquire information about the multiplicity of faiths in our world and come to see similarities among faith groups. By reading books, viewing films, listening to music, watching dramatic presentations, and listening to storytellers, children and adolescents may strengthen their own convictions, as well as develop tolerance and appreciation for the beliefs of others.

Genres of Children's Literature

High quality fiction and nonfiction books offer authentic ways to address faith traditions of the past and present. The books we review in this chapter are a sampling of child and adolescent literature teachers can use to develop content knowledge and open-mindedness toward religious diversity. Books were selected from reviews from Children's Literature Comprehensive Database, consultations with university librarians, the National Council for the Social Studies Notable Trade Books for Young People, and recommendations from religious leaders and practitioners. Criteria for selecting books about faith diversity can be found in Tables 16.1 and 16.2. We have organized the books by the traditional genres of children's literature to demonstrate the many areas in which teachers can address religion and faith. However, several of the books overlap the conventional genre definitions.

In the remainder of this chapter we will examine the major genres of children's literature: traditional literature, modern fantasy, modern realistic fiction, historical fiction, poetry, biography, and informational books. The description of each genre will begin with a definition of the genre, followed by examples of books within that that relate to various faith traditions. Teaching strategies to extend the meaning of the books will also be presented.

Traditional Literature

Traditional literature includes the category of religious stories and myths based on sacred writings of religious traditions. Within the broad category of traditional religious literature, readers will find myths, legends, parables, pourquoi tales (explain natural phenomenon), and hero stories. Although some people may question the classification of religious stories and myth, "myth in this sense can be broadly defined as the quest to discover and share truth concerning the spiritual aspect of existence" (Darrigan, Tunnel, & Jacobs, 2002). The Jakta tales of Buddhism, ancient epics of Hindu heroes, the legends of the Catholic saints, American Indian legends, and the Jewish myth of the Golem are examples of religious stories. The following books contain legends and myths based on religious traditions of the world.

Sacred Myths: Stories of World Religions (McFarlane, 1996) is dramatically illustrated with digital art that brings each story to life. The tales represent Buddhism, Christianity, Hinduism, Islam, Judaism, Native American, and Sacred Earth (indigenous). By reading stories from each tradition,

TABLE 16.1   Evaluating Nonfiction Books About Religious Diversity

In seeking high quality informational books and biographies about religious diversity, teachers and families should consider the following suggestions:

1. Examine the text for stereotypes. Are there any "loaded" words, such as "odd" or "unusual" that hint of a prejudiced or condescending attitude?

2. If the book covers many different religions is each covered fairly and honestly? Check the qualifications of the author. Is this person a member of the faith community about which he or she has written? If not, has the author done adequate research?

3. Has the author included endnotes, time lines, a glossary, tables, maps, and references for adults and children?

4. Did the author use current sources by experts in the field? Is the book organized in a clear way that children or adolescents can follow?

5. Does the book authentically convey depth of content about the religion appropriate for the audience?

6. Does the content have a positive and sensitive focus on values of the religion?

7. Do illustrations and photographs honestly portray religious observances and practices?

8. Are the illustrations free of stereotypes and do they clarify information in the text?

9. Are there any craft activities that might be offensive to members of the religious group? For example, some older books on American Indians suggested that children make totem poles, a sacred symbol.

10. Does the book encourage analytical thinking? For example, some informational books pose thought-provoking questions for discussion.

11. Does the style and format of the book stimulate interest in the religious group?

Sources: Groce and Groce (2005) and Norton (2007).

TABLE 16.2   Criteria for Selecting Fictional Books on Religious Diversity

1. Are the characters portrayed as individuals rather than representatives of a particular religion?

2. Is the writing free of stereotypes and language that might be offensive to members of this religion?

3. Are factual or historical details accurate?

4. Is the religion accurately portrayed?

5. Are the conflicts or problems in the book authentic for the time period and the character?

6. Is the setting authentic to the religious group?

7. Are the illustrations authentic and free of stereotypes?

8. Is the format and content appropriate for the age group for which it is intended?

9. Does the book make a positive contribution toward learning about the religion being studied?

Sources: Galda and Cullinan (2002), Norton (2007).

students can note similarities in values and themes among the religions. McFarland provides a brief introduction to each chapter, a pronunciation guide and a glossary. Children and adults will admire the storytelling style and peaceful illustrations in this volume.

There are many surprises in Heather Forest's *Wisdom Tales From Around the World* (1996). The volume includes Taoist parables, Zen stories, tales from Ancient Greece, Mulla Nasrudin stories from the Muslim Sufi tradition, and tales from Christianity. The parables are pithy stories, often with animal characters, that have a clear, but sometimes surprising message at the end. One of the Christian stories was a biographical piece on John Newton, the slave ship captain who returned to his childhood Christian roots and penned the well-known hymn "Amazing Grace."

Virtually every early culture had its own story of how the earth was formed. *In the Beginning: Creation Stories from around the World* (Hamilton, 1988) is a stunning collection of 21 myths about gods and goddesses, plants and animals, and the first humans. Throughout time, these stories have provided people from sacred traditions with solace, inspiration, and answers to some of the eternal questions of human kind. The dramatic illustrations by Barry Moser and author comments following each myth enrich this comprehensive volume.

Stories of Catholic and Orthodox saints have inspired both adults and children for many centuries. In *Lives and Legends of the Saints,* Armstrong (1995) includes full-page reproductions of famous classical paintings to accompany engaging stories of the lives and heroic deeds attributed to the saints. For example, Armstrong describes Catherine of Alexandria, patron saint of philosophers, ministers, students, wheelwrights, millers, and young women. In an intriguing one-page story, the author illuminates Catherine's steadfast Christianity that led to her torture and death. Armstrong explains the symbols in the art, which date from the Middle Ages and Renaissance. She also includes an index to artists and paintings at the end of the book, making it an excellent resource for art history lessons.

The rich cultural variety found in the folktales and sayings in *Ayat Jamilah: Beautiful Signs,* by Sarah Conover and Freda Crane (2004), will help children and adults realize the diversity found in Islam. The authors, one who is Muslim, wrote their book in order to reach both the secular and Muslim world. Stories and wisdom from cultures as diverse as China, Pakistan, Turkey, West Africa and Indonesia provide humor, insight and cultural perspective. A quote from the Qur'an in the introduction captures the spirit of the book, "Of Allah's Signs, one is that He created you from dust; and lo, you become human beings ranging far and wide" (43:48). The book contains two types of stories: those from the Qur'an and those from the hadiths, words and actions of the Prophet Mohammad. Many of the stories begins with *kan ya ma kan,* meaning "There was and there was not," a Muslim version of "Once upon a time." The stories are told with humor and insights that reveal beliefs and values underlying Islam.

The 32 fables in *Kindness* are often told from the perspective of the Buddha himself or from that of a Buddhist monk or nun. Stories from a variety of Asian countries are included in *The Wisdom of the Crows and Other Buddhist Tales* (Chodzin & Kohn, 1997) and exemplify different aspects of Buddhist wisdom. "The Foolish Boy" is an example of Tibetan humor similar to Western "noodle-head tales." Other stories include gods and goddesses, demons, human and animal characters who illustrate the profound truths of Buddhism. The richly colored illustrations and borders created by Marie Cameron, portray Buddhist art from the country in which the story originated.

Modern Fantasy and Science Fiction

Modern fantasy and science fiction books depict characters, setting and events that could not really happen in the physical world. Although there are few modern fantasy books that directly tell stories about religious beliefs, it is not unusual for books within this genre to have underlying religious themes. A classic example is the *Narnia* series by C. S. Lewis, who was a professor of medieval and renaissance literature at Cambridge and Oxford Universities. Born into Christianity, Lewis became an atheist during his teen years. His reconversion to Christianity at age 31 strongly influenced his writing.

Madeleine L'Engle's characters often struggle with religious themes, such as the power of love and hatred. The Newbery Award book, *A Wrinkle in Time* (1976) and the four books that follow in the series are both science fantasy and religious allegory. Fundamental themes of faith are woven throughout the novels, which include quotations from the Bible, Dante, Pascal, and Shakespeare. L'Engle honors the mysteries in life and conflicts of the human condition we all face.

Phillip Pullman's popular "His Dark Materials" science fiction trilogy takes readers on a trip into a parallel universe filled with daemons, winged creatures, mammoth polar bears, and a substance called dust. The initial volume, *The Golden Compass* (1996) and its sequels present a parallel universe quite similar to our own in which complex characters grapple with universal questions. Some religious conservatives have criticized the series for negatively portraying organized religion. Other readers believe that Pullman portrays the beauty of the world and the value of life within a well-crafted fantasy. Middle school students who read this trilogy might begin to think critically about the authenticity of these claims and read the author's own words. There are several interview clips with Pullman on www.beliefnet.com.

Sandy Eisenberg Sasso, the first woman to be ordained a Reconstructionist rabbi, writes books for young children with inclusive religious themes. *In God's Name* (1994) is a celebration of the diverse ways people have of knowing and naming God. As the poetic story begins, the world has just been created, and every creature has a name, but no one knows the name of God. Boys and girls around the world suggest different names based on their perceptions and beliefs and in the end learn what God's name really is.

Julius Lester is another author who has embraced the topic of religion in his books for young readers. The son of a Methodist minister, Lester converted to Judaism as an adult. He was influenced early in his career by a creative writing teacher who believed that writing was a way of praying. Lester sees his writing as reaching out, not only to a child or adolescent audience, but also to the Divine (Lester, 1999a).

> If in the presence of a book or a person, we feel ourselves … confirmed as human
> beings, and we sense that life itself is being celebrated in this book or person, then
> we are in the presence of the Divine. (Lester, 1999a, p. 55).

Drawing on both African American and Jewish traditions that portray God as having a sense of humor, Lester created two religious fantasy books for children: *What a Truly Cool World* (1999b) and *When the Beginning Began* (1999c). The first is a picture book illustrated with Joe Cepeda's vibrant and humorous paintings. The story opens with a bald, dark-skinned god wearing a yellow robe and green bedroom slippers, admiring his new creation, a blue and brown earth populated with people and animals of many shapes and colors. But his side-kick, Shaniqua, the angel in charge of everybody's business, complains that the new world is too dull. After listening to her suggestions, God brightens the earth with a variety of creations—trees and bushes, flowers and music, vibrant colors and fluttering butterflies. *When the Beginning Began* (Lester, 1999c), draws from the Jewish tradition of the midrash, narratives that inquire into or investigate biblical stories. In a sense the midrashim fill in what is missing, what people wonder about, in the biblical text. For example, Lester explains in his introduction, all the Abrahamic religions (Judaism, Christianity, and Islam) say that God is eternal, that he has always existed. In the short stories Lester has created in this collection, he plays with the idea of what God did before and during the creation.

In a similar vein, Rabbi Marc Gellman creates his own humorous twists on traditional Bible stories in *Does God Have a Big Toe?* (1989). In the short story with the same title as the book, a little girl asks her mother, father, and grandfather if God has a big toe. Each adult is preoccupied and sends her to someone else until her question reaches the king. The king orders everyone in the country of Babel to build a tall tower up to God, so he can see if God has a big toe. Knowing what a waste of time and resources this is, God decides to solve the problem by giving people different languages so that they aren't able to communicate. In the end, the people who speak the same languages move away together and the little girl asks about God's belly button. These would be good stories for reading aloud and discussing the updated messages.

Samsara Dog (Manos, 2006), a story based on Buddhist principles, contains elements of both realism and fantasy. Dog begins his existence as a rough street animal that lives only for himself. After he dies he returns as a mascot of a motorcycle gang. In each incarnation Dog has different responsibilities and characteristics. The more times he returns to life, the more loyal and giving he becomes, until he returns as a companion and teacher to a child who is blind. Once he has given the great gifts of love and compassion to another, he no longer returns to life on earth.

Modern Realistic Fiction

Modern realistic fiction books are invented stories that could actually happen in the real world. They sometimes present dilemmas faced by child and adolescent characters as they grapple with religious convictions. For example, Amal, the teen protagonist in *Does My Head Look Big in This?* (Abdel-Fattah, 2007) is conflicted over the decision of whether or not to wear the hijab (head covering) to her private school in Australia. Students and teachers could discuss some of the stereotypical ideas held by the students in the book about Muslims and see if any of these notions changed as they came to know Amal.

Buddha Boy (Koja, 2003) is a story told from the point of view of Justin, a typical high school student, who somewhat reluctantly befriends a new student, Jinsen. As their relationship develops, Justin learns of Jinsen's past and his conversion to Buddhism. Other students, uncomfortable and intolerant of those who are different, torment Jinsen who refuses to fight back. Both *Does My Head Look Big in This* and *Buddha Boy* are excellent novels to stimulate discussion of pre-conceived ideas about belief systems and the treatment of students from minority religions.

Shouting! (Thomas, 2007) is a picture book for primary children illustrated with exuberant, yet featureless paintings by Annie Lee, that make the reader want to stand up and celebrate. The story is told from the point of view of a young African American girl going to church with her mother. As the preacher begins to wave and thunderously preach and the choir vigorously responds, some of the women rise from their seats and dance with the ghost (Holy Spirit). The girl's mother is among this throng, overcoming her arthritis pain to join other worshippers in the aisles, swaying and shouting "Hallelujah, Amen." At the end of the book, the illustrations show contemporary worshipers joining with African dancers, as they trace their steps back through time. This book could connect with a study of spiritual music and the evolution of dance.

Historical Fiction

Historical fiction books combine an accurate and convincing portrayal of a setting in the past with fictional characters. This genre facilitates children's understanding that history is more than a series of dates, names, and places; history is about the lives of real people. It can help children develop positive attitudes toward history and gain general understanding of different time periods (Norton, 2007). Sometimes realistic events and authentic minor characters are included in well-researched historical fiction. Occasionally historical fiction refers to the religious milieu during a certain era and the impact of various religious movements on individuals and on history.

Gideon's People (Meyer, 1996) is a fictional story for intermediate students set in the late nineteenth century near Lancaster, Pennsylvania. Two adolescent boys learn about each other's religions when Isaac, the son of a Jewish peddler, is injured and stays with Gideon's old order Amish family for several weeks. Both boys experience conflicts about the strict rules of their conservative faiths and their desire to fit in with their English (non-Amish) neighbors. The author describes the Amish Sunday service, the Friday evening Jewish Shabbat, dress codes of each group, differences in diet, and the custom of shunning among the Amish.

In *Brother Juniper*, Diane Gibfried (2006) tells the story of the most charitable friar living in the monastery with Father Francis in the hills of Assisi. Brother Juniper is so generous that when the other friars leave to preach, he gives away the chapel's gold chalice, the priest's vestments, the altar cloth, the stained glass windows, and even the doors and walls of the chapel. When the other brothers return, they find him naked in the hole of what was once their sanctuary (he gave away his robes, as well!). The tale ends with the town's people coming to a hilltop on Sunday morning to thank Brother Juniper for his kindness when they were in need. Readers see that it is people, not walls, windows and ornaments that make a church. Based on writings of St. Francis of Assisi, Gibfried and artist Meilo So, create a charming tale of generosity, which contains elements of both history and legend.

There are numerous books about the role of Quakers in helping slaves escape through the Underground Railroad. One example is *Henry's Freedom Box* (Levine, 2007) in which the main character is shipped north in a wooden crate with the help of Quaker abolitionists. *North by Night* (Ayers, 1998) illustrates how one woman made a decision based on her religious convictions to assist escaping slaves. These books could be used as part of a broader unit on slavery and the role of religion in the abolitionist movement.

Poetry and Songs

The artistic expression, rhythm and imagery of poetry and song lyrics can be a beautiful way to express spirituality. The Psalms from the Judeo-Christian-Islamic tradition are well known examples. The artwork in *The Lord Is My Shepherd* (Wilson, 2003) proclaims the joy and comfort many people find in these verses. Striking colors and swirling abstract shapes provide a visual journey for young readers. In contrast, Tim Ladwig's illustrations for *Psalm Twenty-Three* (1993) show the meaning this poem might have for contemporary urban children. Living in a crowded city, the children find love, comfort, and encouragement from grandparents, teachers, and a school crossing guard. The words of the psalm appear to give them strength to surmount the negative forces in their environment.

Had Gadya: A Passover Song (Chwast, 2005) is one of the best-known songs sung after the Passover Seder. The folk art paintings add to the lightheartedness and cumulative style of this chain folk song. In an afterward for adults, Rabbi Michael Strassfeld explains that the tale may be a metaphor for the history of the Jewish people. He believes that the song relates to the oppression of Jews and final liberation by God (an interpretation that may be controversial among contemporary Jews). Music and words in Aramaic are provided at the end of the book.

Kadir Nelson's illustrations for *He's Got the Whole World in His Hands* (2005) suggest an immense, beautiful world, as a child might see it. The multiethnic family depicted in Nelson's paintings show gratitude for the world and for each other by swimming in the ocean, fishing, and admiring the night sky. A delightful DVD accompanies the book.

Ramadan Moon (Robert, 2009), written in narrative verse, describes holiday preparations, prayers, and celebration of a modern Muslim family, told from a child's point of view. The delightful mixed media illustrations of Shirin Adl, show the changing phases of the moon that accompany the family through The Month of Mercy (Ramadan).

A recent noteworthy publication, *On My Journey Now,* by Nikki Giovanni (2007), chronicles African American history through the music of spirituals, beginning with music brought across the Atlantic from Africa and continuing through the years of slavery, the Civil War, and on to today. Lyrics to some of the verses of the spirituals are included in the text and complete lyrics are included at the end of the book. Many of these spirituals and other hymns from the African American Christian tradition are included in Gloria Pinkney's *Music from Our Lord's Holy Heaven* (2005) and the accompanying compact disc.

Biographies

Biographies, autobiographies, and first person accounts are an especially valid way for students to learn about the lives and courageous acts of individuals, conflicts real people try to resolve, as well as history and culture. Biographies of religious leaders such as Gandhi, Thich Naht Hanh, Mother Teresa, Martin Luther King, Jr., Black Elk, Mahalia Jackson, Billy Graham, Muhammad and the lives of the Sikh Gurus give children insight into the religious history and exemplars of spiritual commitment.

Becoming Buddha: The story of Siddhartha (Stewart, 2005) is a stunning biography of Siddhartha Gautama. Illustrator Sally Rippen's bold paintings, fabric, and gold outlines are dramatic against a black background, enriching the text and providing the reader with appreciation for the life and teachings of this religious leader. The seamless story recounts the life of the Buddha from prophesies of his birth to his enlightenment and his early teaching.

Gandhi, written and illustrated by Demi (2001), concentrates on the spiritual and political leader's ethical decisions, his respectful defiance, and the "insatiable love of humankind that guided his life" (unpaged). Throughout the stages of Gandhi's life depicted in words and paintings, the reader sees growth in his religious convictions.

Flora Geyer's *Saladin: Muslim Warrior Who Defended His People* (2006) with its maps, replicas of Muslim art, and timeline, would be an excellent resource for learning about the Crusades. The book also provides a hero to be compared to many contemporary Muslim warriors.

Dalai Lama (Worth, 2004) includes a chapter on Tibet under Communism that could be a focus for understanding the continuing conflict between the Communist regime in China and the traditional Buddhist faith that led to the Dalai Lama's exile from his native Tibet. Both of these books might help students learn more about underlying causes of religious and political conflicts.

Do Re Mi: If You Can Read Music, Thank Guido d'Arezzo (Roth, 2006) begins by informing readers that if they had lived a thousand years ago and heard a song they wanted to learn to sing, they would have to listen very carefully and memorize it. Roth goes on to tell the story of "The Father of Music," first as a choirboy and later as a monk, struggling with little encouragement to convey musical pitches in written form. He finally has his epiphany and the world of music changed forever. Roth's charming collages of torn and cut paper and an array of musical scores provide a perfect complement to this inspiring story.

Informational Books

Informational (nonfiction) books on faith traditions reviewed here contain documented facts in a format that is appealing to children and youth. Most contemporary informational books on religion contain photographs of holy sites, devotees engaging in religious practices or festivals, and artifacts used in worship. These images help young readers gain a visual concept of the religion and its followers. There is a trend among publishers to produce series of books on different world religions. Some books are general, whereas others focus on a specific aspect of religion, such as houses of worship or the way different religions commemorate life transitions.

A Faith Like Mine (Buller, 2005) is a large-format picture book that addresses the six major world religions. It also includes a section on traditional beliefs and a final chapter on "other faiths" that have smaller followings and may not be well known. Each page contains several photographs of religious symbols, worshippers, or houses of worship. Small pictures of children accompany quotations from them about their beliefs and practices. Short segments of text and an abundance of photographs from around the world make this an appealing introductory book for many age groups.

The Usborne Encyclopedia of World Religions (Meredith & Hickman, 2005) has a similar format to *A Faith Like Mine,* but includes more text and is written for older readers. It is also a good resource for teachers and families. The authors address thirteen religions that are practiced today, as well as historical belief systems, such as those of Ancient Egypt, Greece, and Rome. Maps of the world's religions and a time chart that shows when various religions began and died out are also included. Internet links allow students to go on a virtual Hajj when reading the chapter on Islam or take a picture tour of a Korean Buddhist temple.

DK Publishing produces a series of Eyewitness Books that includes several volumes on world religions (Bowker, 2006), Christianity (Kindersley, Wilkinson, & Tambini, 2006), Islam (Wilkinson, 2005) and Judaism (Charing, 2003). Each double page spread focuses on a topic about that religion. In the book on Islam the topics include Islamic culture, scholarship and teaching, and festivals and ceremonies. Following an introductory paragraph for each section, the remainder of the information is in the form of detailed captions accompanying photographs. The final pages in the book are a section called "interesting facts," a glossary, questions and answers, and a timeline. *World Religions: The Great Faiths Explored* (Bowker, 2006), also published by DK, is a visually appealing book, covering 11 faith traditions.

Faith (Ajmera, Nakassis, & Pon, 2009) is a nearly wordless book that conveys its message through stunning photographs and succinct text describing the many ways in which children around the world express their faith. Each photograph is accompanied by a brief identification of the religious practice and location where it is occurring in the photo. Authors' notes, providing a longer description of the elements of faith, and a thorough glossary, provide useful information for teachers and students.

Author Anita Ganeri and illustrator Rachael Phillips have collaborated on six books in the series "Traditional Religious Tales" for Picture Window Books: *Buddhist Stories* (2006a), *Christian Stories, Hindu Stories* (2006b), *Islamic Stories* (2006d), *Jewish Stories* (2006b), and *Sikh Stories* (2006e). Each slim volume contains about eight illustrated stories, a glossary, index, and lists of print and online resources. Other helpful features are that children and adults can search by ISBN number on www.facthound.com to locate further age-appropriate informational on a particular religion and the "Did you know" inserts, containing information and pictures that extend the story or religious concepts contained within it.

The World Religions series (Nardo, 2010a, 2010b; Raatma, 2010; Rosinsky, 2010a, 2010b), consisting of six books representing major organized religions around the world, is appropriate for upper elementary or middle school students. Each book follows the pattern of beginning with the story of a teen or young adult of the faith, followed by chapters that answer a particular question, such as, "What do Muslims believe?" and "What are the origins of Sikhism?" An appealing feature of this series, especially for older readers, is the "debate" boxes that pose questions that relate to the faith. For example, the book on Islam has a debate box on whether arranged marriage is a good idea.

The Holidays Around the World series (Heiligman, 2006a, 2006b, 2006c, 2006d, 2007a, 2007b, 2007c, 2007d, 2007e, 2007f; Otto, 2007, 2008, 2009), produced by National Geographic, includes 12 books on both religious and secular holidays. Evocative photographs and examples of global traditions make these informative books appealing to children and adults. The back matter includes cooking and craft activities, songs, a glossary, resources for further investigation and a note for adult or older readers. The religious holidays included in the series are Diwali, Christmas, Easter, Hanukkah, Passover, Rosh Hashanah, Ramadan, Eid al-Fitr, and Chinese New Year.

Religion and Spirituality in America (Gay, 2006) is part of the "It Happened to Me" series for teens published by Scarecrow Press. The text is interspersed with photographs and boxes, which include quotations from teens found on religious websites. One example is an entry from a teen who has lived much of her life in a religious commune; another insert quotes nonreligious teens who have been harassed at their school. Chapters address mixing religion and politics, rites of passage, lesser-known beliefs, and a chapter on what agnostics and atheists believe.

The Cultures of the World series (Marshall Cavendish Benchmark, n.d.) are a comprehensive set of books focusing on world geography, history, people, government, and religion. The religion sections are quite comprehensive and (depending on the country) include information on indigenous, as well as contemporary faiths. The books are generously illustrated with colorful photographs.

In Every Tiny Grain of Sand: A Child's Book of Prayers and Praise (Lindbergh, 2000) is a collection of prayers and inspirational sayings from many different faith traditions. Four acclaimed artists use different styles (acrylics, collages, watercolors) to illustrate children from various spiritual traditions. The traditions represented include Native American, Jewish, Muslim, Baha'i, Buddhist, Hindu, African, and Celtic. Arranged in four themes: "For the Earth," "For the Night," "For the Home," and "For the Day," this book is appropriate for families and religious educators to use to help children understand how they are both alike and different from children from other faith traditions.

Many Ways: How Families Practice Their Beliefs and Religions (Rottner, 2006) features colorful and engaging photographs of very young children from around the world worshipping with their families. Families in churches, mosques, synagogues and other places of worship are depicted to show both how families are alike and different. At the end of the book adults are given background information on each of the photographs to help them answer questions.

Teaching Strategies for Books about Religion

The books described in this chapter are exceptional resources for teaching content about religious diversity. There are many approaches teachers can employ to enhance comprehension, expand understanding of character and perspective, and stimulate further reading and research.

Storytelling

Reading aloud and storytelling are logical choices for sharing traditional religious myths and legends that have been transmitted orally from generation to generation within communities. When stories are told rather than read, there is no barrier between the teller and the audience. Listeners incorporate the voice and gestures of the storytelling with their own imaginations to picture the events and characters in their minds. Teachers can model storytelling techniques then teach students to tell their own stories. An outstanding resource for helping children learn to tell stories is *Children Tell Stories: Teaching and Using Storytelling in the Classroom* (M. Hamilton & Weiss, 2005).

Creative Drama

Students might create a play based on one of the Buddhist stories in *Kindness* (Conover, 2005) an Islamic story from *Ayat Jamilah: Beautiful Signs* (Conover & Crane, 2004) or a Pagan tale, such as "The Rebirth of the Sun" retold in *Circle Round: Raising Children in Goddess Traditions* (Starhawk, Baker, & Hill, 1998). They could also dramatize scenes from biographies of religious leaders who advocated nonviolent protests, such as Gandhi's Salt March to the Sea or a discussion between Martin Luther King, Jr., and other religious leaders who supported the civil rights movement.

Graphic Organizers

Graphic organizers help students visualize the way a book is organized and key facts they have learned about the religion. If a class is studying several religions, students might glean facts about each and display them on graphic organizers, such as spider webs, around the classroom. One example might be a web showing houses of worship for different faith communities. For examples of graphic organizers and ways to use them see www.readwritethink.org.

For younger children, drawing scenes or helping construct a mural may help them focus on details or sequence of a story. Character maps are a helpful way for students to think about and record the feelings of a character and reasons he or she behaves in a certain way. Graphic responses to literature can be appropriate for any fictional genre.

Upper elementary and middle school students could create graphic organizers to compare and contrast creation myths from different cultures. A good resource for this particular exercise is *In the Beginning: Creation Stories From Around the World* (V. Hamilton, 1988). Social studies students might research the geography and culture in which folktales originated.

KWL

Before reading an informational book about a religious group, students and their teacher could develop a KWL chart. In the "K" column list what students think they *know* about a certain religion. In the "W" column write what they *want to know*, and when they have completed their study, write what they have *learned* in the "L" column. This approach can be used with individual students or a group. Teachers can apply the KWL approach with a single book or with a longer unit of study.

Writing

Creative modern fantasy books may inspire children to write their own imaginary myths or stories to explain natural phenomenon such as lightning or volcanoes. Children's writing and artwork can be published at websites such as www.kids-space.org, a safe, commercial-free website for publishing students' stories and pictures from all over the world.

Writing point of view pieces can help students take the perspective of religious leader from an historical or contemporary time. "I poems" can be written about oneself or students can write from the point of view of the subject of a biography they have read. For example, after reading a biography of Thich Naht Hanh, a student could determine his values, beliefs, interests, and hobbies and construct an "I poem" about him. (See www.readwritethink.org for "I poem" templates.)

Students could synthesize what they have learned about various religious groups by writing original poems based on their reading and research. Because poetry is meant to be heard, it is an excellent genre for choral reading, where groups of children read different lines. Students could practice choral reading and perform for another class at school.

Literature Circles

Literature circles could provide a forum for students to discuss books such as those described above in small groups of peers. To prepare for literature circle discussions students take notes on the book, make personal connections to the story, and sometimes do further research on some aspect of the book. Group meetings are characterized by open, natural conversations, honest, open-ended questions, and a spirit of playfulness and fun (Daniels, 2002). In reading books such as *Does My Head Look Big in This?* (Abdel-Fattah, 2007) and *Buddha Boy* (Koja, 2003) students might discuss the religious beliefs of the protagonists and how those beliefs influence their decisions. As students research related information about Buddhism, it might lead to a discussion about the current conflicts between China and Tibet involving Buddhist monks. Likewise, *Does My Head Look Big in This?* could be connected to news items in which school girls and teachers have been prevented from wearing the hijab (head covering). This discussion could also lead middle school students to debate the wearing of other religious symbols in public schools in the United States and other countries.

Visual Arts

Many teachers today share "author studies" with their students. This approach could be expanded to "illustrator studies," where students learn about the lives of artists, as well as the media and styles they use. Illustrators' websites frequently include video clips showing work in progress and demonstrations of techniques. Students can try their own hand at collage, photography, charcoal, scratchboard, or various types of paint.

Many informational books about religion focus on visual arts and music. Religious art is some of the finest and most revered art ever created. Christian painting, sculpture and architecture dominated the art of Medieval Europe. The rich and varied culture of Islam is reflected in the architecture of mosques, decorated ceramic tiles, the beauty of their calligraphy, pottery and carpets; and detailed geometric, floral, and vegetative designs. One way for students to understand

Buddhism is to study the symbolism in the different physical positions of the Buddha depicted in sculptures. Children's literature that includes information on religious art can be a way for students to develop a deeper understanding of particular religions.

Biography Boxes

Students might demonstrate their understanding of Gandhi's life by creating a "biography box" (a decorated box or other container in which the student places objects that relate to the subject of a biography). A biography box for Gandhi might include a British flag to represent his years of schooling in London, salt to represent the salt marches, homespun cloth to represent the right of Indians to spin their own cotton, a piece of fruit to symbolize vegetarianism, and rose petals, which were scattered after his death.

"You Are There" Dramas

To extend their understanding of biographies, students might create "You Are There" dramas based on important historical events documented in the biographies they are reading. An example might be a dramatization of the civil rights event in which Martin Luther King, Jr. and Rabbi Abraham Joshua Heschel prayed and marched together, as depicted in *As Good as Anybody* (Michelson, 2008). In these presentations student take on roles of different historical figures in a biography and write a script about a memorable scene to perform for others. Students might dress in simple costumes, if they choose.

Higher level thinking skills will be applied when teachers and students stage imaginary conversations between two people from the same time period or different times (Norton, 2007). For example, what would The Buddha and Harriet Tubman talk about if they were to meet? Although completely fictional, these discussions would have to be well grounded in an understanding of each person's philosophy and religious beliefs. Students could also study interview techniques and stage a mock interview with a famous religious character from the past.

Conclusion

Because religion and spiritual traditions are so important in understanding past and present cultures around the world, it is essential for teachers to include the topic of faith traditions in their classrooms. Both the national guidelines and state curriculum standards for social studies include the teaching of religious and spiritual traditions under many topics (National Council for the Social Studies, 1998). These include families and communities around the world, holidays, current events, exploration and discovery, and colonial settlements. In addition, teachers need to validate the cultural differences, including the religious and spiritual beliefs, of the children and adolescents in their classroom. Teaching strategies that use children's literature to explore diverse cultures can also provide opportunities to open the window on the diversity of religions within the United States and the world. These strategies, in turn, will enable children and adolescents to reflect and think with greater depth and broader understanding about their own cultures and faith traditions.

References

Baestrup, K. (2007). *Here if you need me*. New York, NY: Little, Brown.

Bruchac, J. (1996). *Roots of survival: Native American storytelling and the sacred*. Golden, CO: Fulcrum.

Buxbaum, Y. (1994). *Storytelling and spirituality in Judaism*. Northvale, NJ: Jason Aronson.

Daniels, H. (2002). *Literature circles: Voice and choice in book clubs and reading groups*. Portland, ME: Stenhouse.

Darrigan, D. L., Tunnell, M. O., & Jacobs, J. S. (2002). *Children's literature: Engaging teachers and children in good books*. Upper Saddle River, NJ: Merrill Prentice Hall.

Galda, L., & Cullinan, B. (2002). *Literature and the child* (5th ed.). Belmont, CA: Wadsworth/ Thomson Learning.

Gangi, J. M. (2004). *Encountering children's literature: An arts approach*. Boston, MA: Pearson Education.

Groce, E., & Groce, R. (2005). Authenticating historical fiction: Rationale and process. *Education, Research and Perspectives, 32*(1), 99–119.

In memoriam: Madeleine L'Engle (2007). *Journal of Children's Literature, 33*(2), 78.

Lester, J. (1999). Writing about Religion. *Book Links, 9* (2), pp. 54–56.

Marshall Cavendish Benchmark. (n.d.) Retrieved from http://www.marshallcavendish.us/marshallcavendish-us/benchmark/catalog/social_studies/cultures_of_the_world_second_ed/index_fr.xml

National Council for the Social Studies. (1998). *Study about religions in the social studies curriculum*. Retrieved from www.socialstudies.org/positions/religion

Norton, D. E. (2007). *Through the eyes of a child* (7th ed.). Upper Saddle River, NJ: Pearson Merrill Prentice Hall.

**Children's Literature Cited (P = Primary Level,
I = Intermediate level, M = Middle School Level)**

Abdel-Fattah, R. (2007). *Does my head look big in this?* New York, NY: Orchard. (M)

Armstrong, C. (1995). *Lives and legends of the saints*. New York, NY: Simon and Schuster Books for Young Readers.

Ayers, K. (1998). *North by night*. New York, NY: Delacorte. (M)

Bowker, J. (2006). *World religions: The great faiths explored and explained*. London, England: DK (I, M)

Buller, L. (2005). *A faith like mine*. New York, NY: DK. (P, I, M)

Charing, D. (2003). *Judaism*. New York, NY: DK Eyewitness Books.

Chodzin, S., & Kohn, A. (1997). *The wisdom of the crows and other Buddhist tales*. Bath, England: Barefoot Books.

Chwast, S. (Illustrator). (2005). *Had Gadya: A Passover song*. Brookfield, CT: Roaring Brook Press. (P)

Conover, S. (2005). *Kindness: A treasury of Buddhist wisdom for children and parents*. Spokane, WA: Eastern Washington Press. (I)

Conover, S., & Crane, F. (2004). *Ayat Jamilah: Beautiful signs*. Spokane, WA: Eastern Washington Press.

Cultures of the world. (various authors, 2009). New York, NY: Marshall Cavendish Benchmark. (I, M)

Demi. (2001). *Gandhi*. New York, NY: Scholastic. (I)

Forest, H. (1996). *Wisdom tales from around the world*. Little Rock, AR: August House. (P, I)

Ganeri, A. (2006a). *Buddhist stories*. Mankato, MN: Picture Window Books. (P)

Ganeri, A. (2006b). *Christian stories*. Mankato, MN: Picture Window Books. (P)

Ganeri, A. (2006c). *Jewish stories*. Mankato, MN: Picture Window Books. (P)

Ganeri, A. (2006d). *Hindu stories*. Mankato, MN: Picture Window Books. (P)

Ganeri, A. (2006e). *Islamic stories*. Mankato, MN: Picture Window Books. (P)

Ganeri, A. (2006f). *Sikh stories*. Mankato, MN: Picture Window Books. (P)

Gay, K. (2006). *Religion and spirituality in America*. Lanham, MD: Scarecrow.

Gellman, M. (1989). *Does God have a big toe?* New York, NY: HarperCollins (P, I)

Geyer, F. (2006). *Saladin: Muslim warrior who defended his people*. Washington, DC: National Geographic. (I)

Gibfried, D. (2006). *Brother Juniper*. New York, NY: Clarion. (P)

Giovanni, N. (2007). *On my journey now*. Cambridge, MA: Candlewick. (M)

Hamilton, M., & Weiss, M. (2005). *Children tell stories: Teaching and using storytelling in the classroom*. New York, NY: Richard C. Owen.

Hamilton, V. (1988). *In the beginning: Creation stories from around the world*. San Diego, CA: Harcourt, Brace, Jovanovich. (I, M)

Heiligman, D. (2006a). *Holidays around the world: Celebrate Diwali: With sweets, lights, and fireworks*. Washington, DC: National Geographic.

Heiligman, D. (2006b). *Holidays around the world: Celebrate Hanukkah: With light, latkes, and dreidels*. Washington, DC: National Geographic.

Heiligman, D. (2006c). *Holidays around the world: Celebrate Ramadan and Eid al-Fitr*. Washington, DC: National Geographic.

Heiligman, D. (2006d). *Holidays around the world: Celebrate Thanksgiving: With turkey, family, and counting blessings*. Washington, DC: National Geographic.

Heiligman, D. (2007a). *Holidays around the world: Celebrate Christmas: With carols, presents, and peace*. Washington, DC: National Geographic.

Heiligman, D. (2007b). *Holidays around the world. Celebrate Easter: With colored eggs, flowers, and prayer*. Washington, DC: National Geographic.

Heiligman, D. (2007c). *Holidays around the world: Celebrate Halloween*. Washington, DC: National Geographic.

Heiligman, D. (2007d). *Holidays around the world: Celebrate Independence Day: With parades, picnics, and fireworks*. Washington, DC: National Geographic.

Heiligman, D. (2007e). *Holidays around the world: Celebrate Passover: With matzah, maror, and memories*. Washington, DC: National Geographic.

Heiligman, D. (2007f). *Holidays around the world: Celebrate Rosh Hashanah and Yom Kippur: With honey, prayers, and the Shofar*. Washington, DC: National Geographic.

Koja, K. (2003). *Buddha boy*. New York, NY: Farr, Straus, and Giroux. (M)

Ladwig, T. (1993). *Psalm twenty-three*. Grand Rapids, MI: Eerdmans Books for Young Readers. (P)

L'Engle, M. (1973). *A wrinkle in time*. New York, NY: Dell. (I, M)

Lester, J. (1999b). *What a truly cool world*. New York, NY: Scholastic. (P)

Lester, J. (1999c). *When the beginning began*. New York, NY: Harcourt/Silver Whistle. (I, M)

Levine, E. (2007). *Henry's freedom box*. New York, NY: Scholastic. (P, I)

Lewis, C. S. (1950). *The lion, the witch, and the wardrobe*. New York, NY: Macmillan. (I)

Lindbergh, R. (2000). *In every tiny grain of sand: A child's book of prayer and praise*. Cambridge, MA: Candlewick Press. (P, I)

Manos, H. (2006). *Samsara Dog*. La Jolla, CA: Kane/Miller Book.

McFarlane, M. (1996). *Sacred myths: Stories of world religions*. Portland, OR: Sibyl. (P, I)

Meredith, S., & Hickman, C. (2005). *The Usborne encyclopedia of world religions*. London, England: Usborne House. (I, M)

Meyer, C. (1996). *Gideon's people*. San Diego, CA: Harcourt Brace.

Michelson, R. (2008). *As good as anybody*. New York, NY: Alfred A. Knopf.

Nelson, K. (2005). *He's got the whole world in his hands*. New York, NY: Dial Books for Young Readers. (P)

Nelson, K. (2005). *He's got the whole world in his hands*. New York, NY: Scholastic DVD. (P)

Otto, C. B. (2007). *Holidays around the world. Celebrate Kwanzaa: With candles, community, and the fruit of the harvest*. Washington, DC: National Geographic.

Otto, C. B. (2008). *Holidays around the world: Celebrate Valentine's Day: With love, cards, and candy*. Washington, DC: National Geographic.

Otto, C. B. (2009). *Holidays around the world: Celebrate Chinese New Year: With fireworks, dragons, and lanterns*. Washington, DC: National Geographic.

Pinkney, G. (2005). *Music from our Lord's holy heaven*. New York, NY: Amistad/HarperCollins. (P, I)

Pullman, P. (1996). *The golden compass*. New York, NY: Alfred A. Knopf. (M)

Robert, N. B. (2009). *Ramadan moon*. London, England: Frances Lincoln. (P)

Roth, S. (2006). *Do, re, mi: If you can read music, thank Guido d'Arezzo*. Boston, MA: Houghton Mifflin.

Rotner, S., & Kelly, S. (2006). *Many ways: How families practice their beliefs and religions*. Minneapolis, MN: Millbrook Press (P)

Sasso, S. E. (1994). *In God's name*. Woodstock, VT: Jewish Lights. (P, I)

Starhawk, Baker, D., & Hill, A. (1998). *Circle round: Raising children in Goddess traditions.* New York, NY: Random House. (I, M)

Stewart, W. (2005). *Becoming Buddha: The story of Siddhartha.* Torrance, CA: Heian. (P)

Thomas, J. C. (2007). *Shouting!* New York, NY: Hypernium. (P)

Wilkonson, P. (2005). *Islam.* New York, NY: DK Eyewitness Books.

Wilkonson, P. (2006). *Christianity.* New York, NY: DK Eyewitness Books.

Wilson, A. (Illustrator). (2003). *The Lord is my shepherd.* Grand Rapids, MI: Eerdmans Books for Young Readers. (P, I)

Worth, R. (2004). *Dalai Lama (Tenzin Gyatso).* Philadelphia, PA: Chelsea House.

Neighbourhood Ethnic Diversity Buffers School Readiness Impact in ESL Children

Chassidy Puchala, Lan T.H. Vu, and Nazeem Muhajarine

Research surrounding children's successful transition from home to school has received much recent attention because of the subsequent impact on academic, social, emotional and mental health outcomes.[1,2] School readiness has been defined as "a child's ability to meet the demands of school",[3] in part indicating a successful transition from home to school. Systematic and consistent differences in school readiness have been linked to characteristics of the child, including male sex, Aboriginal ancestry, being from an ethnic minority and age of school entry.[4-7] A child's lack of facility with the primary language of instruction (which is often English, in Saskatoon), as indicated by English as a second language (ESL*) status, is expected to be a strong predictor of school readiness,[8] although this is relatively under-explored within the published school readiness literature.

This paper explores factors contributing to poor school readiness among ESL children. Children are classified as ESL if they are currently learning to use and study English, but their mother tongue is a language other than English. Gaining a better understanding of the relation between ESL status and school readiness is of particular importance because of the high proportion of ESL individuals (children and adults) in Canada (approximately 20%), which is consistently rising each year with increasing

---

* For the purposes of the current study, the term ESL is used. However, it should be noted that recently the term English as an alternative language (EAL) has been used to reflect the fact that for some children/families, English is not a second language but rather one of several alternative languages.

rates of immigration.[9,10] The process of acculturation presents many challenges to ESL students entering kindergarten as they must adapt to learning in an environment that uses language practices significantly different from those used in their home and cultural community, in addition to coping with many broader cultural, psychological and socio-economic issues.[11] Perhaps as a result of such challenges, ESL children are at risk of many negative academic, social and emotional outcomes.[12,13]

In terms of the ability to meet the demands of school, ESL children have poorer school readiness outcomes than their non-ESL counterparts, particularly in the communication skills and general knowledge domain.[1,8,14,15] It is expected that ESL children will score more poorly in these domains, which directly assess children's ability to use and listen to English, communicate with and understand others, and answer general questions about the world.

While ESL status influences school readiness, recent evidence indicates that many contextual variables also affect school readiness and, moreover, may mitigate the relation between individual risk factors and school readiness.[8,16-19] Contextual factors are those that describe the physical, social and economic environment of a geographical place in which people live and, through various mechanisms, that are expected to influence outcomes in the individual. These include safety in neighbourhoods, availability of services or amenities, social variables such as level of unemployment among adults, household income and transiency. Therefore, it is not simply the characteristics of the child that shape his or her school readiness but, rather, the combination of both individual- and contextual-level factors.

The aim of the current study is to examine the individual and contextual factors related to school readiness and to ascertain whether the relation between child ESL status and school readiness may be buffered by contextual factors based on community-defined neighbourhoods in Saskatoon, Saskatchewan. Neighbourhoods in Saskatoon are well defined geographical entities, have known boundaries, are meaningful to residents and are comprehensively planned units that can be efficiently serviced and maintained over the long term.[20]

Method

Setting
Data were collected for three cohorts of kindergarteners in 2001, 2003 and 2005 in Saskatoon, Saskatchewan. The City of Saskatoon has a total of 86 neighbourhoods, 63 of which are considered residential.

Measurement

School Readiness
The Early Development Instrument (EDI) is a tool that measures kindergarten students' school readiness. It consists of 103 questions falling into one of five domains: physical health and well-being, social competence, emotional maturity, language and cognitive development, and

communication skills and general knowledge. Scores for each domain range from 0 to 10. The EDI is completed by kindergarten teachers for each student midway into the kindergarten year over a two-week period of time.

Individual-level Factors

The EDI also captures basic demographic information for each child as reported by the kindergarten teacher, in part based on school records. Seven individual level characteristics were examined: ESL status, sex, age, Aboriginal status,* special needs status and the presence of special skills† and special problems.‡

Contextual-level Factors

The EDI data are analyzed and reported at the population level and can therefore be linked to other population-level databases, such as the national census, conducted by Statistics Canada. The Canadian census collects reliable, detailed data on every resident of Canada, allowing analyses to be conducted for areas, such as a neighbourhoods. The 2001 Census special tabulations provided information on seven characteristics for each of Saskatoon's neighbourhoods: percentage of families falling below Statistics Canada's low income cut-off (LICO), ethnic diversity, percentage of the population with Aboriginal status, percentage of the population greater than 19 years with education under grade 9, percentage of the population 24 to 64 years old who are employed, percentage of the population who had moved within the previous year and the percentage of single parents.[8,16-19] The LICO is a standard used by Statistics Canada to relate family income to living expenses for various sizes of families living in urban and rural settings in Canada. A family falls below the LICO if it spends more than 20% of its average income on basic necessities such as shelter, food and clothing. Neighbourhood ethnic diversity is based on Statistics Canada's Single and Multiple Ethnic Origin Response table. The diversity index is calculated at the neighbourhood level and indicates the heterogeneity of ethnic group presence in each neighbourhood.[20] First, the population of each given ethnic group in a neighbourhood is compared with the population of the same ethnic group within the city as a whole to create

---

* The Aboriginal status of the child is proxy-reported by the kindergarten teacher. On the basis of Statistics Canada's definition of Aboriginal identity, generally, a declaration of Aboriginal status would involve a child having parentage of Aboriginal ancestry (i.e., Registered Indian, Treaty Indian, Métis or Inuit).

† Developers of the EDI include these skills as special: numeracy, literacy, arts, music, athletics/dance, problem-solving and other. Each of these skills is simply scored as yes or no.

‡ Developers of the EDI consider special problems to include physical disability, visual impairment, hearing impairment, speech impairment, learning disability, emotional problem, behaviour problems and problems at home. These are scored in the same way as special skills.

a ratio. Next, these ratios are summed across ethnic groups to create a diversity index for each neighbourhood. Higher sums are indicative of more ethnically diverse populations.

Statistical Approach

To test the hypothesis that ESL children have lower EDI scores than non-ESL children, we applied multiple linear models to estimate the adjusted difference in EDI score for all five domains, controlling for age, sex, special needs status, Aboriginal status, special problems and special skills. Multi-level modeling examined the buffering effects of individual risk and neighbourhood factors on the relation between child ESL status and EDI domain scores. Three hierarchical models were estimated using HLM (hierarchical linear modelling) software version 6.07 (Scientific Software International, Inc.), each building on the previous model and thus increasing in complexity and explanatory power.[21] The interaction between the variable ESL status and individual risk factors and neighbourhood factors was examined.

Results

The average age of the entire study sample (N=6,144) was 5.65 years (SD=0.36); there were 135 ESL children, 5,833 non-ESL children and 176 children whose language status was unknown. ESL children accounted for 2.2% of the entire sample. Children missing two or more domain scores were classified as having non-valid EDI data and were excluded from the analysis. After excluding children with non-valid EDI, 127 ESL children and 5581 non-ESL children remained in the analysis. Children with non-valid EDI did not differ demographically from those with valid EDI, with the exception of Aboriginal status. Significantly more Aboriginal children (62.9%) than non-Aboriginal children (37.1%) had non-valid EDI. No significant differences were found with respect to demographic characteristics (sex, age, special needs status) between ESL and non-ESL children, with the exception of Aboriginal status. There were significantly more ESL children in the non-Aboriginal group (2.6%) than the Aboriginal group (0.5%). The average number of special skills and special problems for the entire sample was 0.42 and 0.26, respectively.

Average EDI domain scores were as follows: 8.63 (SD=1.32) for physical health and well-being, 8.30 (SD=1.77) for social competence, 7.95 (SD=1.57) for emotional maturity, 7.67 (SD=2.09) for language and cognitive development and 7.63 (SD=2.35) for communication and general knowledge. After all other available child characteristics had been controlled for, ESL children had significantly lower scores on all EDI domains, the largest difference being in the communication and general knowledge domain (see Table 17.1). The association between ESL status and EDI scores was mitigated by individual and contextual factors only for the communication skills and general knowledge, and the emotional maturity domains. The final multilevel models for these two domains are presented in Table 17.2 and Table 17.3.

At the individual level, older children and children with more special skills had higher scores on emotional maturity, and communication and general knowledge. Males, children

TABLE 17.1   Comparison of EDI Domain Scores Between ESL (n=127) and Non-ESL (n=5,581) Subgroups in a Kindergarten Population, Saskatoon, Saskatchewan, 2001, 2003, 2005

EDI Domain	ESL Mean (SD)	95% CI	Non-ESL Mean (SD)	95% CI	p
Physical health and well-being	8.34 (1.49)	8.07–8.60	8.63 (1.32)	8.60–8.66	0.013
Social competence	7.71 (1.91)	7.37–8.05	8.29 (1.76)	8.24–8.33	0.000
Emotional maturity	7.40 (1.32)	7.17–7.64	7.96 (1.57)	7.92–8.00	0.000
Language & cognitive development	6.61 (2.28)	6.21–7.02	7.69 (2.07)	7.64–7.74	0.000
Communication skills & general knowledge	4.53 (2.61)	4.07–4.99	7.69 (2.29)	7.63–7.75	0.000

EDI=Early Development Instrument; ESL=English as a Second Language; CI=confidence interval

TABLE 17.2   Estimated Coefficients From Final Hierarchical Linear (Multi-level) Modeling: EDI Communication Skills and General Knowledge Domain Score Regressed on Child and Neighbourhood Factors (n=5,722)

Variable	Coefficient	Standard Error	p
Child characteristics (level 1)			
Age	0.46	0.09	0.002
Sex (0=female, 1=male)	−0.45	0.05	<0.001
Aboriginal status (0=non-Aboriginal, 1=Aboriginal)	−1.26	0.12	<0.001
Special needs status (0=no, 1=yes)	−1.54	0.17	<0.001
Number of special skills	0.52	0.03	<0.001
Number of special problems	−0.99	0.05	<0.001
Cross-level interaction between child and neighbourhood characteristics			
ESL status – intercept	−2.85	0.29	<0.001
Neighbourhood ethnic diversity	0.71	0.23	0.004
Neighbourhood characteristics (level 2)			
Intercept	7.44	0.06	<0.001
Percentage of movers during previous year	−0.22	0.08	0.010
Percentage employed	0.14	0.05	0.013

TABLE 17.3   Estimated Coefficients From Final Hierarchical Linear (Multi-level) Modeling: EDI Emotional Maturity Domain Score Regressed on Child and Neighbourhood Factors (n=5,690)

Variable	Coefficient	Standard Error	p
Child characteristics (level 1)			
Age	0.21	0.07	0.002
Sex (0=female, 1=male)	−0.75	0.04	<0.001
Aboriginal status (0=non-Aboriginal, 1=Aboriginal)	−0.43	0.07	<0.001
Special needs status (0=no, 1=yes)	−0.22	0.10	0.034
Number of special skills	0.18	0.02	<0.001
Number of special problems	−0.77	0.04	<0.001
Interaction: ESL × sex	0.70	0.21	0.002
Cross-level interaction between child and neighbourhood characteristics			
ESL status – intercept	−0.51	0.11	<0.001
Neighbourhood ethnic diversity	0.23	0.11	0.027
Neighbourhood characteristics (level 2)			
Intercept	7.88	0.03	<0.001
Percentage of movers during the previous year	−0.13	0.05	0.008

of Aboriginal status and those with special needs or problems had lower domain scores. An interaction between sex and ESL status was found for the emotional maturity domain, meaning that for males, compared with females, there was a larger difference in EDI score between ESL and non-ESL children. At the neighbourhood level, children from neighbourhoods with a lower percentage of employment among adults had lower EDI scores in the communication and general knowledge domain. Children from highly transient neighbourhoods, with a higher percentage of the population who had changed residences within the previous year, had lower EDI scores on the emotional maturity and on the communication and general knowledge domains.

Importantly, children from neighbourhoods with high ethnic diversity had higher scores on communication skills and general knowledge, as well as emotional maturity, even if they were ESL speakers. As shown in Figures 17.1 and 17.2, the adjusted mean difference on these domains between ESL and non-ESL children is attenuated for ESL children in neighbourhoods with high ethnic diversity and exacerbated for ESL children in neighbourhoods with low ethnic diversity.

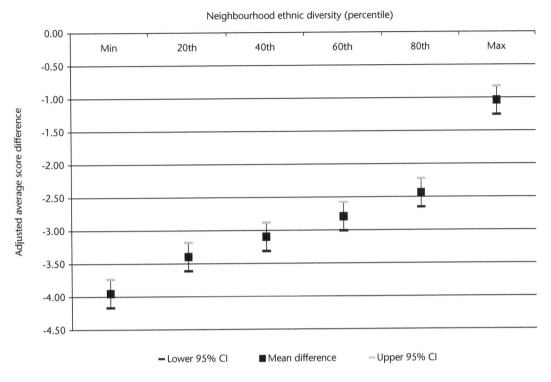

FIGURE 17.1 Adjusted Average Difference in EDI Communication and General Knowledge Scores Between ESL and non-ESL Children by Neighbourhood Ethnic Diversity

Discussion

The current study explored the individual and contextual factors associated with poor school readiness and child ESL status. Consistent with past research,[8,15,22] ESL children had lower levels of school readiness than non-ESL children on all domains, especially the communication skills and general knowledge domain. Although ESL children are at risk of poor readiness across all domains, only scores on the communication skills and general knowledge, and the emotional maturity domains were mitigated by individual and contextual factors, indicating that different contextual-level factors have varying degrees of association with each domain of school readiness.[8,19,23]

Male ESL children were at risk of lower emotional maturity scores than non-ESL males, whereas the difference was smaller for females. This may be attributed to the gap in emotional development between males and females wherein females, generally, have higher levels of developmental maturity.[24,25] ESL status may further exacerbate this difference if young males are less able to handle the challenges associated with having an ESL status and thus make an even poorer emotional adjustment. Relatively rapid development emotionally among females may actually help them cope with such challenges, which would translate into smaller disparities. In the communication and general knowledge domain no interaction was observed between ESL status and sex. While females have been found to consistently outperform males in this

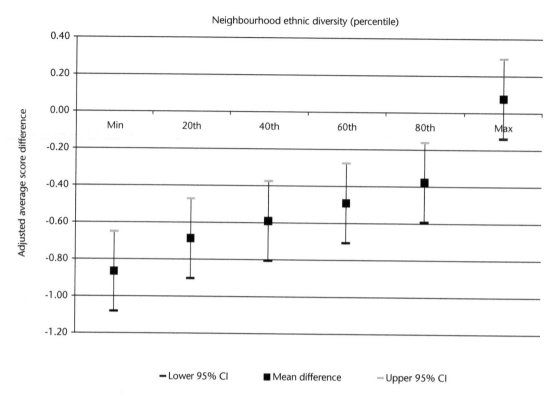

FIGURE 17.2   Adjusted Average Difference in EDI Emotional Maturity Scores Between ESL and non-ESL Children by Neighbourhood Ethnic Diversity

domain,[26,27] it is likely the challenge of using a language other than one's own mother-tongue to communicate that places both sexes at the same level of risk.

The significant relation between neighbourhood factors and performance on the communication skills and general knowledge domain aligns with previous studies.[8,23] The current study offers a unique contribution to the literature by providing evidence that ethnic diversity mitigates the relation between ESL status and EDI performance. It has been suggested that children raised within "neighbourhood language-based enclaves", wherein a majority of parents and community members communicate in one dominant language other than English, may be less likely to acquire English language skills.[8] However, no research has examined the effects of growing up in a linguistically diverse neighbourhood. If ethnic diversity is used as a proxy for linguistic diversity, it may be that high levels of exposure to varying languages facilitate an ESL child's ability to understand and communicate in languages other than his or her mother tongue, such as English. It should be noted that while one may speculate that ethnic diversity is related to exposure to multiple languages, the current study was unable to directly examine neighbourhood linguistic composition.

Previous school readiness research has shown that neighbourhood factors are least associated with scores on the emotional maturity domain.[8,23,28] However, to our knowledge studies have not examined the neighbourhood factor of ethnic diversity. The identification of neighbourhood buffering effects on the emotional maturity domain is a unique contribution to the literature. We found that ethnic diversity buffers the negative association between ESL status and emotional maturity scores. In fact, mean emotional maturity scores did not differ between ESL and non-ESL children when ESL children lived in the most ethnically diverse neighbourhoods.

This finding points to the importance of community in promoting success among ESL children. Ethnic minority families share similar struggles, in that they must adapt to their new host culture while simultaneously maintaining their own unique identities, which may foster interdependence and community. ESL children from communities with high levels of interdependence may be less likely to experience difficulties emotionally. For instance, for some children the ability to empathize with others and a strong social support system may translate into pro-social and helping behaviours within the classroom setting and protect against negative emotionality or poor psychological adjustment (e.g., being unhappy or sad, anxious or fearful behaviour). Therefore, programs directed towards increasing interconnectedness among ethnic minority communities may increase school readiness.

Although the current study added knowledge to the research literature on school readiness among ESL children, there are limitations that should be addressed. First, a two to four year time difference exists between collection of the EDI data (2001, 2003, 2005) and the census data (2001). Although this difference could affect our findings, there is little evidence in Saskatoon that such significant change has occurred during the four years relevant to this study (2001 to 2005). Second, despite the potential contributions of ethnic diversity, the current study did not examine the specific ethnic composition of the neighbourhoods. A third limitation is the inability to assess the English language proficiency of the neighbourhoods under study, which may have an impact on English language acquisition among their children.

In summary, the current study provided some insight regarding how contextual factors may protect ESL children from poor school readiness outcomes. It is clear that although ESL children are at a disadvantage in many areas, neighbourhood ethnic diversity may buffer against this risk specifically within the communication skills and general knowledge, as well as the emotional maturity domains. As a result, community initiatives should focus on these domains in addition to promoting an ethnically diverse and inclusive environment. On the basis of our findings, future research should continue to examine the contextual factors related to ESL status and early child developmental outcomes, particularly focusing on the role of neighbourhood ethnic and linguistic concentration. Such research is vital in order to help communities work together to foster school readiness and, consequently, promote long-term academic success and positive developmental outcomes in this at-risk population.

References

1. Essex MJ, Klein MH, Slattery MJ, Goldsmith HH, Kalin NH. Early risk factors and developmental pathways to chronic high inhibition and social anxiety disorder in adolescence. *Am J Psychiatry* 2010;167:40–46.

2. Silver RB, Measelle JR, Armstrong JM, Essex MJ. Trajectories of classroom externalizing behaviours: Contributions of child characteristics, family characteristics, and the teacher-child relationship during the transition to school. *J School Psychol* 2005;43:39–60.

3. Janus M, Brinkman S, Duku E, Hertzman C, Santos R, Sayers M, et al. The Early Development Instrument: A Population-based Measure for Communities. A Handbook on Development, Properties, and Use. Hamilton, ON: Offord Centre for Child Studies, 2007.

4. Janus M. Validation of the Early Development Instrument in a Sample of First Nations' Children. Hamilton, ON: Offord Centre for Child Studies, 2002.

5. Lloyd J. Province-wide EDI Findings: Aboriginal Children. Vancouver, BC: Human Early Learning Partnership, special tabulation, 2006.

6. Fryer RG, Levitt SD. Understanding the black-white test score gap in the first two years of school. *Rev Econ Stat* 2004;86(2):447–64.

7. Hertzman C, McLean SA, Kohen DE, Dunn J, Evans T. Early Development in Vancouver: Report of the Community Asset Mapping Project (CAMP). Vancouver, BC: Human Early Learning Partnership, 2002.

8. Oliver LN, Dunn JR, Kohen DE, Hertzman C. Do neighbourhoods influence the readiness to learn of kindergarten children in Vancouver? A multilevel analysis of neighbourhood effects. *Environment and Planning* 2007;39:848–68.

9. Statistics Canada. Profile of Languages in Canada: English, French and Many Others. 2001 Census. Ottawa, ON: Statistics Canada, 2002. Available at: http://www12.statcan.ca/english/census01/Products/Analytic/companion/lang/pdf/96F0030XIE2001005.pdf (Accessed September 20, 2009).

10. Statistics Canada. Population by Mother Tongue, by Province and Territory (2006 Census). Ottawa, ON: Statistics Canada, 2007. Available at: http://www40.statcan.ca/l01/cst01/demo11c.htm?sdi=british%20columbia%20mother%20tongue/ (Accessed September 20, 2009).

11. Espinosa LM. English-language learners as they enter school. In: Pianta RC, Cox MJ, Snow KL (Eds.), *School Readiness and the Transition to Kindergarten in the Era of Accountability*. Baltimore, MD: Paul H. Brookes Publishing, 2007.

12. Spomer ML, Cowen EL. A comparison of the school mental health referral profiles of young ESL and English-speaking children. *J Community Psychol* 2001;29(1):69–82.

13. Gertnet BL, Rice ML, Hadley PA. Influence of communicative competence on peer preferences in a preschool classroom. *J Speech Hearing Res* 1994;37:913–23.

14. Guhn M, Gadermann A, Zumbo BD. Does the EDI measure school readiness in the same way across different groups of children? *Early Educ Dev* 2007;18(3):453–72.

15. Wright C, Diener M, Kay SC. School readiness of low-income children at risk for school failure. *J Children & Poverty* 2000;6(2):99–117.

16. Beauvais C, Jenson J. The Well-being of Children: Are There "Neighbourhood Effects"? Ottawa, ON: Canadian Policy Research Networks Inc, 2003.

17. Kershaw P, Forer B, Irwin LG, Hertzman C, Lapointe V. Toward a social care program of research: A population-level study of neighborhood effects on child development. *Early Educ Dev* 2007;18(3):535–60.

18. Cushon J, Vu L, Janzen B, Muhajarine N. Neighborhood poverty impacts children's physical health and well-being over time: Evidence from the Early Development Instrument. *Early Educ Dev* (in press).

19. Muhajarine N, Vu L, Labonte R. Social contexts and children's health outcomes: Researching across the boundaries. *Critical Public Health* 2006;16(3):205–18.

20. City of Saskatoon, Planning and Development Branch. Neighbourhood Profiles, 9th ed. Saskatoon, Saskatchewan: City of Saskatoon, 2008.

21. Raudenbush S, Bryk A, Cheong YF, Congdon R. *HLM5: Hierarchical Linear and Nonlinear Modeling.* Lincolnwood, IL: Scientific Software International, 2000.

22. Janus M, Offord DR. Development of psychometric properties of the Early Development Instrument (EDI): A measure of school readiness. *Can J Behav Sci* 2007;39(1):1–22.

23. Leventhal T, Brooks-Gunn J. The neighborhoods they live in: The effects of neighbourhood residence on child and adolescent outcomes. *Psychol Bull* 2000;126:309–37.

24. Brody LR. Gender differences in emotional development: A review of theories and research. *J Personality* 1985;53(2):102–49.

25. Fischer AH. *Gender and Emotion: Social Psychological Perspectives.* Cambridge, UK: United Press, 2000.

26. Janus M, Duku E. The school entry gap: Socioeconomic, family, and health factors associated with children's school readiness to learn. *Early Educ Dev* 2007;18(3):375–403.

27. Janus M, Duku E. Normative Data for the Early Development Instrument. Hamilton, ON: Offord Centre for Child Studies, 2004.

28. Lapointe V, Ford L, Zumbo BD. Examining the relationship between neighborhood environment and school readiness for kindergarten children. *Early Educ Dev* 2007;18(3):473–95.

Migrant and Refugee Children, Their Families, and Early Childhood Education

Susan Grieshaber and Melinda G. Miller

Population Trends

One of the effects of globalization is the increasing movement of people around the globe. Whether it is due to migration by choice or matters connected to war and persecution that produce refugees and asylum seekers,[1] the transitional displacement of people in the early twenty-first century has meant that 200 million people are living away from their country of birth (Global Commission on International Migration, 2005). According to Adams and Kirova (2006c), Australia, Canada and the U.S. are "three major receiving nations for transnational migrants" (p. 199). The estimated net migration rate for the U.S. for 2009 is 4.32 migrants per 1000 of the population. For Canada it is 5.63/1000 of the population and Australia 6.23/1000 (Central Intelligence Agency [CIA], 2009). These countries also accept quotas of refugees from refugee camps and have long histories of immigration. The U.S. census of 2000 indicated that nearly 46 million people (18% of the population) spoke a language other than English as their first language and of these 29 million (about 60%) speak Spanish (Nieto & Bode, 2008). This diversity is reflected in public school enrolments in the U.S. The school-age population (5–17 years) increased by 17 percent from 1990–2000 and the percentage of English language learners increased by 46 percent during this same time (Nieto & Bode, 2008). However, as Nieto and Bode point out (2008), immigration is one of the "most contentious issues" (p. 7) in the U.S.

Unlike the U.S. which has a long history of immigration, some of the Nordic countries have recently experienced a change in the composition of their population. In

Denmark for instance, migrants now constitute 4.1% of the population and in Norway it is 3%, while in Finland there are over 100 different migrant groups, with most coming from Russia and Somalia (OECD, 2006).

Globalization has also produced changes in the population of several European countries, with an estimated net migration rate in 2009 of 2.19/1000 population for Germany and 2.16/1000 for the UK (CIA, 2009). Australia, which has a much smaller population than the U.S. has recently experienced societal transformation due largely to changes in the source countries of Australia's permanent arrivals since the mid 1990s. In accordance with United Nations priorities, the Australian Humanitarian program resettled approximately 24,000 refugees from the Horn of Africa (notably Sudan and Somalia), the Middle East and South West Asia in 2005 and 2006, and expects to settle a similar number each year for the next few years (Department of Immigration and Multicultural and Indigenous Affairs (DIMIA), 2005). The number of new migrants settling permanently in Australia in 2007–8 increased by 7.3% (Australian Human Rights Commission, 2008).

New theorizing about issues of migration that includes refugees has moved from cultural deficit models, through economic and social reproduction models and explanations of cultural incompatibilities, to current understandings of the complexities of cultural globalization. Such perspectives recognize that overlooking the rich cultural, social and cognitive resources that come with migrants and refugees is counterproductive to all facets of society (Cummins, 2004, p. xv). In his study of the socio-economic environment in the United States, Florida (2004) detailed the conditions under which new migrants contribute critically and creatively to the vibrancy of society. Significantly, feeling safe and valued were paramount and correlated with areas of greatest growth and vitality.

In this chapter we review literature that relates to young migrant and refugee children from birth to age eight, their families and early childhood education. Migrants and refugees are those who have settled permanently in a new country. Having said that, for the most part when reviewing literature, we have used the same descriptors as the authors. For instance, because Adair and Tobin (2008) use the term "immigrant" to describe the parents in their study, we follow suit. This accounts for the variations in use of the terms migrant and immigrant throughout the chapter. We concentrate on literature published between 2000 and 2009, although we do move outside these years on occasion. Our preference was to restrict the literature to empirical research only, but given the small amount of research undertaken in the area of our focus, we draw on a range of publications, some of which relate to primary and secondary education. We do this because of the relevance of certain issues about primary and secondary schooling to young migrant and refugee children and early education contexts.

Initial scans of the literature revealed that most empirical studies have used qualitative methodologies such as case studies. Interview and observation studies have also been undertaken. We draw on a range of literature from around the globe but concentrate on studies from the U.S. and Australia (because we are Australian and the 2009 estimated net rate of migration to Australia is the highest of the countries cited above [CIA, 2009]). Examples are used to illustrate key points and there is no intention of generalizing these to all countries. For the purpose of this chapter we have chosen to focus on three areas of literature: curriculum; relationships with parents, and teacher education. Curriculum was selected because more research has been undertaken in primary and secondary schools about migrants and refugees than in early childhood settings. In addition, little has been written about the education of refugee children (Hamilton & Moore, 2004), and there is "little research about refugee children's educational experiences" (Rutter, 2005, p. 5). Curriculum is an area in which practitioners can make a difference when working with migrant and refugee children. A small section about different approaches to the use of the arts to support migrant and refugee children is included because art therapy is one approach often used as a technique with refugee children who have experienced trauma situations.

The second focus of our review of literature is relationships with parents. Like curriculum, this area of research is small and growing. Relationships with parents is a key focus of most early childhood programs. Developing positive relationships with migrant and refugee parents is an important part of the daily work of early childhood educators because there is a very real likelihood that migrant and refugee parents may hold different views about early childhood education than what their children experience in the programs they are attending (Adair & Tobin, 2008). Teacher education is the third topic of our review of literature. We have selected it because teacher preparation and in-service programs can not only teach about the importance of drawing on the rich cultural, social and cognitive resources that come with permanent new settlers, but also appropriate ways of going about this. As Florida (2004) pointed out, feeling safe and valued is paramount to migrants being able to contribute critically and creatively to their adopted society. However, feeling safe and valued requires understandings of culture that are "multidimensional and complicated and not simply [about] ... artefacts, food, and music" (Nieto, 2004, p. xxvii).

After reviewing the literature and considering relevant theoretical positions for each of these three topics, we discuss implications for researchers, policy makers and practitioners. The chapter concludes with some recommendations about young migrant and refugee children, their families and early childhood education. While research studies about refugee children are dominated by what Rutter (2005) calls the trauma literature, our focus remains educational and encompasses children of migrants and refugees, their families and the early childhood contexts in which they are engaged.

Transnational Migration

Transnational migration brings demographic changes that produce challenges for education and social services. Children from immigrant families have been described as "at-risk" due to the difficulties their parents can experience in finding employment and because, often, they have little knowledge of the official language and culture of their adopted country (OECD, 2006). According to the Australian Research Alliance for Children and Youth (ARACY) (2008) other reasons that make life difficult include "... being part of a minority group in Australia ... experiences prior to migration (for example refugee trauma), the different values and practices ...

the problems ... face[d] having qualifications and experience ratified, and the various forms of racism ... experience[d]" (p. 1). Poverty is another issue often faced by immigrant families (Adair & Tobin, 2008; OECD, 2006). Conditions for migrants and refugees are made more difficult when a number of these factors act in combination.

Racism seems to be something experienced by many migrants and refugees. In the UK, particular conceptualizations of 'race' are integral components of media and public debates about refugees and historically, about migrants (Rutter, 2005). Rutter argues that "older phenotypic notions of 'race' have survived in the popular imagination, as well as among some policy makers" (p. 10). She cites the British National Party as continuing to promulgate "ideas of distinct races, racial separation and repatriation of those who are not white" (p. 10). In Australia, addressing racism has attracted increased media attention and assumed heightened significance since the Sydney 'race' riots in December, 2005, and various other incidents such as a university professor making statements that "Sub-Saharan Africans have an average IQ of 70 to 75" and that "... an expanding black population is a surefire recipe for an increase in crime, violence and a wide range of other social problems" (Roberts, 2005). Like the UK, Australia has historically rooted conceptions about 'race' that transferred to assimilation policies and multicultural approaches to education. However, the more contemporary approach of anti-racist education was not adopted as fervently in Australia as it was in the UK, the U.S. and Canada. Much like the UK, current policies in Australia promote social cohesion and integration; expressions of which, in our view, are really assimilation by another name (see Ho, 2007).

There is a large body of literature about educational concerns associated with migrant children, but young migrant children are not often included in this research because it concentrates on secondary and primary schooling. For parents who have recently migrated, enrolling their child in an early childhood program can be the definitive moment when cultural values of their home and the adopted culture come into contact and, often, conflict (Multicultural Health Brokers Co-op [MHBC], 2004). This means that early childhood settings are often the first context in which migrant parents and their young children come face to face with differences between the culture of home and the public culture of their new country. The potential for tension between families and early childhood settings can arise when curricula are not responsive to children's cultural values and practices (see Adair & Tobin, 2008). In Western countries such as the UK, U.S., Canada and Australia, early childhood curricula have a history of being primarily Eurocentric or monocultural because they are based on developmental psychology, which means that young children from migrant backgrounds are likely to experience forms of marginalization in their early education experiences.

Curriculum

There is a distinct lack of relevant research identifying the educational needs of young children of migrant families (see Adams & Kirova, 2006a), and a growing and serious concern that simply providing regular mainstream education for these young children is not enough (Ariza, 2006).

In this section we consider literature that identifies refugee and migrant children as having special needs and provide field examples from research to illustrate how this notion is produced by teachers' actions and curriculum choices. In the literature, special needs tend to be associated with pre-migration experiences such as trauma. However, as Adams and Kirova (2006c) point out, relocation can also be traumatic, especially if the new arrivals are a "visible minority" (p. 199) in their new community. What follows considers literature about trauma; teachers, practitioners and children in early childhood settings; the use of the arts as curriculum initiatives, and transformational approaches to education.

That refugee children have special needs, especially those who have experienced trauma, is a point that continues to be made in regard to education generally, as well as early education. A corpus of literature addresses the social, medical, political, linguistic and educational issues of refugees, but little has been written about refugee children (see Hamilton & Moore, 2004). In the few studies that have investigated the needs of refugee children, the focus has been on children's traumatic experiences rather than their educational experiences (Rutter, 2005).

One approach to the inclusion of refugee children in early years classrooms is to provide practical strategies and advice for teachers, such as making classrooms more responsive to those who have experienced trauma (Szente, Hoot, & Taylor, 2006). In line with this approach, others have argued for refugee children to be considered as distinct from those who have migrated for other reasons, on the basis that the experiences of refugee children often involve trauma and therefore they have special needs (Waniganayake, 2001). In support of this, strategies put in place by teachers have also been examined, with one study investigating how teachers and practitioners responded to coping behaviors of children who have been traumatized—the results of which concluded that a range of appropriate strategies was developed that supported healing and provided a safe environment (see Sims, Hayden, Palmer, & Hutchins, 2000).

Common initiatives in early childhood settings include providing information about school policies and expectations, and parents' rights being translated into parents' native language. Well planned buddy programs have also met with success, particularly as social isolation and loneliness seem to be experienced by young immigrants irrespective of their racial, ethnic, and linguistic backgrounds (Kirova & Wu, 2002). Appropriate materials for children at various levels of knowledge should always be available and it is essential to provide teachers with adequate professional development opportunities to prepare them to be successful in working with migrant and refugee children and their families. One form of professional development proven to be a productive way to assist teachers to use effective strategies with newly arrived children is mentoring (Adams & Shambleau, 2006).

The extent to which children receive appropriate support can be impacted by the amount of information a teacher receives (or is willing to find out) about children's prior experiences. For example, by law in the U.S., teachers and administrators are not able to ask about immigration status (Szente & Hoot, 2006). These circumstances create particular difficulties for teachers in light of repeated cautions in the literature concerning assumptions about refugee children that can lead to further isolation in interactions and curriculum choices (Szente & Hoot, 2006). While a lack of information about children's backgrounds is problematic for staff, attempts should be made to find out about children's home and previous lives. This aligns with Adams and Shambleau's (2006) reminder about the well known teaching strategy of building on the knowledge and strengths that children bring to the classroom to ensure more inclusive practices are implemented. It is similar to learning about "families' funds of knowledge" (Gonzalez, Moll, & Amanti, 2005), which also refers to their strengths and resources, and how learning occurs in family contexts. This knowledge is then used to create teaching approaches that are linked to children's lives, local histories and community contexts. Nieto and Bode (2008) suggest vigorous family outreach and provide an example of a teacher who visits every family in the two weeks prior to school beginning to learn about the children who will be in her class.

Despite good intentions and effective strategies, the immigrant experience for children remains highly problematic because of learning a new language, the disruption to family life, and learning to live in another culture where things may be very different from home cultures and values (Suárez-Orozco & Suárez-Orozco, 2001). Regardless of the variance in cultural differences, isolating practices can and do occur as seen in a study of children who migrated from mainland China to Hong Kong with their families. The findings revealed that the children experienced segregation, prejudice and marginalization because of their accents and dialects, despite their ethnic similarity to Hong Kong Chinese (Rao & Yuen, 2006). This experience is consistent with migrants who are racially different from the dominant group (Li, 2001; Moreau, 2000). As in Rao and Yuen's study, the approach of school staff in the adjustment process for children is highly significant to educational outcomes for young children. One key difficulty is teachers' unchanging and monocultural conceptualizations of how schooling should be conducted in particular locations regardless of the changing demographic of the student population and the increasing complexity of society generally (see Chong, 2005). Recent research in primary schools in Hong Kong highlights why a monocultural approach is problematic, with reports from teachers working with newly arrived children from mainland China indicating that traditional approaches to teaching and learning are ineffective (Chong, 2005). One implication is that teachers are challenged to move beyond monoculturalism and adopt teaching and learning approaches that are successful with newly arrived children.

These examples show how personnel in early childhood settings may engage in practices that can lead to the marginalization of migrant and refugee children. While these practices can be extensions of the broader curriculum and may be inadvertent, it draws attention to the need for regular professional learning opportunities, appropriate resources and ongoing support for all staff. In an Australian study in before school contexts, Robinson & Jones Díaz (2006) reported that children were judged by staff according to their proficiency with English: "... children's ability to mix effectively with other children ... is measured against the ability to speak English ... what counts as cultural capital for these children is the ability to 'fit' into the monolingual 'English only' setting" (p. 115). Robinson & Jones Díaz found that the majority of long day care practitioner participants "constructed bilingual children's lack of English as a deficit and located children in discourses of 'need'" (p. 115). Accordingly, such children are marked as different (deficit) by practitioners. As Adams and Kirova (2006b) note, practitioners do not always have a correct understanding of children's language abilities and competence. Most migrant children act as language brokers for their parents and other family members and these skills are not always reflected in the classroom or academic achievement (Adams & Kirova, 2006b). McBrien (2003) advised against making assumptions that "students are slow or need special education services because they do not speak fluent English" (p. 78). This advice is exemplary in that it acts as a reminder of how easy it is to fall into deficit approaches, that is, equating a lack of English proficiency with cognitive or other inability.

Other relevant Australian research has shown how a boy (Nate) who had migrated from the Pacific Islands and was in Year 3 (aged 8 years) was categorized by his teachers as performing at a low level and struggling with literacy and numeracy (Grieshaber, 2008a). Nate completed a set computer task of making a maze at a more sophisticated level than all other children in the class. At the same time he engaged in an unsanctioned practice on another window, drawing one of the characters from *Mortal Kombat*, which resulted in a small group of boys watching in awe and discussing what he was drawing, as *Mortal Kombat* was unknown to them. Nate was astute enough to switch back to the maze window when the research assistant moved near him. Despite his multiliteracy talent, the teachers did not see or acknowledge his efforts at the maze, nor did they come to know about the complex digital artefact that he created at the same time as completing the set task. There is a high probability that he remained known by the teachers as a child who was struggling with literacy and numeracy. Other research in secondary and primary school shows that when teachers do interact with students, the questions they ask provide migrant and refugee students with limited ways of responding, which means that they are prevented from becoming actively involved in classroom discussion (Lee, 2002; McBrien, 2005).

The Arts and Children "In Need"

As a specific curriculum area, the arts have received attention in relation to young migrant and refugee children. Art therapy has been used as a technique for refugee children who have experienced trauma situations and are seen as having special needs because of their emotional and psychological fragility (Brunick, 1999). Being mindful of the conditions that enable migrants to flourish in their adopted country (Florida, 2004) means taking care that well intentioned humanitarian discourses do not continue to construct refugees as helpless and in need of support (Rutter, 2005).

In contrast to using art-as-therapy, McArdle and Spina (2007) used art as a language with refugee children aged about eight years in an attempt to move beyond positioning them as deficit because of their differences in "language, culture and social capital" (p. 50). Using art as a language is aimed at building children's identities and social capital as it enables children to communicate with each other and adults without the barrier of language. Art as a language may also be able to help children with language acquisition and other academic achievements, as well as build connections between the worlds of school and family. The children engaged in three visual arts workshops with a practising artist over a three-week period. They experienced the language of art, specific skills, techniques and artistic processes, and an appreciation of particular artists' works. The idea was to provide "exposure to, and experience in the arts as well as an avenue for creative expression" (p. 51). In contrast to popular views about the purpose of art-as-therapy, the children did not represent traumatic experiences that may have been part of their past. Instead they engaged in the set task with the resources and processes required for art-making, and communicated with each other, the artist and the researchers through sharing the art-making. The workshops enabled the teachers, children, artist and researchers to establish meaningful connections and for the children to produce unique three-dimensional portraits. Several of the children were able to communicate that they had hope for the future.

In a slightly different approach, Campey's (2002) suggestion is to use the expressive arts in whole class or whole school approaches in ways that have particular benefit for immigrant and refugee children coping with trauma. The claim is that the coping and resiliency skills of all children would be enhanced in a climate of reducing resources, more curriculum demands, and the increasing difficulty of providing programs for individual children. The strategies about which Campey talks are not unique. What is being suggested is that strategies promoted for migrant and refugee children (such as buddy programs, ensuring that all children can see themselves in the curriculum, recognizing celebrations, providing translations and opportunities for children's self-expression and so on), may benefit all children if used as part of a whole school approach. This idea has merit and is worth considering as others have made similar suggestions. For example, one line of argument that has been pursued by some authors is the transformation of schooling so that it is oriented to the diversity of educational needs of all students, and in the process respects their social and cultural origins, and the abilities they bring to the setting (Blanco & Takemoto, 2006; Neito & Bode, 2008).

To many people, transformation means something monolithic (or systemic) and even revolutionary, which also suggests the idea of significant events that cause change in a relatively short amount of time. Contrary to this idea, Nieto and Bode (2008) locate educational transformation as something that is ongoing and "in progress", which takes time and is firmly within the province of those who work with children and families in classrooms on a daily basis. Globalization has resulted in the presence of migrant and refugee children in many early childhood contexts. While cultural, linguistic and ethnic diversity is not uncommon in early childhood settings, what might be different is the increasing diversity of the source countries of migrants and refugees. Such changes present ongoing challenges to early childhood practitioners, classrooms and schools; curriculum, pedagogies and assessment; organization and management, and the socio-political context in which schools are located.

The idea that transformation is part of what happens on a daily basis in classrooms is a vote of confidence in practitioners but requires sustained hard work. Nieto and Bode (2008) provide many practical strategies for classroom practitioners which are related to all facets of classroom life. These include focusing on human differences and similarities in the preschool years, having high expectations of all children, using the curriculum critically, using pedagogies that engage children in meaningful ways, and using inclusive disciplinary strategies. Among other ideas, Nieto and Bode also suggest respecting student differences, and making differences and similarities an explicit part of the curriculum. This includes talking about skin colour, hair texture and other physical differences to teach children that it is unacceptable to laugh at new class members who speak with an accent; that dark-skinned children can be the princess in role plays, and that it is objectionable for children to refuse to play with dark-skinned dolls because they are "dirty" (see Derman-Sparks & Ramsey, 2006). Many of these strategies are not part of everyday practice in early childhood settings, particularly those that are prefaced on notions of developmental psychology and normative understandings of children's development (these are discussed further in the section about Teacher Education). The presence of migrant and refugee children in early childhood settings is also a unique opportunity to learn about and work with their families.

Relationships with Parents and Families

There is much emphasis in early childhood education about parents as partners in the education process and about transition to school. However, both these bodies of literature (parents as partners and transition to school) do not deal comprehensively or specifically with developing relationships with migrant and refugee parents. Because of this, early childhood programs that serve children of migrants and refugees though generally well intended, may not consider perspectives of the parents. Little research has involved parents of young immigrant and refugee children (see MHBC, 2004; Pryor, 2001) and even less has consulted migrant parents about their values, beliefs, expectations and concerns regarding their young children's education.

The small but growing body of research about migrant parents, their children and early childhood education employs mostly qualitative approaches. On the whole, migrant families tend to value education (Suárez-Orozco & Suárez-Orozco, 2001) even though they may have different opinions and beliefs about specific aspects of it. For example, immigrant parents may be unfamiliar with being involved in their child's educational experiences and may have low levels of schooling themselves (Hernandez, 2004). It is possible that some migrant parents may have had no prior contact with educational settings, while others choose not to become involved in their child's education. Others may not be familiar with the style of instruction (Li, 2006) and some may not be able to communicate with staff or speak openly with them. Some may believe that teachers are the education experts and there is no need to become involved, and others may disagree with testing and assessment procedures (Adams & Kirova, 2006a). Conversely, migrant parents may be familiar with school routines and procedures in the country of settlement such as testing and a competitive academic environment. There are wide parental differences and they are attributable to "culture, prior experiences, and individual personalities" (Adams & Kirova, 2006a p. 9). The teachers in the study undertaken by Adams and Shambleau (2006) recognized the importance of reaching out to newly arrived parents because of cultural differences, and the significance of families and schools working together. However, the case study of a Sudanese refugee family in Buffalo, NY depicted the way in which parents, who were already marginalized because of their 'race' and refugee status, were positioned as powerless by the school their children attended (Li, 2006). The parents were unable to effect any changes to the programs their children experienced and were also excluded from decisions made about their children's education. Canadian research has concluded that too often, programmatic reforms for young children are initiated without input from parents (Pacini-Ketchabaw & Scheter, 2003), and this is particularly true when the parents are migrants.

One approach that has taken parental perspectives into account is the work comparing ideas about preschool held by teachers and immigrant parents (Adair & Tobin, 2008; Tobin, 2004; Tobin, Arzubiaga, & Mantovani, 2007). Tobin (2004) argues that preschool programs are able to serve immigrants better when parents, teachers and other stakeholders talk to each other. The aim of comparing ideas held by immigrant parents and others is to act as "a catalyst for dialogue among parents, practitioners, scholars and policymakers about the problems and possibilities of creating preschool programs that reflect the values and beliefs of both immigrant communities and of the societies to which they have immigrated" (Adair & Tobin, 2008, p. 137). This research is still underway but some ideas that have emerged to date include:

- In many cases immigrants parents hold different views about quality and best practice;
- The technique of watching and discussing a video of a day in the preschool is helpful for facilitating ongoing discussion between staff and parents, and with careful structuring adversarial and contentious situations can be avoided;
- The idea that "We need to learn to hear immigrants' parents expressions of desire for their children to become Americans as something other than assimilationism or capitulation to the agenda of the right" (Adair & Tobin, 2008, p. 149);
- Many teachers of immigrant children do not fully understand the experiences of poverty or the "racism and the discrimination they face, and the feeling of alienation they experience in response to the racism" (p. 149). Even when aware, early childhood staff often do not know what to do about it.

Experiences of racism and discrimination occur inside early childhood educational settings as well as outside them. For staff, dealing with these issues means "working consciously against their own biases and those of the students" (Kirova & Adams, 2006, p. 324). It also means understanding how identity, difference, power and privilege are all interconnected within the socio-political context of society and that decisions about education are never neutral (Nieto & Bode, 2008).

Teacher Education

In teacher education programs course work related to the education of children from culturally and linguistically backgrounds can be limited (see Early & Winton, 2001). When coursework about children from diverse backgrounds is present, it is often located in content about developmental psychology or child study, generally as an adjunct to the topic of "inclusion". For over 15 years critiques of developmental psychology have revealed how normative understandings about children's strengths and areas of need are constructed from uncontested, Eurocentric ideas of developmentalism. Against developmentalism, elements of "difference" are interpreted as developmental delay or deficit (see Burman, 1994; Lubeck, 1996; Ryan & Grieshaber, 2005).

For refugee children in particular, perpetuations of trauma or "at-risk" discourses position them as helpless and traumatised and in need of support from "mainstream" agencies and services including education. The positioning of refugee children as in-need is also evident in the contemporary humanitarian discourse which perpetuates notions of culture as different to that of the mainstream (Rutter, 2005). When this occurs, notions of culture and difference are attached to deficit models rather than being viewed as a resource in mainstream channels (Kalantzis, 2005).

Despite the corpus of work that critiques normative understandings of education and children's development, pre-service teacher education programs often present course work that is grounded in normative or Euro-centric models of teaching and learning (Hickling-Hudson, 2004). Normative models do not offer pre-service teachers extended explorations about curricula that attend to intersections of 'race,' ethnicity, gender, class and sexuality. In early childhood degree programs in particular, subjects about children's development and the inclusion of children with additional needs (of which 'cultural needs' are an adjunct) and which are premised on developmentalism, are more often core or compulsory units, while subjects focussed on cultural diversity are elective and located in broader faculty offerings separate to the early childhood degree program. In instances whereby critiques of developmental psychology are included in course work, preservice teachers may still have little access to exemplars of practice that illustrate transformative approaches to responding to cultural diversity in early childhood curricula (Ryan & Grieshaber, 2005).

Identity Work in Teacher Education

One growing component of teacher education course work related to cultural diversity is 'identity work'. The growth of this field is evident from the plethora of studies conducted since the 1990s that have investigated how and why teacher education courses should prepare pre-service teachers (completing 3–4 year bachelor degrees or graduate diplomas) to teach diverse student populations (for examples see Aveling, 2006; Bernhard, 1995; Brandon, 2003; Cockrell, Placier, Cockrell, & Middleton, 1999; Duesterberg, 1998; Hickling-Hudson, 2004; Jones, 1999; Lawrence & Bunche, 1996; Lin Goodwin & Genor, 2008; Obidah, 2000; Rosenberg, 2004; Santoro & Allard, 2005; Siwatu, 2007; Sugrue, 1997; Tatum, 1992; Vavrus, 2002). These studies generally focus on the need for pre-service teachers to be supported to challenge cultural assumptions in a range of contexts and critically examine their personal beliefs and positioning in society using a cultural framework. These studies vary in their aims, goals and successes. For us, the issue with racism, discrimination and pre-service teachers remains teacher identity formation, or, as Kirova and Adams (2006) have pointed out, "working consciously against their own biases and those of the students" (p. 324). This is by no means easy and requires ongoing work and support.

The focus on teacher identity formation draws from a cultural approach taken up by theorists and researchers interested in understanding how preservice teachers' cultural backgrounds influence their attitudinal stance and ideas about pedagogical practices they intend to employ in the classroom. Because the demographic of the pre-service teaching population in many Western nations comprises white, middle-class females (as seen in the Australian context), identity work has focused largely on how white teachers develop an understanding about their own ethnicity and its impact on how they view and (will) interact with people of a cultural background different to their own. As Graue (2005) states, "the cultural perspective works to identify the tacit, normative, socially developed conceptions of identity and affiliation that shape meaning making for individuals within groups" (p. 159). In this growing body of work, meaning making relates to white individuals' conceptions of identity within the mainstream group.

For pre-service teachers, cross-cultural identity work is important because it creates the likelihood of crisis and confrontation—or "spaces" of confusion and doubt from which possibilities for critical explorations and change are produced (Schick, 2000). In some teacher education programs, ethnicity related course work may be undertaken in conjunction with explorations of interrelated identity constructions that frame individuals' understanding of self including class, gender and sexuality. Combined, all of these perspectives allow for important autobiographical work, although it is critical for this work to be famed sociologically as well as psychologically to ensure that as individuals, pre-service teachers develop understandings of self *in relation to* connections and interactions with others and institutions in their personal and professional lives (Phillips, 2005). This is particularly important for white identity construction work as findings from research in this area often report on the extent to which individual bodies acknowledge their white ethnic status, not inclusive of the ways in which awareness of the influence of their cultural background is also embodied in pedagogical actions and interactions with children and families in specific educational contexts.

Teacher Education and Parental Involvement

When identity construction work focuses on interactions with others as well as self, autobiographical explorations can also support pre-service teachers to explore their disposition toward, and images of, children and families. Of particular salience is their ideas, wonderings and fears about interacting and 'partnering' with children and families from cultural backgrounds different from their own (see Flanigan, 2007). As 'partnership' discourses are given much space in early childhood education course work and literature, pre-service teachers' beliefs about parental involvement and the positioning of parents in the teacher/parent relationship should align with explorations of notions of self in relation to others.

In two recent studies about pre-service teachers' beliefs about relationships with families conducted by Flanigan (2007) and Graue (2005), findings provide insight into how pre-service teachers' beliefs and ideas about partnerships with families contribute to the fragility of home/school relations. While many factors combine to produce a fragile state, including institutionalised practices, both studies call for greater involvement from faculty to provide components in degree programs that afford pre-service teachers opportunities to develop relationships with families in the local community throughout their degree program. It is real-world interactions between pre-service teachers and families that "can provide broader awareness of the issues families face in schooling" (Graue, 2005, p. 183). When faculty commit to parent and community involvement as part of students' clinical experiences (Flanigan, 2007), students have increased opportunities to make links between families' experiences and theoretical concepts that underpin understandings about home/school links (Graue, 2005). This approach to collaborations with families aligns with a service learning model that focuses as much on students as people as potential teachers—a key component also seen in autobiographical work.

While a focus on autobiographical work is critical to pre-service teachers' identity development (Lin Goodwin & Genor, 2008), there will always be a need to be wary of imbalances in the extent to which pre-service teachers' notions of self are disrupted and the extent to which the content they are offered in a degree program comes under greater scrutiny. In drawing from the example provided earlier, it is pertinent to consider Heyning's (2001) viewpoint that "scientific knowledge" (such as developmentalism) provides spaces for pre-service teachers to construct themselves as [future] "experts"—able to make claims about and act as experts in their professional role. The notion of expert is linked to broader discourses of professionalism in which there is an expectation that professional knowledge is located in scientific or standardised realms (Osgood, 2006). In the role of expert, teachers are positioned to rely on objective forms of knowledge that reduce notions of family involvement to that of secondary forms of interaction centered on the idea of parents as clients rather than partners. As stated by Graue (2005), "objective decisions come at the cost of separation from clients and a devaluing of the knowledge of families" (p. 178).

For pre-service teachers autobiographical work can be undermined by overriding influences in course content that create opposing notions of what it is to be and do as an early childhood professional. For children and families from migrant and refugee backgrounds, pre-service teachers' preparation and resulting constructions of self/other and their professional role will impact significantly the foundation on which home/center relationships are forged and how they work (or not) in the interests of both parties. If foundations for relationships devalue the knowledge and participation of families, then "teachers have little to draw on but their own experiences" (Graue, 2005, p. 183). Given that the majority of early childhood teachers are socialised within Eurocentric frameworks, and autobiographical work in teacher education is most often limited to singular subject offerings, these circumstances will contribute to oppressive forms of interactions between teachers and families from diverse backgrounds as well as approaches to teaching and learning afforded to children in early childhood contexts in the future.

Implications

Many nations are affected by transnational migration and educational systems and must respond to these changes and offer the best education possible. That educational institutions and staff have been, and remain challenged by transnational migration is undeniable. The research and examples presented here demonstrate that while early childhood practitioners may require new strategies for dealing with diverse populations who bring a varying range of pre-migration experiences, they should also be aware of the effect of humanitarian discourses. As Rutter (2005) acknowledges about refugees, pity is the "outcome of humanitarian discourses" (p. 9) and succeeds in strengthening the idea that refugees are different from the rest of the population because they are traumatized and dysfunctional. A key understanding about migrant and refugee children is that they do not represent a homogeneous group: "Diversity exists in every group, whether refugees or nations, whether of a single ethnic or cultural group or of a multicultural group" (Kirova & Adams, 2006, p. 323). And while educational settings alone cannot be held responsible for the socialization and acculturation of immigrant children, it is practitioners, educators, early childhood and school contexts that are the "key to facilitating the socialization and acculturation of immigrant children" (Adams & Kirova, 2006a, p. 2). Increasing fundamental theoretical and professional knowledge about the learning needs of particular populations of young children and their families will help to develop high quality and high equity education that aims for success for all students (Luke, Weir & Woods, 2008). We conclude the chapter with suggestions for researchers, policy makers and practitioners, which are not exhaustive.

Suggestions for Researchers

- Invite migrant/refugee parents to be active participants in research;
- Invite migrant and refugee children to be active participants in research;
- Focus on very young children because of the importance of the early years for children's identity and overall development;
- Research the types of professional development that suit early childhood practitioners when exploring cultural diversity;
- Research curriculum, pedagogy, assessment and disciplinary practices that practitioners find successful;
- Research the factors that create successful experiences for young migrant children and their families in early childhood settings.

Suggestions for Policy Makers

- Provide greater scope in coursework about children from diverse backgrounds in curriculum in teacher education;
- Involve, advocate and endorse the involvement of migrant and refugee parents in local and broad policy decisions;
- Advocate for and endorse the involvement of migrant and refugee parents in decision-making at all levels about the curriculum, pedagogy and assessment, as well as in decisions that involve their children;
- Acknowledge the real life experiences of migrants and refugees in terms of the poverty, racism, discrimination and alienation that many face on a daily basis and provide suggestions for how early childhood practitioners might work productively with these factors;
- Recognise that migrants and refugees are not homogeneous and that diversity and difference exist in any group;

- Identify examples of individual and institutional racism and provide suggestions for non-racist practices.

Suggestions for Practitioners

- Learn about individual and institutional racism and discrimination;
- Learn about deficit theories and how they position difference of any sort;
- Learn about your own biases and those of the children in your class, and work conscientiously against them (Kirova & Adams, 2006, p. 324);
- Recognize that migrants are not homogeneous and that diversity and difference exist in any group;
- Focus on strengths and abilities that children and families bring so that culture is viewed as a resource rather than a deficit (see Gonzalez et al., 2005; Kalantzis, 2005);
- Make differences and similarities an explicit part of the daily curriculum (see Nieto & Bode, 2008);
- Recognize that there is no one 'right' way of teaching migrant and refugee children and that a variety of approaches and resources are needed;
- Identify children's learning preferences and use them pedagogically;
- Take up relevant professional development opportunities;
- Share what works with other practitioners;
- Involve and consult meaningfully with migrant and refugee parents in localised practices.

Conclusion

This chapter has reviewed literature about migrants and refugee children and their families, and early childhood educational settings. It has pointed to significant demographic changes to early childhood education contexts that have arisen because of changed global circumstances. At the same time, challenges to the early childhood field provided by these changed circumstances have been highlighted, as have examples of responses in the areas of curriculum, relationships with parents and families, and teacher education. Curriculum and relationships with parents and families are tangible and within the jurisdiction of those who work with children and families on a daily basis. We have faith that practitioners working at the interface with children and families in these unique conditions are more likely to create responsive practices that are potentially transformative, simply because pedagogy and curriculum are shaped by the context as well as the specific children and families with whom practitioners are working (Grieshaber, 2008b). As much of the literature reviewed in this chapter has suggested, starting small is the key. However, there are no easy solutions or recipes to follow that will produce guaranteed results, mainly because the sociopolitical context of society (and therefore education) has altered.

The socio-political environments in which many early childhood practitioners and teacher educators were raised are monocultural. These circumstances underscore the need for practitioners and teacher educators to learn more about the lives and educational needs of migrants and refugees, and also confront their own racism and biases. Teacher education provides a context in which current and future early childhood professionals can commit to learning about a variety of perspectives in order to recognize and acknowledge that there are many ways of seeing and understanding the world. The road for early childhood teacher education is paved with good intentions but these alone cannot engender the changes required in pre-service teacher education. New theorizing about migrant and refugee children and families that affords a view of difference as a resource must permeate content areas in teacher education in place of developmental discourses. When new theorizing is given adequate space in teacher education, current and future early childhood professionals can learn about the ways in which they frame and respond to the educational needs of migrant and refugee children, and how these responses can impact the experiences of migrant and refugee children and their families in early childhood settings.

Note

1. A refugee has been assessed by a relevant national government of international authority such as the United Nations Office of the High Commissioner for Refugees and meets the criteria set out by the *Convention Relating to the Status of Refugees 1951* (Refugee Convention). Asylum seekers claim refugee status but have not been assessed.

References

Adair, J., & Tobin, J. (2008). Listening to the voices of immigrant parents. In C. Genishi & A. Lin Goodwin (Eds.), *Diversities in early childhood education: Rethinking and doing* (pp. 137–150). New York: Routledge.

Adams, L. D. & Kirova, A. (2006a). Introduction to Part I: Global migration and the education of children. In L. D. Adams & A. Kirova (Eds.), *Global migration and education: Schools, children, and families* (pp. 1–12). Mahwah, NJ: Lawrence Erlbaum.

Adams, L. D. & Kirova, A. (2006b). Introduction to Part II: They are here: Newcomers in the schools. In L. D. Adams & A. Kirova (Eds.), *Global migration and education: Schools, children, and families* (pp. 83–86). Mahwah, NJ: Lawrence Erlbaum.

Adams, L. D. & Kirova, A. (2006c). Introduction to Part IV: Far from home with fluctuating hopes. In L. D. Adams & A. Kirova (Eds.), *Global migration and education: Schools, children, and families* (pp. 199–202). Mahwah, NJ: Lawrence Erlbaum.

Adams, L.D., & Shambleau, K.M. (2006). Teachers' children's and parents' perspectives on newly arrived children's adjustment to elementary school. In L.D. Adams & A. Kirova (Eds.). (2006).

Global migration and education: Schools, children, and families (pp. 87–102). Mahwah, NJ: Lawrence Erlbaum.

Ariza, E.N.W. (2006). *Not for ESOL teachers.* Sydney: Pearson.

Australian Research Alliance for Children & Youth (ARACY). (2008). *Achieving outcomes for children and families from culturally and linguistically diverse backgrounds.* Centre for Social Research, Edith Cowan University, Western Australia.

Aveling, N. (2006). 'Hacking at our very roots': Rearticulating white racial identity within the context of teacher education. *Race, Ethnicity and Education, 9*(3), 261–274.

Bernhard, J. K. (1995). Child development, cultural diversity, and the professional training of early childhood educators. *Canadian Journal of Education, 20*(4), 415–430.

Blanco, R., & Takemoto, C.Y. (2006). Inclusion in schools in Latin America and the Caribbean: The case of the children of Haitian descent in the Dominican Republic. In L. D. Adams & A. Kirova, (Eds.), *Global migration and education: Schools, children and families* (pp. 53–66). New Jersey: Lawrence Erlbaum.

Brandon, W. W. (2003). Toward a white teachers' guide to playing fair: Exploring the cultural politics of multicultural teaching. *Qualitative Studies in Education, 16*(1), 31–50.

Brunick, L. L. (1999). Listen to my picture: Art as a survival tool for immigrant and refugee students. *Art Education, 52*(4), 12–17.

Burman, E. (1994). Deconstructing developmental psychology. London: Routledge. *Childhood, 7*(1), 5–14.

Campey, J. (2002). Immigrant children in our classrooms: Beyond ESL. *Education Canada, 42*(3), no page range.

Chong, S. (2005). The logic of Hong Kong teachers: An exploratory study of their teaching culturally diverse students. *Teaching Education, 16*(2), 117–129.

Central Intelligence Agency (CIA). (2009). The world factbook. Accessed 7 June 2009. https://www.cia.gov/library/publications/the-world-factbook/geos/ca.html

Cockrell, K. S., Placier, P. L., Cockrell, D. H., & Middleton, J. N. (1999). Coming to terms with "diversity" and "multiculturalism" in teacher education: Learning about our students, changing our practice. *Teaching and Teacher Education, 15*, 351–366.

Cummins, J. (2004). Foreword. In S. Nieto, *Affirming diversity: The sociopolitical context of multicultural education.* (4th ed.) (pp. xv–xvii). Boston, MA: Allyn and Bacon.

Department of Immigration and Multicultural and Indigenous Affairs [DIMA]. (2005). *Fact sheet 60: Australia's refugee and humanitarian program* [Online]. Retrieved February 4, 2009, from: http://www.immi.gov.au/facts/60refugee.htm

Derman-Sparks, L., & Ramsey, P. G., with Edwards, J. O. (2006). *What if all the kids are white? Anti-bias and multicultural education with young children and families.* New York: Teachers College Press.

Duesterberg, L. M. (1998). Rethinking culture in the pedagogy and practices of preservice teachers. *Teaching and Teacher Education, 14*(5), 497–512.

Early, D. M., & Winton, P. J. (2001). Preparing the workforce: Early childhood teacher preparation at 2- and 4-year institutions of higher education. *Early Childhood Research Quarterly, 16,* 285–306.

Florida, R. L. (2004). *The rise of the creative class : and how it's transforming work, leisure, community and everyday life.* New York: Basic Books.

Flanigan, C. B. (2007). Preparing preservice teachers to partner with parents and communities: An analysis of college of education faculty focus groups. *The School Community Journal, 17*(2), 89–109.

Global Commission on International Migration. (2005). *Final report: Migration in an interconnected world: New directions for action.* Retrieved March 5, 2009, from: http://www.gcim.org/en/finalreport.html

Gonzalez, N. E., Moll, L. C., & Amanti, C. (2005). (Eds.). *Funds of knowledge: Theorizing practices in households and classrooms.* Mahwah, NJ: Lawrence Erlbaum.

Graue, E. (2005). Theorizing and describing preservice teachers' images of families and schooling. *Teachers College Record, 107*(1), 157–185.

Grieshaber, S. (2008a). *Marginalization, making meaning and mazes.* In C. Genishi & A. Lin Goodwin (Eds.), *Diversities in early childhood education: Rethinking and doing* (pp. 83–101). New York: RoutledgeFalmer.

Grieshaber, S. (2008b). Interrupting stereotypes: Teaching and the education of young children. *Early Education and Development,* 19(3), 505–518.

Hamilton, R. & Moore, D. (2004). *Educational interventions for refugee children: Theoretical perspectives and implementing best practice.* London: RoutledgeFalmer.

Hernandez, D. (2004). Children and youth in immigrant families: Demographic, social, and educational issues. In J. A. Banks & C. A. McGee Banks (Eds.), *Handbook of research on multicultural education* (pp. 404–419). San Francisco: Jossey Bass.

Heyning, K. E. (2001). Teacher education reform in the shadow of state-university links: The cultural politics of texts. In T.S. Popkewitz, B.M. Franklin & M.A. Pereyra (Eds.), *Cultural history and education: Critical essays on knowledge and schooling* (pp. 289–312). New York: Routledge.

Hickling-Hudson, A. (2004). Educating teachers for cultural diversity and social justice. In G. Hernes & M. Martin (Eds.), *Planning for diversity: Education in multiethnic and multicultural societies* (pp. 270–307). Paris: International Institute for Education Planning (UNESCO).

Ho, C. (2007). *Father still knows best: The new paternalism and Australian multicultural policy.* Paper presented to the Social Justice in Early Childhood conference: Curriculum as activism. Sydney. 24 March.

Jones, R. (1999). *Teaching racism or tackling it: Multicultural stories from white beginning teachers.* London: Trentham.

Kalantzis, M. (2005). Conceptualising diversity—Defining the scope of multicultural policy, education and research. *Australian Mosaic,* 10(2), 6–9.

Kirova, A. & Adama, L. D. (2006). Lessons learned and implications for the future. In L. D. Adams & A. Kirova (Eds.), *Global migration and education: Schools, children, and families* (pp. 321–326). Mahwah, NJ: Lawrence Erlbaum.

Kirova, A., & Wu, J. (2002). Peer acceptance, learning English as a second language and identity formation in children of recent Chinese immigrants. In A. Richardson, M. Wyness & A. Halvorsen (Eds.), *Exploring cultural perspectives, integration and globalization* (pp. 171–190). Edmonton, AB: ICRN Press.

Lawrence, S. M., & Bunche, T. (1996). Feeling and dealing: Teaching white students about racial privilege. *Teaching and Teacher Education, 12*(5), 531–542.

Lee, S. (2002). Learning "America": Hmong American high school students. *Education and Urban Society, 34*, 233–246.

Li, G. (2006). Crossing cultural borders in the United States: A case study of a Sudanese refugee family's experience with urban schooling. In L. D. Adams & A. Kirova (Eds.), *Global migration and education: Schools, children, and families* (pp. 237–249). Mahwah, NJ: Lawrence Erlbaum.

Li, P. (2001). The racial subtext in Canada's immigration discourse. *Journal of International Migration and Integration, 21*(1), 77–97.

Lin Goodwin, A., & Genor, M. (2008). Disrupting the taken-for-granted: Autobiographical analysis in preservice teacher education. In C. Genishi & A. Lin Goodwin (Eds.), *Diversities in early childhood education: Rethinking and doing* (pp. 201–218). New York: Routledge.

Lubeck, S. (1996). Deconstructing 'child development knowledge' and 'teacher preparation'. *Early Childhood Research Quarterly, 11*(2), 147–167.

Luke, A., Weir, K., & Woods, A. (2008). *Development of a set of principles to guide a P-12 syllabus framework: A Report to the Queensland Studies Authority, Queensland, Australia.* The State of Queensland (Queensland Studies Authority): Brisbane.

McArdle, F., & Spina, N. (2007). Children of refugee families as artists: Bridging the past, present and future. *Australian Journal of Early Childhood, 32*(4), 50–53.

McBrien, J. L. (2003). A second chance: Helping refugee students succeed in school. *Educational Leadership, 61*(2), 76–79.

McBrien, J. L. (2005). Educational needs and barriers for refugee students in the United States: A review of literature. *Review of Educational Research, 75*(3), 329–364.

Moreau, G. (2000). Some elements of comparison between the integration politics of Germany, Canada, France, Great Britain, Italy and the Netherlands. *Journal of International Migration and Integration, 1*(1), 101–120.

Multicultural Health Brokers Co-op (MHBC). (2004). *Mapping the life experiences of refugee and immigrant families with preschool children: A research report presented to the Early Childhood Development Initiative,* Edmonton, Alberta, Canada. Multicultural Family Connections Project.

Nieto, S. (2004). *Affirming diversity: The sociopolitical context of multicultural education.* (4th ed.). Boston, MA: Allyn and Bacon.

Nieto, S. & Bode, P. (2008). (5th ed.). Affirming diversity: The sociopolitical context of mukticultural education. Boston, MA: Pearson.

Obidah, J. E. (2000). Mediating boundaries of race, class, and professional authority as a critical multiculturalist. *Teachers College Record, 102*(6), 1035–1060.

OECD. (2006). *Starting strong II: Early childhood education and care.* OECD: Paris, France.

Osgood, J. (2006). Deconstructing professionalism in early childhood education: Resisting the regulatory gaze. *Contemporary Issues in Early Childhood, 7*(1), 5–14.

Pacini-Ketchabaw, V., & Scheter, S. (2002). Engaging the discourse of diversity: Educator's frameworks for working with linguistic and cultural difference. *Contemporary Issues in Early Childhood, 3*(3), 400–414.

Phillips, J. (2005). Exploring the possibilities. In J. Phillips and J. Lampert (Eds.), *Introductory Indigenous studies in education: The importance of knowing* (pp. 1–8). Frenchs Forest, New South Wales: Pearson Education Australia.

Pryor, C. B. (2001). New immigrants and refugees in American schools: Multiple voices. *Childhood Education, 77*(5), 275–283.

Rao, N., & Yuen, M. (2006). Listening to children: Voices of newly arrived immigrants from the Chinese mainland to Hong Kong. In L. D. Adams & A. Kirova (Eds.), *Global migration and education: Schools, children, and families* (pp. 139– 150). New Jersey: Lawrence Erlbaum.

Roberts, G. (2005). 'Racist' professor cautioned, but launches new attack. *The Australian.* 21 July.

Robinson, K. H., & Jones Diaz, C. (2006). *Diversity and difference in early childhood education: Issues for theory and practice.* Maidenhead, UK: Open University Press.

Rosenberg, P. M. (2004). Color blindness in teacher education: An optical delusion. In M. Fine, L. Weis, L. Powell Pruitt & A. Burns (Eds.), *Off white* (pp. 257– 272). New York: Routledge.

Rutter, J. (2005). *Refugee children in the UK.* Maidenhead, England: Open University Press.

Ryan, S. K. & Grieshaber, S. (2005) Shifting from developmental to postmodern practices in early childhood teacher education. *Journal of Teacher Education 56*(1), 34–45.

Santoro, N., & Allard, A. (2005). (Re)Examining identities: Working with diversity in the pre-service teaching experience. *Teaching and Teacher Education, 21,* 863–873.

Schick, C. (2000). 'By virtue of being white': Resistance in anti-racist pedagogy. *Race, Ethnicity and Education, 3*(1), 83–102.

Sims, M., Hayden, J., Palmer, G., & Hutchins, T. (2000). Working in early childhood settings with children who have experienced refugee or war-related trauma. *Australian Journal of Early Childhood, 25*(4), 41–46.

Siwatu, K. O. (2007). Preservice teachers' culturally responsive teaching self-efficacy and outcome expectancy beliefs. *Teaching and Teacher Education, 23*(7), 1086–1101.

Suarez-Orozco, C., & Suarez-Orozco, M. (2001). *Children of immigration.* Cambridge, MA: Harvard University Press.

Sugrue, C. (1997). Student teachers' lay theories and teaching identities: Their implications for professional development. *European Journal of Teacher Education, 20*(3), 213–225.

Szente, J. & Hoot, J. (2006). Rxploring the needs of refugee children in our schools. In L. D. Adams & A. Kirova (Eds.), *Global migration and education: Schools, children, and families* (pp. 219–235). Mahwah, NJ: Lawrence Erlbaum.

Szente, J., Hoot, J., & Taylor, D. (2006). Responding to the special needs of refugee children: Practical ideas for teachers. *Early Childhood Education Journal, 34*(1), 15–20.

Tatum, B. D. (1992). Talking about race, learning about racism: The application of racial identity development theory in the classroom. *Harvard Educational Review, 62*(1), 1–24.

Tobin, J. (2004). *Children of immigrants in early childhood settings in five countries: A study of parent and staff beliefs.* Unpublished paper submitted to the Bernard van Leer Foundation.

Tobin, J., Arzubiaga, A., & Mantovani, S. (2007). Entering into dialogue with immigrant parents. *Early Childhood Matters, 108,* 34–38.

Vavrus, M. (2002). *Connecting teacher identity formation to culturally responsive teaching.* Paper presented at the National Association of Multicultural Education Annual Meeting, Washington, DC, October 30–November 3, 2002.

Waniganayake, M. (2001). From playing with guns to playing with rice: The challenges of working with refugee children. An Australian perspective. *Childhood Education, 77*(5), 289–294.

Refugee Children's Adaptation to American Early Childhood Classrooms

A Narrative Inquiry

Megan A. Prior and Tricia Niesz

Over 300,000 men, women, and children are currently seeking asylum or have been granted refugee status in the United States. Of course, that number more than triples when we look at refugee migration globally. Over 10 million refugees have looked to other countries to provide a safe haven during times of conflict or persecution in their native countries (United Nations High Commissioner for Refugees [UNHCR], 2011). The large population of refugees in the U.S., as well as around the globe, creates challenges for educators as they determine the best ways to embrace refugee youth and adapt their classroom practices to provide an education that meets the needs of all students. As schools across the U.S. continue to become more diverse, the schooling of refugees is becoming a prominent topic in the field of education.

Educational research on refugee youth and schooling has been critiqued for conflating the adaptation experiences of refugees with those of immigrants (McBrien, 2005).[1] Although both refugees and immigrants are permanently living in a new

---

1   It is important to recognize the difference between a refugee and an immigrant. Refugees have fled their native country due to persecution, war, or other violence. They have sought and received asylum in the country in which they are currently living. Immigrants are those who have left their native country voluntarily. Those who are granted refugee status further differ from asylum seekers who are in some stage of seeking a sanctuary in a country other than their native land. Asylum seekers have not yet been granted the legal rights in their host country as those who have attained the refugee status. The study described in this paper focuses on those who have been granted refugee status.

country, immigrants choose to leave their homeland, whereas refugees often leave due to per-secution, war, or violence. Current research also tends to focus on adult or adolescent refugees and is often removed from educational settings (Hamilton & Moore, 2004; McBrien, 2005). Com-paratively less research examines young refugee children's experiences from their perspectives as they adapt to new settings and situations, especially in the specific context of schools. As Hamilton and Moore (2004) suggest, "there is a paucity of material specifically concerned with refugee children, and only a small proportion of this is about school-based interventions and programmes" (p. xi).

In response to this gap, we designed a study to examine the experiences of refugee children and their families, as shared through their narratives. Our goal was to understand Karen refugees' views on American schooling. More specifically, we were interested in learning how young refugee children and their families narrate their early experiences of American schooling. Megan Prior, the first author, conducted a narrative inquiry into the stories of adaptation to early childhood classrooms told by three young Karen students from Myanmar who were attending Preschool and Kindergarten in the United States. The purpose of our study was to generate understand-ings of the children's views of the early schooling experiences and how these were expressed in narratives. As the teacher of these children, Megan collected children's stories and artwork, which were complemented by family interviews, to investigate what the narratives revealed about the children's adaptation to new communities and new schooling as they entered their first years of formal education.

During the course of this study, Megan conducted initial interviews with the families to provide an oral history of the families' experiences prior to becoming refugees, during the transition, and after arrival in the United States with refugee status. Then, the students created drawings and told stories to share their experiences at school. A second round of family interviews later in the study produced narratives of the families' perceived understanding of their child's adapta-tion to the school and provided an opportunity for families to discuss the children's stories and artwork. At its conclusion, this study provides an analysis of Karen refugee students' narratives in order to promote a greater understanding of the adaptation experiences that these young children share in their stories.

Within the field of early childhood education, research commonly focuses on observation of children within a familiar environment, such as in play, at home,+ or in school. In the case of young refugee students who are unfamiliar with American culture and its formal educational setting, early childhood educators must look toward other methods of research to understand refugee experiences. The use of narratives may provide early childhood educators with an alter-native resource for understanding and considering the experiences of young refugee students.

In what follows, we first present a brief overview of the historic struggles of the Karen in Burma. We then provide a discussion of extant research on refugee youth and adaptation to schooling, concluding with an explanation of why we focused on the stories and artwork of young refugee children. Next we present the methodology of the study. Finally, the remainder of the article is devoted to sharing the study's findings, which are organized by themes in the shared and "storied" adaptation experiences of three young Karen girls and their families.

A Background Note on the Karen State and Burma

The Karen people settled in the hill country of Burma, now known as Myanmar, after migrating from China hundreds of years ago. They have since endured periods of great conflict with the Burmese. During the Konbaung Dynasty from 1752–1885, the Karen people were persecuted, heavily taxed, and enslaved by the Burmese people. In the Burmese war with the British beginning in 1824, many of the Karen people, still exploited by the Burmese, saw the British as allies. It was during the colonial era of the late 19th and early 20th centuries that the Karen people began petitioning the British Empire for separation from Burma. During World War II, open fighting between Burmese nationalists and the Karen began, resulting in the destruction of many Karen villages and massacres of the Karen people. Following the war, Burma was granted independence from Britain in 1948, and the Karen remained subjects to the new Burmese government. Initially, the Karen sought to live peacefully with the Burmese, but this period of calm quickly ended with tensions building on both sides. Burmese militias began invading Karen villages Christmas Eve of 1948. This began a civil war in Burma, and the Karen people have continued to fight and petition for independence (Keenan, 2005). This conflict continued into the 21st century, forcing many Karen people to flee their villages seeking asylum across the Thai border in refugee camps (UNHCR, 2009). As many as 200,000 Karen refugees are reported to have been driven from their homes (Keenan, 2005).

After several decades of living in Thai refugee camps, officials recognized that the Karen people would not be able to go back to their homeland. Beginning in 2006, several countries, including the U.S., opened their borders to Karen refugees. Over the first several years, the majority (at approximately 73%) of Burmese refugees who left Thai camps resettled in the U.S., with most of the remainder moving to Australia, Canada, Finland, and Norway. Yet, most Karen refugees remain in Thailand (Kenny & Lockwood-Kenny, 2011).

Refugee Youth and Schooling

Researchers have noted that schools present refugee youth both an important means of integration into their new communities (Bačáková, 2011; Hamilton, 2004; Mosselson, 2007; Rah, Shangmin, & Thu Suong Thi, 2009) and an immediate challenge. On one hand, as Bačáková (2011) explains, "Much has been written on the importance of education and the school environment in the process of successful integration of refugees" (p. 163). Based on the research literature exploring the role of schooling for refugees, she notes that schools in host countries have been found to "facilitate contact with members of local communities; reintroduce a sense of normality and routine; provide a safe environment; increase self-reliance and empowerment; and foster social, psychological and intellectual development" (p. 163). On the other hand, adaptation to an unfamiliar school environment presents difficulties for refugee youth (Hamilton, 2004; Hoot, 2011).

Much research on refugees and schooling tends to be embedded within the more-developed literature related to immigration and schooling. Gibson's (1997) research, for example, indicates that immigrant youth success in adapting to new cultural norms and practices reflects a variety of factors, which include the society of origin, the society of settlement, and reasons for migrating (see also Ogbu, 1987). Moreover, factors such as age, gender, previous schooling, economic standing, and support in the host country all influence this transition. Additionally, parents and community members can inhibit or encourage the adaptation of refugee and immigrant children (Ascher, 1985; Delgado-Gaitan, 1994; Portes & Rumbaut, 2001). In some cases, parental involvement in schooling provides encouragement for children, helping them bridge the cultural gap between home and school. In other cases, cultural conflicts between family and school create an environment in which borders are created rather than bridges (Erickson, 2001; Phelan, Davidson, & Yu, 1993). Ultimately, as Gibson (1988, 1995) suggests, newcomers who view knowledge of the new cultural practices as an addition to their existing life, as opposed to those who seek to assimilate, are often more successful at adapting to the educational settings of the new country.

Although the research on immigration and schooling provides valuable insights on newcomer youth's experiences in schools, many researchers have pointed to differences between immigrants and refugees, arguing that we need more research that focuses on the specific experiences of refugee youth (McBrien, 2005; Mosselson, 2006). For example, refugees tend to perform better in school than immigrants (Mosselson, 2007). Yet, as Mosselson (2007) notes, they "are more likely than other demographic groups to suffer high rates of depression" (p. 99). Partly due to the conflation of immigrants and refugees in much educational research, the specific educational experiences of refugee groups and individuals have not been sufficiently explored.

Pinson and Arnot (2007) suggest that the research literature on refugees and schooling is rather limited generally, with most research focusing on issues of policy or on "practitioner discourses" relating to the perceived needs of refugee youth in schooling and school-based interventions, "best practice," or practical advice for teachers (e.g., Anderson, Hamilton, Moore, Loewen, & Frater-Mathieson, 2004; Hamilton & Moore, 2004; Hoot, 2011; Szente, Hoot, & Taylor, 2006). Some more recent research also focuses on how schools can work with refugee parents (McBrien, 2011; Rah et al., 2009). A strength of this existing research, much of which is based upon interviews with educators and families, is that it views adaptation as a "two-way street;" instead of putting all of the onus on refugee youth and families to adapt to host country schools, schools themselves are urged to adapt to the needs of their new students and communities.

Despite the development of research on refugee schooling over the past decade, authors of reviews of this research have noted a number of gaps. Pinson and Arnot (2007), for example, argue that the research on refugee youth and schooling needs to be more sociological. McBrien (2005) suggests that in the U.S. we need to pay more attention to specific refugee communities. She writes that "the few noted differences [in refugee populations] indicate the need to research specific refugee groups to discover their particular needs, especially refugee groups arriving in the United States since 1990" (p. 357). Two additional areas in which our understandings of refugee school experiences are limited are early childhood education (Hoot, 2011) and the experiences of young refugee youth in their own words (Mosselson, 2007). Mosselson explains, "Research has delineated perceptions of refugees in schools, and discussions have taken place in the literature on how they adapt; "they," however, are rarely asked themselves" (p. 102). Her work (2006, 2007) and that of others (e.g., Bačáková, 2011; Bash & Zezlina-Phillips, 2006) begins to explore the experiences of adolescents in their own words, but we have not found the voices of very young refugee children represented in the research literature.

Our study was designed to respond to this gap by focusing on the stories that young refugee children tell of their adaptation to American early childhood classrooms. We were inspired by the work of several authors who look to personal stories to document the emotions, sacrifices, and daily life experienced by refugees and immigrants moving to a new country. Florio-Ruane (1997), for example, discusses how stories help us understand self and others in the immigration experience because they highlight the societal and personal implications of cross-cultural experience. This idea is manifested in Igoa's (1995) longitudinal research, which focused on stories told by immigrant youth (aged 10–12). Igoa used what she called a "dual-dialogic approach," reflecting with former students, now young adults, on stories told through filmstrips created while they were students in her class. She analyzed these student and teacher reflections on the making of filmstrips to understand the experiences that children used as inspiration for their work. Analyzing these narratives, Igoa developed a greater understanding of the experiences of immigrant children entering school. Her approach served as inspiration for our study of the reflective artwork and oral stories of the Karen refugee children and their families.

In addition, we were inspired by Fuertes' (2010) work with Karen refugees, in which the refugees' narratives led to a metaphor that extended conversations about their lives and experiences. Through the metaphor, "birds inside a cage," the participants related the difficulties of their lives inside a refugee camp. Some, for example, told of forgetting how to be independent and self-reliant because of the length of their stay inside the camp. We rarely hear the kinds of insights on the refugee experience that Fuertes' work provides. This is especially true in regard to the insights of very young children and their families.

In response to these problems and possibilities, the goal of this study was to explore the stories of a specific group of young refugee children to better understand their views of their adaptation to an early childhood setting in the Mid-West United States. Focusing on the oral stories of young Karen refugee children, their related artwork, and children's and parents' reflection on these, we share lessons learned from the narratives of early school experience.

The Study

Narrative research, Creswell (2007) writes, "begins with the experiences as expressed in lived and told stories of individuals" (p. 54). Interest in narrative inquiry as an approach to qualitative research has surged in recent years, stoked, perhaps, by claims that stories both shape and communicate our understanding of personal experience and the meaning we ascribe to it (Connelly & Clandinin, 1990). This description of the value of stories is reflected in the design of this study. We viewed narratives as a way to learn about how several young Karen refugee children in Megan's school experienced—and "storied"—their first year(s) in American early childhood classrooms. The research question that guided this study was, *What do the stories of Karen refugee children and their families reveal about the children's adaptation to an American early childhood classroom?*

Several distinctly different types of qualitative inquiry are captured under the "narrative inquiry" label. Often these approaches appear to share little other than the interest in "narrative" or "story." Three broad categories in particular shape our understanding of the field of narrative inquiry. Donald Polkinghorne (1995) distinguishes between two of these, contrasting the "analysis of narratives" with "narrative analysis." In his conception, the analysis-of-narratives type of narrative inquiry includes those studies in which "researchers collect stories as data and analyze them with paradigmatic processes" (Polkinghorne, 1995, p. 12). In contrast, the narrative-analysis type of narrative inquiry refers to investigations in which "researchers collect descriptions of events and happenings and synthesize or configure them by means of a plot into a story or stories (for example, a history, case study, or biographic episode)" (Polkinghorne, 1995, p. 12). In addition to these two kinds of narrative inquiry described by Polkinghorne, we would add a third approach. Some narrative inquiry focuses on *how* people tell their stories of experience. This approach is exemplified by Leslie Rebecca Bloom's (1996) study of the shifting narratives told by one woman.

Given the nature of our research question, we designed this study as an *analysis-of-narratives* type of narrative inquiry. We were interested to learn what stories children would tell about their experience in an American early childhood setting and what these stories might teach us about their adaptation. Yet, young children's stories present challenges to narrative researchers, given the children's age and the developmental process of storytelling. As such, the standard interview-based approach to the generation of stories in this kind of narrative inquiry would not suffice for this project.

During the early childhood years, children express their knowledge and understanding through a variety of mediums, including artwork, three-dimensional constructions, language, or other representative means. Moreover, for refugee children with limited exposure to the host country's language, expressing ideas, feelings, and understanding may rely heavily on other forms of communication. For these reasons, Megan not only documented children's oral and written stories, but also collected the drawings that were created to illustrate them. We viewed the artwork not as a supplement to the oral and written stories, but instead as another mode of story-telling. In addition, Megan collected the stories of the children's families to provide a multi-perspective narrative of the children's experience. Finally, she also drew on her observations and experiences with the children as their teacher. Ultimately, for each participating child, we developed narrative cases from their written and oral stories, artwork, teacher observations, and family interviews.

Role of the Researchers

At the time of the study, Megan, the primary researcher, was a teacher in a diverse, suburban early childhood classroom. She wanted to understand the adaptation process of young refugee children in order to raise the quality of education for her students, to ensure the effectiveness of her teaching, and to share these experiences and findings with other educators. Tricia Niesz, the second author, was Megan's graduate school advisor at this time. She helped Megan design a study that was methodologically sound and would respond to her questions and interests. Tricia continued to provide methodological guidance throughout the conduct of the study. In addition, over the course of the data collection, she engaged in peer debriefing with Megan as related to the analysis and interpretation of the narratives. This peer debriefing allowed Tricia to mentor sound research practices, promote Megan's reflexivity, and contribute to the trust-worthiness of the study. Once the study was completed, we developed and wrote this article together, building from Megan's master's degree capstone paper.

Ethics

IRB approval was obtained prior to asking permission from families, children, and the school in which this study took place. Since Megan was also the children's teacher, several steps were taken to maintain voluntary participation and limit undue influence. First, she met with each individual family and a family advocate to discuss the possibility of participating in the study. The families were asked to discuss the study at home with their children in their preferred language so the children had time to understand the study before being approached by Megan. If the families were still interested in participating following these discussions, Megan approached the children, explaining the study by relating it to activities they were familiar with completing during a normal day of school. Their involvement in the study beyond the normal activities of their day was limited to ensure the confidentiality and comfort of the students.

Participants

Megan developed narrative case studies of three Karen children, all girls aged 4–6 and all from her own school, over the course of approximately four months. The children were chosen based on their age, their time spent in a refugee camp before moving to the United States, and the obtainment of refugee status. At the time of the study, all refugees present at the participating school were Karen and only three had been born in a refugee camp and migrated with their families. Megan was a teacher of two of the three children at this time. The three children who met the criteria for participation in the study were Allison,[2] Aurora, and Cindy. Allison, the eldest, was the first from the Karen community to enter the early childhood education setting. Aurora, the next eldest, and Cindy, the youngest, entered school a year and a half after Allison.

All of the participants and their families had several shared experiences before arriving in the United States. The children spoke the same language, were from Burmese Karen families, and were born in the same refugee camp, Tham Hin, in Thailand. Tham Hin is characterized by homes made of bamboo and plastic tarps, rationed food of rice and beans, little to no furniture, and no electricity. The children's parents had little work during this time, as there was no authorized movement in and out of the camp. Additionally, none of the children had received any education prior to their arrival in the U.S. At the time of the study, all had been settled in

---

2   All names are pseudonyms selected by the children themselves.

their current U.S. community for approximately three years. Each family had support from local organizations and a family advocate who assisted them in understanding American culture and living in the U.S. All of the families indicated that they would like to return to their homeland if it becomes possible to be safe and free.

The family advocate was included in all interviews as the primary language used throughout the study was English. The advocate worked closely within the Karen community and was aware of cultural differences, language barriers, and each family's experiences. During the study, the advocate helped ensure understanding between all parties during the interviews to promote accuracy of the narratives shared.

Data Collection

After obtaining IRB approval, selecting the three Karen refugee families with children enrolled in the school, and obtaining the children's assent and parents' permission to conduct the study with the assistance of their family advocate, Megan commenced developing prompts to guide the children's story-telling and art-making sessions. Throughout the course of the study, data were collected through these sessions and included the children's stories with accompanying drawings. All sessions were video and audio recorded. These were complemented by observations of the children in the classroom. To monitor her subjectivity and document her reflexivity, Megan engaged in journal writing and debriefing conversations with Tricia throughout the study.

In addition, we sought to link the children's artwork and stories with the narratives of their families, collected through digitally recorded in-depth English interviews with the assistance of the family advocate. Each family was comprised of the mother and father of the participant, with the exception of one whose father was unavailable throughout the duration of this study. Additionally, during the first family interview for two of the three primary participants, grandparents were involved in telling the families' stories of becoming refugees, living in the Thai refugee camp, and resettling in the United States.

Specifically, during the first phase of the study, Megan conducted and digitally recorded in-depth interviews with the children's families to develop an oral history of each family's experience prior to their arriving in the United States. We used Rubin and Rubin's (2005) "responsive interview model" to guide family interviews, as we found their advice on follow-up questions and prompts, as well as their conversational approach, helpful in generating the kinds of extended stories valued in narrative inquiry. The family interviews were conducted in English with the assistance of the family advocate, who was present to help with any translation or explanation needed by the families. Ultimately, these interviews were successful in providing valuable information regarding the children's histories and experiences as perceived and interpreted by their families.

In the second phase of the study, the students developed four oral stories with artwork guided by prompts, which were based on information from the family interviews. The prompts included starters such as: "Tell me about when you first started school" and "Tell me about a time you were happy at school." Megan also kept observation notes during each of the storytelling sessions with the children. During each session, she developed analytical insights as recommended by Hatch (2002) to guide future interview discussions and storytelling sessions. After the first two storytelling sessions, Megan assessed the data collected through interviews and children's stories to identify missing information and to revise prompts and questions for the second two sessions.

In the third phase of the study, Megan conducted additional interviews with each of the families; these were focused on their perceived understanding of their child's adaptation both at the beginning and end of the study. In these interviews, the families discussed their current understandings of their child's adaptation to the school. They also provided 'member checking' feedback on their child's narratives as Megan shared the children's dialogue and artwork with each family. The families also discussed Megan's initial analyses and interpretations based on her sessions with the children and offered their feedback by adding detail or sharing additional stories.

Data Analysis

We analyzed data throughout the study by recording and developing analytic insights in memos. The formal data analysis that took place later in the study consisted of two stages. In the first stage we analyzed the data to produce a narrative account of each child's experiences over time. We used the stories of each child and her parents to construct a narrative of experiences of adaptation as told from their points of view. To ensure accuracy of the narrative, we transcribed digitally recorded data from all sessions. We then reviewed and transcribed the written data from the family and child sessions for each child in order to develop a narrative case study for each child based on both parent and child narratives. These combined narratives were used as part of the data analysis completed in the second stage.

In the second stage of the data analysis process, we focused on analyzing each of the combined parent and child narratives compiled in the first stage to identify themes present across all the children's experiences. We categorized the data into emerging themes by using codes to compare across all of the parent and child narratives (Hatch, 2002; Merriam, 1998; Rubin & Rubin, 2005). Examples of categories that emerged from the inductive analytical process included "not understanding," "friendship," and "frustration." Throughout the analysis, we studied the material in these categories to develop themes associated with the processes of adaptation that were reflected in child and family's perceptions of these processes. Several of these themes are discussed in the sections that follow.

Findings

A number of themes developed from the analysis of the children's stories, drawings, reflections, and family interviews. The stories of the children's experiences were diverse in nature, of course, but we can see several commonalities across what the children and their families shared. First, all of the children presented a narrative of change over time. Depictions of sadness or anger at the beginning of the school year were transformed over time, with all of the children describing happiness in school by the time of the study. Second, sharing their strategies of adaptation to the classroom, each of the children focused their stories on experiences that bridged home and classroom or on similarities with other children. Finally, in sharing specific experiences that were particularly difficult for the children early on, the children's families contributed narratives that the children themselves did not express through their artwork and stories. In the sections that follow, we develop each of these themes with reflections, stories, and artwork of the children and their families.

Reflections of Change Over Time

The stories and artwork of the children, along with the interviews with parents, presented narratives of experiences that changed over time. Drawing themselves on the first day of school, each child (independent of the others) drew a picture of herself with a frowning face. Although each of the children depicted emotions of sadness, anger, and loneliness as they were beginning school, their representations of their school experience later in the year were marked by smiles and stories of friends. Writing and drawing about the first day of school, for example, Allison appeared to be expressing sadness at being alone. Struggling to identify the term for this emotion, Megan offered the term, "lonely," and defined it for her. After being given the definition of "lonely," Allison used this term to label how she felt: "I was alonely in school." Indeed, Allison often played alone at that time, both in school and, as family reported, at home as well. Her mother noted, "When she started school, she just did [played] alone. She don't want no one with her."

The other two children's stories shared some similarities to Allison's. Aurora, whose stories were generally marked by a strong resiliency and much less conflict than those of Allison or Cindy, represented her initial days in school as somewhat mixed. She described feeling sad, but then drew her family happy that she was going to school and her teacher and peers happy as she got to school. She then continued to draw and tell how she was happy and playing at school. What Aurora described seemed to be her hesitancy about coming to a new place, but also how quickly she began playing. Her story suggested that she was comforted by the apparent happiness of her family and peers at school.

Cindy, however, expressed somewhat more difficulty. Like Allison, she initially had difficulty finding a word that expressed her feelings. Telling the story of her introduction to her new school, she drew what she could not explain about how she felt (Figure 19.1):

Megan: Can you tell me, how did you feel here at the beginning of the story?
Cindy: [*purses up face and squints eyes*] Ummmm mmmmm
Megan: Do you know the word for that?
Cindy: A happy sad.
Megan: A happy sad?
Cindy: Ok, my face said, "don't" ... my face ... [*points to picture*] (see Figure 19.1)

Cindy's illustration showed her with an "X" for her mouth; her body was in red. She described a strong feeling that she referred to as "don't," an emotion that might best be described as anger.

Despite representing their early days in the new school as sad or angry, each of the children presented stories indicating a change in experience and orientation towards school over time.

In marked contrast to the frowning faces drawn early on, all of the stories the children shared and drew in the later sessions showed them interacting with their peers and enjoying school. Each of the children's families also remarked upon how much their child enjoyed going to school, even if they were afraid or did not want to go at the beginning. Allison reflected on the change over time, commenting, "That was when I was sad at school. I don't want to go to school when I was four. That was when I was four. So the next morning, I was five now. It was my birthday and I went to kindergarten like this." As she reflected on this, she viewed the pictures of a story she wrote (Figure 19.2). On the first page was a picture of a sad girl, and on the second one, a picture of a happy one.

What happened in between the difficult first days and the smiles later in the year? In the next section, we describe the adaptation strategies depicted by the children's stories and artwork.

FIGURE 19.1 Cindy's Depiction of her First day of School. As She Drew it, She Explained, "My Face said, 'don't'."

FIGURE 19.2 Allison as Sad and as Happy.

Building Bridges Between Home and School

Each child seemed to use a different strategy to manage early difficulties and begin to adapt to the classroom. Yet, all had to do with building connections through friendship with peers and bridging home and school. Indeed, a commonality across all three of the children's stories was the importance of having something from their home environment represented in their classroom.

When Allison first started school she told about how she played almost exclusively with the dollhouse, pretending the dolls were bears like hers at home. She appeared to use the comfort of toys similar to the ones she had at home to help her transition into the classroom. Allison also told stories of experiences with friendship in the classroom. In two cases, she described a friend who had something that was the same as her: first, a child who was also in preschool with her and who then turned 5 and was in her Kindergarten class; second, she described someone who loved playing the same magic game as she did, making flowers appear and then disappear. Ultimately, her stories suggested that her adaptation to the classroom was promoted by identifying similarities in her peers, and building friendship and connection with others.

Similarly, the stories Cindy chose to tell about positive experiences at school all depicted her interacting with another child in play through some common interest. In stories in which she was enjoying play with friends, she drew them playing with worms, re-enacting a favorite story, and playing outside on the playground—all areas of common interest between herself and her friends (Figure 19.3). Figure 19.3 shows how Cindy represented herself and her friends (a) digging for worms and (b) playing on the playground. These common interests provided opportunities for Cindy to develop friendships with her peers and adapt to the school. Similar to Allison's stories, Cindy's stories also revealed her adaptation in the classroom as being facilitated through similarities with others and building connections.

Aurora's stories indicate that, of the three children, she had the easiest time adapting to the school experience. Even her parents reflected that transitioning between home and school was not difficult for Aurora: "[It's] been easy, she's been in America. It's been easy because she little." Interestingly, her family's presence at school was common among several of her stories. In one of her stories, Aurora drew her mom coming to school to watch her sing. She said, "He [we] singing and family come. Family come and is so happy to see to sing their special song. My mommy is happy to see teacher." Additional examples were present in other stories of school, suggesting the importance of these experiences for Aurora. For example, she drew her family being present at school during family events and the picture of her family that hung in the classroom throughout the year. The presence of her family at school and her family's attitude toward school shaped Aurora's stories. They suggested a strong link between home and school that appeared to provide comfort as Aurora adapted to the American school context.

Indeed, the stories suggest that each child built bridges from home to school through familiar items, family, or developing connections with peers in the class through their similar interests or similar experiences. Although the time frame and process was different for each child, this was a thread that was woven through all of their experiences. Slowly, through bridges and connections of these kinds, the children appeared to feel at home in their American school.

FIGURE 19.3   Cindy's Playing with Friends Through Engaging in (a) Digging for Worms and
(b) Playing on the Playground.

Friendships with other children were often highlighted in stories, artwork, and reflections. The representations the children drew changed over the course of the study from showing them playing by themselves or playing with other Karen children to playing with their peers in the classroom. Allison's stories shifted from depicting her playing by herself with the doll house to sharing the games she played with all her friends in Kindergarten. Reflecting on when she was older and in Kindergarten she said, "I have a lot of good friends and they play with me at every day." Additionally, Cindy and Aurora originally drew pictures of play alongside their peers in the initial stories about school, but showed themselves interacting with peers in their later stories. Their stories began to show integration with their American peers in play as bridges were built between home and school.

Dialogues on Dissonance

We do not want to suggest that the children's and their families' stories of adaptation to the classroom represented a simple linear transition. Families in particular noted difficult experiences, experiences that we have come to think of as "culturally dissonant," with which the children struggled at particular times during the year. Although the children's stories did not tend to highlight these events, listening to their families' stories created a more complete picture of the children's adaptation to the American classroom. In dialogue with Allison's family, discussions concerning a period of time when Allison would speak only English provided evidence of a culturally dissonant experience. Her family told of how Allison refused to speak Karen in preschool and into the beginning of her Kindergarten year. Her mother reflected, "She just speak English. [Her father and I] just tell [her], we are the same people and we love you." Allison's family advocate added that her father encouraged her family to let it be: "His words were, 'She's in America; she needs to speak English.'" She added that she did encourage Allison to use her native language at home. "I told her how beautiful I thought it was when I heard her speak Karen to her mother and father, because I want her to love both cultures."

Although the time frame when she would not speak Karen was included in Allison's narratives and drawings, she did not share this experience herself. Instead she focused her drawings on how she felt alone during preschool. When Allison entered preschool, she was immersed, for the first time, in the American culture. Discussing her drawing, Allison reflected, "That was, I was sad at school. I don't want to go to school when I was four. I had no friends, no friends played with me." Interestingly, looking at Allison's and her family's stories, we can see that the period when Allison talked about making friends in Kindergarten aligns with the time that her family noted she began to speak Karen again.

A culturally dissonant experience Cindy related in her drawings was her struggle when she did not understand the actions or words of the other children in her class. While drawing about an experience putting on a Rapunzel puppet show with her peers, Cindy quoted herself asking her peers, "Why did you do that? It hit me." In the retelling of Rapunzel, her peers had knocked over the old lady, Cindy's puppet, as Rapunzel made her escape from the tower. Her peers, talking in English, verbalized the action with Rapunzel's escape, but this eluded Cindy. She did not understand their play and struggled to understand their words. When discussing Cindy's experiences beginning school, her mother noted that school was "scary and then her [*shakes head for no*] understand, so hard for her." Reflecting on Cindy's drawings, the dialogue with her family, and observations in the classroom, it becomes evident that Cindy struggled when she could not understand her peers. Cindy's response to this was to confront the children to find out more. She initiated conversations because she wanted to understand her peers.

During these culturally dissonant experiences, looking at the children's artwork in combination with the family dialogue created a fuller understanding of what was happening during this time in the children's lives. Through the pictures, the children related the circumstances or their feelings; however, the families provided the broader context around each of these events. Cindy's family reported seeing her difficulty communicating at school leading up to the story she shared about re-enacting Rapunzel with her peers. Allison focused on how she felt and expressed those feelings in her artwork, but her family reflected on her behavior at home during this time, providing insights into why she expressed feeling alone in preschool. Throughout the interviews, combining both the family's narratives with the children's artwork and stories provided additional insight into children's experiences as they entered the early childhood setting. Listening to both the children and their families formed a more comprehensive representation of the children's adaptation to the American classroom.

Discussion: Listening to Children's Experiences in Context

This study was inspired by an interest in the stories that young refugee children tell about their early experiences in an American school. The stories, accompanied by artwork and reflection, as well as their families' reflections on their experiences, highlighted a change in orientation to the school over time. They also revealed strategies that the children used in bridging home and school and in building friendships in their classroom. Not surprisingly, the children sought familiarity, identifying objects similar to objects they knew from home, focusing on family in the classroom, or relating to children with similar interests or experiences. Importantly, viewing the children's narratives through the stories of their families created a more holistic view of what the children experienced during the time span discussed in this research, especially during periods of cultural dissonance.

Although the stories of the children and families sounded these similar notes, it is important to emphasize that the children's strategies and timelines differed. Allison initially pulled away from all friends, both at home and at school, and took over a year to develop friendships and appear comfortable in the classroom. Cindy also felt strong emotions when she could not understand the new environment at school, but confronted the situation and resolved the conflict quickly in comparison. In contrast, Aurora and her family suggested that she eased into the American school fairly easily. In addition, she told stories that focused on times when she was happy at school or enjoying her friends even though she realized they did not always get along. This reminds us that stories are tellings of experience that do not necessarily represent a reality—or even experience—directly; instead, they are representations shaped by a number of factors.

Yet, to some extent, these differing narratives reflect their refugee community's timeline. Allison was the first Karen student to come to the school. Through her experience, the family learned more about the American school and shared what they learned with other families. For example, in the Karen community, mothers generally feed their children until they are 4 or 5 years old. However, when Allison started school, she became responsible for feeding herself during lunchtime. Her family then changed their practices at home and began giving utensils to the children during meals. As shared in the families' narratives, other families in the Karen communities heard about this and began having their children feed themselves in preparation for school. In this way and others, the Karen community adapted to ensure that their children were more successful in American schools. This reflects the findings of J. Lynn McBrien and others who have found adaptation to be a "two-way street" (2011; Rah et al., 2009). It is probable that the school also learned more about the Karen culture and community in the period reflected in the stories presented by the children and their families. The relatively short amount of time it took the younger children to adjust to school may reflect the mutual learning experiences across the school and the new Karen community.

Through the themes presented in the stories collected, Allison, Cindy, and Aurora focused their stories on finding commonalities with peers and those experiences that created connections or built bridges to their homes in order to facilitate their adaptation into the classroom. Similarly, Alejandro Portes and Ruben Rumbaut (2001) found that parental involvement in schooling can help children build bridges over the cultural gap between home and school (see also Ascher, 1985; Delgado-Gaitan, 1994; McBrien, 2011; Rah et al., 2009). These findings can be translated into experiences that educators offer all children to help them adjust to a new environment. Providing young children experiences that promote the commonalities among all students and including families in children's education may aid their adaptation to the early childhood setting.

The stories shared by the children through their artwork, dialogue, and reflection are powerful sources of understanding the processes of adaptation experienced as each of the children encountered U.S. schools. The stories and reflections may not reflect an "objective" reality, but they do relate how the children come to make meaning of their experiences. How refugee children make meaning of their world is important for educators to understand. Observing how children "story" their cross-cultural experiences teaches us what they find meaningful; this kind of learning allows us to provide them additional meaningful experiences.

In future narrative research we would stress the importance of both generating multi-modal (oral, written, and art-based) stories from children and collecting narratives from families to develop a richer and more multi-faceted understanding of "storied" experience. The art provided ways to extend the researcher-child conversation about experience. As for the family narratives, parents were more likely to focus on periods of cultural dissonance or difficulty, providing meaningful context for our understanding of the children's stories.

A limitation of this project, however, was that Megan did not speak the native language of the children and their families. This provided an obstacle to the sharing and generation of narratives in the study. Megan responded to this limitation by including the family advocate in interviews to provide a liaison between the Karen community and the American school, as she is someone who is familiar with both communities. Additionally, although the fact that Megan was a teacher of two of the three children who participated in the study added to the trust and rapport necessary for this kind of study, some might view this existing relationship as a limitation because of the potential for children and families to feel coerced into participating or to feel the need to tell Megan only positive stories about their experience. To ensure that children and families did not feel this way, Megan discussed the research first only with the participants' families. When the families expressed interest in participating, they were asked to discuss the research with their child prior to Megan asking the children if they would like to participate. In addition, she assured the families that all stories were confidential and shared her own stories to establish an open relationship with the families. Because the children and families told stories of difficulty and wanted to share their stories with other teachers and educators, we believe that this potential limitation was minimized.

Future research should include the use of narrative inquiries of young children and families, supplemented by the children's artwork, to provide greater understanding of the adaptation experiences across a range of refugee groups. In addition, other qualitative studies on the adaptation experiences of young refugees using greater numbers of participants could provide a more robust understanding of the young refugee's experience. Mixed method studies that include diverse groups of refugee participants could also broaden educators' understanding of the experiences of refugee youth in school. Together, these three recommendations for future research could capture the breadth and depth of refugee adaptation experiences and teach educators how to adapt their own classrooms to support refugee students.

As a greater number of children and families are finding refuge in new communities across the globe, it is essential for educators to understand how refugees of all ages are making meaning of their experiences and provide them with opportunities to tell their stories. These can teach us how to support children's and families' adaptation into a new community, how to foster smooth transitions, and how to adapt our classrooms to provide students with the best educational experiences possible.

References

Anderson, A., Hamilton, R., Moore, D., Loewen, S., & Frater-Mathieson, K. (2004). Education of refugee children: Theoretical perspectives and best practice. In R. Hamilton & D. Moore, (Eds.), *Educational interventions for refugee children: Theoretical perspectives and implementing best practice* (pp. 1–11). New York, NY: RoutledgeFalmer.

Ascher, C. (1985). The social and psychological adjustment of Southeast Asian refugees. *Urban Review, 17*(2), 147–152.

Bačáková, M. (2011). Developing inclusive educational practices for refugee children in the Czech Republic. *Intercultural Education, 22*(2), 163–175.

Bash, L., & Zezlina-Phillips, E. (2006). Identity, boundary and schooling: Perspectives on the experiences and perceptions of refugee children. *Intercultural Education, 17*(1), 113–128.

Bloom, L. R. (1996). Stories of one's own: Nonunitary subjectivity in narrative representation. *Qualitative Inquiry, 2*(2), 176–197.

Connelly, F. M., & Clandinin, D. J. (1990). Stories of experience and narrative inquiry. *Educational Researcher, 19*(5), 2–14.

Creswell, J. W. (2007). *Qualitative inquiry & research design: Choosing among five approaches* (2nd ed.). Thousand Oaks, CA: Sage.

Delgado-Gaitan, C. (1994). Russian refugee families: Accommodating aspirations through education. *Anthropology & Education Quarterly, 25*(2), 137–155.

Erickson, F. (2001). Culture in society and in educational practices. In J. Banks & C. M. Banks (Eds.), *Multicultural education: Issues and perspectives* (pp. 31–58). Boston, MA: Allyn and Bacon.

Florio-Ruane, S. (1997). To tell a new story: Reinventing narratives of culture, identity, and education. *Anthropology & Education Quarterly, 28*, 152–162.

Fuertes, A. (2010). Birds inside a cage: Metaphor for Karen refugees. *Social Alternatives, 29*(1), 20–24.

Gibson, M. A. (1988). *Accommodation without assimilation: Sikh immigrants in an American high school*. Ithaca, NY: Cornell University Press.

Gibson, M. A. (1995). Promoting additive acculturation in schools. *Multicultural Education, 3*(1), 11–54.

Gibson, M. A. (1997). Complicating the immigrant/involuntary minority typology. *Anthropology and Education Quarterly, 28*(3), 431–454.

Hamilton, R. (2004). Schools, teachers and education of refugee children. In R. Hamilton & D. Moore (Eds.), *Educational interventions for refugee children: Theoretical perspectives and implementing best practice* (pp. 83–96). New York, NY: RoutledgeFalmer.

Hamilton, R., & Moore, D. (Eds.). (2004). *Educational intervention for refugee children: Theoretical perspectives and implementing best practice.* New York, NY: RoutledgeFalmer.

Hatch, J. A. (2002). *Doing qualitative research in education settings.* Albany, NY: University of New York Press.

Hoot, J. (2011). Working with very young refugee children in our schools: Implications for the world's teachers. *Procedia Social and Behavioral Sciences, 15*, 1751–1755.

Igoa, C. (1995). *The inner world of the immigrant child.* Mahwah, NJ: Lawrence Erlbaum Associates.

Keenan, P. (2005). *The museum of Karen history and culture.* Retrieved from http://www.ibiblio.org/obl/docs3/karenmuseum-01/index.htm

Kenny, P., & Lockwood-Kenny, K. (2011). A mixed blessing: Karen resettlement to the United States. *Journal of Refugee Studies, 24*(2), 217–238.

McBrien, J. L. (2005). Educational needs and barriers for refugee students in the United States: A review of literature. *Review of Educational Research, 75*(3), 329–364.

McBrien, J. (2011). The importance of context: Vietnamese, Somali, and Iranian refugee mothers discuss their resettled lives and involvement in their children's schools. *Compare: A Journal of Comparative & International Education, 41*(1), 75–90.

Merriam, S. B. (1998). *Qualitative research and case study applications in education.* San Francisco, CA: Jossey-Bass.

Mosselson, J. (2006). Roots & Routes: A re-imagining of refugee identity constructions and the implications for schooling. *Current Issues in Comparative Education, 9*(1), 20–29.

Mosselson, J. (2007). Masks of achievement: An experiential study of Bosnian female refugees in New York City schools. *Comparative Education Review, 51*(1), 95–115.

Ogbu, J.U. (1987). Variability in minority school performance: A problem in search of an explanation. *Anthropology & Education Quarterly, 18*, 312–334.

Phelan, P., Davidson, A. L., & Yu, H. C. (1993). Students' multiple worlds: Negotiating the borders of family, peer, and school cultures. In P. Phelan & A. Locke Davidson (Eds.), *Renegotiating cultural diversity in American schools* (pp. 52–88). New York, NY: Teachers College Press.

Pinson, H., & Arnot, M. (2007). Sociology of education and the wasteland of refugee education research. *British Journal of Sociology of Education, 28*(3), 399–407.

Polkinghorne, D. E. (1995). Narrative configuration in qualitative analysis. In J. A. Hatch & R. Wisniewski (Eds.), *Life history and narrative* (pp. 5–23). Abingdon, OX: RoutledgeFalmer.

Portes, A., & Rumbaut, R. (2001). *Legacies: The story of the immigrant second generation.* Berkeley, CA: University of California Press.

Rah, Y., Shangmin, C., & Thu Suong Thi?, N. (2009). Building bridges between refugee parents and schools. *International Journal of Leadership in Education, 12*(4), 347–365.

Rubin, H. J., & Rubin, I. S. (2005). *Qualitative interviewing: The art of hearing data.* Thousand Oaks, CA: Sage.

Szente, J., Hoot, J., & Taylor, D. (2006). Responding to the special needs of refugee children: Practical ideas for teachers. *Early Childhood Education Journal, 34*(1), 15–20.

United Nations High Commissioner for Refugees [UNHCR]. (9 June 2009). *Thailand: Recent arrivals from Myanmar.* Briefing Notes. Retrieved from http://www.unhcr.org/cgibin/texis/vtx/search?page=search&docid=4a2e38216&query=karen

United Nations High Commissioner for Refugees [UNHCR]. (2011). *Refugee figures.* Retrieved from http://www.unhcr.org/pages/49c3646c1d.html

Discussion Questions

1. What challenges do immigrants face in our society today?
2. What are some of the major challenges that immigrant students may face when attending school in the United States?
3. In what major ways do the present migrations of people affect our education system, especially in early childhood education field?
4. How would you introduce the topic of immigration to young children?

Activity

Please interview early childhood professionals, and find out what they consider most relevant when working with children with culturally diverse characteristics.

CPSIA information can be obtained
at www.ICGtesting.com
Printed in the USA
FSHW020400051220
76602FS